Microfinance

A Practitioner's Handbook

Consulting Editor **Ranajoy Basu**

Consulting editor
Ranajoy Basu

Publisher
Sian O'Neill

Editor
Carolyn Boyle

Production
Russell Anderson

Publishing directors
Guy Davis, Tony Harriss, Mark Lamb

Microfinance: A Practitioner's Handbook
is published by
Globe Law and Business
Globe Business Publishing Ltd
New Hibernia House
Winchester Walk
London SE1 9AG
United Kingdom
Tel +44 20 7234 0606
Fax +44 20 7234 0808
Web www.globelawandbusiness.com

Printed by CPI Group (UK) Ltd, Croydon, CR0 4YY

ISBN 9781905783977

Table of contents

Foreword

Ranajoy Basu
Reed Smith LLP

Over the last 20 years, much literature has been written on the subject of microfinance. During this time, however, the sector has been continuously evolving. It has survived the risks posed by the global economic crisis and the controversy of the industry's mission. Amid changing perceptions of microfinance as a panacea to eradicating global poverty, many positives remain in the quest to achieve a sustainable microfinance sector, which combines its social objectives with the demands of the commercial world in which it operates. In the age of technology, social media and crowd funding, the microfinance sector has transformed itself in seeking to achieve its objective of bringing financial services to the world's poorest people. In bringing this book together, we were reminded of how fast the sector is evolving.

In determining the structure of the book, I felt that it was important that you, the reader, have the perspectives of microfinance practitioners, regulators, economists, academics, investors and lawyers, and essentially hear the voices of the various participants in the microfinance industry and see the sector through their eyes.

If you are new to the microfinance sector, this book is intended to provide a broad and varied overview of this dynamic, multi-faceted industry. For those with more experience in the sector, I hope that the views, perspectives and often candid thoughts of the authors will offer new insight and perspectives to broaden your existing knowledge base. I hope that this book will be an ongoing resource for you to use.

The book is divided into five parts. Part 1 provides an introduction to the basics of microfinance, the key challenges and hurdles facing the industry, and the most common types of organisation and business models involved in providing microfinance services today. This is followed by analysis of key developments in the microfinance sector, including the growth of the microinsurance industry, *shari'a*-compliant microfinance and the move from the microcredit model to the more sustainable livelihoods model. This is critical in the microfinance sector's quest for sustainability.

Part 2 addresses the view of the microfinance sector from the investor's perspective. With an ever-increasing investor base focused on entering the sector, this is of critical importance for the growth of the sector going forward. The first chapter discusses the gap between demand and supply of financial services and analyses the reasons for this gap. It also explores the types of investor and investment available in the market. The following chapter discusses the ever-increasing use of capital markets as a means for funding the microfinance sector and the ways in which its true potential may be unlocked.

Part 3 then deals with the key issues and basis of governance and sustainability of the microfinance sector and microfinance institutions, and explores what is meant by the concept of governance and why it is of increasing importance in the microfinance industry today. In the aftermath of the global financial crises, and specific microfinance crises in a number of countries, the need for regulation has become increasingly urgent. This is followed by a discussion of the balance between government intervention and self-regulation.

Part 4 is dedicated to impact analysis and includes a discussion of the key issues for the economic empowerment of rural women through microfinance, followed by an interesting and often controversial chapter on the measurement of social performance by microfinance investment vehicles. The last chapter in this section discusses the strength of social networks and the role that they play in creating social capital.

Part 5 is themed "Developments and trends", and looks at the road ahead for the microfinance industry – in particular, the effects of the global financial crises and the crises in the microfinance sector in certain countries. This part includes a topical chapter on the microfinance crisis in India and how microfinance institutions in India are emerging in its aftermath. This section also assesses the impact of mobile banking in microfinance, which is an important topic for bringing microfinance to the remotest parts of the world. The chapter on the future of microfinance is a personal account of a microfinance practitioner, who has spent several years working in the sector. The last chapter of the book discusses the continued evolution of microfinance, and ends on an optimistic note by proposing ways in which one may get involved in the microfinance industry.

I am delighted to have been given the opportunity to work with Globe Law and Business on this publication. It has been an honour and privilege to collaborate with the contributors, who include academics, lawyers, microfinance practitioners and people at the heart of the microfinance industry. I have thoroughly enjoyed debating and sharing thoughts with them on the topics covered.

I believe that I speak on behalf of all of the contributors when I say that we feel very fortunate and humbled to have been able to work in our own ways in this exciting and ever-evolving sector. We hope that this book conveys the passion and enthusiasm for microfinance, as well as providing the reader with a practical and useful guide.

An introduction to microfinance

Ranajoy Basu
Reed Smith LLP

"The core of development is the enjoyment of freedom – the freedom of individuals to lead valuable lives" (Amartya Sen)

1. Introduction

At its core, microfinance aims to address the fundamental issue that the poor do not have access to traditional sources of financial services provided by banks and commercial institutions. Working on the basis that such access would improve the financial condition of the poor, organisations and individuals have come up with many ways to bring this about. This provision of financial services is called 'microfinance', and we discuss various aspects of the term in this chapter.

The last two decades have witnessed a rapid evolution and transformation of the microfinance sector. What began as a simple idea to provide business loans to the poor has today evolved into a far-ranging and dynamic sector. It now includes institutions that provide savings and remittance services, insurance and mobile banking for a wide range of purposes. There are now many models for the provision of microfinance.

The provision of microfinance now entails a range of possibilities and a variety of models. Recent estimates suggest that microfinance has reached 195 million individuals worldwide.[1] However, according to research conducted by McKinsey, there are roughly 2.5 billion people without access to banking around the world;[2] there is thus still enormous demand for financial services for the poor.

However, microfinance is not without its fair share of myths, theories and controversy. In recent years the sector has been embroiled in criticism about its mission. Yet it has shown remarkable resilience and has survived global economic and country-specific crises, and today is at crossroads. It is against this backdrop and through the emergence of such controversy that we examine the meaning of microfinance today.

2. A brief history of microfinance

The concept of microfinance is by no means new. Savings and credit groups have operated for centuries, ranging from 'susus' in Ghana to 'chit funds' in India, 'tandas'

---

1 Microcredit Summit Campaign Report, 2013.
2 'Cross-country variation household access to financial services'. *Journal of Banking and Finance*, 2008, Vol 32, No 11.

in Mexico, 'arisan' in Indonesia, 'cheetu' in Sri Lanka, 'tontines' in West Africa and 'pasanku' in Bolivia.

2.1 The early years, 1700–1800

Formal credit and savings institutions for the poor have also existed for centuries. These have provided customers who were traditionally neglected by commercial banks with a means of obtaining financial services through cooperatives and development finance institutions.

The Irish Loan Fund system, initiated in the early 1700s by the author and nationalist Jonathan Swift, provided small loans to the rural poor with no collateral. By the 1840s, Jonathan Swift's ideas had led to a network of around 300 funds across Ireland. The main purpose of these funds was to make small loans with interest for short periods. At their peak they were making loans to 20% of all Irish households annually.

In the 1800s, Friedrich Wilhem Raiffeisen, a German mayor and cooperative pioneer, and his supporters developed the concept of credit unions in the western world. This altruistic action was motivated by a desire to help the rural population break free from their dependence on moneylenders and to improve their welfare. From 1870, credit unions expanded rapidly over a large sector of the Rhine Province and other regions of the German States. The cooperative movement rapidly spread to other countries in Europe and North America, and eventually to developing countries, supported by the cooperative movements in developed countries and with assistance from donors. Various types of larger and more formal savings and credit institutions began to emerge in Europe, organised primarily among the rural and urban poor. These institutions were known by a variety of names, such as people's banks, credit unions, and savings and credit cooperatives. Indonesia provided an example of early microfinance in Asia with the emergence of the Indonesian People's Credit Banks and the Bank Perkreditan Rakyat (BPR) in 1895.

2.2. The years of rapid development and growth, 1900–2000

Adaptations of these models began to appear in parts of rural Latin America in the early 1900s. While the goal of such rural finance interventions was usually defined in terms of modernising the agricultural sector, there were usually two specific objectives:

- increased commercialisation of the rural sector by mobilising 'idle' savings and increasing investment through credit; and
- reducing oppressive feudal relations enforced through indebtedness.

In most cases, these new banks were not owned by the poor themselves as they had been in Europe, but by government agencies or private banks. Over the years, these institutions became inefficient and, in some cases, abusive.

Between 1950 and 1970, governments and donors focused on providing agricultural credit to small and marginal farmers, in the hope of raising productivity and incomes. These efforts led to governments providing credit through state-owned development finance institutions or farmers' cooperatives, which received concessional loans, which they then lent to customers at below-market interest. Subsidised schemes like these were rarely successful. Because of the subsidised lending rates and poor repayment levels, rural development banks suffered from a large depletion of their capital base. Funds did not always reach the poor and often ended up in the hands of better-off farmers.

From the 1970s onwards, experimental programmes in Bangladesh, Brazil, India and a few other countries extended small loans to groups of poor women to invest in micro-businesses. This type of credit was based on group lending where every member of the group guaranteed the repayment of all the group's members. These microenterprise lending programmes were almost exclusively focused on providing credit for income-generating activities (in some cases accompanied by forced savings schemes), and targeted very poor, often female, borrowers. In the 1970s, government agencies were the predominant method of providing productive credit to those with no previous access to credit facilities. These were generally people who had been forced to pay usurious interest rates or had been subject to rent-seeking behaviour.

A pioneering early fund, Accion International, was founded by Joseph Blatchford, a law student, to address poverty in Latin American cities. It was initially run by student volunteers in the shantytowns of Caracas using $90,000 raised from private companies. Today it is one of the world's leading microfinance organisations, with a network of lending partners that spans Latin America, the United States and Africa.

In 1972, the Self-Employed Women's Association (SEWA) registered as a trade union in Gujarat, India. Its main objective was to "strengthen its members' bargaining power to improve income, employment and access to social security". In 1973, to address women's lack of access to financial services, SEWA established the Mahila SEWA Co-operative Bank using shared capital generated by women. Since then, it has provided banking services to poor, illiterate, self-employed women and has become a viable financial venture with around 30,000 active clients.

In Bangladesh, Professor Muhammad Yunus – often considered the father of modern microfinance – used an action-research scheme to address the banking problem faced by the poor. With his graduate students in Chittagong University in 1976, he designed an experimental credit programme that spread rapidly to hundreds of villages. Making use of a special relationship with rural banks, he disbursed and recovered thousands of loans. However, at the end of the pilot phase, in spite of his success, the bankers refused to take over the project, arguing that it was too expensive and too risky. Eventually, and with the support of donors, Professor Yunus founded the Grameen Bank in 1983. Grameen Bank's initial success stimulated the establishment of several other giant microfinance institutions (MFIs) in Bangladesh, including BRAC, ASA and Proshika. Professor Yunus's model has changed radically over a 30-year period. What began as a small pilot project with the features of an NGO has become a well-established financial institution with the legal status of a cooperative that serves more than six million clients in Bangladesh. Grameen's model of microcredit has been emulated by organisations worldwide.

Microfinance gained popularity in the 1980s in response to a greater demand for finances for farmers and the lack of state-delivered subsidised credit. From the mid-

1980s, the subsidised targeted credit model supported by many donors came under steady criticism – most programmes accumulated large loan losses and required frequent recapitalisation to continue operating. It became increasingly evident that market-based solutions were needed. This led to a new approach that considered microfinance as an integral part of the overall financial system. The emphasis shifted from the rapid disbursement of subsidised loans to target populations to the building up of sustainable local institutions to serve the poor.

Meanwhile, microcredit programmes throughout the world improved their original methodologies and defied conventional wisdom about financing the poor. First, they showed that poor people, especially women, had excellent repayment rates among the better programmes. In fact, repayment rates appeared to be better than the formal financial sectors of most developing countries. Second, the poor were willing and able to pay interest rates that allowed MFIs to cover their costs.

In the 1990s, high repayment and cost recovery interest rates allowed some MFIs to achieve a sustainable funding model and reach large numbers of clients. Enthusiasm for microfinance as a strategy for poverty alleviation grew through the decade. The microfinance sector blossomed in many countries, leading to multiple financial services firms serving the needs of micro-entrepreneurs and poor households. These gains, however, tended to concentrate in urban and densely populated rural areas.

It was not until the mid-1990s that the term 'microcredit' began to be replaced by a new term that included not only credit, but also savings and other financial services. 'Microfinance' emerged as the term of choice to refer to a range of financial services, including insurance and remittances.

Accion, referred to above, helped found BancoSol, the world's first commercial bank dedicated solely to microfinance. Today, BancoSol offers a large client base a wide range of financial services that includes savings accounts, credit cards and housing loans. Just a decade ago such products were only accessible to Bolivia's upper classes. BancoSol is no longer unique, and more than 15 Accion-affiliated organisations are now regulated financial institutions.

2.3 Expansion, crisis, turmoil and the emergence of the modern microfinance sector

Figure 1 illustrates the evolution of the microfinance sector since 2003. It shows the sector's high growth between 2003 and 2009. Growth slowed after 2009, due to the effects of the global crisis and regional economic crises, such as those in the state of Andhra Pradesh in India.

The Indian crisis was markedly severe and has become a contemporary reference point for the state of the microfinance sector in India. Once a purely not-for-profit sector, microfinance in India rapidly grew with the economy and was transformed as many operations shifted to profit-focused non-bank finance companies (NBFCs). These NBFCs, which were a hybrid form of microfinance institution, emerged and experienced exponential growth in India.

In 2010 a number of institutions faced allegations of abuse by profiteering, using coercive recovery practices and making multiple loans to borrowers. Four major microfinance institutions closed 50 branches between them as a result. Links established between the practices of some microfinance institutions and the suicides of a number of defaulting borrowers further contributed to these tensions, leading to an ordinance being passed by the government of Andhra Pradesh to protect vulnerable borrowers. The impact of the ordinance has generally been regarded as negative, slowing down institutions' operations and creating an unstable political and prohibitive regulatory climate. Customers began to question their repayment obligations in the face of mass default and negative perceptions of the industry. The microfinance market in India shrunk and around 8% of loans were written off. In order to generate confidence in the industry, there was a push to override disparate state laws and regulate the industry at national level. Although this led to a draft bill based on the recommendations of the Malegam Committee report, three years after the crisis the bill has still not been passed by Parliament and the industry continues to suffer.

The crisis, which was triggered by uncontrolled market growth, excessive lending and a lack of suitable regulation and supervision,[3] shook the foundations of the microcredit sector in India and has had an adverse impact on the microfinance sector around the world. Following

The Andhra Pradesh crisis prompted questions at the national and international levels about the direction of the sector and the possibility of scaling back the employment of profit as 'an end in itself' to achieve social impact objectives for fear of losing sight of those objectives (commonly referred to as 'mission drift).[4]

Figure 1: Evolution of the microfinance sector since the 2000s[5]

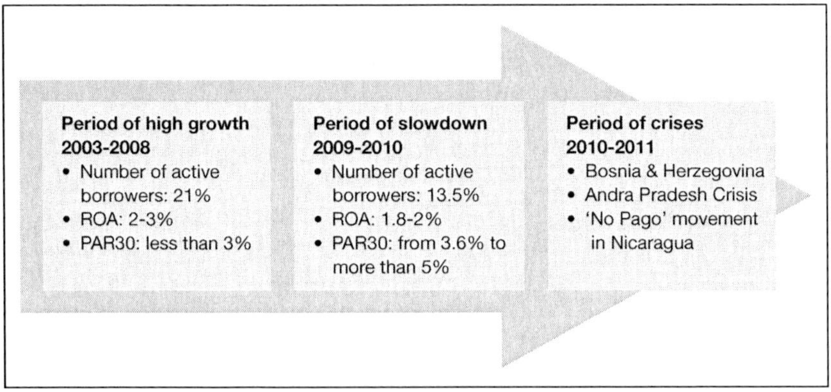

Period of high growth 2003-2008
- Number of active borrowers: 21%
- ROA: 2-3%
- PAR30: less than 3%

Period of slowdown 2009-2010
- Number of active borrowers: 13.5%
- ROA: 1.8-2%
- PAR30: from 3.6% to more than 5%

Period of crises 2010-2011
- Bosnia & Herzegovina
- Andra Pradesh Crisis
- 'No Pago' movement in Nicaragua

2.4 Microfinance today

In the aftermath of the crisis, practitioners and donors today are increasingly focused on expanding financial services to the poor in frontier markets and on integrating

3 For a detailed analysis: C Lützenkirchen and C Weistroffer (2012). 'Microfinance in evolution', *Deutsche Bank Research.*

4 Please see the chapter on the crisis in Indian microfinance for more detail.

5 The diagram relies on information from Lützenkirchen and Weistroffer, 'Microfinance in evolution'; Microrate and Luminis, 'The State of Microfinance Investment 2011: MicroRate's 6th Annual Survey and Analysis of MIVs', available at www.microrate.com/; and the MixMarket website, www.mixmarket.org.

microfinance into the development of financial systems. Recent microfinance approaches, emphasise institutional stability and a favourable policy and regulatory environment[6] in order to improve the overall effectiveness of microfinance interventions. Organisations are increasingly focused on providing sustainable financial solutions for the poor rather than interim fixes.[7] However, many challenges remain, especially in rural and agricultural finance and other frontier markets. Today, both the microfinance industry and the wider development community share a view that permanent poverty reduction means addressing poverty in all its dimensions. For the international community, this means working towards the United Nations' Millennium Development Goals in education, women's empowerment, health and other issues. For the microfinance sector this means viewing microfinance as an essential part of a country's financial system.

3. Changing attitudes towards what microfinance is

The Consultative Group to Assist the Poor (CGAP) defines 'microfinance' as "the supply of loans, savings, and other basic financial services to the poor".[8]

However, the term has come to mean different things to different people. Most people have traditionally considered microfinance to be confined to microcredit – that is, small-scale loans to people who lack access to traditional financial institutions – but this is a misconception, as microcredit is only one subset of microfinance. Recent controversies around microfinance have mainly been associated with microcredit.

Broadly speaking, microfinance is a set of practices developed with the objective of increasing the provision of financial services to low-income clients. Typically, these clients come from the poor 'unbankable' population of the world, to whom traditional sources of finance (lending in particular) are unavailable as they do not satisfy the lending criteria applied by institutions providing traditional sources of finance. The long-term objective of microfinance is to allow low-income groups to generate their own income and become more financially self-sufficient.

Microfinance has always divided opinion, and contemporary attitudes demonstrate a wide spectrum of views, from exuberance to cynicism. A major section of the development sector views it as a panacea for poverty alleviation, and it has therefore become a favourite tool for development institutions. Others believe that the potential of microfinance to close the gulf between the wealthy and the poor is heavily overstated. Such views are often supported by examples of usurious practices, where certain microfinance practices have actually ended up doing more damage to their underlying clients. Whether or not microfinance is indeed the force for good it was intended to be, such polarised views have led to a perception among many of microfinance being fragmented and inconsistent in its approach towards providing financial services to the poor.

---

6 Please see the chapters on 'Governance and the sustainability of microfinance institutions' and 'Microfinance regulation' for more detail.

7 Please see the chapter 'From microfinance to livelihoods'.

8 http://cgap.org.

3.1 Expanding the basic premise

As mentioned above, microfinance has generally been understood to be synonymous with microcredit. 'Microcredit' broadly entails offering very small loans to low-income clients for self-employment, often with the simultaneous collection of small amounts of savings. Many microfinance practitioners have also long viewed microfinance as a 'one size fits all' solution. Just because a certain model has worked in a particular country does not mean that it will be equally successful in another. What 'small' or 'poor' means will differ from country to country, and is heavily dependent on a particular individual's circumstances and the society he or she lives in – a poor villager in a remote part of India will have different relative circumstances and surroundings to a poor person in South America, Africa or Europe.

Various social, economic, political and even religious factors may affect the success or failure of a certain model. When considering a microfinance model that has worked in a certain country, it is therefore important also to examine the broader environment in which it operates, in order to determine the reasons for its success.[9]

Microfinance programmes therefore vary, depending on the model, target group and services offered. Not all programmes labelled as 'microfinance' will meet everyone's understanding of the term. Research indicates that emerging programmes should be benchmarked against other microfinance programmes with regard to outreach, impact and financial self-sufficiency to ensure they offer similar services to similar target groups. But there is no 'one size fits all' model in microfinance.

3.2 Features of microfinance programmes

In view of the foregoing, microfinance programmes need to be assessed against the relevant social, economic and political factors. Some of the more typical features of a microfinance programme include:

- 'micro' or small-scale provision of financial services. Small in this context is relative. However, microloans may be made for as little as $2 a day. A key component of a microfinance programme is that loans remain below a certain 'manageable' size, but there is still a question over what size of loan best serves the dual needs of the clients and the institution. A balance must be found between preserving the interests of clients and maximising the impact of their borrowing, while ensuring that institutions are able to manage their loans. Some argue that a greater diversity of loan products in terms of size is only beneficial up to a point, as it may become unmanageable for institutions and confusing for the client. Accordingly, other products, such as savings and insurance, have emerged as effective complements or substitutes for loans;
- financial services targeted at the poor. Defining 'poor' is not without its challenges, as individuals' experiences of poverty differ widely in various parts of the world. This is particularly important now in view of recent legislation from the US Congress that requires the United States Agency for International Development to restrict funding to programmes that focus on

9 See the chapter 'Evolving business models of microfinance' for more detail.

the poor. Some argue that microfinance should focus on the 'economically active poor', or those just at or below the poverty line.[10] The opposing view is that microfinance institutions (MFIs) should try to reach the indigent;[11]

- unsecured and collateral-free loans. Such small loans are generally, granted for entrepreneurial activities, typically for working capital, and are usually unsecured and collateral free;
- informal appraisal of borrowers and investments;
- collateral substitutes, such as group guarantees or compulsory savings. These have been criticised recently for discouraging the poor from participating in microfinance initiatives, and for having a smaller than predicted effect on repayment rates;
- access to repeat and larger loans, based on repayment performance. This has required microfinance institutions to grow in order to meet demand and provide sustainable funding to its clients;
- streamlined loan disbursement and monitoring;
- secure savings products;
- group lending;
- focus on underserved communities such as women or disabled people that (depending on the social setup or jurisdiction) face severe restrictions in accessing finance. It has been argued that women repay their loans more often and direct a higher share of enterprise proceeds to their families;[12]
- simple, accessible application processes for loans; and
- market-level interest rates.[13]

It is not necessary for a microfinance programme to have all of the above features. However, it is typical for them to have at least some if not most of the above. Initially, microfinance gained popularity for having introduced solidarity groups and village banking with joint liability, mostly among women borrowers. The multitude of approaches that have developed in the last 30 or so years have attracted both praise and criticism.

4. Types of microfinance services

As suggested by its name, 'microfinance' clearly extends beyond credit alone. Many microfinance programmes today include savings products, remittance services (with an increasing use of modern technology such as mobile banking) and insurance. These are becoming popular innovations. It is also no longer exclusively development-focused institutions that offer microfinance services. Commercial banks and insurance companies are beginning to diversify their operations to reach new markets.

---

10 Robinson, M (2001). The Microfinance Revolution: Sustainable Finance for the Poor. Washington DC:IBRD/The World Bank

11 S Daley-Harris (2005). State of the Microcredit Summit Campaign Report.

12 See the chapter on 'Microfinance and the empowerment of women' for more detail.

13 List derived from J Ledgerwood: Microfinance Handbook: An Institutional and Financial Perspective (Washington, DC: World Bank).

Although microfinance's origins are in microcredit, microcredit today is a subset of microfinance. Over the past decade, the almost exclusive attention on microcredit has evolved into a broader vision captured by the use of the word 'microfinance' instead. This takes into account the fact that the unbanked poor need other financial services, not just credit. These include savings, insurance, remittances and financial intermediation.

It is sometimes argued that skills training provided to microfinance customers should also be included as part of the definition of microfinance, since without it customers are unable to move towards sustainability. So far, however, such vocational and financial training has remained outside the definition of microfinance since these services, although they promote the success of microfinance initiatives and encourage better borrowing practices, are not strictly financial. This argument appears increasingly less relevant as institutions must become more client-focused. In future the balance of services provided will be led far more by customers' demographic profile and income levels, the use of subsidy, regulation and government structures, and the breadth and quality of services offered. While lending remains the core activity, it is fair to suggest that all initiatives should have an integral training component appropriate for the type of product and target customer.

In view of the above, the various ways in which microfinance aims to empower low income groups may be broadly classified into the following three categories:

- microcredit;
- microsavings; and
- microinsurance.

4.1 Microcredit

This includes providing funds to customers, typically in the form of small loans. Repayment models can be classified into the following types (each based on a differed risk-sharing method):

- *Solidarity groups.* This is the classic microfinance model, often referred to as the 'Grameen model' after Grameen Bank, which pioneered it. It involves five-person solidarity-groups, in which each group member guarantees the other members' repayment. If any group member fails to repay their loan, the other members must repay for them or face losing out on future credit.
- *Village banking.* This expands the solidarity group concept to a larger group of 15–30 women or men who are responsible for both managing the loan and making and collecting loans to and from each other. India's self-help groups operate according to a similar format.
- *Individual lending.* This is simply the provision of microfinance services to individuals instead of groups. It is similar in form to traditional banking and can be hard to distinguish from it. This is particularly true in cases where MFIs require collateral to guarantee loans, as collateral-free lending has traditionally been one of the hallmarks of microfinance.

It is important to note that micro-lenders themselves are moving away from providing just small loans and group loans, and are starting to offer a wide variety of products. MFIs need to be successful at both extending loans to poor borrowers and developing cost-efficient lending practices.

4.2 Microsavings

It is a common misconception that the poor are incapable of saving. Poor people can and do save, in all kinds of ways. Studies have shown that the poor are as capable of saving just as anyone else.[14] The options and criteria for saving are just different, and diverse. Although microfinance has traditionally focused on expanding access to credit, village savings and loan associations (VSLAs) are savings-led.

Grameen and other similar organisations worldwide typically offer two types of microsavings facility:

- a 'compulsory savings' account, which can be withdrawn if and when the client leaves the organisation, on condition that the client has saved for at least five consecutive years; and
- a 'voluntary savings' account, which, at least in principle, offers microsaving clients the possibility of withdrawing from the accounts at any time during the duration of loan cycles.[15]

In 1991, the NGO CARE pioneered what has proven to be one of the world's most effective informal savings methods, the VSLA. VSLAs allow members to save flexibly, access small loans for investment, and build a social fund to strengthen their resilience to external shocks such as illness or drought. Participation in a VSLA boosts member's average incomes and household assets, and also brings non-economic benefits such as increased self-esteem, particularly for the 70% of participants who are women.[16] Today, CARE's VSLAs reach an estimated 3.1 million people in 26 African countries. Approximately 3 million more participate in VSLAs supported by other development organisations around the world.[17]

(a) How does a VSLA work?

The primary purpose of a VSLA is to provide simple savings and loan services to a community that does not have access to formal financial services. A VSLA is formed by a self-selected group, all of whose members save money in the form of shares. The savings are invested in a loan fund, from which members can borrow money at a reasonable rate of interest. Members also contribute a small sum to a compulsory insurance fund, which can be used to provide grants or no-cost loans to members in distress.

All transactions are carried out at regular meetings in front of all members, with each member holding their own individual passbook. This promotes both transparency and accountability. The cycle of savings and lending is time bound. At

---

14 D Collins, J Murdoch, S Rutherford and O Ruthven (2009). *Portfolios of the Poor: How the World's Poor Live on $2 a Day*. Princeton: Princeton Univesity Press.

15 I Murray and E Lynch (2003). 'What do microfinance customers value?', *Women's World Banking*, Vol 1, No 1.

16 Based on periodic analysis of data from Care's VSLA management information system.

17 Current figures according to The SEEP Network, www.seepnetwork.org/savings-groups-global-outreach-pages-20015.php

the end of an agreed period the accumulated savings and interest earnings are shared out among the members.[18]

4.3 Microinsurance

This can be described as a 'back-to-basics' campaign for insurers that enables them to reach an under-served market. It is also a mechanism that enables government social protection schemes to extend coverage to workers in the informal economy who lack benefits such as health insurance and pensions. Microinsurance is increasingly being used by groups that have a range of ideologies and approaches, but a common objective to protect the vulnerable and insure their low-income members.[19]

5. Who are microfinance's providers?

Microfinance is offered by a number of different organisations. This is still an evolving space, and new participants are always entering the sector. There have also been many innovative methods of getting finance available to the poor.[20]

The various types of microfinance provider are covered in further detail in the chapter 'Evolving business models of microfinance', but they can be summarised as follows:

- non-governmental organisations;
- self help groups;
- credit unions;
- mobile banking organisations;
- microfinance institutions; and
- commercial banks and other market-specific models.

MFIs may be NGOs, savings and loan cooperatives, credit unions, government banks, commercial banks or non-bank financial institutions.

A recent development is the use of crowd-funding – that is, the collective raising and pooling together of funds, usually via the Internet – to support efforts to provide financial solutions to the poor. This also includes innovative payments and remittance platforms that are being currently developed.[21]

6. Who are microfinance's clients?

It is difficult to categorise microfinance clients, as the essential objective of microfinance is that they will use it to start a small business of their own. However, they are typically self-employed, and are often traders, street vendors, small service providers (eg, hairdressers, rickshaw drivers) and artisans.

Although MFIs tend to target micro-entrepreneurs, not all of them require this as a condition for a loan. Some MFIs visit borrowers' places of business to verify that

---

18 Care (2013). *Connecting the World's Poorest People to the Global Economy: New models for linking informal savings groups to formal financial services.*

19 Please see the chapter 'Microinsurance' for a detailed discussion on this topic.

20 Please see the chapter on 'Microfinance from an investor's perspective' for more detail.

21 One such innovative solution is the donations platform that has been established by SharedImpact, www.sharedimpact.org.

their loans have been utilised for entrepreneurial activities, while others disburse loans with few questions asked, operating more like consumer credit lenders. Some MFIs also require collateral or collateral substitutes such as household assets that are valuable to the borrower but of less value than the loan.

Many MFIs offer individual loans to their established clients and even to first-time borrowers. Grameen, one of the pioneers of the group lending model, has since shifted to individual lending.

7. The road ahead for microfinance

Notwithstanding the impact of the global financial crisis on financial markets worldwide,[22] a number of features can be observed about recent developments in microfinance:[23]

- *The continual increase of participants and services.* Whereas microcredit dominated the sector in its early years, the market now encompasses a full spectrum of products and services;
- *The continuing breakdown of barriers between international and domestic markets.* The international market is becoming increasingly integrated, with investors from the international community playing a much greater role than ever before.
- *The increasing use of technology and media solutions.* Crowd-funding and mobile banking are increasingly being used to raise funds and increase access to communities in the remotest parts of the world. Much work still needs to be done in this area to capitalise fully on the potential of technology to those low income populations who use mobile technology but cannot access traditional banking services. However, there are very positive signs of innovative techniques being applied to use the Internet, app technology and alternate forms of currency in this regard.

7.1 Some recent innovations

Thanks to field practitioners, microfinance innovations have grown exponentially. Begun by what is often referred to as 'civil society', microfinance was largely built upon initiatives from NGOs and cooperatives. BancoSol, for example, started as a small NGO in 1986 and is now a commercial bank serving over 100,000 Bolivian clients.[24]

In 2009 Musoni leveraged the popularity of M-PESA, a popular local mobile money transfer service, to launch the first 100% mobile microfinance institution, Musoni Kenya. With all repayments, deposits and disbursements carried out over mobile phones, and with tablets used for field-based data capture, Musoni takes advantage of the latest technologies to enhance the traditional microfinance model for the benefit of its clients.[25]

---

22 D Rozas (2011). 'Weathering the Storm: Hazards, Beacons and Life Rafts: Lessons in Microfinance Crisis Survival from Those Who Have Been There'. Centre for Financial Inclusion at Accion International, http://centerforfinancialinclusionblog.files.wordpress.com/2011/07/weathering-the-storm_center-for-financial-inclusion_final.pdf.

23 Please see the chapters on 'The Future of Microfinance' and 'Microfinance 3.0'.

24 B Armendariz and M Labie (2011). *The Handbook of Microfinance.* Singapore: World Scientific Publishing.

25 See the chapter on 'Microfinance and the impact of mobile banking' for more detail.

CCACN (*Central de Cooperativas de Ahorro y Crédito Financieras de Nicaragua*) markets 'Agriculture Salary' savings product to farmers. The goal is to smooth the flow of income from the proceeds of an annual or semi-annual harvest. Each credit union works with its farmers to identify their individual expenses and determine a monthly 'salary' (a portion of harvest proceeds on deposit combined with an above-market interest rate), which can be withdrawn from the credit union.

Caja los Andes in Bolivia offers loan repayment options that fit to the cashflow of various agricultural activities. These include an end-of-term payment for both principal and interest that fits single crop activities, and unequal payments at irregular intervals for farmers who have planted several crops with different harvesting periods. Flexibility is also provided in loan disbursements, and farmers can receive the agreed loan amount over a number of instalments.

Unibanka, a Latvian commercial bank, used to view microfinance loans as too costly to deliver. Now, however, branch staff use scorecards to evaluate microfinance loan applications quickly, which has reduced the cost of review and made microfinance lending profitable.[26]

7.2 Conclusion – the quest for sustainability

Microfinance is at a crucial juncture in its evolution, not only in terms of growth and financial sustainability, but also with respect to its underlying promise to effect social change by alleviating poverty. If the sector wants to maintain its impressive growth rate, donors' money will not be sufficient. Commercialised microfinance has been an enduring promise in the field, but it has not been without controversy. Those who argue that commercialisation should be the path for microfinance tend to dismiss concerns that it can compromise social achievement. Instead they tend to focus on how it can expand scale. Others argue that compromises between financial and social goals are manifest. There is growing interest in the sector among investors, particularly those with an interest in socially responsible investing. It remains to be seen whether this will translate into a contribution in earnest and help the industry meet its outreach objectives at a faster pace without compromising its social mission.

Nevertheless, recent experiences, particularly the crisis in Andhra Pradesh, suggest that the practices of microfinance institutions do not always respect basic ethical standards. An increased incidence of irresponsible lending and commercialisation that loses sight of the core objectives of microfinance could put the whole sector at risk. It is therefore likely that the sector's sustainability will not only depend on the financial results achieved by the MFIs, which will facilitate the entry of new actors, but also on social sustainability. In the wake of the crisis in Andhra Pradesh, regulation has been welcomed by the sector to address the issues brought about by its unprecedented growth. However, one needs to be careful as, over-regulation by local governments could limit growth and potential.

Securing meaningful and sustainable growth for microfinance is a pursuit both fraught with difficulty and brimming with opportunity. Although the last 30 years have seen many accomplishments, much more remains to be done. Many feel that

26 D G Salazar (2004). 'Credit Scoring', *CGAP IT Innovation Series*.

moving the sector forward requires a dialogue between institutions and other participants to foster a collective ownership of and responsibility for microfinance. Making space for key stakeholders in what is an increasingly complex and diverse market will require a coordinated effort from all the sector's various emergent and established factions.

The author would like to thank Marcus Fedder, Cameron Goldie-Scot, Christopher Bernard, Aditi Kapoor and Ayesha Patwardhan for their thoughts, comments and assistance with the content and editing of this chapter. The author would also like to thank Sian O'Neill and Nidhi Misra Basu for their support and guidance.

Microfinance: hurdles and key issues

Sam Mendelson
Financial inclusion & microfinance consultant

1. Introduction

It is approaching three years since the foundations of the microfinance industry (and I choose this term advisedly) were severely shaken. This was not so much due to the events in Andhra Pradesh (AP) *per se* – concerning as some stories of alleged client mistreatment were. It was rather the emergence of this negative narrative into the global mainstream press; the contagious perception that microfinance – far from being a panacea for alleviating poverty – was not even meeting the hippocratic threshold of "do no harm".

This narrative is true in parts, untrue in others, but most of all it is an extremely complex story. The low point came on November 17 2010 when the *New York Times* ran a cover story entitled "Indian Microcredit Faces Collapse from Defaults" – and the die was cast. Almost three years later and the acute crisis has passed. While certain markets continue to struggle with an overindebtedness that had settled deep into the industry, on the whole I hope we can say that the crisis is over.

However, what the 2010 AP crisis (and the specific market crises in Bosnia, Nicaragua and Morocco, among others) gave way to was a series of larger issues about the future of microfinance. Some of these are focused:

- Which social performance management (SPM) framework (the methodologies for determining social impact of microfinance) should dominate?
- Who should be the main providers of agri-insurance?
- What – if any – margin or rate caps are appropriate?

Some are much more general, even philosophical.

Typically, a multi-author book such as this would tuck the 'challenges' chapter somewhere in the back. The narrative thus goes from promoting an argument or product and then doing the minimum to say "however..." towards the end. It is pleasing that this chapter has been front-loaded. This means that all the interesting stuff to come – on microfinance investment vehicles (MIVs) and SPM and technology and product innovation – is underpinned by a clear recognition of the challenges to be overcome.

The corollary to this is that it is impossible to address all the issues in more than cursory depth. So this short chapter will introduce some of the challenges ahead, but will equally foreshadow the subsequent chapters of the book, which will address many of the same issues in greater depth.

There is much to be positive about within microfinance today. After almost four decades of back slapping, self-congratulatory complacency about microfinance as a miraculous solution for poverty, realism is having its time in the sun. What might have been heresy only a few years ago is orthodoxy today:

- microfinance is a 'tool', not a poverty panacea;
- the provision of 'one-size-fits-all' credit to the poor probably does not help – and may quite possibly do harm;
- a reliance on heart-warming anecdotes in place of robust and transparent analysis helps nobody;
- savings and insurance are probably more important than credit in bringing the un(der)banked into the financial system in a useful, sustainable way; and
- microfinance is about neither purely commercial access to new markets nor purely social poverty alleviation for the poor. It has dual roles, which sometimes come into conflict and sometimes complement one another.

Only six or seven years ago, the SPM framework that we see today – with Universal Standards designed by the Social Performance Task Force, the Client Protection Principles of the SMART Campaign, the Seal of Excellence for Poverty Outreach in Microfinance being promoting by the Microcredit Summit Campaign, and UNPRI's Principles for Investors in Inclusive Finance (let alone the continued evolution of the rating agencies and the social reporting submitted to the MIX Market) – would have been hard to imagine. Mobile banking (the ability to save, remit and transact money stored on a mobile phone – a phenomenal tool for the unbanked) was barely a glint in the Department for International Development (DFID)/Safaricom's eyes, nor was much of the most exciting work being done within microfinance in livelihood or value chain finance, 'last-mile' energy finance, food security or financial education.

So only a couple years from the 'Chicken Licken' scenario brought about by front-page headlines of Indian suicides and the disaster of the SKS IPO, I am excited about the future.

Of course, you cannot talk about challenges and issues without success or failure – and you cannot discuss these without considering what success actually is. As argued in the introduction, every writer in this book will have a different definition of 'microfinance' because there is no single one. Each will have a different idea of what success for the industry looks like.

For me, it is not about poverty alleviation as a direct objective. I am generally pleased with the sea change which has heralded a focus on financial inclusion. I truly believe that the provision to the poor of appropriate, demand-led, ethical, scalable and potentially profitable financial services, leveraging new technologies and provided in conjunction with financial education is a good thing. Diversifying the industry's funding among government, development finance institutions, retail social investors, savings mobilisation, local bank funding and institutional investors is a good thing. And regulating not only the lenders (the microfinance institutions (MFIs)) but also the funders (investors) recognises the role that a surfeit of cheap funding chasing too few clients – a key driver of the Indian crisis – can have in overheating a market and bringing the whole thing crashing down.

However, if long-term success is a stable and sustainable industry of institutions providing quality, useful services to the poor, this remains a long way off: there are risks to mitigate on the journey ahead. Without claiming to be an exhaustive list – and with the caveat that this is a think-piece and not an academic journal article – here are some of the key issues along the way.

2. Banana skins ahead

As co-author since 2009 of the annual Microfinance Banana Skins survey, my colleagues and I get a good feel for the risks facing the industry, and the way that perceptions move over time. Banana Skins – an industry wide, forward-looking, qualitative and quantitative survey of risk – asks respondents to predict the risks facing the industry as a whole (although many undoubtedly focus only on their own market) over the coming three to five years. While we try to look beyond the medium to the long-term health of the industry, the results from the last couple of Banana Skins are revealing – and worth a short summary.

Microfinance Banana Skins 2012 (2011 position in bracket)			
1	Overindebtedness (-)	11	Mission drift (9)
2	Corporate governance (4)	12	Back office (13)
3	Management quality (7)	13	Macro-econimic risk (17)
4	Credit risk (1)	14	Staffing (8)
5	Political interference (5)	15	External risks (-)
6	Quality of risk management (-)	16	Technology management (11)
7	Client management (-)	17	Too litle funding (23)
8	Competition (3)	18	Interest rates (21)
9	Regulation (6)	19	Too much funding (22)
10	Liquidity (16)	20	Foreign exchange (24)

The 2011 survey was conducted in late 2010. As expected, the crisis in India – along with problems in Morocco, Bosnia and Pakistan – dominated responses. Our introduction reflected some of these fears: "In the last two years, microfinance has found its enviable reputation under attack for a number of perceived reasons: its growing commercialism, as evidenced by an increasing focus on size and profitability, a decline in standards, particularly in the area of lending, and a sense that the industry may be drifting away from its original 'double bottom line' purpose."

Many respondents cited AP specifically, and many more expressed concern at the issues being raised there: overconcentration, collection practices, mission drift and pricing.

The 2011 survey showed dramatic shifts. 'Reputation' rose 15 places to second overall (out of 24). 'Political interference' rose five spots to fifth and 'mission drift' climbed 10 to ninth place, revealing an industry paying extremely close attention to

India and concerned about the future. Movement was not just relative but absolute. In terms of severity, respondents felt the risks were getting worse. There was, in late 2010, genuine concern for the future – or the value – of microfinance.

Around the same time, a lot of quasi-scientific speciousness was being trumpeted by Milford Bateman, whose book *Why Doesn't Microfinance Work?* was being widely read – and widely disputed. The UK government's All-Party Parliamentary Group on Microfinance, quoted him thus: "The MF movement... has failed to provide robust evidence that is it meaningfully associated with poverty reduction... many specialists [now believe] that microfinance actually undermines the process of sustainable poverty reduction and 'bottom-up' economic and social development."

What was previously heresy (questioning microfinance's positive impact on poverty) was becoming more prevalent. A DFID study failed to find any evidence of positive impact. The perception that microfinance has failed to do what it should have these past decades – to prove its worth, instead of self-congratulating with heart-warming anecdotes – was spreading. AP did not cause this, but it certainly helped it along.

Just over a year later, the 2012 Banana Skins survey showed much more self-awareness among practitioners and funders. Awareness of risk is, after all, a "precondition to coping" as one survey respondent noted, and a first step in beginning to manage and move beyond the hurdles ahead. The high rankings of overindebtedness, quality of risk management, and client management – all new entries – bodes well.

However, despite greater confidence in practitioners' preparedness for challenges and much greater awareness of the Responsible Finance agenda, the survey results did raise important questions about MFIs' capacity to rise to the occasion, and in particular the capacity of management and staff to cope with the complexities of the new operating environment.

According to more optimistic observers though (myself included), microfinance has already begun to emerge from this difficult period and is in a stronger state, having learned (some) lessons and resolving to do better. Nonetheless, questions remain over the industry's direction. Can it find a future which combines its social objectives with the more demanding commercial world in which it operates? As it navigates its way forward, what are the hurdles that it faces? The overall message from the 2012 survey was that the immediate risks posed by the global economic crisis and by the controversy over the industry's mission have eased – but that larger questions about the future direction of microfinance remain. This book addresses many of these larger questions.

The Banana Skins survey has its uses, but looks only to the short to medium term, and is a line-of-best-fit of the agendas of a disparate group of respondents: non-governmental organisations (NGOs), non-bank MFIs, commercial banks, MIVs, development finance institutions (DFIs) and regulators among others – most with a specific geographical focus.

I would like to take a few of the general themes that have been consistently raised, and look beyond the comments of Banana Skins respondents and beyond the medium term. I will briefly look at five key issue areas, 'hurdles' which I think the industry will have to surmount:

- reputation;
- institutional issues;
- the client;
- products; and
- funding.

3. Reputation

Critics see MFIs allowing their business and ethical standards to slip as they pursue business targets, disregarding the interests of their customers, and putting the industry at risk. As well as the reputational consequences of this shift, there is the practical concern that certain investors and donors – DFIs in particular – could become less willing to fund an industry whose main objective is perceived to be profit.

The big money flowed into certain microfinance markets in the mid-2000s, as MIVs scrambled to achieve double-digit returns in new markets, and the recipient MFIs scrambled to find new clients to make the profits to generate that return. That trend, despite the collapse (and now partial recovery) in Indian microfinance, has not stopped. The money is still there, still active, and the question remains: "Is the industry as a unit able to sufficiently keep those destructive flows in check?"

Much will turn on how effective are measures in place to stop future bubbles. The risk is of a combination of reputational fallout with a credit failure. That is, there is only so much more market deterioration that the sector can handle, because it remains hugely dependent on foreign money (with the exception of a few well-developed markets such as Bangladesh, India, Peru and Mexico) from DFIs, social investors, MIVs and multilaterals. That tipping point has not been reached, but there is the possibility that a couple more market disasters, and it will be all over. In an ideal world, savings mobilisations and local bank funding would take up the slack, but reducing dependence on foreign funding takes time – especially in the many markets that are in the early institution-building stages of development. It is ironic that tapping capital markets was supposed to be the great leap forward for microfinance. It may be its undoing.

What would being "all over" look like in practice? If the DFIs lose their appetite for investing in the industry, it will be serious. Microfinance is a small part of DFIs' portfolios, but this small part comprises a large part of non-deposit microfinance funding. And that's just debt; equity is also dominated by foreign money, even more so.

Reputation has two sides to it, of course. There is the reputation of the industry as a relatively low-risk, relatively high-return alternative investment class, and there is the social reputation – microfinance's mission of helping the poor by providing useful financial access (and unshackling them from the much-hated moneylenders). Future empirical evidence on whether microfinance works will affect this social reputation, especially with divergence of view on what microfinance is for. Either way, preserving both reputations – financial and social – will be a big hurdle to overcome for the long-term future.

One Banana Skins respondent put this issue well: "Is microfinance primarily about financial inclusion or poverty alleviation? Is microfinance primarily a business opportunity or a development intervention? Does microfinance really meet both financial and social return expectations? Is it an 'either or'? Or has microfinance many faces? Whatever the answers, the industry's reputation will never be the same."

4. Institutional issues

Over the past decade or two, there has been a general trend from an initially NGO-led sector, to an industry in which non-bank MFIs and increasingly commercial banks are the dominant institutions. The objectives can and should change: now the objective is a full range of useful financial services for those currently unserved or inadequately served. The goal is not to have lots of profitable MFIs. This is like saying you should have profitable departments in a bank, rather than embedding an international perspective in the whole of what the bank does.

There are thousands upon thousands of MFIs in dozens of countries today. But the MFI – typically the non-bank financial institution (NBFI), although we should include semi-formal credit and savings groups, NGOs and some banks in this – need not be the foundation of the microfinance industry. The next stage in the evolution of microfinance will include considering what lies beyond MFIs. This is the osmosis of microfinance products or services into the broader economy and not MFIs for their own sake.

The emergence of the MFI over the past four decades was, as with many organic developments, messy, unplanned and sub-optimal. When anything starts, it begins in its own bubble, away from the rules that disallow it. So while there is some case to make that savings should really have started before insurance, which in turn was before credit, there are perfectly clear reasons why it happened the way it did. Savings are slow and hard. Credit is quick and easy. And people wanted a big impact fast.

However, among the most interesting discussions about what future success (within the definition of 'financial access' I gave at the start) looks like is the institutional issue. Do we want all retail banks to go downscale to reach microfinance clients themselves? Do we want the non-bank MFIs going upscale so they do not have to hand off their best, profitable clients who are just on the cusp of paying back all that investment as a small and medium-enterprise (SME) owner? This is the 'graduation'. The gap between micro and SME-finance remains, for the most part, a chasm.

So who do we want the players to be? Does microfinance become the charitable leftovers for those who mainstream banks fail to reach? Is the goal that everyone is served, and as big a proportion as possible served by private sector, by a bank, with infinite graduation possibility? Or is the goal that the institution looks beyond lending money, calculating its risk and charging interest?

If the goal is indeed to go beyond merely increasing financial access, let me give a short example.

A 'rickshaw loan' given by some MFIs in India is a good example of credit customised for a specific purpose. Eight million livelihoods depend on this low-cost, all weather, environmenttally friendly vehicle; but they are rarely owned by those who pull them. Typically the owners collect rent from the pullers, leaving little for them to live on. The Centre for Rural Development (CRD) therefore designed the rickshaw loan.

An improved, ergonomically efficient vehicle was designed. This rickshaw was made available on lease (hire purchase) to rickshaw pullers. The condition was that they should be in joint loan groups (JLGs) of five members and function in a cluster – called a garage – of five JLGs. The loan of Rs10,500 included not only the cost of the vehicle, but two years licence and insurance costs. The insurance covered not only the rickshaw, but the puller's life and third-party injuries/death due to accident.

A small instalment of hire rental of Rs25 per day is charged over 520 days, over 18 to 24 months. The overall recovery made is Rs13,000. CRD generates revenue by hiring the rear of the rickshaw for advertisements. The revenue from this source is Rs5,000 per annum, which is used towards a part of the loan, making it possible to collect only Rs13,000 against interest and principal from the rickshaw puller. After all the instalments are paid, the rickshaw become the property of the puller. The lease rental charged is no more than the hire paid to owners by pullers otherwise.

This case study bears such close analysis because it cuts across sectors, encompassing asset building, livelihood development, credit and title support. An institution that does not allow itself to go beyond being just a financial institution would not be able to achieve this on behalf of its clients. The challenge is to create organisational enablers in order to give those working as loan product designers in banks or MFIs the scope to liaise with solar companies, energy companies, advertisers, property developers, food manufacturers, market owners, builders or architects in order to come up with solution that really achieve the client's purpose.

For the most part, this is still pie in the sky. Not enough time has been spent defining 'success' in microfinance. If we spent more time on this, we might realise that building big MFIs is not the goal, it is a stage. But the trend is in the right direction, and getting the MFI beyond being just a pseudo-bank for the reasonably poor will take time, courage and immense vision by practitioners.

5. Understanding the client

When microfinance historians of the future look back to the late 2000s and early 2010s, they will recognise one of the most important developments as having been the burgeoning recognition of the importance of understanding clients. This is not to say that this was something previously dismissed out of hand, but it reflects an increasing understanding of the complexities of the financial lives of the poor, and the risks of supply-led products ill-suited to the actual needs of the underserved.

Understanding one's client (or KYC, in the parlance) is rapidly evolving. The proliferation of responsible finance initiatives, the 'financial diary' approach pioneered in *Portfolios of the Poor*, the use of new (often branchless) delivery channels, more credit bureaux, energy products and exciting ideas in education and livelihood reflects this. However, despite piecemeal progress, it remains the case that not only do the underserved need financial services more than anyone else, but that those they do receive are worse than anyone else's.

Mainly, the underserved rely on informal tools, but the tools available and the behaviour they affect are not always well matched with needs. As Stuart Rutherford and I argued in the first session of my Citi/DFID fellowship last year, there are three big needs:

- The daily grind – managing money on a day-to-day basis to ensure there is food on the table every day and not just on days when income comes in (eg, money to buy a child an ointment on the day she gets conjunctivitis and not when the infection has already damaged her eyes for life);
- Big expenditures – this means forming sums big enough for life's big spends (eg, lifecycle events like birth, education, marriage, death, homemaking and furnishing, as well as big assets such as fans, televisions or bicycles, and business assets); and
- Emergencies – these include private emergencies like ill health, and public ones like fires, floods and cyclones. Poor countries – virtually by definition – are more susceptible to these emergencies, or shocks. Dealing with emergencies requires activity similar to those for big expenditures but with the added complication that their timing and their nature (mostly) cannot be foreseen.

The trouble is that those excluded from the formal financial system typically suffer volatility of income. This leads to difficulty affording charges of financial services providers (a higher proportion of small loans need to be paid as interest; savings may yield no financial returns or entail handling charges). Volatility also means smaller and more regular transactions, so higher costs for providers and higher rates for the end client.

The excluded also have to absorb other transaction costs such as bus fares for repayments – although the emerging of m-banking will mitigate this – and the opportunity cost of travelling to a MFI or bank branch, arranging for someone else to look after the shop, animals or children while the adult spends a few hours transacting. Moreover, the (un)suitability of financial products offered is a problem (eg, minimum balance requirements; or the poor household needs a loan of a smaller amounts or for a shorter duration than the financial organisation is interested in).

In addition, there is the struggle of making a commitment. Standard microloans need to be repaid in equal weekly repayments, and making such commitments either causes significant stress, or the borrower opts for the lowest possible denominator to be safe from wide income/ expenditure fluctuations.

These are some of the issues facing clients. But what is the 'hurdle' which needs to be overcome by the industry for it to prosper by the definition I originally set out? It is the problem that product design is not evolving at a rate to match our increased knowledge of the financial lives of the underserved. What is needed is the better translation of increased client understanding into appropriate market segmentation and the design of financial products that meet the needs of these market segments in a fair, sustainable and profitable way.

6. Product design

So what products do meet these criteria? This is an especially complex area as products must vary as considerably as the needs they are designed to meet. A soy farmer with a family in a village in sub-Saharan Africa who wishes to add value to his produce and sell it in an urban market has manifestly different product needs to an unmarried rickshaw driver in a Pakistani city. The traditional microfinance product – the 'vanilla' loan – seldom meets clients' actual needs. As Graham Wright and I argued in the second session of the fellowship programme, as a bare minimum poor people probably need a suite of products that include:

- a transaction or very basic savings account (linked to a reliable and efficient payments/remittance system that is not too costly);
- recurring deposit accounts for different goals (perhaps with an attached overdraft);
- a general short-term (up to one year) loan (which can be used for working capital as well as for consumption smoothing and education);
- a credit life insurance policy and possibly health, livestock or asset coverage; and
- a longer-term loan to facilitate purchase of large assets such as housing or a vehicle (secured against assets).

For most of the history of modern microfinance, product design has rested on the assumption that a single microcredit product would do for most purposes. It was framed in terms of microenterprise support (buying cheaper inventory, expanding a small business, investing in better transport and the like) while tacitly understanding that it would be used as much for so-called consumption smoothing.

There is no doubt whatsoever that for some individual microfinance clients this has been very helpful – something tiresomely promoted in MFIs' promotional literature and on the conference circuit. However, we understand now that matching appropriate products to market segment needs is the essential element of industry success.

Credit has been the staple of microfinance since inception, for the obvious reasons that it is easier to offer, and more profitable too. However, savings and, increasingly, insurance are arguably more important to clients than credit (something which Mosleh Ahmed outlines in detail in Chapter 18). Seeing microinsurance as a standalone product may be a mistake, though. It is not disassociated from the insurance market continuum: it is simply the lower end – or as Richard Leftley of MicroEnsure prefers to call it, "mass market insurance". In the same way that insurers deal completely differently with multinational corporations like Shell Oil than they do with middle income homeowners, they need to figure out how to deal with the low-income market.

The difference is not just a lower premium for a lower sum insured. To 'crack' the microinsurance problem (and the difficulty thus far in providing insurance beyond credit life means it is a problem) mandates a different approach to:

- controls – forgetting the long list of exclusions and extensive requirements for claims settlement;

- marketing – the industry needs to build trust and convey information in a way that has an impact on the low income market;
- agents – traditional agents are not effective in selling microinsurance;
- policy documents – making them easier to understand for clients with low literacy;
- product features – making them flexible in terms of the needs of the market;
- understanding the market – with no more individual underwriting, insurers need to understand the clients and their risks and needs, as well as market-segment underwriting, as individual underwriting is too expensive for this market; and
- delivery – how to get products out to millions of people efficiently and effectively.

Implementing this approach may be the hardest part of next-generation product design. Insurers need to:

- design simple products that are understandable and easy to administer (with few exclusions);
- educate the consumer base and sales force (which often have a negative understanding of insurance in general);
- handle massive volumes – with robust technology to handle the back-office requirements of scale as margins are thin; and
- pay claims quickly – within days, not weeks.

Encouraging savings and providing the right tools to do so is equally important. For one thing, lending that is funded by savings is less susceptible to the whims of foreign investors and the vicissitudes of the global markets. Second, a lot of consumption smoothing (in this case helping the financially excluded to deal with fluctuations in income and expenditure to help them with a stable path of consumption) can be achieved with diligent saving instead of borrowing at high interest rates. Third, saving may be more appropriate than insurance in some situations, especially in cases like endowment insurance products, which punish missed premiums and can be decimated by high inflation.

Despite this, only around half the world's households have access to a savings account. As the World's Bank Consulting Group to Assist the Poorest (CGAP) has outlined in its extensive work on the subject, most poor people use a variety of informal savings instruments – from putting cash in the mattress, savings clubs, investing in livestock or saving with family – to manage their small, unpredictable incomes. A lot of the time, there is a risk of loss, theft or depreciation.

Providing savings products is no easier than insurance. The smallest accounts are costly for financial institutions to maintain. The poor – especially those in rural areas – are often geographically isolated from bank branches and unable to make the frequent, small deposits they need. Branch opening hours can be a problem – as MicroSave has reported, there is higher interest in business correspondent models and m-banking.

The good news is that economies of scale and technology-based innovations can bring down costs. A recent CGAP study shows that the high operating costs linked to small-balance savings mobilisation can be more than offset by the profits generated through cross-sales of loans and other products to the small savers, as well as by fee income from savings accounts and the use of technology.

Credit is the most established financial product offered to the poor, so it is unsurprising that there are more variations offered around the world. If there is something that useful, high-quality credit products have in common, it is that they accommodate demand-side rather than just supply-side concerns. The better credit products have been those that were adequate for the purpose, with assured continued availability of credit, supply of next loan after the current one was paid off and regular collection of repayments from the borrower – with procedures for repayment flexibility in cases of shock. In terms of good products, their quality stems from their strong fit to both the purpose and the borrower.

As Wright has said, some products can be good in some circumstances, but do not work everywhere all the time. In India, some MFIs have offered the weekly instalment loans, which were fine for trading activities that generated daily/weekly cash incomes – but no good for small crop production or where income was generated with a time lag. One-year loans are good for purposes with a seasonal cycle of less than one year, but not for investments that pay back over a longer period. The real future of credit to the underserved, it can be argued, is in the thoughtful, well-researched, demand-led design of specific-purpose credit products – rather than general 'enterprise' credit unmatched to the needs of the client.

So where does this uneven product landscape leave us? It leaves us with a vision for how to move forward. Overall, the industry must offer the poor a range of savings, credit, payments and insurance products tailored to their needs, aspirations and mental accounting (and not just minimalist versions of traditional products). It must communicate the products and the opportunities it offers in clear, concise client language – often with integrated training or financial education integrated. And it must leverage new technologies to deliver these products in a convenient, accessible, reliable and affordable manner.

7. Funding issues

When the big money started flowing into the microfinance industry, the great plan was to connect MFIs to capital markets. While this has allowed scale in some markets in a productive, controlled and beneficial way, it is far from a completely rosy picture. There is not scope in this chapter to examine the behaviour and roles of MIVs in detail (Chapters 6, 11 and 15 are devoted to this) but the long-term success of the industry must start with the question of where we want the capital for serving the poor to come from, to be most sustainable? We want sustainability and stability for the institution and the client. And yet we often see that the inistitution's liquidity issues has an enormous impact on borrowers. A client of an MFI struggling to tap further debt funding, who cannot get the next cycle of loan after having used the previous one to invest in inventory or staff, may be in a much worse position than if there had been no loan in the first place. This is not acceptable when dealing with the vulnerable poor.

Capital markets have facilitated a lot of outreach. But in crisis, you get flight to quality, with investors scared of risk in a portfolio – microfinance bonds were perceived as risky after the Lehman Brothers collapse. So some investors that had been excited about the double bottom-line possibilities within microfinance (eg, Morgan Stanley) fled back to Triple-A corporates. This means that bond prices shot up for MFIs and became their most volatile source of capital. They in turn had to increase interest rates or make clients wait for their loans while they waited for donor money to come in.

The supposed success of going from a credit fund supported by DFID or a foundation, to a licensed bank, to being a regular borrower in capital markets, may be a highly questionable path – especially as there is nothing safer, more affordable, and more conductive to financial prudence than having most of an MFI's funding coming from its own clients' savings. The disadvantage of course if that the institution cannot leverage it up to do much on the credit side. However, as it may have behoved the global banks to know back in 2008, stability can be an underrated quality.

Blame must not be thrown around flippantly. Investing in microfinance has its own set of challenges and bottlenecks sometimes emerge because of the lack of investable institutions on the ground (when actual double bottom-line due diligence has been carried out). Reaching the poor may in part be gridlocked by the need for more high-quality MFIs in the countries where so many of the unbanked are – in Africa and Asia.

Sometimes the difficulty is regulatory rather than institutional. There is huge demand for microfinance outreach in the Philippines, for example, but the onerous Central Bank regulation disincentivises social MFIs from getting involved. This is true in Indonesia too – the fourth biggest country in the world by population, where 60% of the adult population of 140 million people remains unbanked.

There will be ups and downs within the funders of microfinance. There will be cycles of investment and redemption. Investors' objectives will continue to vary, from the pension funds with a primarily fiduciary duty to their own members (the 'financial-first' group) to the social investors who want to see evidence of benefit (the 'impact-first' contingent). MIVs will continue to offer a range of options, from the high return on equity targets at Blue Orchard's private equity fund Bamboo Finance, to more socially-minded MIVs, such as Triodos or Agora. Managing these disparate interests is an unenviable task, and that is without solving the biggest issue of all – that of the principal agent, which concerns the misalignment of interests and power between the client, the MFI and the investor (something outlined well in Hugh Sinclair's *Confessions of a Microfinance Heretic*).

A final anecdote. Last year I was at a big microfinance conference in Europe. I sat through a panel workshop on the investment landscape within microfinance. On the panel were several MIV representatives and private bankers marketing MIV funds as investments for their clients. After presentations, the room was opened up for questions. Someone put the following question to one of the private bankers: "Can you please tell us what you think about the importance of client protection?" The banker seemed pleased with the question, and confidently replied: "We always take all possible measures to ensure that our clients are protected from foreseeable risks."

If this is at all typical of the new microfinance investors, the hurdles ahead might be daunting.

8. Looking ahead

It is a tired metaphor, but microfinance is at a crossroads. It is – rightly, I believe – no longer thought of as a panacea for poverty alleviation. It is an industry buzzing with innovation in some areas (social performance management, m-banking and value chains among them) but moribund in others (regulation, spread of credit bureaux, credit product design). It remains as a whole too dependent – and thus, beholden – to foreign investors, not all of whom have the best interests of the clients at heart, and only some of whom really understand those clients' needs. Too many MFIs follow the same old story of rolling out while failing to critically appraise their effectiveness. Microinsurance beyond credit life is generally yet to reach scale. The graduation issue has not yet been cracked and the so-called 'Bottom of the Pyramid' is far from being reached in a sustainable way. Microfinance as a whole remains urban-focused, when it is the rural poor who need it most. Consumer finance (for non-productive items) is pushing enterprise finance aside.

At the same time, currency risk seems to have been mostly hedged out of the industry. Open-source management information systems are allowing tiny MFIs to computerise their back office. A wealth of free material is available for training clients, trainers and loan officers. The so-called 'last mile' problem is being addressed. The mobile phone is every bit the emancipatory tool it was hoped it would be. Empirical academic rigour in testing assumptions is, if not commonplace, growing. A holistic perspective on the relationships between health, financial access and education is allowing fantastic opportunities in livelihood development. Education on pricing transparency has increased by an order of magnitude. And savings mobilisation is being widely encouraged – if not yet widely practised.

I remain optimistic that the possibilities within the latter paragraph will vanquish the disappointments of the former. And I generally subscribe to David Roodman's thesis that even if the best guess as to the poverty-alleviating effect of microcredit alone is zero, this does not mean there is not much to commend. Microfinance has built institutions and infrastructure and networks in hard-to-reach places, which will all ready for when microfinance learns to be what it was supposed to be. (It is this network of infrastructure and people across the world, and not the place of the profit motive, which is why I called microfinance an 'industry' and not a 'sector' in the opening paragraphs). And finally, control of one's finances, like other forms of development, can (emphasise can) be freedom itself.

Despite this, the business models have not yet been found to offer small savings and useful insurance products well and cheaply. Postal banks, and village savings and loans associaitons do some good work, but banks are yet to be able to bring it to scale. A lot of innovation on both the business model and the technology side will be to allow small-scale savings and insurance.

So those like me who believe in microfinance's continued transformational potential know there is much to be done. In reputation, the industry will have to do better to explain itself. In terms of honesty it must rigorously and candidly test its own assumptions and claims. Existentially, it will need to continue to ask itself what microfinance is, and what it is for. Technologically, it will have to grasp opportunities and innovations, even when there is a cost in doing so. Financially, it may have to forego the largesse of foreign investment and refocus on savings and local bank funding. And pragmatically, it must learn from its mistakes. The reckless conceits of adolescence must now have passed. Adulthood awaits.

With thanks to Rosalind Copisarow, Deborah Drake, Marcus Fedder, Dan Rozas and Sheetal Walsh for their thoughts on the content of this chapter.

Evolving business models of microfinance

Pete Power
Angkor Mikroheranhvatho Kampuchea Co, Ltd

'Microfinance' is typically defined as the provision of financial services to low-income clients who historically have lacked access to banking and related financial services, due to the high transaction costs required to service this market.

Pioneered by Muhammad Yunus and Grameen Bank in Bangladesh, microfinance has gained attention and sometimes notoriety in recent years with large and lucrative public offerings at institutions such as Compartamos in Mexico and SKS in India. Reports of over-indebtedness and client suicides led to the collapse of the microfinance sector in the Indian province of Andhra Pradesh in 2010 and tarnished the sector's reputation internationally. Some of this bad press is deserved, as there are a small number of microfinance actors that use social mission as a cloak to cover inefficient practices and unnecessarily high interest rates and client charges.

However, there also exists a complex ecosystem of other microfinance service providers, ranging from non-government organisations (NGOs) to credit unions to mobile banking companies, which are quietly expanding the reach of financial services in the developing world. These providers have radically different legal structures and business models, and many transform from one legal structure and business model into another as they grow and evolve.

This chapter covers the following broad topics:

- the most common types of organisations and business models that provide microfinance services today;
- the evolution of microfinance institutions as they grow, with a focus on the quiet revolution that is going on in many microfinance institutions as they wean themselves off overseas funding and become more balanced, self-financed and client-centric organisations; and
- how innovative technologies and delivery models are beginning to transform the sector.

The essay will draw primarily on the experiences of Angkor Mikroheranhvatho Kampuchea Co Ltd (AMK) in Cambodia, but will also refer to other markets and institutions, where appropriate.

1. Providers of microfinance

A large range of organisations provide microfinance services today. This chapter describes the most common actors:

- NGOs;

- self-help groups (SHGs) and rotating savings and credit associations (ROSCAs);
- credit unions;
- microfinance institutions (MFIs);
- commercial banks;
- mobile banking companies; and
- other market specific models.

1.1 Non-governmental organisations

NGOs have been involved in providing microfinance services from a very early stage. Most microfinance institutions in the world today can trace their roots back to a founding/sponsoring NGO.

Most NGOs view the provision of financial services as one of the key elements necessary for effective livelihood development programming. In most cases, their efforts are based at grassroots level (where their primary target beneficiary groups are located) and involve the provision of social protection payments and the set-up and support of groups such as SHGs and ROSCAs.

(a) NGO transformation motive

Most NGOs have found, however, that legal transformation is necessary if they want to scale up their microfinance activities to regional or national levels. In some cases this transformation is mandated by local regulatory authorities. Almost all NGOs are non-profit institutions. Most of their funding comes in the form of donor grants rather than client generated revenue. The legal and non-profit status of NGOs means that they cannot usually raise the external equity or debt financing that is critical to growing a microfinance operation. As a result, many NGOs that do want to expand their microfinance operations will transform them into a commercial company and/or registered MFI. This allows the new company to make and retain profits, and makes it possible for it to take on external debt and equity. Many NGOs will retain an equity stake in the resulting MFI but these are typically minority stakes that become further diluted as the MFI takes on the additional equity it needs to grow.

In addition to these legal and financing benefits, such transformations are often accompanied by a cultural shift within the newly formed MFI. Income/revenue now comes from clients rather than donors, eliminating the concept of non-paying beneficiaries. Work practices and compensation models may change radically – performance-based compensation is quite common among MFIs, but is almost unknown in the NGO sector.

This shift in focus and compensation has led some NGOs to view the MFI model as too profit-motivated. While this is true in some cases, MFIs that follow a dual social and financial bottom-line approach effectively pursue the same poverty alleviation goals as NGOs. While the means may be different, the social mission of 'real' MFIs is very close to that of the NGO sector.

1.2 Self-help groups and rotating savings and credit associations

SHGs usually comprise up to 20 members. The group may be formed under the guidance of an NGO, or it may evolve from a traditional ROSCA or other locally initiated grouping. Members typically make a savings contribution to a central pool, from which other members can take loans. Interest rates are set by the group. SHGs and ROSCAs are usually independent and unregistered.

Because they are sponsored by NGOs, most SHGs have a broad agenda to alleviate poverty – promoting school enrolment, for example, or improving nutrition. Financial intermediation is generally viewed as a means to these other goals rather than as a primary objective. Since most SHGs are independent, their financial impact is limited to the amount of capital contributed by the village.

However, more successful SHG operations have begun lending across SHGs. Some SHG federations effectively function like formal MFIs. Such consolidations have been most successful in India, where there is a SHG-bank linkage programme. This allows SHGs to borrow from banks once they have accumulated a base of their own capital and have established a track record of regular repayments.

1.3 Credit unions

Credit unions are best described as member-owned financial cooperatives. Membership is usually limited to individuals with a common interest, such as a professional (teachers or civil servants) connection or geographic limitation. They differ from other financial institutions in that the members of the union (in other words, people with accounts there) are also its owners. Members usually democratically elect their board of directors.

Credit unions are typically savings led, but allow regular saving members to take loans from the credit union. Interest rates are typically lower than those for MFIs and commercial banks, and profits are usually distributed to the members at the end of each year. Many commentators maintain that the credit union membership model mitigates risky growth strategies and the pursuit of excessive profits.

Credit unions have not grown as quickly in most of the developing world as MFIs in recent years. Many see their common interest limit on membership and their democratic management structure as barriers to growth and innovation. Nevertheless, credit union membership is high in certain developing countries, most notably in West Africa.

1.4 Microfinance institutions

In some markets MFIs are referred to by other names, such as non-banking financial institutions, and other associated terms. For the purposes of this chapter, I refer to all such institutions as MFIs.

(a) Real MFIs: balancing social and financial performance

MFIs are typically structured as commercial companies. Most also have a clear social mission to provide services to the poor and help alleviate poverty. They do this by providing services on a commercial basis, the goal being to ensure financial sustainability. In theory, most MFIs attempt to balance social and financial returns.

This is sometimes difficult to achieve, and some manage it better than others.

Much has been written recently about the high interest rates charged by MFIs, and their generation of high equity returns, sometimes in excess of 30%. Such returns are probably not sustainable in any market and do not in general represent a healthy financial/social balance.

Much of the recent crisis in Andhra Pradesh in India was driven by excessive growth, high portfolio yields and unsustainable profit goals. In many cases, this growth was transaction driven: over-ambitious promoters extracted large premiums from incoming shareholders with the promise of continued exponential growth. In turn, new shareholders sought high returns to justify their overpriced investments. Like all bubbles it was just a question of time before this one burst.

However, some MFIs have put specific controls in place to try to enforce the social/financial balance. Cambodia's AMK, for example, uses a senior management incentive compensation system that emphasises social and financial performance goals but dis-incentivises excessive profits. The expectation is that once an optimum level of profits has been achieved, interest rates and other client charges should be lowered.

Staff incentives are also critical to balancing social and financial performance. Such incentives need to be carefully designed, since there is a large risk of unintended consequences. Some MFIs, for example, indirectly encourage client officers to push up loan sizes because staff incentives are linked to loan portfolio sizes and disbursement targets. AMK uses an alternative system that incentivises aspects such as working in a difficult area (remote rural areas, areas with frequent flooding or droughts) and efficiency, measured by client caseload levels and portfolio quality rather than loan portfolio size and interest income.

Tempering financial returns is only half the challenge. A social mission with clear social goals must be accompanied by a way of measuring social performance. Financial performance measures have been around for centuries, but the concept of social performance is relatively new and still under developed today.

Some MFIs claim that such a concept is too complicated to be worthwhile, and throw their hands up in exasperation. Others do the minimum possible to get by, drafting organisational policies that recommend social performance but provide no effective way to measure it. Others implement tools borrowed directly from other countries or markets, with little thought into whether they are relevant.

It is revealing to note that few MFIs score highly on both social and financial ratings. This is a reflection of the challenge this balance presents, and the lack of success there has been in maintaining it to date.

AMK has tried to take responsibility for social performance directly. It gathers client-specific information and preferences and uses them to develop new products. A full-time research department has been created, as well as a principal component analysis methodology for poverty assessment, and a client well-being score specific to Cambodia. AMK has applied this methodology since 2003 and conducted hundreds of client and non-client interviews every year. In doing so, it has created a vast database of client information.

AMK measures changes to client wellbeing over time to try to ensure that its microfinance services are having a positive effect on clients' lives. Clients and non-clients are interviewed on a periodic basis (usually every three years), and detailed assessments are made of their income, assets, education and overall levels of livelihood. So far, these surveys have indicated a small but consistent improvement in the livelihoods of AMK's clients. AMK clients also fare better than non-AMK clients surveyed in the same period.

However, many MFIs feel that they are being forced by their external funders and donors to adopt certain social performance models. Indeed, AMK has been offered substantial funding to implement certain models, and has been told that this funding is not available for the development of customised context, or client-driven approaches. Imposed from outside, social performance models can be a painful overhead that does not add value. However, rationalised internally, with a focus on client intimacy and corresponding product development, they can transform an organisation.

(b) *Wolves in microfinance clothing*

Balancing social and financial performance may be key to determining if an organisation is a 'real' microfinance institution, or whether it is a wolf masquerading in microfinance clothing.

In some markets, profit-maximising institutions share the same microfinance license designation as socially motivated microfinance institutions. Depending on the regulator some companies may hold an MFI licence, but not provide financial services to low-income clients. They may have taken advantage of the lower capital requirements for MFIs to allow them to pursue commercial lending.

The issue of classification has had a detrimental effect on the sector. A small number of MFIs with predatory high interest rates, portfolio yields and returns have gained much press attention, and have tarnished the reputation of the entire sector. Microfinance investment vehicles (MIVs) sometimes exacerbate this problem by using social investment funds to fund the wrong types of institutions.

One positive result of the recent crises within the microfinance industry is that regulators and funders are becoming much more discerning about who they allow to operate and who they will fund.

(c) *MFI lending methodologies*

Most microfinance institutions are or have been credit led. This bias towards credit is driven by several considerations:

- in most developing markets there is still a high demand for credit among the poor;
- in regulated environments, it is often easier to obtain a micro-credit licence; and
- credit is typically easier to configure and sell than more complex products such as micro-savings and micro-insurance.

Most MFIs offer two broad categories of loans: group and individual loans. There are multiple methodologies within each.

Grameen Bank in Bangladesh is credited with pioneering the solidarity group lending methodology. Typically, clients are organised into groups who meet with an MFI representative at regularly scheduled meetings in their village. Group members make a commitment or moral guarantee to oversee the repayment of loans made to other members of their group.

The group guarantee concept has been widely adopted around the world, with small variations for different markets. Some MFIs lend to the group, meaning that all group members are joint and severely liable for the loan. Other MFIs, including AMK, lend to individual members of a group, with the other group members providing a mutual/cross guarantee. Although they differ slightly in their legal and delivery perspectives, both models rely on a moral rather than collateral guarantee for the loan. Some MFIs also impose a mandatory savings deposit (loans linked to savings), which can also serve as collateral.

For larger loan amounts MFIs will often offer individual loans that do not rely on the group methodology. These usually require collateral and/or an independent guarantor. Collateral requirements may be waived in some cases for longstanding customers. Some MFIs have also experimented with individual loans with no collateral or reduced collateral in environments where the group lending methodology does not work (eg, urban slums, migrants, unregistered/displaced clients).

(d) *Non-financial services*

Some microfinance providers offer additional or non-financial services in addition to their standard offering. Examples include financial education, or livelihoods, health and other service provision. The provision of such services is controversial.

While financial education is necessary where clients have no experience with the formal financial sector, repetitive basic education can be a waste of time in competitive markets where most prospective clients have experience with formal credit and savings products. Indeed the reaction of AMK clients who have received financial literacy training from other providers is that such training is patronising and its content is too basic to be useful. Nevertheless, financial education is widely viewed as necessary in remote markets where formal financial products have never previously been available.

Some MFIs also offer business advisory or planning services in conjunction with larger business start-up loans. In many cases, this may be an appropriate part of the loan assessment process. It also reduces the risk of business failure and associated loan loss to the MFI. In order to be effective, however, these services must be provided by skilled staff. They cannot be bolted on to a regular client officer's job description, as sometimes happens.

However, MFIs who become involved in non-financial services run the risk of diluting their organisational focus and becoming ineffective at delivering microfinance services and/or the other additional services they are trying to provide. Health, education and other social services are typically the responsibility of governments and/or NGOs. MFIs are not designed to deliver such services and are usually not good at doing so. With a few exceptions, those MFIs heavily involved in such additional services are not efficient providers of microfinance and are invariably financially unsustainable. They end up caught somewhere between being a client-driven commercial business and a donor-driven charity. Like most middle grounds, this can be a precarious place to be.

(e) Organisational characteristics of MFIs

Most MFIs are still credit led. Most credit-led organisations share the following characteristics:

- standardised products and operational processes, as discussed above;
- a reliance on overseas debt and equity financing, with associated currency hedging issues;
- an executive focus on funding and portfolio growth; and
- social performance metrics, focusing primarily on credit outreach.

Reliance on overseas debt and equity financing is necessary since credit-led institutions do not normally have regulatory approval to raise deposits. The domestic capital markets in most developing countries are not strong and have historically targeted higher return businesses. This leaves most MFIs reliant on overseas funding, with a limited number of multilateral organisations and MIVs providing the bulk of the funding.

Because leverage is relatively high, most funding comes in the form of relatively short-term debt. A three-year tenor is typical. Until recently, many MIVs were unable to lend in local currency, creating a situation where much MFI debt is denominated in reference currencies such as euros or US dollars. The MFI is then forced to hedge with the local currency and/or accept the currency risk. Organisations such as The Currency Exchange are now offering hedging products for various exotic currencies, but their emergence has by no means solved this problem.

Credit-led organisations require additional funding to finance portfolio growth, which in turn is seen to create economies of scale in the MFI's operating costs. As a result, executive focus in many MFIs revolves around growing the portfolio and obtaining funding. These can be challenging goals.

Throughout the early 2000s, multilateral and MIV debt funding was readily available to large, well-known MFIs. Additional pressure was therefore placed on large MFIs to continue growing their portfolios even in markets that were approaching saturation. Much has been written about the problems this may have caused; see for example, the 2010 ADA paper "Can Bad Microfinance Practices be the Consequence of Too Much Funding Chasing Too Few Microfinance Institutions?".[1]

On the other hand, the focus of MIVs on the larger and more established players means that smaller and often more innovative MFIs struggle to raise funding. MIV risk aversion and the skewing of capital allocation decisions continue to be a problem. In the aftermath of the Andhra Pradesh crisis, MIVs have become more conservative in their lending practices. They now impose a wide variety of exposure limits, loan covenants, default clauses and so on. Loan negotiations have become

1 See www.microfinance.lu/fileadmin/media/Publications/downloads/Discussion_Paper/ADA_DiscPaper2_EN.pdf.

more protracted, and MIVs often now commit smaller amounts for shorter terms.

These pressures have meant that, for much of the last 10 years, MFI executive time and attention has been focused on portfolio growth and the negotiation of funding. The most important operational functions have therefore tended to be treasury management and credit operations. The sector at large has tended to focus on measures such as portfolio growth, portfolio at risk, client outreach, client poverty profiles and multiple loans. In many organisations, 'client' has been synonymous with 'borrower'. Frontline staff have tended to be credit officers rather than officers who might service multiple products.

(f) *The quiet revolution*

The recent crises have taught the sector some important lessons:

- Focusing too much on portfolio growth is a dangerous strategy;
- There has not been enough innovation in the microfinance sector in the last ten years, with the vast majority of revenue still coming from traditional solidarity group and collateralised individual loan products;
- International financing is not a reliable long-term strategy because of multilateral and MIV home country funding issues, risk aversion and a lack of in-depth knowledge of local markets.

It is clear that changes are necessary, and some of these appear to be happening already. Commentators can point to big global initiatives such as the Universal Standards for Social Performance Management[2] and the Seal of Excellence for Poverty Outreach in Microfinance,[3] both of which are indeed helpful.

However, the real change must happen at the 'coal-face', within those organisations that are actually delivering microfinance services.

A quiet revolution is occurring in many markets, and many MFIs are changing fundamentally. This revolution is not a legal transformation in the sense of the 'NGO to MFI' or 'MFI to Commercial Bank' transformations discussed earlier. Nevertheless, a series of strategic, operating model and organisational structure changes are currently underway in many MFIs around the world.

From a strategic perspective, MFIs are reducing their focus on portfolio growth, in recognition that at some point their credit markets will become saturated. More and more investment is being made in product development, in the search for innovative products and delivery methodologies.

Key to this trend is a reduced focus on loan products and a greater focus on savings, remittances, payments, insurance and other products. This strategic shift is changing MFI revenue streams, which have historically relied almost exclusively on portfolio yield. Increasingly, savings financing spreads and transactions fee revenue are also adding to MFI bottom lines.

Focusing on savings has the twin benefit of putting the MFI in control of its own funding and lessening its reliance on overseas funding. In most cases, deposits are

---

2 See http://sptf.info/spstandards1.

3 See www.microcreditsummit.org/about/the_seal_of_excellence/.

made in the local currency, thereby reducing the hedging cost associated with overseas funding. Less overseas funding also frees managers from time-consuming external negotiations and allows (or even forces) them to focus on designing client-centric products. In effect, it is an opportunity for MFIs to take control of their destinies.

Key effects of the quiet revolution on MFI operations are:

- a drive for savings mobilisation;
- more focus on demand driven product development;
- innovation in low cost delivery channels and methodologies; and
- an increased use of mobile technology.

Savings mobilisation is a very different challenge to the provision of credit. While group-lending methodologies have created certain efficiencies in credit operations, the cost of service for low transaction amounts in savings, money transfer and microinsurance is a major hurdle, especially in remote areas. Traditional approaches will not usually work unless they are heavily subsidised. As a result, MFIs have begun to innovate, especially in the areas of mobile banking and branchless/agent-based banking.

Organisationally, this translates into more complex organisational structures. Credit operations are balanced by other operations, such as product development, savings, money transfer, insurance and so on. This means hiring new staff who have experience in savings mobilisation, mobile technology, branding and marketing. Many of these staff come from commercial banking, mobile telecommunications companies and so on, and bring with them the ability and confidence to develop new products and delivery methodologies from scratch. Such people give MFIs new confidence and a healthy scepticism for the types of old ideas being recycled by many international microfinance 'consultants' and technical assistance providers.

1.5 Commercial banks

Some commercial banks have evolved from MFIs. Such a transformation typically involves much higher minimum capital requirements, enhanced systems that are capable of performing more complex regulatory reporting, and regulatory approval to sell more complex products. Additional capital usually requires additional investors, who in most cases are interested in profit maximisation.

Nevertheless, many commercial banks are actively involved in microfinance. Banks that have evolved from MFIs, such as Acleda Bank in Cambodia, retain many of their original microfinance customers and continue to offer microfinance services.

Other commercial banks are increasingly moving downstream. In many developing countries, the high-net-worth, business and even middle class markets are limited. The bottom of the economic pyramid makes up the vast majority of the population. As commercial banks start to saturate their primary markets, many are beginning to move down-market and compete directly with MFIs.

Commercial banks usually have strong brands, systems and branch networks. Although they are not necessarily designed to serve the bottom of the pyramid, and in many cases lack an explicit social mission, commercial banks increasingly are seeing profit potential in the large low-income market of many countries. In some cases, as with the recent acquisition of Sathapana MFI in Cambodia by Marahun Japan Bank,[4] commercial banks are actually acquiring MFIs in an effort to expand their reach. Such consolidation and competition can only be positive for the sector, and ultimately for the microfinance customer.

1.6 Mobile banking companies

Mobile banking technology is increasingly being used to enhance existing business models, and in some cases to create brand new operating models.

Mobile technology enables the concept of branchless or agent banking. With it, MFIs and banks can 'outsource' certain activities to non-salaried agents who process transactions using low cost mobile phone technology. This increases outreach and avoids the costs of establishing and staffing bricks-and-mortar branches. Agents, who are usually shopkeepers or mobile airtime vendors, are compensated with a share of any transactions fees charged to the customer. This makes financial services viable for the first time in very remote, low-income areas.

Many would classify Kenya's M-PESA as a microfinance provider as it has made low cost money transfer and bill payment services accessible to those at the bottom of the economic pyramid. The highly liquid M-PESA agent network has allowed other microfinance providers to adapt their operating models in innovative ways. Several lenders now disburse loans and accept repayments through M-PESA, thereby greatly reducing their operating costs.

MFIs such as Musoni in Kenya have gone totally mobile, and use mobile money transfer services for all loan repayments and disbursements. Clients can top up their M-PESA account at any national agent, and then send payments to Musoni at their own convenience. Once the funds have been sent, they are deposited within seconds into Musoni's M-PESA account, while the client receives an automated text message confirming that their transaction has been successful.[5]

Once seen as expensive cutting-edge technology, mobile banking is becoming increasingly affordable. Open source systems such as Cyclos,[6] developed by the Social Trade Organisation,[7] greatly reduce the capital investment necessary to establish a mobile banking platform.

1.7 Other microfinance models

Other models have evolved to meet local market dynamics and customer needs.

The Susu collector network in Ghana allows low income individuals to make small savings deposits on a daily basis. Susu collectors normally operate near markets and collect deposits directly at their clients' homes or businesses, or at a dedicated kiosk. Small deposits are taken on a periodic or daily basis over the course of a month. At the end of the month the Susu collector returns the accumulated savings to the client, keeping one day's savings as commission. Some Susu collectors in

4 See www.phnompenhpost.com/2012110259531/Business/maruhan-japan-bank-buys-stake-in-mfi.html.
5 See www.microfinancegateway.org/p/site/m/template.rc/1.11.131997/.
6 See www.cyclos.org.
7 See www.socialtrade.org.

Ghana are now using mobile technology to record deposits and provide their clients with SMS receipts.

Many similar practices, some with longstanding traditional roots, some resulting from recent innovations, are active in microfinance around the world. Such practices hold great promise for the sector.

2. The future

The old maxim that 'that which does not kill us makes us stronger' seems to be true in microfinance. In some countries, the sector is evolving, diversifying its product offerings, revenue streams and associated risk. In Cambodia, certainly, MFIs are becoming more competitive and are hiring more experienced managers and staff. Clearer measures of social performance are being put in place, with tools such as the Mix Market and MF Transparency allowing investors and funders to make much better investment decisions and to support true double-bottom-line institutions.

MFIs themselves are beginning to incorporate new technologies such as mobile banking and agent-based services into their delivery methods. These are leading to new business models, with companies like Musoni using mobile banking providers to handle much of their customer interactions. As their respective target markets begin to overlap, MFIs are entering into competition with commercial banks. MFIs, commercial banks, mobile banking companies and other market participants are all competing for staff as well as customers.

In many markets, the sector is beginning to grow up and stand on its own feet. It is becoming less reliant on international MIVs and technical assistance providers. Many MFIs are listening to their clients and designing products accordingly, rather than implementing the latest model from India or Bangladesh. Progress is by no means uniform and there is still a lot of work to do, but the signs are beginning to look good for microfinance and for its customers.

Microinsurance – the next step towards financial inclusion

Mosleh Uddin Ahmed
Microinsurance Research Centre

---

1. What is microinsurance?

Poverty reduction does not only mean generating incomes for the poor. These incomes also need to be protected through effective risk-management. Insurance is an *ex-ante* risk management tool that provides financial protection to individuals and businesses. There are many market-based insurance products and processes designed to address the lifecycle risks faced by people on a daily basis. Microinsurance is one such product designed for people at the bottom of the pyramid.

Insurance for low-income communities is not a new idea. The industrial insurance that was popular in Europe and the United States in the 19th and early 20th centuries is the predecessor of today's microinsurance. Although the word 'microinsurance' first appeared in the microfinance context in the 1990s, the concept has been around for more than 40 years. La Equidad, a Columbian cooperative, began offering microinsurance to its members in 1970. Gono Shayestho Kendra, a healthcare provider in Bangladesh, launched a health microinsurance programme for the rural poor in 1972. Delta Life Insurance Company Limited, a regulated insurance company in Bangladesh, developed its Grameen Bima product – life insurance with savings for the rural poor – in 1988.

Put simply, microinsurance is the provision of insurance to low-income households. However, despite its 40 years of existence there is still no standard definition of the concept.

Different stakeholders see microinsurance from the point of view of their own use, and define it from that angle. Governments see it as social protection. Donors focus on its potential to secure poverty reduction. Commercial insurers see its potential as a way of reaching large under-served markets. Analysts use it to highlight the size of the market at the 'bottom of the pyramid'. Academics see it as an essential financial service for sustainable economic growth. Microfinance practitioners see it as the 'next step forward' in financial inclusion. The poor, finally, consider it an 'unnecessary' expenditure that they find hard to finance from their scarce cash resources.

All of the above definitions are similar to those for conventional insurance, except for the clearly prescribed target market: low-income people. This changes the whole character of microinsurance. The definitions also indicate that microinsurance should be funded by premiums and managed on generally accepted risk-management principles. Microinsurance therefore excludes both social welfare and emergency assistance provided by governments. It is a tool that can be used to increase the social protection of the low-income population.

Microinsurance is not charity – it is business. However, it requires insurers to change their thinking. It challenges insurers to go back to the drawing board and find quick, cheap and simple solutions to provide cover for people who have very little ability to pay. Microinsurance business operations can be sustainable. If appropriately designed and delivered, they can play an important role in reducing the vulnerability of the poor and open profitable markets for commercial insurers. Finally, just like microcredit proved that the poor are creditworthy, microinsurance proves that low-income people are insurable.

2. The purpose of microinsurance

Poverty and vulnerability reinforce each other in a downward spiral. Exposure to risks results not only in substantial financial losses for the poor, but also the ongoing uncertainty about whether and when a loss might occur. Because of this perpetual apprehension, the poor are less likely to take advantage of income-generating opportunities that may arise and reduce their poverty.

Vulnerability results from the inability of the poor to deal with the losses or costs that result from a risk event. They are more vulnerable to many of these risks than the rest of the population, and they are less able to cope when they do occur. The role of microinsurance is to reduce this vulnerability. The vulnerability of the poor and the inefficiency of the traditional risk-management techniques they employ are the two main factors that have motivated its development.

Microinsurance is normally offered to people who do not have access to conventional insurance policies and who live in more vulnerable conditions. It aims to reach low-income people by offering insurance at lower premiums and with more rapid payouts than are available under traditional policies. By doing so it extends financial inclusion to the insurance domain. The objective of financial inclusion is to give individual consumers – particularly those currently excluded from formal financial sector services – sustainable access to financial services that are appropriate to their needs and provided by regulated service providers.

The target population for microinsurance can be defined by exclusion: those families or people whose income is so low that they are excluded from standard insurance markets. However, many people within the target population of microinsurance are not in such extreme poverty that they fit into social security and income-transfer programmes (Churchill, 2006). The target is the poor and the vulnerable poor, rather than the ultra-poor or the destitute. The state is responsible for the ultra poor and the destitute; they lie outside the scope of microinsurance.

3. Why do the poor need microinsurance?

Uninsured risk leaves poor households vulnerable to serious or even catastrophic losses. It also forces them to undertake costly strategies to manage their incomes and assets in the face of risk, lowering their ability to earn income. The welfare costs arising from shocks and lost earning opportunities are substantial, and contribute to persistent poverty in many developing countries (Murdoch, 1990).

Microinsurance has the potential to reduce these financial shocks, uncertainties and welfare costs. By offering a payout when an insured loss occurs, it avoids other costly ways of coping with the shock, leaving future income earning opportunities intact.

Three categories of risk-managing financial products are available to low-income households:

- using liquid savings to reduce the effects of an economic stress;
- emergency loans; and
- microinsurance.

Of these three options, insurance, which pays compensation after the event has taken place, is the only one that can be pre-planned in accordance with household income.

While microcredit helps people to grow economically and to move out of poverty, microinsurance helps to make this growth sustainable and prevents them from falling back into poverty. It is a safety net that pushes people back above the poverty line with financial compensation whenever they suffer a financial loss due to a risk event. Because of this fundamental link with credit, microinsurance is often sold by microcredit organisations, and often offered in combination with loans. Some microfinance institutions sell insurance as an additional service. Others make insurance compulsory for their clients, for reasons ranging from reduced credit risk to building an insurance culture.

The low-income households are exposed to a variety of risks throughout their lives. Figure 1 shows the lifecycle needs and perils faced by the poor.

Figure 1: Lifecycle risks and needs of the poor (based on a presentation by Microinsurance Centre)

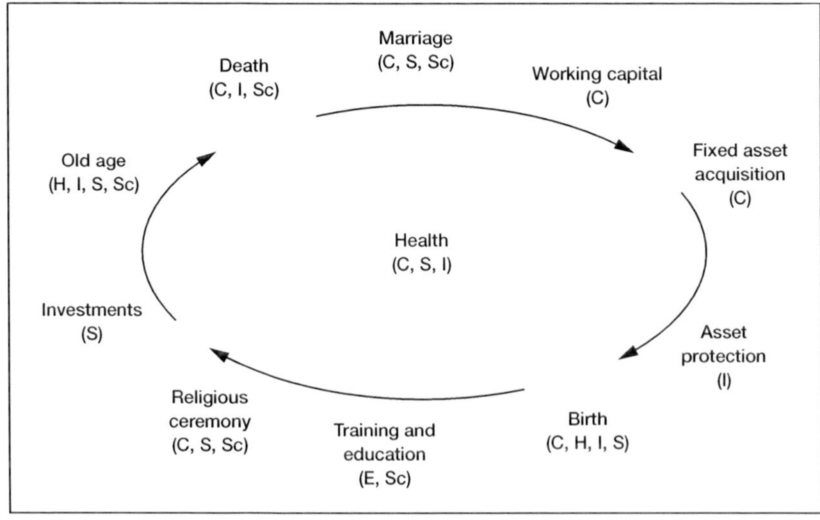

C = Credit; E = Education; H = Healthcare; I = Insurance; S = Savings; Sc = Social Services

Of all the risks shown above, the following affect low-income households most adversely:

- illness or injury (health);
- death (of a breadwinner or close family member); and
- loss of valuable assets through fire, natural disaster or theft (asset protection).

The financial cost to a household that loses a valuable asset or a breadwinner is reasonably clear and can be substantial. The impact of ongoing uncertainty about whether and when a loss might occur is not easily understood, but it is nonetheless more damaging. Uncertainties make low-income households hesitant and prevent them from taking advantage of economically beneficial opportunities. The security that comes with being insured allows low-income people to take timely decisions and avoid costly risk-management strategies, with a positive impact on poverty reduction.

4. Microinsurance stakeholders

A range of players and institutions are involved in the microinsurance value chain. Each is a stakeholder. They include insurance regulators, risk carriers, administrators, policyholders, delivery channels, technology platforms and related service providers. The microinsurance value chain has three distinctive levels at which the stakeholders interact with each other; these are shown in Figure 2.

Figure 2: Microinsurance value chain (based on a presentation made by Microinsurance Centre)

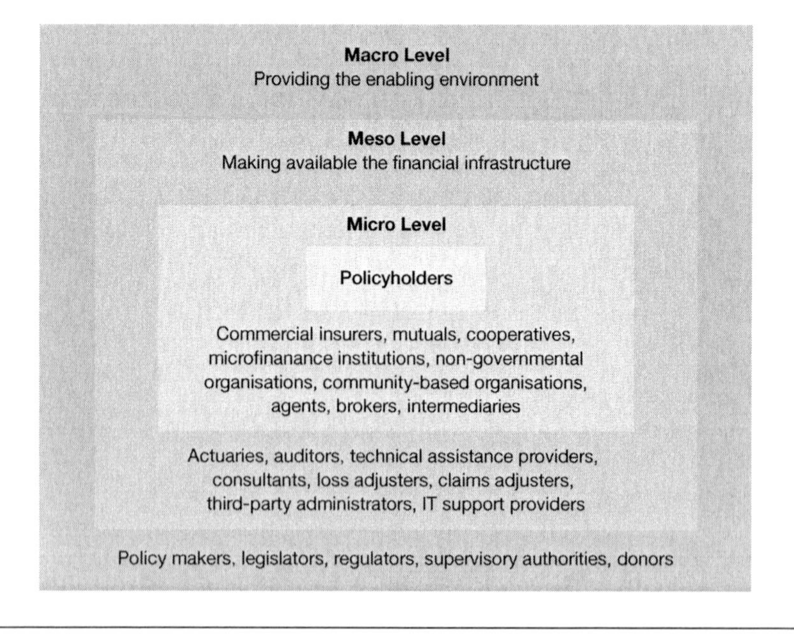

4.1 The micro level

At the micro level the policyholders are at the centre. Everything revolves around them. Policyholders may be individuals, members of an organised group or the group itself. When provided on a 'group basis', the underwriting process is simplified and the cost of microinsurance is reduced substantially.

The next important player at the micro level is the insurance provider. While microfinance institutions (MFIs) or non-governmental organisations (NGOs) enter the market for the benefit of their members, commercial insurers are in microinsurance for a number of reasons. Through a multiple-choice questionnaire conducted in 2011, Coydon and Molitor found that 39% of commercial insurers are in the microinsurance business in order to enter a new market, 27% entered in expectation of financial profit, 23% entered due to corporate social responsibility, 21% are in it for image/brand recognition and 16% entered to expand to new countries.

The provider may be a single institution that carries the risk, markets or distributes the products, and administers the policy. In other cases these tasks are carried out by separate organisations. The insurer might carry the risk and another organisation, such as an MFI, NGO, community-based organisation (CBO) or cooperative, may distribute the product and collect the premium. A specialist administration provider called a third-party administrator might undertake the administration of the service. Administrators offer specialist back-office support and/or claims processing in the supply chain. The risk carrier or delivery channel may also perform these functions. Dividing responsibilities often reduces costs and thereby reduces the overall premium. This helps to make microinsurance more affordable to low-income households.

The microinsurance industry is constantly innovating new connections between various players at the micro level. Many initiatives have been launched by major supporters of microinsurance to encourage the development of new microinsurance concepts and encourage support from other stakeholders, practitioners and policy makers to contribute to new innovations and to further the extension of microinsurance to all low-income households.

4.2 The meso level

Meso level activities in a microinsurance value chain facilitate the micro-level activities. They provide the critical support required for the smooth functioning of microinsurance schemes. They include actuaries, claims adjusters, IT providers, software providers, information system providers, trainers and other facilitators. They are often the link between micro level and macro level players and effectively drive these two levels. Technology platforms enable the processing of services across the chain and include electronic media, such as personal digital assistants and mobile phones, and social mechanisms, such as group-based premium collection.

4.3 The macro level

Stakeholders at the macro level are governments and donors. The government needs to establish the right legal environment under which microinsurers can operate.

Insurance regulators play a vital role in protecting consumer interests and instituting a legal and policy framework for microinsurance. Donors lobby the government to create the right environment and provide financial and technical support. The main aims of both stakeholders are to protect the microinsurance policyholders and develop the industry. Governments also need to establish supervisory mechanisms so that they can ensure that the various players operating microinsurance schemes in the country are complying with the law.

The government may also play a role in establishing consumer protection by setting up an ombudsman or a mechanism for registering grievances from dissatisfied microinsurance policyholders and helping them to obtain an equitable solution.

5. The demand for microinsurance

The demand for microinsurance arises from the risks and risk-management strategies of low-income households. Client demand is an essential prerequisite for any microinsurance programme. Demand is often assumed to be present, and is misunderstood or over-simplified by most microinsurance providers. In many microinsurance programmes this misunderstanding has resulted in products and services that have not met the needs of low-income households. Many insurance providers assess the demand based on what is available in the market, rather than establishing through research what low-income households actually require. Demand research reveals the need among low-income clients to find more effective ways to cope with risks, even though clients rarely see insurance itself as a way to bridge this gap.

Insurers often use existing market studies and surveys as a base from which to quantify client demand and design suitable microinsurance products. Such products, however, must be customised to suit the varying requirements of the local population. They must be simple, available, affordable, accessible and flexible; they must be need-based and demand-based. Serving the low-income market requires insurers to develop and promote customised products to meet the localised needs of their clients. However, since client need is location-specific and is based on a given point in time, generalising demand across countries and regions will result in inappropriate microinsurance products.

Analysis of demand for microinsurance is extremely important to formulating policies and strategies for the low-income sector. An adequate knowledge of the extent, determinants and elasticity of microinsurance demand is essential to ensuring that the existing resources are properly used, and to improve the quality of services. Analysis of demand is also crucial for designing strategies that aim to make a programme financially sustainable.

The challenge for microinsurance is turning risk-management from a reactive process into a proactive one. This begins with an understanding of demand for a particular microinsurance product.

6. Microinsurance products

A variety of microinsurance products for the poor are available today. The appropriateness of some of them is questionable. Many have been developed based on the needs of the poor as they are perceived by insurers. NGOs and MFIs mainly offer credit-life insurance to protect their own loan portfolios. Many commercial insurers entering the market prefer to scale down their existing products rather than develop new, responsive products for the sector. Microinsurance products offered by commercial insurers are usually limited to life insurance and accidental death and disability because these are the least risky for the insurance providers and therefore the most likely to be profitable.

Such products can be relatively expensive and inaccessible to low-income households, who are often wrongly sold them through unethical practices. In most cases poor households are unable to continue payment beyond a few years, resulting in a lapsed insurance policy and the loss of their hard-earned cash.

The microinsurance product that most poor people have contact with is credit-life insurance. This must be purchased with microcredit and other borrowing. It can be very profitable for the insurer, since borrowers are often unaware that they have purchased insurance with their loans. Anecdotally, those insured with simple credit-life cover suggest that the product is not for their benefit, but rather the lender's. Such products may not be the ones in highest demand from the poor. Considering that very few loan defaults are due to death of the borrower, they are also rarely needed.

Some of the microinsurance products that are available today and the countries in which they are offered are shown below.

- Credit-life/life/endowment:
  - Bangladesh, Cambodia, India, Indonesia, Laos, Nepal, Pakistan, Philippines, Sri Lanka, Vietnam;
  - East Africa, South Africa, West Africa; and
  - Brazil, Colombia, Guatemala, Mexico, Nicaragua, Peru, Venezuela;
- Health/critical illness:
  - India, Bangladesh, Cambodia, China, Laos, Pakistan, Philippines;
  - East Africa, South Africa, West Africa;
  - Colombia, Mexico; and
  - Georgia, Russia;
- Crop/weather:
  - India, Philippines;
  - Ethiopia, Kenya, Malawi; and
  - Haiti, Mexico, Nicaragua;
- Property/asset/livestock:
  - Bangladesh, India, Mongolia, Nepal;
  - East Africa, South Africa; and
  - Albania;
- Funeral:
  - East Africa, South Africa, West Africa; and
  - Colombia, Mexico;
- Integrated package:
  - India;
- Rural insurance schemes:
  - India;

- Group personal accident:
  - West Africa;
- Unemployment:
  - East Africa; and
- Flood:
  - China, Indonesia.

6.1 Life insurance

Life insurance pays out benefits to designated beneficiaries upon the death of the insured. There are three broad types of life insurance coverage: term, whole-life and endowment. Term-life insurance policies provide a set amount of insurance coverage over a specified period of time, such as one, five, 10 or 20 years. This insurance is appropriate when the policyholder's need for coverage is temporary. It is the most widely used life insurance policy in low-income communities in developing countries and the least complicated for the provider to offer. Whole-life insurance is a cash-value policy that provides lifetime protection. Endowment life insurance pays the face value of insurance if the policyholder dies within a specified period. Microcredit lenders have invented credit-life insurance to protect their own loan portfolios. This is a term-life policy that is tied to the term of the loan. It pays off the balance of the loan if the borrower dies before the full repayment of the loan. In actual fact it is a loan protection policy for the benefit of the lender rather than the borrower. In most cases the risk is taken in-house by the lender. Unfortunately the majority of microinsurance policies in existence today are credit-life insurance.

6.2 Health insurance

Health insurance provides coverage against illness and accidents that result in physical injuries. NGOs and MFIs have realised that expenditures related to health problems are a significant cause of defaults and people's inability to improve their economic conditions. Although coverage varies, many providers cover limited hospitalisation benefits for certain illnesses, and for the costs of physician visits and medicine. Some also make primary healthcare services available. Health insurance is complex and is difficult to operate; the risk of moral hazard is high and safeguarding against such risk is expensive. Very few insurers or NGOs and MFIs offer this product.

6.3 Crop insurance

This typically provides policyholders with protection in the event of their crops being destroyed by natural calamities, such as floods or droughts. The experience with crop insurance in developing countries and even in the developed economies has been unsatisfactory. It is difficult and expensive to prove whether the loss is due to insured perils or due to negligence by the insured. A derivative of crop insurance is index insurance. Very few insurers or NGOs and MFIs offer this product.

6.4 Property insurance

Property insurance covers against loss or damage of assets, including huts, houses, shops, contents and livestock. Providing such insurance is difficult because of the need to verify the extent of damage and determine whether loss has actually occurred. It is difficult for most insurers and NGOs or MFIs to guard against such moral hazard. A few, however, do provide such coverage. A derivative of property insurance is index insurance.

6.5 Index insurance

Index insurance has been developed as a solution to the problems of crop and property insurance. It is especially designed for drought and excessive rainfall in the agricultural sector and catastrophic risks such as floods, earthquakes, typhoons and severe cold weather. An index insurance policyholder is not compensated on the basis of the loss but on a pre-determined index such as rainfall level or earthquake magnitude or temperature level. Once an index has been calibrated and correlates well with actual losses, underwriting and claims verification costs for the insurer are minimal and moral hazard and fraud are virtually eliminated. Using donor support several countries are experimenting with various index products. Very few have reached sustainability, however.

6.6 Crop and weather insurance

These products are more complex and as a result very few organisations offer them. Life insurance products are relatively easier and are more popular.

7. Microinsurance distribution

A distribution or delivery channel is an individual or an organisation that takes or helps to take an insurance product or an insurance service to the policyholder and provides all the after-sale services. Any organisation that already makes financial transactions with the poor and has their trust is best suited to act as a microinsurance distribution channel. Distribution may involve several different organisations, including insurance companies, NGOs/MFIs/CBOs, cooperatives, outsourced administrators, third-party payment providers, and client aggregators such as brokers and retailers. Microinsurers prefer to use existing distribution channels rather than agents for the following reasons:

- to gain credibility by exploiting the relationship that distribution channels have with low-income households;
- to generate sufficient commission to sustain a livelihood, which is difficult for full-time agents because microinsurance premium-based commissions are too small to interest them;
- because most microinsurance channels do other things as their main business, such as providing loans, selling groceries or distributing agriculture inputs; and
- because the microinsurance business model has a greater chance of success if risk carriers can achieve scale quickly, which they can do by working in partnership with a distribution channel such as an NGO/MFI/CBO/cooperative that already aggregates large numbers of low-income persons.

Distribution is a much wider concept than simply getting the insurance product to the client. It refers to all interactions between the insurer and the policyholder. This includes handling policy applications, policy delivery, premium collection and policy administration, as well as all marketing, sales and handling claims activities. It is thus a much wider service than just the selling of insurance.

The cost of selling, underwriting and administering an insurance claim does not decrease in proportion to the value of the policy. When they use traditional channels and processes, insurance companies cannot write policies with values below a certain threshold without pricing them unrealistically. Moreover, microinsurance is a low-cost, high-volume business. Achieving scale through an efficient distribution system is therefore crucial.

Cost-effective distribution is one of the biggest challenges faced by insurers in low-premium environments. Customers are typically unfamiliar with insurance products and are often sceptical about providers. In an effort to reach as large a client base as possible, the emphasis is increasingly falling on innovative new distribution models as alternatives to traditional microinsurance distribution approaches. Typically, the new models rely on distribution through microfinance institutions.

Distribution channels are essential for bringing products to clients for whom insurance may be fundamentally new. Microinsurance generally engages NGOs and MFIs as distribution channels. Because of the scale involved, and because NGOs and MFIs are already working with low-income households and can deliver microinsurance at no additional cost, a premium-based commission is attractive to such organisations. In addition to NGOs and MFIs, organisations such as post offices, cooperatives, labour unions, employers and other institutions with large networks have the potential to reach significant numbers of clients at low cost.

A 2011 Coydon and Molitor report shows the following distribution of delivery partners:

1. MFI/rural bank	30%
2. Agents	14%
3. NGOs	11%
4. Retailers, service providers, funeral parlours	11%
5. Brokers	10%
6. CBOs	10%
7. Government and semi-government	8%
8. Employers	7%

continued overleaf

9. Faith-based groups	6%
10. Cooperatives	5%
11. Others	9%

Retail channels such as grocery and clothing stores are an interesting new innovation because they can be either formal or informal. The formal retail chains have the advantages of a well-known brand, client data and transaction systems, but they are often less convenient than informal retailers. Informal outlets – like 'mom and pop' shops – may have the advantage of proximity and frequency of use, but they have so far not been very successful with regard to sales volumes. This may be because people do not expect to buy insurance at the same place as they get their milk and bread, or top up their mobile phones. Insurers have also found it difficult to develop an effective value proposition for informal retailers, leaving them with limited motivation to sell insurance (Smith *et al*, 2010).

In recent years there has been a dramatic rise in the use of mobile phones among low-income people in most developing countries. Mobile technology has therefore emerged as an innovative channel for reaching low-income people and carrying out financial transactions. In countries like Brazil, Ghana, India, Kenya and the Philippines there is an increasing trend to use mobile phone service providers as distribution channels. In a number of developing countries, mobile phone network operators have made it possible for customers to pay for their premium using their existing mobile account. The advantage of this payment mechanism is that it can be used by any customer with a mobile phone.

A number of niche players, like Bima, MicroEnsure and Trustco, have emerged as specialists in bridging the gap between insurance companies and network operators. Their products make use of airtime dealers and mobile money agents as channels for sales, premium collection and claims payment.

Because microinsurance premiums are small, distribution channels are more often institutions than individual agents. An agent can earn a much higher commission from selling a conventional insurance product than a microinsurance product, whereas an NGO, MFI or retailer is already working with a large group of people and can convert its clients into microinsurance clients a little additional cost. A variety of businesses and organisations are engaged in microinsurance and they often join forces in diverse, and at times, innovative ways to deliver services to clients. Typical distribution/delivery models include:

- partnerships between commercial insurers and MFIs and other delivery channels;
- regulated insurers that serve low-income clients directly, often with separate agents;
- healthcare providers offering a package, which includes both insurance and healthcare service;
- CBOs, which pool risks and/or funds of members;

- MFIs that offer insurance to their clients and act as risk carriers themselves; and
- public-private partnerships – government or donor partners with insurers/NGOs/MFIs to provide microinsurance to NGO beneficiaries.

A variety of institutions can and do sell insurance products to the poor. The challenge is to minimise the trade-offs in each model and ensure that different entities are able to offer services that are customised for the poor population. In one new innovation insurers are partnering with institutions traditionally not involved in insurance. These alternative distribution model partners have a community presence larger than insurers could achieve on their own. Their infrastructure may be physical, such as store buildings, or virtual, such as mobile-phone networks.

Other recent innovations include:

- cash-based retailers such as supermarkets and clothing retailers offering simplified personal accident and funeral insurance products;
- credit-based retailers, such as furniture and electronic goods stores offering credit-life, extended warranties, personal accident and life insurance products;
- utility and telecommunications companies offering disability, unemployment, personal accident and, in some cases, household structure insurance; and
- third-party bill payment providers offering personal accident and life insurance products.

Another distribution channel that has recently entered the market is the microinsurance intermediary. This is an organisation that transfers the insurance risk from an NGO, MFI, cooperative or self-help group to an insurance company. They can also provide back-office services. Intermediaries work for a commission or a flat fee, and examples include MicroEnsure, First Microinsurance Agency Pakistan and PlaNet Guarantee. Commercial intermediaries that have ventured into microinsurance include Aon, Marsh and Guy Carpenter.

Another new innovation is distribution channels in which insurers do not collect premiums from customers at all. Instead, service providers or product manufacturers cover the cost of insurance or include the cost of the insurance in their service charge or product cost. Such schemes generate customer loyalty, to the benefit of both the insurer and the service provider or product manufacturer. The insurance policy in such a model is normally renewed every month, as long as the customer continues to buy the service or product. When they stop, the insurance benefit is forgone. Loyalty programmes reward, and therefore encourage, buying behaviour, and this is valuable enough to the service provider or product manufacturer to justify subsidising the cover. A key success factor for such programmes is that they make customers aware of the potential benefits of the insurance cover they are receiving.

The following list summarises the characteristics of a good distribution channel (McCord and Roth, 2006):

- regular transactions with low-income people;

- convenience and good customer service;
- client trust;
- a large volume of customers who are potential policyholders;
- trustworthy to both the insurer and the low-income population;
- secure and efficient systems to collect and deliver premiums; and
- transparent information on the cost of insurance services, coverage and other performance.

8. Benefits of microinsurance

Insurance services reduce the vulnerability of low-income households to risks against which they cannot afford to protect themselves. The risk-pooling mechanism of insurance makes protection more affordable. There is a further, indirect benefit of insurance: it creates financial incentives for insurance companies to encourage risk prevention. These financial incentives can lead to tangible development benefits that are produced by the private insurance market without prodding or funding from donors.

The following are some of the benefits of microinsurance for the various stakeholders:

- benefits for low-income households:
  - products adapted to client needs;
  - products adapted to client capacity to pay;
  - products focused on loss of life and livelihood;
  - reduced vulnerability to natural and other disasters; and
  - improved ability to cope with loss;
- benefits for intermediaries:
  - new line of business;
  - larger policyholder base;
  - improved morale among employees;
  - corporate social responsibility;
  - enhanced corporate image;
  - increased commission earnings; and
  - training and capacity building;
- benefits for insurers:
  - new line of business;
  - larger policyholder base;
  - improved morale among employees;
  - corporate social responsibility; and
  - enhanced corporate image;
- social benefits:
  - improved morale in rural communities;
  - increased ability to face problems; and
  - escape from cycle of poverty.

9. Challenges of microinsurance

Despite the success of many microinsurance schemes, there are still many challenges in providing insurance protection to low-income households. These challenges are especially salient for the more complex forms of insurance, such as health, property and crop insurance.

9.1 Restrictive regulatory environments

Insurance regulations in many developing countries are unintentionally biased against microinsurance providers. Regulations such as those involving minimum capital requirements, solvency, licensing, distribution and investment restrictions are often designed for large insurance companies serving the middle and upper-income segments of the market. These regulations are restrictive for insurers trying to serve the low-income market.

9.2 Limited interest of commercial insurers

Commercial insurers in many developing countries are often unwilling to provide insurance for the low-income market, possibly because of traditional biases and beliefs regarding the attractiveness of low-income households as customers. As long as these traditional biases persist, they will continue to limit the participation of commercial insurers in low-income markets and will thereby slow the development of microinsurance.

9.3 Minimising transaction costs

Low transactions costs are key for both the policyholder and the institution. If the costs are too high and applying for insurance, paying premiums and submitting claims are inconvenient, low-income households will be unwilling to purchase the insurance, regardless of its benefits. At the same time, microinsurance providers need to minimise their costs to ensure insurance premiums are affordable for poor households.

Integrating insurance into existing credit distribution systems has successfully reduced transactions costs for basic credit insurance. However, packaging insurance alongside a credit product means that the client only has coverage when he or she has a loan. Many poor people would like insurance cover without having to be in debt.

9.4 Experience with insurance

Poor households are slow to understand the concept of insurance and are reluctant to commit to regular premium payments for a future intangible benefit. Poor people do not have the surplus cash to pay for a risk-management service, especially one they hope they will not need. It is difficult for them to justify paying premiums until after a risky event has occurred. Unfortunately, at that point it is too late.

The level of trust required for an insurer to sell its products is greater than for other financial services. In the case of credit, the institution has to trust that the borrower will be willing and able to repay the loan. With savings, the roles are reversed: clients have to trust that the institution will safeguard their deposits, but they can test this relationship by periodically withdrawing money. With insurance, the level of trust required of policyholders exceeds that required of depositors and savers, because the client does not know whether the insurer will keep its promise until some uncertain time in the future when they or their dependents make a claim. In addition, prospective clients in some areas have been subject to aggressive sales tactics by commercial insurers and now harbour a dislike or distrust of all insurance providers.

9.5 Irregular household income flows

Traditional insurance products generally require a fixed amount to be paid on a regular basis. However, low-income households can struggle to maintain a regular contribution schedule, given the substantial fluctuations in their income. Such households require flexible premium payment options that will not jeopardise their household budget.

9.6 Affordability of premiums

Microinsurers face the challenge of offering insurance coverage at a price that is affordable to poor households, while ensuring their own financial sustainability. One response to this is to limit the coverage provided. This may not meet the needs of the low-income households, however.

A number of pilot projects are being run to establish what types of insurance can be offered profitably and to which policyholders. Early indications suggest that well-designed life insurance products can sustainably serve a broad spectrum of clients. There is insufficient evidence, however, to draw even tentative conclusions regarding the depth of outreach for health and property insurance.

9.7 Differential pricing for different risks

Most microinsurance providers charge a flat-rate premium for their policies. Although this increases the simplicity of the products and lowers the premium, it prevents the insurer from setting premiums in line with the actual risk levels of individual policyholders. As a result, low-risk policyholders pay more than they should, effectively subsidising the high-risk policyholders.

9.8 Limited understanding of insurance needs

Low-income households are highly exposed to many risks. Little effort has been made, however, to understand how this exposure translates into a need for insurance. Understanding this translation is further complicated by households' unfamiliarity with the concept of insurance. Without this understanding, microinsurers run the risk of offering poorly designed and unsuitable products.

9.9 Limited financing

Where financially strong partners are not available, microinsurers must finance the total cost of product development during the start-up phase. Until sufficient scale has been achieved, client acquisition costs and initial claims expenses for new insurers can also easily exceed revenues from premium payments. Funding this start-up phase requires access to financing or reinsurance to act as a capital reserve. Lack of access to these sources can either prevent an insurer from beginning operations altogether or constrain its growth.

9.10 Lack of actuarial expertise

One of the most significant obstacles facing NGOs, MFIs or CBOs that intend to act as full-service insurers is the actuarial expertise required to set premiums and determine benefits accurately. Without this knowledge, potential microinsurers run the risk of setting premiums either too low or too high.

9.11 Limited products

Today's poor households require a range of insurance products to mitigate the risks they face. Unfortunately, most of them are offered only life insurance products like credit-life insurance. Very few insurers offer the health or property insurance that poor people need most.

9.12 Climate change

Weather-related insurance has always posed a challenge to the insurance sector. These difficulties may be exacerbated by the increasing risk and unpredictability of extreme weather associated with climate change. Climate change will probably increase the demand for insurance, while at the same time increasing its cost. The challenge will be to find ways to make insurance more affordable by reducing administrative costs.

10. The next step

Microinsurance is still a new and evolving area for experimentation and research. Experience so far provides some useful lessons and highlights where further innovation, change, and experimentation are needed. Each challenge represents an opportunity for further research into innovative solutions. Additional research is also needed to understand and assess the developmental impact of various types of microinsurance product.

Although it is too early to predict what impact microinsurance will have on low-income households and the institutions that work with them, various pilot projects and experiments have garnered a lot of interest among stakeholders in furthering the development of microinsurance. Governments and donors need to focus more on the enabling environment, and commercial insurers need to focus on developing low-cost and need-based products and innovative distribution channels.

Sharia-compliant microfinance

Atif Hanif
Edana Richardson
Allen & Overy

Allah will not change the condition of a people until they change what is in themselves. *Qur'an, 13:11*

1. Introduction

Conventional microfinance provides access to financial services to entrepreneurial but collateral poor customers who might otherwise be excluded from the formal banking system.[1] Rather than offering charity, microfinance institutions provide financial assistance for people to help themselves, to work their way out of poverty and to contribute to the economy.[2] Like conventional banking, conventional microfinance services also involve the collection of interest.[3] Indeed, due to the greater risks involved in financing micro-entrepreneurs and the smaller economies of scale on which microfinance institutions operate, the interest rates charged by these institutions are often higher than those charged by commercial banks.[4]

The Islamic finance industry, however, is founded on unique structural restrictions. These represent the outer limits of financial activity that is acceptable under Islamic law (or *Sharia*[5]). They include a prohibition on charging or receiving interest. As such, conventional microfinance is not compatible with Islamic law. Islamic microfinance – that is, microfinance that adheres to the teachings of Islamic law – therefore fills a gap by addressing the needs of unbanked members of society whom conventional microfinance fails to accommodate.[6]

This chapter provides an overview of the Islamic microfinance industry. It considers the theoretical aspects of Islamic microfinance and the sources of Islamic law, the underlying principles of Islamic microfinance, the structures available to

1 Wilson, Rodney (2007) "Making Development Assistance Sustainable through Islamic Microfinance", *IIUM Journal of Economics and Management*, Vol 15, No 2, pp 197–217, at 198–199; Obaidullah, Mohammed (2008) *Introduction to Islamic Microfinance*. India: IBF Net (P) Limited, p 4.

2 Rahman, Abdul Rahim Abdul (2006) "The Islamic Microfinance Potential", *New Horizon Magazine*, No 162, pp 9–12, at 9.

3 Ahmed, Habib (2012) "Organizational models of Islamic microfinance", *Shari'a Compliant Microfinance*, ed S Nazim Ali. New York: Routledge, pp 17–32, at 17.

4 Sultan, Hussam (2012) "Islamic microfinance; Between commercial viability and the higher objectives of shari'a", *Shari'a Compliant Microfinance*, ed S Nazim Ali. New York: Routledge, p 46–59, at 50.

5 This chapter will follow other commentators, scholars and participants in the Islamic finance industry by using transliterations of Arabic terms when relevant. There is of course, no single correct means of expressing Arabic words and sounds in the Latin alphabet. Throughout this chapter, quotations and the official names of products and organisations that contain a transliteration and use of italicisation which are different from that used in this chapter, are reproduced without adjustment.

6 Karim, Nimrah, Tarazi, Michael and Reille, Xavier (2008) "Islamic Microfinance: An Emerging Market Niche", *CGAP Focus Notes*, No 49, p 1.

Islamic microfinance institutions, and *Sharia* supervision. It then looks at Islamic microfinance in practice and, through illustrative case studies, discusses how Islamic microfinance has been implemented in certain Muslim states. These countries have been chosen in order to provide a broad overview of Islamic microfinance and cover the implementation of this financial sector in East and South Asia, the Middle East and Africa.

2. Islamic microfinance – the underlying principles

The Islamic banking and finance industry has developed rapidly over the last 40 years, and particularly in the last decade. With global assets now worth over $1 trillion,[7] Islamic finance has assumed more mainstream relevance, and *Sharia*-compliant financial products are now available for both wholesale, sophisticated financial activity and retail-level transactions. Indeed, the first successful and innovative development in contemporary Islamic banking – Mit Ghamr in rural Egypt – provided financial services to small-scale, rural customers and shared some characteristics with microfinance.[8]

The connection between *Sharia* and Islamic finance ensures that the distinguishing features of this industry are broadly ethical in nature, concerned more with the well-being of the parties and the community than with individualism and materialism.[9] Islamic finance therefore represents a value-heavy system that seeks to uphold the Islamic worldview by emphasising cooperation, personal responsibility, morality, brotherhood and fairness.[10] The prohibitions of *riba*, *gharar*, *maysir* and *haram* activities, which are discussed below, represent the external application of *Sharia*. Adherence to these financial rules is essential to establishing a legitimate Islamic banking and financial system. In addition, the objectives of *Sharia* (maqasid al-*Sharia*) and its socio-economic goals are part of the institutional fabric of the Islamic financial sector.[11] Economics and religion are thus closely interwoven.[12]

The broader pursuit of ethical goals in Islamic finance would appear to present this financial sector as an ideal mechanism for implementing microfinance.[13] Notions of equity, social justice and a disavowal of exploitation are already ingrained in Islamic finance and do not need to be newly adopted. In practice, Islamic

---

7 Richter, Frederik (2009, April 8) "Islamic finance assets seen at $1.6 trln by 2012", *Reuters*. Available from www.reuters.com/article/2009/04/08/islamicfinance-growth-idUSL894329020090408.

8 Allen & Overy LLP (2009) *Islamic Microfinance Report*. International Development Law Organisation, p 13.

9 Rice, Gillian (1999) "Islamic Ethics and the Implications for Business", *Journal of Business Ethics*, No 18, pp 345–358, at 346.

10 Chapra, M. Umer (2000) "Is it necessary to have Islamic economics?", *Journal of Socio-Economics*, No 29, pp 21–37, at 29.

11 See generally, Siddiqi, Mohammad Nejatullah, Keynote Speech, *Round table on: Islamic Economics: Current State of Knowledge and Development of the Discipline*, held at Jeddah, Saudi Arabia on May 26-27, 2004, under joint auspices of the Islamic Research and Training Institute, Jeddah and the Arab Planning Institute, Kuwait. Available from www.siddiqi.com/mns/Keynote_May2004_Jeddah.html.

12 Kahf, Monzer (1989) "Islamic Economics and Its Methodology", *Readings in the Concept and Methodology of Islamic Economics*, ed. Aidit Ghazali and Syed Omar. Petaling Jaya: Pelanduk Publications, pp 40–48 at 44; Rice (1999), p 346.

13 Dhumale, Rahul and Sapcanin, Amela (1998) *An Application of Islamic Banking Principles to Microfinance, A Technical Note*. Washington DC: Regional Bureau for Arab States, United Nations Development Programme, p 1.

microfinance has not been widely implemented and the ostensible compatibility between Islamic finance and microfinance notwithstanding, examples of a fusion between the two are somewhat limited.[14] A survey of Islamic microfinance undertaken in 2007 by the Consultative Group to Assist the Poorest (CGAP) concluded that Islamic microfinance institutions reached 380,000 customers in 15 countries, accounting for just 0.5% of global microfinance outreach.[15] Nevertheless, CGAP has itself stated that "Islamic microfinance has the potential to expand access to finance to unprecedented levels throughout the Muslim world".[16]

2.1 Principles of Islamic financial contracts

Islamic law is inclusive in its scope and its edicts deal with both the explicitly religious and seemingly secular aspects of its adherents' lives. Religious principles thus form the standard against which every facet of a Muslim's private, social and commercial life will be judged.[17] Islamic law is not, however, a codified body of teachings contained in a single source. Instead, the rules of *Sharia* (including those relating to financial activity) are spread, piecemeal, throughout a number of different sources.

Sharia is revealed to Muslims in its primary sources: the *Quran* (the holy book of Islam)[18] and the *Sunnah* and *hadith* (the utterances and actions of the Prophet in light of this revelation). The non-divine sources of Islamic law are developed through human effort (*ijtihad*).[19] These derivative roots comprise *qiyas* (analogy) and *ijma'* (consensus of legal scholars), and are used principally as a means of deducing rules of Islamic law where the *Quran* or *Sunnah* are not explicit in their teachings.[20]

Neither the *Quran* nor the *Sunnah* contains a single, discernible theory guiding contractual relations generally, or financial transactions specifically. Verses relating to contract and commerce are instead scattered throughout the texts.[21] Nevertheless, Islamic law is not devoid of principles relevant to contracts and contractual relationships.[22] Rather than developing a single theory of contract, Islamic law has been

---

14 Ali, Nazim (2012) "Introduction", *Shari'a Compliant Microfinance*, ed S Nazim Ali. New York: Routledge, pp 1–6 at 1; Islamic Finance Project (2008) *Microfinance: Toward a Sustainable Islamic Finance Model: A Short Report*, p 1. Available from http://ifp.law.harvard.edu/login/view_pdf/?file=Microfinance.pdf&type =seminars; Dusuki, Asyraf Wajdi (2008) "Banking for the poor: the role of Islamic banking in microfinance initiatives", *Humanomics*, Vol 24, No 1, pp 49–66 at 50.

15 Karim, Tarazi and Reille (2008), pp 1 and 5.

16 *Ibid*, p 1.

17 Crane, Robert, "The Essence of Islamic Law," *The American Muslim*, ed. Kareema Altomare. Available from www.theamericanmuslim.org/tam.php/features/print/the_essence_of_islamic_law/.

18 Al Omar, Fuad and Abdel-Haq, Mohammed (1996) *Islamic Banking Theory, Practice and Challenges*. New Jersey: Zed Books, p xvi.

19 *Ijtih d* is defined by Weiss as "the process of extracting or deriving (*istinbat, istithmar*) legal rules from the sources of the Law"; Weiss, Bernard (1977–78) "Interpretation in Islamic Law: The Theory of Ijtih d", *American Journal of Comparative Law*, No. 26, pp 199–212 at 199–200. The continued use of *ijtih d* among Islamic scholars is an area of controversy; see Hallaq, Wael B. (1984) "Was the Gate of Ijtihad Closed?", *International Journal of Middle East Studies*, Vol 16, No 1, pp 3-41.

20 L J Potter in the UK Court of Appeal noted that "most of the classical Islamic law on financial transactions is not contained as 'rules' or 'law' in the *Qur' n* and *Sunnah* but is based on the often divergent views held by established schools of law formed in a period roughly between 700 and 850 CE", *Beximco Pharmaceuticals Ltd v Shamil Bank of Bahrain EC* [2004] 1 Lloyd's Rep 1, at 30.

21 Hassan, Hussein (2002) "Contracts in Islamic Law: The Principles of Commutative Justice and Liberality", *Journal of Islamic Studies*, Vol 13 No 2 pp 257–297 at 257–258.

22 Doi, 'Abd ar-Rahman (2008) *Shariah Islamic Law*, revised and expanded by 'Abdassamad Clarke. London: Ta-Ha Publishers, at 550ff.

interpreted by scholars as setting out generalised conditions which are present in valid contracts as well as elements which must be avoided in *Sharia*-compliant contracts.

The roots of Islamic law have thus been interpreted by these scholars as establishing basic precepts to which Islamic finance services and products should adhere: the prohibition of *riba* (etymologically, *riba* signifies increase or growth but is, in practice, generally translated as interest), the avoidance of *maysir* (gambling and speculation in financial activity), the requirement that *gharar* or uncertainty in a contract is limited and, finally, the prohibition of involvement in certain *haram* (forbidden) activities and industries. These principles represent the parameters within which all Islamic financial activity – including Islamic microfinance – must operate. They are, quite simply, the pre-conditions for compliance with *Sharia* rules for Islamic finance transactions, and they distinguish Islamic finance activity from conventional, secular alternatives.[23]

2.2 Structures available in Islamic microfinance

Unlike conventional financial activity, Islamic finance contracts and transactions are thus constrained by obligatory suprasocial, non-temporal principles. The prohibitions of *riba*, *maysir*, *gharar* and *haram* activities require Islamic market participants to consider issues other than maximum economic success when developing and using financial instruments. It is precisely because of these prohibitions that a series of Islamic structures has been developed by Islamic scholars to allow Muslims to participate in financial activity without breaching the parameters of Islam's teachings. These structures continue to form the contractual basis for the contemporary Islamic finance industry and are broadly divided into sale-based structures, partnership structures and lease structures. The activity for which financing is sought often determines the type of structure used.[24] Beneficial or interest free loans (*qard hasan*) can also be offered and received without violating the teachings of Islamic law, although no interest can be charged, or any tangible benefit received, as a result of making such loans.

As will be discussed in Section 4, some of these structures are currently used in Islamic micro-credit and micro-saving ventures.

(a) Sale-based structures

Explicitly sanctioned by the *Quran* as the *Sharia*-compliant means of earning a profit without taking *riba*, sale has been categorised as the prototype Islamic contractual structure.[25] As an arrangement in which parties can exchange goods on the spot by way of barter or in exchange for money, a sale-based arrangement avoids *riba*. In contemporary Islamic microfinance arrangements, sales contracts most frequently take the form of *murabaha* (or sale with a mark-up), although *salam* (pre-paid forward sale) may also have potential in relation to Islamic microcredit.[26]

---

23 Ayub, Muhammad (2007) *Understanding Islamic Finance*. Chichester: John Wiley & Sons, p 43.
24 Ahmed (2012), p 22.
25 Schacht, Joseph (1964) *An Introduction to Islamic Law*. Oxford: Clarendon Press, p 151.
26 Obaidullah (2008), p 46, noting that the *mur baha* contract involving deferred repayment is "the most popular product among Islamic microfinance institutions".

Murabaha is a cost-plus-profit economic arrangement[27] in which a seller adds a defined profit margin to the price he or she originally pays for an object, disclosing both the cost price[28] and any mark-up to the purchaser.[29] When a *murabaha* is used as an Islamic financing contract, a customer will instruct a financier to purchase a particular asset. That asset is then sold to the customer by the financier at a mark-up price with that marked-up price paid in instalments on a deferred basis.[30] As such, *murabaha* gives a customer the opportunity to purchase an object which he or she wants, without having to pay the full purchase price immediately.[31] At the same time, the financier can earn a profit through the mark-up portion of the arrangement. This profit is not *riba* because it is not payable as a result of the deferred payment of the purchase price but rather because the financier assumes ownership of the object before the sale and so bears the risks of that ownership. The combination of a credit sale, mark-up and the ability of the seller to set the level of that mark-up have resulted in the widespread contemporary use of *murabaha* arrangements as an alternative to interest-based loans.[32] According to CGAP, *murabaha* now accounts for 70% of Islamic microfinance funding provided globally.[33]

Salam sales are the inverse of *murabaha* and involve payment in advance for an asset to be delivered in the future.[34] In order to avoid *riba* and speculation, the agreement for future delivery can only be made in relation to fungible objects whose quantity and quality have been specified at the time of contracting.[35] Though not yet widely used in Islamic microfinance, it is suggested that *salam* structures have potential in *Sharia* compliance microfinance contracts in farming or cottage industries. Here the microfinance institution would buy the future output of the farm or workshop in exchange for cash. This would provide the farmer or manufacturer with immediate capital. Once the output is available it could be sold by the microfinance institution, allowing that institution to recover the initial capital paid to the microfinance customer.

---

27 Saleh, Nabil A (1992) *Unlawful Gain and Legitimate Profit in Islamic Law*, 2nd ed London: Graham & Trotman, p 117; Ayub (2007), p 213.

28 See Ibn Rushd (1996) *Bidayat al-Mujtahid wa Nihayat al-Muqtasid* [*The Distinguished Jurist's Primer*], Vol II, trans. Imran Ahsan Khan Nyazee. London: Garnet Publishing, pp 256–257 for a discussion of the views of scholars relating to what can and what cannot be included as costs.

29 Vogel and Hayes note that *mur baha* is now most commonly used in a composite form identified as "*al-mur baha lil-amir bi-al-shira*". This translates as "the *mur baha* of the one who orders or commissions another to purchase"; Vogel, Frank E. and Hayes, Samuel L (1998) *Islamic Law and Finance, Religion, Risk and Return*. The Hague: Kluwer Law International, p 140; Ayub (2007), p 213; Usmani, Muhammad Taqi (1995) "Methods of House Building Finance According to *Shar 'ah*", in *Islamic Banking Modes for Building Financing*, Proceedings of a Workshop organized in Khartoum by the Islamic Research and Training Institute of the Islamic Development Bank, October 27–29, 1999, Seminar Proceedings Series No 28, ed Mahmoud Ahmad Mahdi. Jeddah: Islamic Research and Training Institute, Jeddah, pp 61–74 at 63.

30 Vogel and Hayes (1998), p 140.

31 Ahmad, Abu Umar (2010) *Theory and Practice of Modern Islamic Finance: The Case Analysis from Australia*. Florida: BrownWalker Press, p 193.

32 *Ibid*, p 204.

33 Karim, Tarazi and Reille (2008), p 8.

34 Mohammed, Noor (1988) "Principles of Islamic Contract Law", *Journal of Law and Religion*, Vol 6, No 1, pp 115–130 at 124.

35 Al-Zuhayli, Wahbah (2003) *Financial Transactions in Islamic Jurisprudence*, trans. Mahmoud el-Gamal. Damascus: Dar al-Fikr, p 239, notes that scholars are in agreement that *salam* is "permissible for all commodities measured by volume, weight, length, or number of similar items (eg, nuts, eggs, etc)".

(b) *Partnership structures*

The emphasis in Islamic law on trade and the assumption of commercial risk has led Islamic scholars to place stress on an equity-based system of profit-and-loss sharing as the alternative "of choice"[36] to fixed or variable interest-based lending.[37] Relying on the Islamic maxim which confirms that "gain accompanies liability for loss", the philosophical underpinning of partnership financing rests on the idea that a financier looking to make a profit must be prepared to share the risks and rewards with the entrepreneur.[38] Rather than offering the financier guaranteed returns, partnerships bring together several parties in a mutually beneficial relationship. They can be used as a way to provide a customer with funds without contravening the prohibitions of *riba* and *gharar*.[39] Islamic partnership arrangements thus offer a financial structure through which entrepreneurial but collateral-poor customers can obtain financing. As such, this structure would appear to be aligned in purpose with conventional microfinance, albeit in a manner consistent with *Sharia*. Two broad categories of partnership exist: *mudaraba* and *musharaka*.

Mudaraba is a form of participatory arrangement between at least two parties: a finance partner (*rabb al-mal*) and a management partner (*mudarib*) (that is, the party seeking financing). When used in Islamic financial activity, the finance partner, which may be a bank, supplies all the capital needs of a venture.[40] The customer (the *mudarib*) supplies no capital but provides expertise and management necessary to ensure the ultimate success of the investment. As *mudarib*, the customer manages the *mudaraba* arrangement and invests the capital according to criteria agreed by the parties. Once a successful *mudaraba* generates income, the *mudarib* returns to the rabb al-mal the principal sum invested, plus an agreed-upon share of the venture's profits – rather than a pre-arranged fixed lump sum.[41] If the enterprise is unsuccessful, the parties bear that loss in proportion to their investment. Because the finance partner invested capital, he or she bears any pecuniary losses and may not be able to recover all or any of the initial investment. The *mudarib* will lose the time and effort he or she expended in the venture. However, except in the case of fraud or negligence, the *mudarib* will not be held financially liable for any loss.[42]

In *musharaka*, all parties contribute to the partnership in cash or in kind.[43] Unlike

---

36 Warde, Ibrahim (1999) "The Revitalisation of Islamic Profit-and-loss Sharing", Paper presented at Third Harvard University Forum on Islamic Finance; *Local Challenges, Global Opportunities*, Cambridge, Massachusetts, October 1.

37 Wilson, Rodney (1997) "The Issue of Interest and the Islamic Financing Alternatives", *Journal of International Banking Law*, Vol 13, No 1, pp 23–29 at 25.

38 Warde (1999).

39 Ray, Nicholas Dylan (1995) *Arab Islamic Banking and the Renewal of Islamic Law*. London: Graham & Trotman, p 70; Lewis, Mervyn and Algaoud, Latifa M. (2001) *Islamic Banking*. Cheltenham: Edward Elgar, p 43.

40 El-Ashker, Ahmed Abdel-Fattah (1987) *The Islamic Business Enterprise*. London: Taylor & Francis, cited in Klein, Daniel (1994–5) "The Islamic and Jewish Laws of Usury: A Bridge to Commercial Growth and Peace in the Middle East", *Denver Journal of International Law and Policy*, Vol 23, pp 535–554, at 539.

41 Khan, Mansoor H. (1997) "Designing an Islamic model for project finance", *International Financial Law Review*, Vol 16, pp 13–16 at 15.

42 Usmani, Muhammad Taqi (2002) *An Introduction to Islamic Finance*. The Hague: Kluwer Law International, p 13.

43 Abdul-Basser, Taha bin Hasan (2003) "The Centrality of Fiqh, An Introduction to *Shar'ah*-Compliant Finance", Paper presented at the Fifth Harvard University Forum on Islamic Finance; *Islamic Finance: Dynamics and Development*, Cambridge, Massachusetts, April 6.

mudaraba structures, therefore, the financier (such as a bank) and the customer in *musharaka* arrangements may both contribute capital to the venture.[44] Any profits generated by the enterprise are shared between the parties, either in proportion to their investment or in accordance with a pre-agreed ratio. As well as sharing profits, every partner must bear the risk of the venture's failure in proportion to their capital contribution. As a result both the financier and the customer may lose some or all of their initial investment.[45] The parties to a *musharaka* therefore interact as partners to a transaction, both contributing and both enjoying similar rights, benefits and liabilities.[46]

(c) *Lease-based structures*

The final category of Islamic finance structure to be considered is *ijarah*, or leasing arrangements. *Ijarah* are similar in structure and function to conventional leases and are widely used in contemporary Islamic finance products.[47] When used in the context of assets, *ijarah* involve the sale[48] of an asset's usufruct (that is, the use of the asset) to the lessee for a period of time. Title and ownership remain with the lessor, who charges the lessee rent for the right to use and benefit from the underlying tangible asset.[49] Thus, while the lessee will be responsible for expenses and costs incurred in the day-to-day operation of the property and any loss caused by the lessee's negligence or misuse, the lessor must retain full ownership of the property together with all the responsibilities of ownership.[50]

2.3 *Sharia* supervision

Compliance with the dictates of Islamic law is the central premise of the Islamic finance industry. The disparate nature of many of Islamic law's teachings and the absence of a single authoritative interpretation of those teachings may make it difficult,

---

44 The Shafi'i school represents the strictest position in relation to acceptable contributions, insisting that capital is the only possible form of investment in a partnership (Jaziri, *al-Fiqh 'ala al-madhahib*, Vol III at 76, in Saleh (1992), p 115). The Hanafis and Hanbalis have adopted a more liberal approach to investment, accepting contributions in the form of cash, labour or a combination of these even if the contribution involves mixing of unlike currencies (Ibn Qudama, *al-mughni*. Riyadh, cited in Ray (1995), p 60). Finally the Maliki School has adopted a midway approach by permitting investments in cash and labour but insisting that the currencies be of the same type (Ibn Rushd (1996), pp 302–304).

45 Iqbal, Munawar and Molyneux, Philip (2005) *Thirty Years of Islamic Banking; History, Performance and Prospects*. Basingstoke: Palgrave Macmillan, p 20; Ibn Qudamah, *Al-Mughni*. Beirut: Dar-al-ktab-al-'arabi, cited in Usmani (2002), p 8.

46 Al-Harran, Saad, "Musharakah Financing Model", *Iqtisad al Islamy* [*Islamic Economics*]. Available from www.Islamic-world.net/economics/musharakah.htm.

47 Warde, Ibrahim (2010) *Islamic Finance in the Global Economy*, 2nd ed Edinburgh: Edinburgh University Press, p 144.

48 Though *ij rah* represent leasing contracts, in Islamic finance, the lease of a good is considered to be the sale of the good's use; Vogel and Hayes (1998), p 143.

49 *Ibid*, p 103; Al-Zuhayli (2003), p 424.

50 Recommendations of the Workshop, Proceedings of a Workshop organized in Khartoum by the Islamic Research and Training Institute of the Islamic Development Bank, October 27–29 1999, Seminar Proceedings Series No 28, ed Mahmoud Ahmad Mahdi. Jeddah: Islamic Research and Training Institute, Jeddah, p 275; Issa, Nabil A. and Campos, Patrick (2007) "Challenges in Structuring Non-Recourse Islamic Financing for Energy Projects in Saudi Arabia", *Texas Journal of Oil, Gas and Energy Law*, Vol 2, 452–469, at 454.

51 Al-Rifai, Tariq (2009) "Development of the Shari'a-compliant fund market and the role Shari'a scholars played," *Euromoney Encyclopedia of Islamic Finance*, ed Aly Khorshid. London: Euromoney Books, pp 70-78 at 73; Garas, Samy Nathan and Pierce, Chris (2010) "Shari'a supervision of Islamic financial institutions", *Journal of Financial Regulation and Compliance*, Vol 18, No 4, pp 386–407 at 388.

however, for market participants and customers to determine for themselves if financial activity is *Sharia*-compliant.[51] A lack of awareness of the nuances of Islamic law may make it particularly difficult for microfinance retail customers to determine the compatibility of financial products with the dictates of a consumer's faith.

The Islamic finance industry has relied upon two mechanisms for the religious oversight of an entity's activity. The first is government-level supervision involving centralised, official oversight through the development of *Sharia* standards by the legislature and use of the courts as an organ for vetting activity for compatibility with Islamic law. The second is private *Sharia* supervision implemented at institutional level by *Sharia* supervisory boards.

Institutional *Sharia* supervisory boards have become the preferred mechanism for facilitating supervision across the Islamic finance industry. However, among those countries considered below, national boards are the dominant *Sharia* supervisory mechanism. Centralised *Sharia* boards operate in Indonesia, Malaysia, Bangladesh, Pakistan and Sudan. These national boards advise their respective governments and central banks on religious issues relating to Islamic finance, review and determine the *Sharia*-compliance of products or instruments developed for the Islamic banking industry, and resolve disputes or uncertainties within institutional *Sharia* supervisory boards on interpretations of Islam.[52]

In the absence of universally accepted interpretations of *Sharia* standards, the *Sharia* supervisory boards and scholars, whether appointed at a national or institutional level, will continue to represent a unique but widespread feature of the Islamic finance and microfinance industries. In recognition of this, the executive director of Akhuwat (an Islamic microfinance institution based in Pakistan) proposed at the Global Islamic Microfinance Forum in Dubai in 2012 the establishment of a specialist *Sharia* Supervisory Committee, "to cope with the *Sharia* challenges encountered by Islamic Microfinance Institutions".[53]

3. Case studies

3.1 East Asia

(a) *Malaysia*

Early examples in East Asia of micro-style finance that is compliant with *Sharia* principles exist in Malaysia, a jurisdiction which has now developed into a hub for large

52 Pakistan has established "the *Shari'ah* Board" that advises the State Bank of Pakistan (Habib, Ahmed (2011) *Product Development in Islamic Banks*. Edinburgh: Edinburgh University Press, p 66). Malaysia's Central Bank has established a national Shariah Advisory Council (SAC) (Central Bank of Malaysia Act 2009, section 51ff) and its Securities Commission has developed its own Shari'ah Advisory Council (SAC) for non-banking Islamic financial activity. The Central Shariah Board for Islamic Banks of Bangladesh was established in 2001; Ahmad, Abu Umar Faruq (2010) *Developments in Islamic Banking Practice: The Experience of Bangladesh*. Boca Raton, FL: Universal Publishers, p 136. A National *Shar 'ah* Board also exists in Indonesia and a Higher Sharia Supervisory Board advises the Sudanese Central Bank; Central Bank of Sudan, *Higher Sharia Supervisory Board*. Available from www.cbos.gov.sd/en/node/544.

53 Meyers, Drew (2013, January 3) "MFI's of 27 Countries unified for the development of Islamic Microfinance", *MyKRO*. Available from www.mykro.org/mfis-of-27-countries-unified-for-the-development-of-islamic-microfinance/2013/01/?utm_source=feedburner&utm_medium=feed&utm_campaign=Feed%3A+Mykro+%28myKRO.org%29.

scale Islamic financial activity and retail-level Islamic banking. Malaysia's initial inroads into *Sharia*-compliant finance began in 1969 with the establishment by Act of Parliament of the Lembaga Tabung Haji Malaysia (Pilgrims Management Fund Board). This was created to help poorer Muslims perform the hajj by investing their savings using investment mechanisms approved by *Sharia*, and paying those savers a profit share rather than interest.[54] As a form of Islamic micro-saving the Lembaga Tabung Haji Malaysia relied on the concept of wadiah (or safekeeping). This was a means by which savers would deposit their cash with the institution, giving it authority to invest the cash using *musharaka*, *murabaha*, *mudaraba* and *ijarah* arrangements.[55] If the investment produced a profit, a portion of this profit was paid to the savers, thereby providing them with a *Sharia*-compliant return on their invested capital.

The Malaysian government and Malaysia's central bank (Bank Negara Malaysia or BNM) have recently sought to encourage microfinance, including Islamic microfinance, in Malaysia.[56] A number of organisations operating under the aegis of the government now offer financial assistance that complies with Islamic legal principles to small and medium enterprises and entrepreneurs. Permodalan Usahawan Nasional Berhad (PUNB), for example, offers financial products to Bumiputera entrepreneurs in the retail and small and medium enterprise sectors.[57] The 'Core PROSPER' programme was created by PUNB to "develop and assist Bumiputera entrepreneurs to increase their participation in the national economy and to contribute to the formation of a high-income society by 2020".[58] The type of Islamic product available to a PUNB customer depends of the requirements of their proposed business. In compliance with Islamic law, however, financing may take the form of a *qard hasan*, *musharaka*, or bai al inah or bai bithaman ajil (both similar to *murabaha* arrangements).[59] Agro Bank, another government-linked institution, offers the Ar Rahnu or Islamic pawnbroker's scheme. This offers short-term interest-free loans to those in financial difficulty.[60] Under this scheme, the customer provides collateral in exchange for instant cash, and the bank charges a fee for the safekeeping of the collateral but does not charge interest.[61]

Islamic microfinance in Malaysia is further facilitated by the guarantee

---

54 Islamic Development Bank (1995) "Tabung haji as an Islamic Financial Institution, The Mobilization of Investment Resources in an Islamic Way and the Management of Hajj", *IDB Prize Winners' Lecture Series*, No. 4. Jeddah: Islamic Research and Training Institute, pp 9–14; Thani, Nik Norzrul, Abdullah, Mohamed Ridza Mohamed and Hassan, Megat Hizaini (2003) *Law and Practice of Islamic Banking and Finance*. Malaysia: Sweet & Maxwell, p 11.

55 Islamic Development Bank (1995), pp 9–14.

56 Bank Negara Malaysia (2007) *Small and Medium Enterprises Annual Report*. Available from www.bnm.gov.my/index.php?ch=109&pg=611&ac=66&yr=2007&eId=box2.

57 Nawai, Norhaziah, Shariff, Mohd Noor Mohd (2011) "The Importance of Micro Financing to the Microenterprises Development in Malaysia's Experience", *Asian Social Science*, Vol 7, No 12, pp 226–238 at 230.

58 Permodalan Usahawan Nasional Berhad, *PROSPER Core*. Available from www.punb.com.my/v2/index.php?option=com_content&view=article&id=118&lang=ms.

59 SME Corp Malaysia, *The National SME Development Council*, available from www.smecorp.gov.my/v4/node/215; Nawai and Shariff (2011), p 23; Latip, Hamrila A. (2012) "Social Capital and Entrepreneurship: Building a National Entrepreneurial Capacity for Sustainable Development", *International Conference on Economics, Business and Marketing Management*, Vol 29, pp 158–162 at 158.

60 Agro Bank, *Ar Rahnu*. Available from www.agrobank.com.my/ar-rahnu.

61 Allen & Overy LLP (2009), p 22.

programmes offered by the Credit Guarantee Corporation Malaysia Berhad. Established in 1972 by BNM, the corporation provides guarantees for funds paid to small and medium enterprises by financial institutions, particularly in circumstances where those businesses would not otherwise qualify for credit facilities due to lack of collateral.[62] A strategic partnership between the corporation and Islamic financial institutions has made a number of these guarantee schemes available for both Islamic and conventional microfinancings offered by Malaysian institutions.[63]

Islamic financing offered to SMEs represented 9.6% of total SME financing outstanding in the Malaysian banking sector in 2006[64] and Islamic microfinance has formed part of the Malaysian authorities' goal of promoting the growth of Islamic finance in general. As well as fostering Malaysia as a centre for large-scale Islamic finance transactions, therefore, BNM has also acknowledged that Islamic finance should be inclusive and accessible to all, "particularly the lower income groups and small businesses".[65] This imperative "translates into the need and demand for more Islamic microfinancial products".[66] The governor of BNM has noted that "Islamic microfinance, if supported by micro-takaful (Islamic micro-insurance), has the potential to provide a more comprehensive, sustainable and accessible financing and protection solution for the lower income groups and small businesses".[67]

(b) *Indonesia*

Indonesia operates a dual financial system in which conventional and Islamic financial activities are formally recognised and co-exist.[68] This dual approach extends to the Indonesian microfinance market, where both conventional and *Sharia*-compliant microfinance options are available.[69] Indeed, one commentator has suggested that Indonesia is a country with possibly "the greatest diversity of both conventional and Islamic microfinance".[70]

Islamic microfinance itself is offered by a number of different types of institution in Indonesia:

- the microfinance department of Indonesia's Islamic banks;
- *Sharia*-compliant rural banks (Bank Perkreditan Rakyat Syariah or BPRS); and
- Islamic financial cooperatives (Baitul Maal wat Tamwil or BMT).[71]

While the first two institutions are supervised and regulated by the Indonesian

---

62 Saad, Norma Md and Anuar, Azizah, (2009) "'Cash Waqf' and Islamic Microfinance: Untapped Economic Opportunities", *Islam and Civilisation Renewal*, Vol 1, No 2, pp 337–354 at 340.

63 Bank Negara Malaysia (2006) *Small and Medium Enterprise (SME) Annual Report 2006*. Kuala Lumpur: Bank Negara Malaysia, p 137.

64 *Ibid*, p 137.

65 Zeti Akhtar Aziz (2012) Governor's Opening Address at the 2nd ISRA Colloquium 2012, *Islamic Finance in a Challenging Economy: Moving Forward*. Kuala Lumpur: Sasana Kijang. Available from www.bnm.gov.my/index.php?ch=en_speech&pg=en_speech_all&ac=452&lang=bm.

66 *Ibid*.

67 *Ibid*.

68 Law No 10 of 1998 on Amendment of Law No 7 of 1992 on Banking, Law No 23 of 1999 and Law No. 21 of 2008, see also, Bank Indonesia, *Islamic Banking in Indonesia in Brief*. Available from www.bi.go.id/web/en/Perbankan/Perbankan+Syariah/.

69 Obaidullah (2008), p 57; Karim, Tarazi and Reille (2008), p 9.

70 Seibel, Hans Dieter (2012) "Islamic microfinance in Indonesia: The challenge of institutional diversity, regulation and supervision", *Shari'a Compliant Microfinance*, ed S Nazim Ali. New York: Routledge, pp 147–169 at 147.

central bank (Bank Indonesia), the third exists outside the formal financial sector and is not officially regulated.[72] All three institutional types are considered below. A state-owned pawning company, Perum Pegadaian, also operates in the microfinance sector and provides *rahn* (pledge) and *amanah* (safe keeping) services that are compliant with the principles of Islamic law.[73]

Indonesia's Islamic commercial banks offer Islamic microfinance within the formal Islamic banking sector.[74] The impact of commercial banks on the microfinance sector is perhaps less pronounced in Indonesia than in other countries, however, because of the range of other institutions that offer financing and credit facilities to collateral poor entrepreneurs. Nevertheless, in 2011 the US Agency for International Development signed an agreement with Bank Muamalat – Indonesia's oldest Islamic bank – under which it agreed to guarantee $1.15 million in *Sharia*-compliant micro-loans made to low-income Indonesian female entrepreneurs.[75] As well as offering micro-loans to individuals, Bank Muamalat also offers working capital financing to BPRSs and BMTs to help them provide *Sharia*-compliant microfinance.[76] These working capital products are offered on a *mudaraba* and *musharaka* basis and can be provided for a term of up to five years.[77]

More common in the Islamic microfinance sector are Indonesia's *Sharia*-compliant rural banks. In 2011, 154 BPRSs operated 362 offices within Indonesia.[78] Their mission is "to help the enterprising poor, particularly small traders and micro-entrepreneurs",[79] and they focus on rural entrepreneurs, particularly in the agricultural sector.[80] These rural banks are privately owned and are subject to Indonesia's banking laws of 1992 and 1998.[81] As in many other aspects of Islamic finance, although a variety of *Sharia*-compliant financing structures are available,[82] *murabaha* arrangements dominate the micro-credit portion of these BPRS activities,[83]

---

71 Sakai, Minako, Marijan, Kacung (2008) "Harnessing Islamic microfinance", *Australian Indonesia Governance Research Partnership, Policy Brief*, p 1, Obaidullah (2008), p 57; Karim, Tarazi and Reille (2008), p 9.

72 Obaidullah (2008), p 57.

73 Pegadain, *Sharia Services, Rahn.* Available from www.pegadaian.co.id.

74 Seibel (2012), p 148.

75 USAID (2011, August 23) *United States Will Help Indonesian Women Develop Businesses In Partnership With Bank Muamalat.* Available from http://indonesia.usaid.gov/en/USAID/Article/583/United_States_Will_Help_Indonesian_Women_Develop_Businesses_In_Partnership_With_Bank_Muamalat.

76 Bank Muamalat, *Working Capital Financing Islamic MFI* (BPRS/BMT/Cooperative). Available from www.muamalatbank.com/home/produk/pembiayaan_lkms.

77 *Ibid.*

78 Bank Indonesia (2011) *Statistik Perbankan Syariah* (Islamic Banking Statistics), p 1.

79 Seibel, Hans Dieter (2004) *Islamic Microfinance in Indonesia.* Eschborn: Deutsche Gesellschaft für Technische Zusammenarbeit, p 24.

80 Lindsey, Tim (2012) "Between Piety and Prudence: State Syariah and the Regulation of Islamic Banking in Indonesia", *Sydney Law Review*, Vol 34, pp 107–127 at 111.

81 Law No 7 of 1992 on Banking and Banking Amendment Law 1998, the licensing of BPRSs is subject to government oversight: PBI No 6/17/PBI/2004 on Rural Banks is based on Syariah Principles, as is the prudential supervision of such banks: PBI No 6/18/PBI/2004 on Earning Assets Quality for Syariah Rural Banks. See generally, Lindsey (2012).

82 Allen & Overy LLP (2009), p 21. Bank Indonesia confirmed in its Codification of Islamic Banking Products that a range of Islamic financing arrangements were available to BPRSs; Bank Indonesia (2008) *Codification of Islamic Banking Products.* Available from www.bi.go.id/NR/rdonlyres/1DFA882B-16DB-44C9-8461-5CA3D8C637A5/16893/CODIFICATIONOFISLAMICBANKINGPRODUCTS.pdf.

83 In October 2011, *mur baha* represented Rs2,079,543 million while *mush raka*, the next most prevalent method, represented only Rs263,986 million; Bank Indonesia, *Statistik Perbankan Syariah* (Islamic Banking Statistics) (October 2011), p 19.

with *wadiah* (safekeeping) and *mudaraba* both widely used in micro-savings schemes.[84]

Finally, BMTs are organisations which set out to help the enterprising poor in a *Sharia*-compliant manner. As grassroots organisations they are not subject to formal supervision by the Indonesian government or central bank. Some BMTs function like cooperatives, and are registered with the Ministry of Cooperatives, Small and Medium Enterprises, while others are registered with PINBUK (Centre for Micro Enterprise Incubation).[85] The activities of BMTs are divided into two separate services. *Baitut Tamwil* activities promote saving within the community. These savings are used to help finance economic activities within the community through *Sharia*-compliant working capital and other financing products. Such financing is generally provided on a *murabaha* basis, although the profit and loss sharing arrangements of *musharaka* and *mudaraba* are also used.[86] The Baitul Maal activities relate to *Zakat* (alms giving), *infaq* and *sadaqah* (both charitable contributions in this context), which are accumulated before they are distributed to the poor on the basis of *qard hasan* loans.[87]

The Indonesian government has also made a conspicuous effort to promote microfinance and to reduce poverty. PNPM Mandiri, for example, is a national programme of poverty reduction that focuses primarily on community empowerment. It is supported by the Islamic Development Bank, which has stated its intention to introduce a *Sharia* Microfinance Programme under PNPM Mandiri before 2014.[88] However, while Indonesia has taken positive steps to encourage Islamic microfinance, a Bill on Microfinance Institutions drafted in 2001 was only presented to the House of Representatives in 2010. It has yet to be enacted.

3.2 South Asia

(a) Bangladesh

Bangladesh was one of the first countries to introduce both conventional and Islamic microfinance, and it now has the world's largest outreach of microfinance products. Both conventional and Islamic products are available, although most are conventional.[89] Between 2010 and 2012 alone, Islamic microfinance in Bangladesh grew 16-fold to constitute 8.38% of the country's Islamic finance market.[90] Yet although Bangladesh is a Muslim majority country, its key microfinance success has

---

84 Bank Indonesia (2011) *Statistik Perbankan Syariah [Islamic Banking Statistics]*, p 15; Karim, Tarazi and Reille (2008), p 9.

85 Seibel (2012), p 164.

86 *Ibid*, p 165.

87 Ersa Tri Wahyuni (2008) "The Accountability of Islamic Microfinance Institutions: Evidence from Indonesia", *Islamic Finance for Micro and Medium Enterprises*, ed. Mohammed Obaidullah and Hajah Salma Haji Abdul Latiff. Islamic Research & Training Institute, Islamic Development Bank and Centre, pp 339–354 at 342; see also: Pinbuk Indonesia, *Understanding the Vision and Mission of BMT*. Available from http://pinbuk.org/index.php/sekilas-bmt/pengertian-visi-dan-misi-bmt.

88 Islamic Development Bank (2011) Member Country Partnership Strategy, Republic of Indonesia: Harnessing the Regional Potential, 2011–2014, p 20.

89 Karim, Tarazi and Reille (2008), p 7.

90 *The Daily Star* (March 21 2012) "Islamic microcredit going great guns". Available from www.thedailystar.net/newDesign/news-details.php?nid=227109.

been in the conventional sector, through Grameen Bank. The Grameen Bank model is a way for small loans to be provided to borrowers who cannot provide collateral.[91] Instead of providing physical collateral for a loan, a borrower joins a group of other borrowers, each of whom has an interest in ensuring repayment by the other borrowers. Failure by any one member of the group to repay his or her loan not only results in that member being disqualified from the group and from new loans, but also disqualifies the whole group from receiving new capital. This repayment format has been replicated across the microfinance industry, creating social collateral through the peer pressure of making timely repayment.[92]

By December 31 2010, Grameen Bank had provided microfinance services to 8.34 million customers in Banglasdesh.[93] However, Islamic microfinance in Bangladesh has developed more modestly. The UK-based non-governmental organisation (NGO) Muslim Aid began providing a *Sharia*-compliant microfinance programme in the country in 1993.[94] It continues to offer interest free micro-loans based on *qard hasan*, *murabaha*, *bai-muajjal* and *musharaka* financial structures, and by the end of 2010 had nearly 70,0000 customers[95] and a recovery rate of 99.65%.[96] Muslim Aid's goal is to help "the poorest section in the community"[97] in Bangladesh, and it has formed partnerships with a number of organisations to increase the range of Islamic microfinance services available. Among these, the Shah Jalal Islami Bank offers *Sharia*-compliant financing products based on *murabaha*, *bai-muajjal* and *salam* to small enterprises and female entrepreneurs.[98] In partnership with other microfinance and Islamic organisations, Muslim Aid now provides a range of *Sharia*-compliant services, including a micro-credit programme, a hardcore poor programme, a small and medium-sized enterprise (SME) programme, and agro-based financing and investment programmes.[99]

The Islamic microfinance structure operated by Islami Bank Bangladesh Limited (IBBL) combines Islamic financial principles with the group-based structure used by Grameen Bank. Although IBBL is a commercial Islamic bank, it has introduced the "Rural Development Scheme" to address the finance and investment needs of Bangladesh's rural and agricultural sectors.[100] The Rural Development Scheme brings together five individuals from villages within a 10km radius of a branch of IBBL.[101]

---

91 Ahmed, Habib (2002) "Financing Microenterprises: An Analytical Study of Islamic Microfinance Institutions", *Islamic Economic Studies*, Vol 9, No 2, pp 27–64 at 31.

92 Wilson (2007), p 199.

93 Maes, Jan P and Reed, Larry R (2012) *State of the Microcredit Summit Campaign Report 2012*, Washington, DC: Microcredit Summit Campaign, p 47. Available from www.microcreditsummit.org/pubs/reports/socr/2012/WEB_SOCR-2012_English.pdf.

94 Muslim Aid, *Microfinance and Small and Medium Enterprise (SME)*. Available from www.muslimaid.org.bd/index.php?option=com_content&view=article&id=134&Itemid=206.

95 Maes and Reed (2012), p 49; Muslim Aid, *Microfinance and Small and Medium Enterprise*.

96 Muslim Aid, *At a Glance*. Available from www.muslimaid.org.bd/index.php?option=com_content&view=article&id=136&Itemid=208.

97 Muslim Aid, *Microfinance and Small and Medium Enterprise*.

98 Shahjalal Islami Bank Limited, *Prottasha for Small Enterprises*. Available from www.shahjalalbank.com.bd/sme_ise.php and Shahjalal Islami Bank Limited, *Prottasha for Women Entrepreneur*, available from www.shahjalalbank.com.bd/sme_women.php.

99 Muslim Aid, *Microfinance and Small and Medium Enterprise*; see also Sultan (2012), p 54.

100 Sarker, Abdul Awwal (2009) "Country Focus: Islamic finance progress in Bangladesh", *New Horizon*, No. 170, pp 24–28 at 28.

Each member of the group then opens a personal *mudaraba* savings account with the bank into which regular deposits must be made.[102] IBBL provides financing to members of the group using *musharaka* or *bai muajjal* structures. Each member of the group who receives financing must repay the capital received from IBBL over a period of time; however, each member is also responsible for ensuring repayment to IBBL by the other members of the group who received financing. Default by one member will result in the other members being held financially responsible.[103] As of August 31 2012, the scheme was operated by 195 branches of the bank, covering 14,569 villages across Bangladesh and had nearly 700,000 members.[104] Although IBBL's Islamic microfinance activities remain focused on Bangladesh's rural poor, the "Urban Poor Development Scheme" was launched in May 2012 with the aim, among others, of "alleviat[ing] urban poverty through investment in income generating activities".[105]

In March 2012, the governor of Bank Bangladesh, the country's central bank, called on Islamic banks and the Islamic windows[106] of conventional banks in Bangladesh to promote and provide Islamic micro and SME financing in order to reduce poverty and increase financial inclusion.[107] Speaking at the World Islamic Economic Forum, the governor stated that "[t]here is ample room for Islamic microfinance to flourish, given the growing popularity of Islamic finance among both Muslims and non-Muslims."[108] He also noted that the Islamic Development Bank was to establish an Islamic microfinance institution in Bangladesh.[109] This institution has yet to be established, although the Islamic Development Bank is producing a "Member Country Partnership Strategy for Bangladesh, 2013–2016" that will anchor its activities in Bangladesh.[110]

Until recently, Bank Bangladesh has had little direct involvement in promoting and supervising Islamic microfinance. Its explicit support for Islamic microfinance in 2012 came at a time of noticeable growth in this financial sector. Together with cooperation from the Islamic Development Bank, it suggests that Islamic microfinance may continue to develop in Bangladesh, now boosted by official sanction.

---

101 Islami Bank Bangladesh Limited, *Modus Operandi*. Available from www.islamibankbd.com/rds/modus_operandi.php.

102 *Ibid.*

103 *Ibid.*

104 Islami Bank Bangladesh Limited, *Performance of RDS*. Available from www.islamibankbd.com/rds/performance.php.

105 Islami Bank Bangladesh Limited, *UPDS*. Available from www.islamibankbd.com/rds/upds.php.

106 An Islamic window is a section of a conventional bank that is dedicated to the provision of *Shar 'ah*-compliant financial services.

107 *The Financial Express* (March 21 2012) "Atiur calls for promotion of Islamic microfinance". Available from www.thefinancialexpress-bd.com/more.php?news_id=124210&date=2012-03-21.

108 *Ibid.*

109 *Ibid.*; see also Jan, Fouzia (May 2012) "Islamic Microfinance: India as an Emerging Potential Market", *New Horizon*. Available from www.newhorizon-islamicbanking.com/index.cfm?section=features&action=view&id=11415.

110 *The Financial Express* (August 2 2012) "IDB to initiate MCPS to extend BD's need-based lending". Available from www.thefinancialexpress-bd.com/more.php?date=2012-08-02&news_id=138739.

(b) *Pakistan*

Along with Iran[111] and Sudan,[112] Pakistan is one of the few countries where official attempts have been made to make the financial system fully *Sharia*-compliant. In practice, the total islamisation of the economy has not been straightforward. Recent years have seen a the development of a parallel financial system in which both conventional and Islamic finance operate side by side. In line with its goal of strengthening the Islamic finance sector domestically, the Pakistani government has introduced legislation, regulations and guidelines relating specifically to Islamic financial activity and institutions. These include the Guidelines for Islamic Microfinance Business by Financial Institutions (the Islamic Microfinance Guidelines), also released by Pakistan's central bank (State Bank of Pakistan or SBP). These guidelines complement and must be read in conjunction with the existing regulatory framework established by SBP for both Islamic and conventional banks, and for microfinance banks.[113]

The criteria and conditions set for conventional microfinance banks in the Microfinance Institutions Ordinance 2001[114] must be adhered to when establishing a dedicated Islamic microfinance bank in Pakistan. These include the establishment of a depositors' protection fund,[115] and the maintenance of specific liquidity[116] and reserve ratios.[117] A number of additional characteristics must also be present for Islamic microfinance banks. The include the requirement that all the institution's financial transactions be "in accordance with the injunctions of *Sharia*"[118] and the appointment of a suitably qualified *Sharia* adviser.[119]

In practice, this institutional option has not yet been adopted in Pakistan. The SBP Islamic Microfinance Guidelines do, however, permit a number of other institutions to offer Islamic microfinance. The first is Islamic commercial banks. These are encouraged to offer Islamic microfinance products as they can not only "bring additional value streams" to Islamic banks, but also "help in building their image of fulfilling ... social responsibility and working for the cause of poverty alleviation."[120] These banks can offer Islamic microfinance products through

---

111 Amin, Sayed Hassan (1986) *Islamic Banking and Finance: The Experience of Iran*. Tehran: Vahid Publications; Binder, Leonard (1986) "Islam, Ethnicity, and the State in Pakistan: An Overview", *The State, Religion and Ethnic Politics; Afghanistan, Iran and Pakistan*, ed A Banuazizi and M Weiner. Syracuse: Syracuse University Press, pp 259–266; Rahnema, Ali and Nomani, Farhad (1990) *The Secular Miracle – Religion, Politics and Economic Policy in Iran*. London: Zed Books Ltd, pp 236–292, Amuzegar, Jahangir (1993) *Iran's Economy under the Islamic Republic*. London: I B Tauris Publishers, pp 15-18; Khan, Mohsin S and Mirakhor, Abbas (1990) "Islamic Banking, Experiences in the Islamic Republic of Iran and in Pakistan", *Economic Development and Cultural Change*, Vol 38, No 2, pp 353–375 particularly 358ff.

112 Tripp, Charles (2006) *Islam and the Moral Economy, The Challenge of Capitalism*. Cambridge: Cambridge University Press, p 140; Iqbal and Molyneux (2005), p 43–44.

113 State Bank of Pakistan (September 10 2007) *Guidelines for Islamic Microfinance Business by Financial Institutions*, Islamic Banking Department, Circular No 05, p 1. Available from www.sbp.org.pk/ibd/2007/Annex-c5.pdf.

114 State Bank of Pakistan (2001) Microfinance Institutions Ordinance 2001 (As amended up to 1 July 2007). Available from www.sbp.org.pk/l_frame/MF_Inst_Ord_2001.pdf.

115 State Bank of Pakistan (2001), Article 19.

116 State Bank of Pakistan (2001), Article 18(1).

117 State Bank of Pakistan (2001), Article 18(2).

118 State Bank of Pakistan (2007), p 2.

119 *Ibid.*, p 2.

120 *Ibid.*, p 3.

dedicated Islamic microfinance counters in existing branches, or by opening standalone Islamic microfinance branches, establishing independent Islamic microfinance subsidiaries or developing links with microfinance banks licensed by SBP and NGO-microfinance institutions.[121] In each case, the Islamic bank must submit the approval of their *Sharia* adviser of the products, mechanisms and agreements that relate to Islamic microfinance to the SME and Microfinance Department of SBP, as well as confirmation that the products can be provided in a *Sharia*-compliant manner.[122]

Finally, the Islamic Microfinance Guidelines provide a framework for conventional institutions to provide Islamic microfinance facilities. Conventional commercial banks may provide such services if they have been issued with an Islamic banking branch licence by SPB. Conventional commercial banks that want to offer Islamic microfinance services must therefore appoint a *Sharia* adviser who can confirm that the bank's activities are *Sharia*-compliant. Conventional microfinance banks can also provide Islamic services where they have received permission to do so by SBP.[123] If permission is granted, the microfinance bank must set up an Islamic Microfinance Division at its head office in Pakistan, appoint a *Sharia* adviser, carry out internal *Sharia* reviews and adhere to statutory liquidity and cash reserve requirements.[124]

In practice, the existence of a coherent regulatory regime has not encouraged the widespread development of dedicated Islamic microfinance banks in Pakistan.[125] Indeed, interest in Islamic microfinance services has primarily come from conventional financial institutions, and non-bank institutions and NGOs which are not regulated by SBP. In 2011 Tameer Bank, a conventional microfinance bank, announced its intention to open an Islamic microfinance division.[126] This would offer four Islamic microfinance products on the asset side (*murabaha*, *bai al inah*, *ijarah* and *musharaka*), three products on the liability side (current/checking account, *mudaraba* and *mudaraba* certificates) and one *takaful* product (health micro-insurance).[127] The bank envisaged the establishment of one fully operational Islamic branch and 19 Islamic counters at existing branches of Tameer bank by the end of 2013.[128]

Several Islamic microfinance schemes are available in the non-banking sector. The NGO Naziran Yousaf Memorial Trust, for example, is certified as an Islamic microfinance organisation by the SPB and offers *murabaha*-based financing and Islamic Enterprise Loans on a *qard hasan* basis. The organisation focuses on urban

---

121 *Ibid*, pp 3-4.

122 *Ibid*, p 4.

123 *Ibid*, p 6.

124 *Ibid*, pp 8 and 9.

125 Khaleeqquzzaman, Muhammad and Shirazi, Nasim Shah (2011) "Islamic Microfinance – An Inclusive Approach with Special Reference to Pakistan", Paper presented at the *Second European research Conference on Microfinance*, June 16–18 2011, Groningen, the Netherlands; see also Hussein, Maliha Hamid (2009) *State of Microfinance in Pakistan*. Institute of Microfinance, p 16. Available from www.microfinancegateway.org/gm/document-1.9.45537/State%20of%20microfinance%20in%20pak.pdf.

126 Mustafa, Shahid (2011, Mrch 25) "Islamic Microfinance Challenge: Profiling Tameer Bank, Pakistan", *CGAP*. Available from www.cgap.org/blog/islamic-microfinance-challenge-profiling-tameer-bank-pakistan.

127 *Ibid*.

128 *Ibid*.

and semi urban areas of Pakistan, with the goal of raising "the living standard and empowerment of low-income communities on [a] sustainable basis through providing quality micro finance services".[129] *Akhuwat*, another non-banking institution, operates a unique system developed in Pakistan in 2001. It offers interest free *qard hasan* microfinancing to individuals at the cost of a 5% administration fee.[130] Rather than relying on financial assistance from international donors or financial institutions, Akhuwat depends upon local, small-scale donations. This is helped by the fact that loans and information connected with the organisation are distributed in local religious spaces.[131] By the end of 2012, Akhuwat had 94,061 active loans and had disbursed in excess of PRs3 billion (approximately $30 million)[132] in the form of Islamic microfinance assistance.[133]

Finally, Pakistan's Islamic banks have also entered the Islamic microfinance market. This is, however, by way of financial assistance to NGOs rather than through the direct provision of microfinance. In 2009 Meezan Bank, an Islamic commercial bank signed a memorandum of understanding with Islamic Relief, an NGO that has provided *murabaha* based microfinancing to individuals in Pakistan since 2001.[134] According to the memorandum, Meezan Bank would "assist Islamic Relief to further enhance its Islamic Microfinance operations in Pakistan by capacity building, training and product development support."[135] A similar memorandum of understanding was also signed with HSBC Amanah (HSBC's Islamic arm), under which HSBC Amanah would fund Islamic Relief's Islamic microfinance projects in Rawalpindi.[136]

As for the Islamic finance sector, the SBP has tailored a regulatory regime to Islamic microfinance and the institutions that offer it. In addition to this regulatory oversight, Islamic microfinance knowledge and best practice standards are supported in Pakistan by the Centre of Excellence in Islamic Microfinance[137] and the Islamic Microfinance Network,[138] both of which are headquartered in the country. Although Islamic microfinance services are available in Pakistan, however, many of these services operate outside of the SBP's regulatory guidelines. Instead, the key Islamic microfinance institutions in Pakistan are non-bank organisations and NGOs, funded at the local level or by Pakistan's Islamic banks. Nevertheless, the commitment of

---

129 Naziran Yousaf Memorial Trust, *Microfinance & Enterprise Development*, available from www.naymet.org/microfinance-enterprise-development.

130 Allen & Overy LLP (2009), p 20.

131 Munir, Kamal (February 9 2012) "Akhuwat: Making Microfinance Work", *Stanford Social Innovation Review*. Available from www.ssireview.org/blog/entry/akhuwat_making_microfinance_work.

132 Converted at an exchange rate of $1 = 98.1099PRs.

133 Akhuwat, *Progress Report up to 31 November 2012*. Available from www.akhuwat.org.pk/progress_report.asp.

134 Allen & Overy LLP (2009), p 21; *New Horizon* (October 1 2009) "Meezan Bank partners with Islamic Relief". Available from www.newhorizon-islamicbanking.com/index.cfm?section=news&action=view&id=10835.

135 Meezan Bank, "Meezan Bank Limited and Islamic Relief sign MOU". Available from www.meezanbank.com/NewsDetail.aspx?iNewsID=113.

136 *AME Info* (July 17 2008) "HSBC Amanah to launch pilot Islamic microfinance programme with Islamic relief". Available from www.ameinfo.com/163835.html.

137 *Al Huda* (July 12 2012) "'Centre of Excellence in Islamic Microfinance' Established". Available from www.alhudacibe.com/pressrelease1.php.

138 Islamic Microfinance Network, available from www.imfn.org.

Pakistan's authorities to Islamic microfinance has been impressive and may well provide a platform for further institutional development within this sector.

3.3 Middle East and North Africa

Mit Ghamar in Egypt represented an early example of Islamic microfinance in the Middle East and North Africa. Nevertheless, the outreach of Islamic microfinance in Arab countries has been less extensive than in other parts of the world.[139] CGAP has noted that microfinance institutions offering Islamic microfinance in the Arab world frequently reach between 2,000 and 7,000 active borrowers, while conventional microfinance institutions in the same region "reach tens and hundreds of thousands active borrowers using conventional microfinance".[140] Nevertheless, levels of financial exclusion in the Arab world are "exceptionally high",[141] and one report has suggested that the provision of Islamic microfinance services "may be a powerful means of expanding outreach to otherwise excluded populations".[142] This has led to some notable developments in Islamic microfinance in the region.

Yemen, for example, issued in April 2009 the Microfinance Banks Law No 15.[143] This law applies to both conventional and Islamic microfinance banks, and Article 18 notes that "[b]anks established under Commercial Firms Law, Banks Law and Islamic Banks Law are entitled to exercise banking microfinance business as one of its usual activities in accordance with provisions [contained in the Microfinance Banks Law]".[144] The provisions of this law complement, and must be read in conjunction with, the provisions of Yemen's other banking laws, including those relating to Islamic finance.[145] As such, the Microfinance Banks Law is neither detailed nor exhaustive. It acts rather as a framework for those financial institutions that offer microfinance services but that are already governed by of one of Yemen's more extensive financial institutions laws. The Microfinance Banks Law therefore contains certain carve-outs where its provisions are inconsistent with Yemen's Islamic banking regime. Most notably, Article 7 sets out activities in which microfinance banks cannot engage – such as possessing shares in projects – but goes on to confirm that an Islamic microfinance bank may still carry on those activities permitted by the Islamic banking law, even where, it would seem, these are inconsistent with this article.[146]

A number of dedicated Islamic microfinance institutions have in fact been

---

139 Karim, Nimrah and Khaled, Mohammed (2011, February 23) "Taking Islamic Microfinance to Scale", *CGAP*. Available from www.cgap.org/blog/taking-islamic-microfinance-scale.

140 *Ibid.*

141 Akhtar, Shamshad and Pearce, Douglas (2010) "Microfinance in the Arab World: The Challenge of Financial Inclusion", *MENA Knowledge and Learning Quick Notes Series*, Vol 25, No 4. Washington, DC: World Bank, p 1.

142 Abdel-Baki, Ranya, Zain, Shaimaa, Cordier, Charles (2011) *MIX Microfinance World: 2010 Arab Microfinance Analysis & Benchmarking Report*, p 4. Available from www.themix.org/sites/default/files/2010%20Arab%20Microfinance%20Analysis%20Benchmarking%20Report%20-Final_2.pdf.

143 Microfinance Banks Law No 15 of 2009.

144 Microfinance Banks Law No 15 of 2009, Article 18.

145 That is, Law No (21) for 1996 regarding Islamic Banks.

146 Microfinance Banks Law No 15 of 2009, Article 7.

147 UN-HABITAT noted in 2005 that "A large proportion of microfinance initiatives in Yemen is based on Islamic financial principles." United Nations Human Settlements Programme (UN-HABITAT) (2005) "Paper 8: Islamic Credit and Microfinance", *Islam, Land & Property Series*. Kenya: UN-HABITAT, p 13.

established in Yemen.[147] One example is the 'Hodeidah Microfinance Programme', launched in 1997. This programme relies on a group lending model based on *murabaha* structures.[148] Potential customers form groups, which are then evaluated by a credit officer. If the credit officer is satisfied that entering into *murabaha* arrangements with members of the group is feasible, he or she purchases goods identified by each member of that group. In line with the *murabaha* nature of the Hodeidah arrangements, the credit officer then sells those goods purchased to the groups' members at the original cost price plus a mark-up. Both payments can be made in deferred instalments.[149] As with other group-based microfinance projects, the members of the Hodeidah groups act as a form of social pressure to encourage repayment.

More recently, *Al-Amal* Microfinance Bank was established under *Al-Amal* Bank Law No. 23 of 2002. *Al-Kuraimi* Islamic Microfinance Bank was re-registered in 2010 under the Microfinance Banks Law.[150] Both banks offer *Sharia*-compliant micro-savings services, microfinancing based on *murabaha* and *ijarah* structures, and micro-takaful products. *Al-Amal* is not actually established under the Microfinance Banks Law, but has been particularly successful as a microfinance institution in Yemen. It has developed the *ijarah*-based arrangement as a way for tradesmen to buy equipment and other tools. The pilot of this programme won Al-Amal the Islamic Microfinance Challenge 2010, an award sponsored by CGAP, Deutsche Bank, Grameen-Jameel Pan Arab Microfinance and the Islamic Development Bank. The challenge sought "ideas for sustainable, scalable, and authentic Islamic microfinance business models to meet the financial needs of the Muslim poor",[151] and received applications from 140 microfinance institutions in 23 countries. Al-Amal was named the winner as the first microfinance bank in the Arab world to offer only *Sharia*-compliant products. It was also noted that Al-Amal had developed "creative solutions to self-finance its banking activities and has demonstrated that micro-entrepreneurs can be reached with diverse Islamic finance tools on a large scale."[152] Al-Amal subsequently won the Grameen-Jameel Award for Sustainable Growth in 2012, and by December 2012 had disbursed over $14million using Islamic microfinance arrangements.[153]

As in Yemen, a dedicated microfinance law (the Microfinance Decree) has been established in Syria under which institutions may accept deposits, and provide

---

148 Al-Zam Xami, Ahmed and Grace, L. (2002) *Islamic Banking Principles Applied to Microfinance, Case Study: Hodeidah Microfinance Programme, Yemen*. New York: United Nations Capital Development Fund, pp 4 and 6; Obaidullah, Mohammed (2011) "Islamic Microfinance: The Way Forward", *Islamic Capital Markets: Products and Strategies*, ed. Kabir Hassan, Michael Mahlknecht. West Sussex: John Wiley & Sons, Ltd, pp 415–428 at 419.

149 Al-Zam Xami and Grace (2002), p 4.

150 Mansour, Adel (2011) *Small and Micro Enterprises Development in Yemen and Future Prospects*. Yemen: Social Fund for Development, p 27.

151 Karim and Khaled (2011).

152 Henry Azzam, quoted in Thomas, Jeanette (2011, February 15) "Al Amal Microfinance Bank of Yemen Named Winner of the Islamic Microfinance Challenge 2010", *CGAP*. Available from www.cgap.org/news/al-amal-microfinance-bank-yemen-named-winner-islamic-microfinance-challenge-2010.

153 Al Amal Bank, *Monthly Reports*. Available from www.alamalbank.com/index.php?option=com_content&view=article&id=237&Itemid=269&lang=en.

micro-credit and micro-insurance.[154] However, unlike the Microfinance Banks Law in Yemen, the Microfinance Decree does not contain tailored carve-outs for Islamic banking activity. Indeed, Article 12 of the decree prohibits microfinance institutions from owning real estate. This contradicts Article 9 of Syria's Islamic banking law, which provides that Islamic banks may acquire, sell, exploit, lease and rent movable and immovable property. In practice, key examples of Islamic microfinance in Syria have been situated in the non-banking sector, which is not covered by the Microfinance Decree.[155]

The Jabal Al Hoss Rural Community Development Project is an Islamic microfinance initiative in rural Syria supported by the United Nations Development Programme (UNDP). It creates self-reliant local financial institutions (*sanduq*, plural: *sanadiq*) in villages. The first *sanduq* was established in 2000. These institutions are initially funded by the share capital of their members. If they operate successfully for three months, the UNDP provides an additional capital injection.[156] The accumulated capital is used to offer short-term microfinancing. Following a preference expressed by the communities in Jabal Al Hoss, this microfinancing is offered on a *Sharia*-compliant basis through *murabaha*-based contracts. These allow customers to repay on an instalment basis while also providing the *sanduq* and its members a *Sharia*-compliant return in the form of the *murabaha* mark-up.[157] By the end of the project's first phase (2000–2002), 22 *sanadiq* had been established, with 4,691 members and a shareholder equity of $130,000.[158] During the second phase (2003–2007), support was also given by the Japanese government. Nevertheless, the success of the Jabal Al Hoss project is open to question. In 2008, one commentator noted that "[w]ith the current capital base the project can maintain the current level of operations, but cannot extend new loans". There also appears not to have been a third phase in the project's development. Nevertheless, the concept was replicated in the Idleb Rural Development Project, funded by the International Fund for Agricultural Development. This also involves *murabaha* loans provided by village-based institutions. By 2010, 30 villages in Idleb had established *sanadiq*, with more than 6,600 shareholders and repayment rates of 98%.[159]

Despite these developments, in light of the ongoing turmoil in Syria it is unclear how, and indeed if, the domestic Islamic microfinance industry will progress in the future.

---

154 The General Microfinance Decree (Act No 15 of 2007), Article 2.

155 NGOs, for example, operate under the Associations and Private Institutions Law rather than the Microfinance Decree.

156 Buerli, M. and Aw-Hassan, A (2004): "Microfinance in marginal dry areas: Impact of village credits and savings associations on poverty in the Jabal al Hoss region in Syria", talk given in the *Proceedings of Deutscher Tropentag 2004 on Rural Poverty Reduction through Research for Development and Transformation: international research on food security, natural resource management and rural developments*, October 5–7, Berlin, Germany, Humboldt-Universität.

157 Al Asaad, Mahmoud (2008) "Village Funds: The Experience of Rural Community Development at Jabal al Hoss, Syria", *Islamic Finance for Micro and Medium Enterprises*, ed. Mohammed Obaidullah and Hajah Salma Haji Abdul Latiff. Brunei: Islamic Research and Training Institute, Islamic Development Bank and Centre for Islamic Banking, Finance and Management, pp 197–210 at 198.

158 *Ibid*, p 197.

159 International Fund for Agricultural Development (2012) *Islamic microfinance: Unlocking new potential to fight rural poverty*, p 3. Available from www.ifad.org/operations/projects/regions/pn/factsheets/nena_islamic.pdf.

3.4 Africa

Like Pakistan, Sudan islamised its financial system in the 1980s and 1990s. Unlike Pakistan, however, where both Islamic and conventional finance now operate in parallel, Sudan is the "only country that [has] managed to successfully complete the project of Islamising its entire financial sector."[160] Following the secession of South Sudan, the financial system of Northern Sudan remains fully *Sharia*-compliant. The only financial products available are those which are consistent with the teachings of Islam.[161]

The Interim National Constitution of the Republic of the Sudan declares poverty alleviation as an explicit aspiration of the Sudanese government, noting that:

> *[t]he overarching aims of economic development shall be poverty eradication, attainment of the Millennium Development Goals, guaranteeing the equitable distribution of the nation's wealth, redressing income disparities, and achieving decent living standards for all citizens.*[162]

Consistent with this statement, the Central Bank of Sudan established a dedicated and independent Microfinance Unit in 2007.[163] Its purpose is to draw up microfinance policies and develop socio-economic banking "with a view of encouraging the establishment of effective microfinance institutions and activities to alleviate poverty in society".[164] As the Central Bank no longer regulates banking in South Sudan,[165] these policies would appear to affect only the microfinance sector in the North and, as such, microfinance which is *Sharia*-compliant. Among the policies issued by the Central Bank relating to microfinance, Circular number 05/2008 recognises the validity of non-conventional guarantees "appropriate to the nature of micro-finance". These include the group-based guarantees used in the Grameen Bank model.[166] The Central Bank of Sudan Policies for the Year 2012 also require each bank in Sudan to allocate 12% of its finance portfolio to "financing the projects and programmes of the small finance, micro finance, mini finance and the small finance with a social dimension".[167] These policies pledge to "exempt... micro finance projects from all Federal and State taxes throughout the repayment period"[168] of the financing allocated to those projects. The Aman Microfinance Portfolio has been established under the administration of the Central Bank of Sudan. Sudanese banks can contribute into this some of the 12% of their finance portfolio that must be

---

160 *New Horizon* (April 1 2009) "Country Focus: Sudan – Forgotten centre of Islamic finance". Available from www.newhorizon-islamicbanking.com/index.cfm?section=features&action=view&id=10774.

161 The Central Bank of Sudan Policies for the year 2012 noted that the methods of finance available for financial institutions were *mur baha, mush raka, mud raba* and "the other Islamic finance modes such as Salam ... Ijarah, Istisna'a and Crop Sharing"; Central Bank of Sudan (2012) *Central Bank of Sudan Policies for the year 2012*. Available from www.cbos.gov.sd/en/node/3324.

162 Article 10 of Chapter 2 of the Interim National Constitution of the Republic of the Sudan.

163 MFU Microfinance Unit (Central Bank of Sudan), *Microfinance Unit Overview*. Available from www.mfu.gov.sd/en/content/microfinance-unit-overview.

164 *Ibid.*

165 Central Bank of Sudan, The Main Objectives of the CBOS. Available from www.cbos.gov.sd/en/node/110.

166 Central Bank of Sudan (March 10 2008), Non-conventional Guarantees related to Micro-finance Operations, Circular No. 05/2008, Ref. CBOS/BSODD/BAD/23. Available from www.mfu.gov.sd/sites /default/files/2._circual_no.__05-2008_.pdf.

167 Central Bank of Sudan (2009) *Central Bank of Sudan Policies for 2009*. Available from www.cbos.gov.sd/en/node/70.

168 Central Bank of Sudan, *Central Bank of Sudan Policies for the year 2012*.

allocated to microfinance activity.[169] As of 2011, the portfolio was worth S£56.7 million (nearly $13 million[170]) and aimed to support poor families that "possess economic activity potential".[171]

In practice, it is non-governmental and community-based projects that have been most involved in providing Islamic microfinance in Sudan. The North Kordofan Rural Development Project (NKRDP) and the South Kordofan Rural Development Programme (SKRDP), for example, offer Islamic micro-credit to the rural poor. Both are supported by the International Fund for Agricultural Development. Like the Jabal Al Hoss Rural Community Development Project in Syria, these programmes have established *sanadiq* (183 by the NKRDP and one federated *sanduq* by the SKRDP) through which funds are disbursed at the community level. By 2007 the NKRDP had disbursed approximately $1.4 million and by 2010 the SKRDP had disbursed approximately $80,000, at a 100% repayment rate.[172] The *sanadiq* structure is also used by other development projects throughout Sudan that base their financing on *murabaha, musharaka* and *ijarah* structures.[173] More recently, an agreement signed between a Sudanese-based NGO – the African Charitable Society for Mother and Child Care – and the Islamic Solidarity Fund gave the African NGO access to $100,000 funding. This capital will be used to establish 225 microfinance projects in the areas surrounding Khartoum.[174]

The Central Bank of Sudan has thus made the development of microfinance a key policy for the Sudanese banking system. As in other countries in which Islamic microfinance is offered, *murabaha* dominate the Sudanese Islamic microfinance industry. However, in 2012, the Central Bank described one of its policies as "encouraging... banks to use Islamic financing modes without concentration on the Murabaha mode."[175] The practical impact of this policy, and the effectiveness of the 12% allocation that banks must make to microfinance activity, remain unclear. Nevertheless, official support for Islamic microfinance in Sudan suggests that there may be scope for further expansion of the country's existing microfinance industry.

4. Conclusion

The growth of the Islamic finance industry around the world has been well publicised. The emergence and development of an Islamic microfinance industry has been more muted, however. Nevertheless, Islamic finance lends itself well to microfinance activity because of its emphasis on equity and fairness. It offers collateral poor but entrepreneurial customers access to financial services in

---

169 Central Bank of Sudan (2011) *50th Annual Report 2010*, p 44, available from www.cbos.gov.sd/sites/default/files/annual_e_10.pdf.

170 Converted at an exchange rate of $1 = 4.41129 S£.

171 Microfinance Africa December 14 (2011) *Sudan: Microfinance – Between Noble Intentions and Complexities of Implementations.* Available from microfinanceafrica.net/tag/central-bank-of-sudan/page/2/.

172 IFAD, Promotion of Sanduqs into formal Microfinance Institutions. Available from www.ifad.org/nena/retreat/rural/sanduqs.htm.

173 Badawi, Osman, Bazalgette, Evelyn, Benbouali, Abdenour, El Samani, Mohamed and Hamza, Amel (2002), *Terminal Evaluation of Area Development Schemes (ADS) and Area Rehabilitation Schemes (ARS) in Sudan*, Vol I United Nations Development Project, p 21.

174 Sudan Vision (2012, December 23) African Maternity Society Signs Agreement with Islamic Solidarity Fund. Available from http://news.sudanvisiondaily.com/details.html?rsnpid=217547.

175 Central Bank of Sudan, *Central Bank of Sudan Policies for the year 2012.*

circumstances where their religious beliefs may otherwise prevent them from seeking financing.

The case studies presented in this chapter demonstrate that governments and central banks in Muslim countries are increasingly accommodating and encouraging Islamic microfinance rather than focusing only on macrofinance for corporates and the wealthier members of society. Although it is still primarily NGOs and other non-bank institutions that offer Islamic microfinance, commercial banks and dedicated microfinance banks in many Muslim countries are now offering *Sharia*-compliant services. As the Islamic finance industry matures, increasing focus may be placed on greater financial inclusion and, as a result, on Islamic microfinance. Recent conferences dedicated to Islamic microfinance held in financial centres such as Dubai suggest that this sector, though still niche, may be beginning to attract more mainstream interest.

From microfinance to livelihoods

Olly Donnelly
Shivia
Malcolm Harper
M-CRIL; Cranfield University

1. Introduction

Microfinance is often promoted as a remedy for poverty. The preceding chapters have shown that most microfinance institutions (MFIs) only provide small loans. In fact, the original term for the movement, initiated in the late 1970s by Muhammad Yunus and others in Bangladesh, was microcredit. Since the mid-1990s this word has become replaced by microfinance. Yet most MFIs still focus on credit, rather than the full range of microfinancial services, including savings (except as a qualification and security for loans), and insurance (except when it is a compulsory life product to reduce the risk of default).

There are of course an increasing number of exceptions. Some MFIs are licensed to mobilise demand deposits, for example, as they appreciate that their clients need to save, and can also pay for additional services such as insurance and both domestic and foreign remittances. Mobile money is also becoming more widely available, dramatically reducing the heavy transaction costs involved in small value savings deposits and withdrawals.

Poverty, however, is about more than financial services, even if these services are broadly defined. It is about the lack of what we sometimes call a livelihood, a means of making a living. It is very unlikely that any of this book's readers are poor, or that they are potential microfinance clients. All of us have some sort of livelihood that enables us not to be poor. But if we think about why we are so fortunate – what factors have enabled us to escape the poverty that blights the lives of billions of people across the world – it is unlikely that any of us would identify any kind of financial service as the critical input. Certainly it is not the only input that enables us to enjoy our relatively well-off status.

It is useful to be able to save money securely and accessibly, to borrow it when we need to, to transfer money to others or to receive transfers from them, and to insure ourselves against sickness, or accidents or other calamities. But these financial services are not the 'assets' that have made a critical difference to our lives. They are much less important than our education, our family, our health, the communities to which we belong, our physical security, communications and so on.

Some readers may be self-employed, and microfinance is said to be particularly valuable for people who run their own small business, or 'micro-enterprises'. Most people prefer to have jobs, to be employed by others, rather than create their own businesses. Millions of poor people, however, have no choice. There are no jobs, or at least no jobs that are accessible to them, and there are many heart-warming stories of women whose micro-enterprises have benefited from microfinance loans. Such stories remain, in fact, the staple content of the worldwide appeals for charitable donations to start or expand MFIs. This is in spite of the fact that the same or similar MFIs and their promoters are also making large profits.

Yet even these 'heroines of microfinance' owe their success to more than microcredit. It has helped, and it may have been the final catalyst that helped them to be successful, just as a last minute multi-million dollar investment may catalyse a new business venture. The money on its own would not have been sufficient, however.

It is obvious that successful livelihoods depend on more than financial services alone. One tool that makes this point in particular is the so-called 'sustainable livelihoods framework'.[1] This proposes five types of 'capital' necessary for a sustainable livelihood:

- natural capital, or air, water and land;
- human capital, or health and skills;
- social capital, or community and society;
- physical capital, or housing, roads and communication infrastructure; and
- financial capital, or financial services.

Readers of this book can obtain the last of these from banks, insurance companies and other institutions. Poorer people, however, can usually only turn to microfinance institutions or local moneylenders and other informal and often unreliable providers.

The sustainable livelihood framework is not totally satisfactory, and others have suggested that faith is a vital sixth capital, or that security and the rule of law merit a separate capital of their own. The model does show, however, that financial services make up only one of several types of 'capital' that are needed.

Microfinancial services are generally very different from their 'mainstream' equivalents. Clients are usually served only in groups, and they often have to guarantee each others' loans. Men may be excluded. Loan amounts are standardised. Clients are often not allowed to 'rest' – that is, not to be in debt – for more than a few weeks. Finally, the cost of loans is rarely less than 2% a month, and may be twice that or more. Such restricted and low quality financial services are even less likely than mainstream services to be the sole basis of a successful livelihood.

An increasing number of MFIs no longer believe in the promotional rhetoric of their peers. They recognise that putting poor people into debt, even if that debt is less expensive and less onerous than the moneylender loans that it has replaced, is not sufficient for a satisfactory livelihood. Clients and their families need the other four 'capitals', including skills, markets and supplies for their businesses or jobs, as well as more fundamental assets such as health, education and social support.

It is a great deal easier, however, and potentially more profitable, to sell credit

1 See Chambers, R and Conway, G 'Sustainable Livelihoods for the 21st Century,', IDS Discussion Paper 296, IDS, 1991.

and other financial services to people who have previously had no access to formal services of this kind, than to fill the other gaps in their livelihood capitals.

Every household has different resource endowments, and different needs. Much of what is required is either non-marketable, such as social networks, or long-term, such as skills and education. Other assets that are more directly related to self-employment, such as markets, equipment or supplies, are not usually under the control of microfinance institutions. Such institutions are also not often equipped to provide training, other than in the basic procedures required to enable a client to make use of the financial services that the institution itself supplies. It is not feasible for any institution to provide all the services and markets which its clients may need. The most that it can do is to 'facilitate' their supply from other specialised institutions – which may be the government, non-governmental organisations (NGOs) or commercial businesses. 'Facilitation' is a vague term, however, and conceals an immense variety of potential functions.

As a result of the complexity and indeed near-impossibility of supplying clients with all the capitals that they need, most MFIs accept that they can only supply financial services. They may attempt to introduce their clients to other service providers, but as microfinance itself becomes more regulated and more competitive it is not unreasonable for MFIs to focus on their 'core competence' in financial services, and to hope that other institutions will fill the gaps.

There have been some notable exceptions, however. BRAC of Bangladesh is generally accepted to be the world's largest development organisation, as measured by its outreach within Bangladesh. It also works in 10 other countries, including Afghanistan, Sierra Leone and Liberia. BRAC started as a rural reconstruction organisation after the liberation war in 1971, but soon became involved in microfinance.

BRAC's management realised that financial services alone were not enough to significantly alleviate poverty in Bangladesh. As a large and well-managed organisation, BRAC can provide many if not most of the five capitals listed above. It currently provides a range of health services; primary, secondary and university education; legal services and community development. BRAC is also itself involved in business, and operates a large retail and export handicraft business, an information technology company and a commercial bank that specialises in services to small business and businesses that work with poor producers. BRAC also supplies inputs and veterinary services to village poultry farmers and other local micro-enterprises.

Bangladesh is a large, poor and relatively homogeneous nation. Its people are generally ill-served by other service providers, apart from MFIs. BRAC itself started not as a financial service provider, but as a holistic development institution. As a result it has come closer than any other institution, anywhere, to providing the full range of livelihood capitals. Smaller MFIs elsewhere cannot generally follow this path, and must find different ways to assist their clients to achieve sustainable livelihoods.

2. Different approaches to livelihoods development

There are a number of different ways to help poor people to improve their livelihoods. Some are unrelated to microfinance or any kind of business, except perhaps for an organisation such as BRAC, which is large and flexible enough to become involved in a totally holistic way. Yet even BRAC has kept away from politics and government, which is for some, aside from the 'five capitals', often the only route to major systemic change. As the recent problems of Grameen Bank illustrate, politics can be dangerous in Bangladesh.

Many NGOs and other groups work on particular generic problems for small producers, often through what is known as 'advocacy'. These may include the reduction of bureaucratic burdens and corruption, the rationalisation of regulatory problems, creating better roads or fairer taxes, or similar issues. These are not usually appropriate areas for MFIs, however, whose main business involves regular field-based client contact and financial management. Some MFI associations, such as MFIN in India, ASOMIF in Peru or the Pakistan Microfinance network, do lobby government and financial regulators, but this is usually on behalf of MFI members themselves, rather than the wider client population.

Another more business-related approach to livelihood development is the promotion and support of producer groups. These may be formal cooperatives, producer companies or other types of group organisation, depending on local regulations and the risk of government interference in the management of cooperatives. Such agglomerations of small farmers and artisans are by no means always successful. Often the only motive for their formation is to 'cut out the middleman', with little idea of how to replace his (or her) services. When they do succeed, however, they can bring enormous and sustainable benefits to small producers. The Amul dairy group in India, for instance, has more than three million members and has made it possible for India to be the world's largest milk producer.

Credit and finance play an important part in cooperative initiatives of this kind, and many credit and savings cooperatives have assisted their members to start producer groups. Again, however, this is not a typical role for a microfinance institution. Cooperative groups such as Ocean Spray Cranberries and Sunmaid raisins in the United States, and their members, require a wide range of financial services, including large capital funds for processing and distribution. These fall well beyond the usual range of microfinance. Such cooperatives did not start as or originate from anything resembling a microfinance institution, or indeed a financial institution of any kind.

The main problem faced by such producer cooperatives is usually marketing. Small producers do not have business or even social links to buyers other than those in their immediate neighbourhood, and 'getting rid of the middleman' often means getting rid of the market altogether.

3. Value chains

Such groups need to become part of a complete value chain, from the original producer, perhaps even the businesses which supply the producer with inputs such as seeds, fertilisers and other raw materials, through the whole sequence of brokers, traders, exporters, importers, wholesalers and retailers to the final consumer. Such value chains, however, are usually created and led by large corporations which have the financial and managerial strength to control, or at least to influence significantly, every link in the chain. They may be producers, such as the Amul dairy cattle owners, who are mostly women who own two or more often only one animal. More frequently, they are consumer goods manufacturers that can access materials and components, and can supply larger wholesalers and retail chains such as Wal-Mart with large volumes, on time and in standardised qualities.

Value chain relationships of this kind are often regarded as exploitative and inevitably weighted against small producers. This can be true, but it is usually in the long-term interest of all the parties in the chain if each benefits from belonging to it. Gross exploitation can backfire, as many garment and other importers have discovered to their cost when their suppliers in South Asia and elsewhere mistreat their labour.

Every link in the chain needs finance, if only to cover the period between initial harvest or production and when the goods are paid for by the consumers. Finance is often an essential lubricant to making such a chain function effectively. Small farmers are particularly likely to need short-term crop finance, as well as longer term loans for land development, irrigation and so on. For this reason a number of MFIs have become involved in value chains.

It is unusual, however, for an MFI to attempt to improve its clients' livelihoods by actually organising a value chain. One publication on this subject[2] describes and analyses 13 cases where microfinance for small producers has played an important part in the success of a value chain. In only two of these cases, however, did the MFI actually initiate the development of the value chain. In the remaining cases NGOs, an international development project or a commercial business invited a local MFI or other financial institution to become involved. As the five capitals model suggests, financial services are important, but they or their providers are not usually central players in value chains or any other business transactions. In spite of what has been called the 'financialisation' of many aspects of modern commerce, money only facilitates 'real' transactions; it does not control or initiate them.

The two exceptions are K-Rep, a pioneer of microfinance in Kenya, and BASIX, a similarly innovative microfinance group in India. The managers of both these institutions realised soon after they were established that microfinance on its own could not eliminate or even significantly alleviate poverty, except for a minority of clients. These clients were generally those who were somewhat better off and already had the skills and connections to make profitable use of their loans.[3] These two institutions concluded that they could not expect their clients to depend on other institutions for the remaining four 'capitals'. They themselves had to become involved in the non-financial aspects of livelihood promotion.

K-Rep became involved with small-scale traditional honey producers in the Kitui district of Kenya. It had some success, and helped producers form cooperatives and take over and revive a derelict honey processing plant which had earlier been set up by a government agency. This initiative has played a major role in catalysing the

---

2 *Value Chain Finance, Beyond Microfinance for Rural Entrepreneurs*, KITT/IIRR, Amsterdam, 2010.

3 Harper, Iyer, Rosser, "Whose sustainability counts? BASIX's long march from microfinance to livelihoods", Kumarian, Sterling VA, 2011.

development of small-scale home-based honey production in Kitui, both by the groups it promoted and by other commercial operators, NGOs and church-based institutions. K-Rep itself, however, found it necessary to set up a specialised agri-business development company, known as Juhudi Kilimo, to undertake this type of value chain and livelihood development work; honey and microfinance did not mix.

4. The BASIX livelihoods experience

The BASIX group in India started in 1996, offering traditional microcredit. However, an evaluation of its impact in 2000 showed quite clearly that small loans, or 'micro-debt' as Professor David Hulme calls it,[4] do not on their own make much difference to poor people's livelihoods. Indeed, the poorest benefit the least.

As a result of these findings BASIX attempted in 2001 to re-orient its whole emphasis to livelihoods. It called itself a livelihoods rather than a microfinance institution and its field credit staff were re-labelled as 'livelihood service advisers'. The conversion was presented as the 'Livelihood Triad', and comprised three segments: finance, livelihoods, and institutional development. These correspond more or less with the five capitals framework. Finance is of course financial services, institutional development is the 'formal' side of social capital, such as cooperatives and their ilk, and livelihoods constitutes business aspects such as skills and supply, and market linkages.

BASIX's major activity continued to be the provision of microcredit, with the addition of savings in a local area bank, for which BASIX obtained a banking licence in 2001. This covered only a relatively small part of its total operations, but the company made several efforts to implement its new commitment to livelihoods promotion.

A large number of BASIX's borrowers were small-scale dairy farmers. These were usually women, owning one or two buffalos. These borrowers took loans to buy new animals, but they also needed additional services such as veterinary care, artificial insemination and above all more remunerative and secure buyers for their milk. BASIX did not itself become involved in the milk business, but it identified a local state sponsored dairy cooperative, the Andhra Pradesh Dairy Development Cooperative Federation, which was operating well under its capacity because of a shortage of supply. Borrowers were also linked to local government veterinary services, which had previously been more or less dormant.

BASIX helped the cooperative to identify a competent manager and to install a new electronic fat content machine that automated the previously inaccurate milk pricing system. It also linked dairy borrowers to the newly revived milk reception point. As a result, the society, which had been previously scheduled for closure because of continuing losses, crossed its break-even point and became profitable. BASIX borrowers were able to sell and be properly paid for their milk, and were thus able to repay their loans.

After some time, however, the cooperative became affected by management

---

4 'Is micro-debt good for poor people?', in Dichter and Harper (Eds), *What's wrong with microfinance?*, PA Publishing, Rugby 2007.

problems at the state level. The new manager left, and service levels at the plant declined. In 2006 BASIX turned to a private sector alternative, Reliance Fresh, which was rapidly developing a chain of supermarkets in cities throughout India. Reliance needed a reliable source of milk, and they collaborated with KBSLAB, the local area bank in the BASIX group, in the installation of a number of local milk collection points. These were able economically to collect, measure and pay for very small deliveries of liquid milk from BASIX borrowers and other cattle owners. The milk was then shipped to bulk chilling plants and thence to the company's retail outlets in neighbouring Hyderabad.

In this case the BASIX bank actually appointed and supervised the owner/managers of the local collection points, rather than 'facilitating' the operation. The capital costs of the collection equipment were covered by Reliance, who paid BASIX a fee of about two cents per litre for the milk they collected. This covered BASIX's direct costs, as well as a small commission to the owners of the collection points. The institutional development role which BASIX played was effectively cross-subsidised by the profits from its loans. Borrowers who owned good quality animals, with regular veterinary care and a secure market, were able to repay more regularly than those who did not enjoy this level of support. BASIX also offered livestock insurance to cover owners' losses, and their outstanding loans, if their animals died.

BASIX also became involved in a value chain in the state of Jharkhand in the north east of India. Frito Lays, a subsidiary of PepsiCo, the large multinational food and beverage company, operated a potato crisp plant in Kolkata that required a regular year-round supply of high-quality chipping potatoes. Locally harvested supplies were not available in October and December, and the company had to bring in potatoes at great cost from farmers in the state of Gujarat, almost 2,000 kilometres (km) away.

The soil and climate conditions in Jharkhand, a backward and largely 'tribal' state about 200 km from Kolkata, were ideal for the required potatoes. Nevertheless, the local tribal farmers had no experience of supplying a large demanding buyer such as FritoLays, and BASIX was asked to facilitate the transactions and the necessary development which would have to precede it. BASIX staff organised the farmers into producer groups and arranged for the supply of suitable seed from Gujarat. The farmers were also instructed in how to grow this new crop, and BASIX and PepsiCo agreed on operational details such as farmer supervision, inspection and quality standards. BASIX also provided crop loans to the farmers, and its costs were covered by a charging a small margin on the seeds, by service fees from the farmers, and by an agreed fee from PepsiCo, in addition to BASIX's normal margin on its loans.

The operation started in 2005 with some 400 farmers. In 2006 the number increased to about 1,000, who planted about 500 acres with potatoes for Frito Lays. The BASIX staff and their colleagues from Pepsi felt justifiably proud in their achievement; they had successfully linked some of the most backward smallholders in Asia with one of the world's most sophisticated and demanding corporations.

During that year and in 2007, however, in spite of a further increase in the acreage and the number of farmers, the relationship went seriously wrong. There were numerous disputes about the quality and timing of potato deliveries to the FritoLays plant, and many of the farmers refused to pay the agreed fee to BASIX because they felt that FritoLays had not kept its side of the bargain. Eventually the arrangement was discontinued, at a substantial loss to BASIX.

Although the Reliance Fresh collaboration appeared initially to be successful, such experiences show the dangers for a microfinance institution, and its clients, if the 'leadership' of the value chain, such as PepsiCo, or Reliance or the Andhra Pradesh Dairy Development Cooperative Federation, are not under the control of the financial institution attempting to promote the livelihoods of its clients. Such arrangements also depend on there being a large number of clients in one area who are engaged in a particular activity, such as dairy, or growing a particular crop. An MFI usually aims to serve the needs of as many as possible of the relevant client population in a given area, and to spread its risks over a number of different activities. These arrangements went directly against this practice.

Most MFI clients are small-scale traders, such as tailors, shopkeepers and teashops. These micro-enterprises are the 'last mile' link in the distribution chain for many consumer goods manufacturers, and play an important part in their value chains. Yet there is no role for a microfinance institution in these value chains as a whole. Companies such as Unilever or Colgate can finance their own operations, and those of their distributors if necessary, or they can arrange such 'value chain finance' through a bulk loan more effectively than an external financial institution can lend directly to the farmers.

BASIX management and field staff realised, however, that independent small-scale traders and artisans share many common non-financial problems. There are many small-scale activities, such as raising household poultry, where village people's incomes could be substantially increased, or their costs reduced, by the adoption of a few simple improvements.

BASIX therefore introduced a number of very simple 'livelihood packages'. For tailors this included some basic training and advice, along with a few simple patterns and accessories. Shopkeepers were advised on improving their displays and on basic cleanliness. Each package included some one-on-one advice, sometimes with brief classroom training and some basic materials. The packages were sold for about ten dollars each, which covered the direct costs of the materials included and the time of the adviser or trainer. Most of the clients were also credit customers; BASIX management anticipated that the overheads associated with these packages would be covered by the improved repayments.

By early 2010 around half a million BASIX clients, or around half the total number of borrowers, were receiving some sort of livelihood assistance, either as members of a dairy or other value chain, or as purchasers of a livelihoods 'package'. The following table summarises the performance:

Business	Numbers buying the service
'Kirana', local grocery shops	55,000
Tailoring	120,000
Dairy cattle owners	180,000
Various crop farmers	100,000
Hotels	15,000
Mushroom growers	25,000
Sheep and goat farmers	5,000

Source: Harper, Iyer, Rosser (2011), p 92

In late 2010, however, the Andhra Pradesh crisis overtook BASIX as it did all the other MFIs with significant operations in the state. The livelihoods operations were not genuinely sustainable on their own. In spite of its efforts since 2001 to re-orient itself BASIX was still perceived mainly as a microfinance institution, and its clients in the state defaulted heavily. A separate company was set up to provide livelihoods packages to non-credit clients, or in areas where BASIX financial services were not offered. Most of the buyers of these livelihood packages and the participants in the value chains were also borrowers, however, and BASIX could not afford to maintain the livelihoods services on their own. Many of them had to be discontinued.

BASIX had to close down most of its offices in Andhra Pradesh and dismiss several thousand staff, including the livelihood service advisers who handled credit and the livelihood services. Large numbers of buyers of the livelihood packages remained in other areas, such as neighbouring Orissa, where the poultry and mushroom packages had been particularly successful. BASIX's overall experience in livelihoods promotion seemed to demonstrate, however, that it was difficult to make a profitable business out of livelihoods promotion alone. The value chain initiatives were over-dependent on the chain leaders, who were beyond BASIX's control, and the income from the livelihood packages was insufficient to make them profitable unless they were accompanied by credit.

The dairy collaboration between Reliance Fresh and the KBSLAB Bank continued to be successful. Indian bank regulations do not allow banks to engage in non-banking businesses, so BASIX had to form a separate company, BKSL, to undertake livelihoods operations in the three districts where it had been permitted to operate as a licensed bank. This new company struggled to break even, another powerful argument against the involvement of MFIs in livelihoods promotion.

Microfinance clients need secure and flexible savings products as much or more than credit. Where possible, they should be served by full-service banks. If banks are not permitted to offer livelihoods services, they must either start separate companies to do so, which is not always possible, or they must rely on other institutions which are not under their control.

BASIX's experience was of course distorted by the Andhra Pradesh crisis, which makes it difficult to draw definitive conclusions. Shivia, however, is another much smaller institution working in West Bengal, outside BASIX's areas of operations. It has successfully taken on and adapted the BASIX livelihood package approach to enable its poor clients in the rural areas north of Kolkata to improve their livelihoods, and their nutritional status.

5. Shivia

Shivia is a UK charity founded in 2007 with operations in India and Nepal. It was originally engaged in supporting microcredit schemes, but in 2011 it adopted BASIX's 'backyard poultry farming' package as a way to improve the livelihoods of poor farmers in West Bengal, India. As with K-Rep in Kenya and BASIX in India, Shivia's management quickly realised that providing credit and training alone was not making the intended positive socio-economic difference to the lives of the poor. Villagers are not necessarily entrepreneurs, the loans were typically spent on consumption rather than productive purposes, clients were engaging in supply rather than market-driven enterprises, such as the trades their families had been engaged in for generations, the loans – which were accompanied by intensive training and annual social impact assessments – were expensive to administer so interest rates had to be high, previous 'social collateral' was affected by too many lenders flooding the market place and the breakdown of group systems, commercial players introduced aggressive lending tactics to make a profit, and there was no exit route for the client nor lender. To move away from mere money-lending, the Shivia team researched various agricultural enterprises with a local demand in which to engage clients. If the products couldn't sell, the clients would then be able to keep them for household consumption, unlike tailored products or baskets, for example, which would sit unused at home. So as to avoid the challenges listed above the team was keen to introduce an initial model in which credit was not necessary.

The first enterprise chosen was backyard poultry farming. Research by both BASIX and Shivia showed that backyard poultry contributes to household livelihoods in multiple ways – food, cash and a source of security for farmers. The sale of eggs is a regular source of income and birds are sometimes sold for cash to cover expenditure such as school fees and medical bills. Consumption of eggs and meat is a valuable source of protein and poultry litter is a good source of manure. In the context of livelihoods, chickens contribute to both social and human capital. They are often taken care of by women and children – an equitable allocation of resources within the household – and activities of this kind do not displace prior household activities and income streams, nor do they prevent children from attending school.

Experience has shown that minor changes in technique and infrastructure are required if farmers are to generate significant returns from backyard poultry farming. Services aimed at increasing productivity in terms of bird live-weight and eggs laid are necessary, as well as ones that decrease bird mortality. Chickens face predation by rodents and snakes, requiring farmers to build low-cost poultry sheds or create some space in the home. Climate is also a problem, especially in the monsoon time when the chickens frequently drown; for this reason ducks are often supplied instead. Local challenges in West Bengal included rising costs of grain. At Shivia's two project sites, grain prices rose from Rs18 per kilogram (kg) in November 2011 to Rs33 per kg in September 2012, making the packages more costly for Shivia to provide.

The BASIX poultry package used by Shivia consists of 10 one-day-old chicks or ducklings, initial feed, initial vaccinations and medications. Most importantly it includes training in how to raise and keep chickens at home. The training takes place in two phases. The first comes immediately after registration, before the packages are distributed. It involves seven or eight visits from Livelihood Service Providers with regard to housing, brooding, low-cost poultry diet and alternative feed such as Azolla cultivation. Like microfinance, the training is primarily aimed at women, since in 95% of cases it is women and children who take care of the chickens and ducks. The second phase comes after the packages have been distributed. It comprises 15 household visits which cover topics such as how to feed and water poultry, vaccinations and veterinary care, and predator attacks. Both phases involve discussions, demonstrations, video and photographic presentations with special emphasis on the socio-economic livelihood benefits of poultry farming.

First-time packages are typically sold for Rs450, or about £5. BASIX-Shivia research has shown that this is the maximum that the farmers are prepared to or can afford to pay. The initial package has no credit attached. Farmers usually borrow money from family members or friends and pay in instalments – 50% on registration and 50% on delivery of the package, a month later.

The birds are sourced from Keggfarms Pvt Ltd, which has developed the 'Kuroiler'. This is a dual-purpose, multi-coloured, hardy, village bird, capable of producing 150–240 eggs per year and of achieving a marketable body weight in eight weeks. The birds are typically sold in local markets. Shivia's work in year one has resulted in an increase in household income of up to 30% for these poor farm households. The adult members of these households are typically agricultural labourers who work 200–250 days per year and earn approximately Rs100 (around £1.15) per day.

The BASIX model was imported from the neighbouring state of Orissa (Odisha) with aim of developing a self-financing model for Shivia in West Bengal. An important realisation has been the need to understand local livelihoods and the difficulties of replicating models – as also witnessed in the microfinance industry. Shivia's clients are the very poorest households. They are farmers who simply cannot or will not pay the required amount to make the model self-financing, as is desired by microfinance and social enterprise practitioners who are still influenced by the so-called 'Washington consensus'.

The table on the next page shows the average cost of a Shivia package.

In addition to this cost is the time of the livelihood service providers, which costs an average of Rs700 per package. Distribution costs are a further Rs30 per package. In total a package therefore costs an average of Rs1015, or 2.25 times more than the home-farmers will pay.

Avg cost per kit (Rs)	April 2012	May 2012	June 2012	July 2012	August 2012	Sept 2012	Oct 2012	Nov 2012
Chicks	184	194	186	190	192	168	195	208
Feed	35	45	31	41	62	60	46	57
Vac/med	44	26	135	23	34	60	39	21
Total	262	264	353	253	288	287	280	286

The situation in Ossia is different. There, farmers are prepared to pay up to Rs500 for a package of eight chicks. The costs of the livelihood service providers are also considerably lower. It is clear from Shivia's first year results that farmers in West Bengal do value the expert advice and skills – the 'human capital' – that they receive. Once they have acquired these skills, however, they are unwilling to contribute as much for second and subsequent packages. These are sold for Rs250, or just one quarter of the cost of the package to Shivia. The culture in West Bengal differs from that in Orissa in that the lure of jobs in Kolkata means the livelihood service providers have to be paid more. Farmers' dependence on state handouts after 32 years of Communist party rule also makes it hard to convince them to pay for poultry and services that they have, in the past, received for free.

The scheme also shows that the fees that really poor people are willing and able to pay are rarely enough to make operations self-financing, especially with inputs such as grain which are rapidly rising in price. The model has high fixed costs and must be permanently subsidised if it is to help those who need it most. The good news, however, is that packages like this can create a sustainable source of income for the poor they are designed to help. Payments made by farmers for training and packages are at least one step away from handouts. This was the original premise of microfinance, which was originally never expected to be profitable. Farmers who wish to expand backyard poultry beyond a batch of ten chickens will need to invest in infrastructure, and Shivia will look into providing or assisting with access to finance. Like regular microfinance this should be self-financing, but will have a clear focus on a particular group of clients. Indian-based livelihood organisations such as Pradan and Suguna, working with less poor farmers who have 300–400 and 2,000–4,000 birds, respectively, and in more favourable states, have shown that this is possible. Shivia's experiences so far, however, suggest that the first step on the ladder to a sustainable livelihood must be subsidised.

BRAC probably offers the widest range of livelihood and microfinance products of any institution, anywhere. It also tries to make as many of its programmes as possible into self-sustaining businesses. Nevertheless, it has concluded that it is not possible to bring those the so-called 'ultra-poor' out of poverty without substantial subsidy. In 2002, BRAC initiated the programme "Challenging the Frontiers of Poverty Reduction Targeting the Ultra Poor", which is specifically designed to meet the needs of ultra-poor households. These are households too poor even to access benefits from traditional development interventions such as microfinance. The programme was the result of three decades of learning from rural poverty alleviation programmes. It helps the very poorest through grants or soft loans and life skill training so that in time, usually two years or so, they can participate in BRAC's mainstream development programmes. Several hundred thousand women have been brought out of abject poverty as a result of the programme, at a cost of around $300 each. These women are now clients of BRAC and other regular microfinance institutions, and the programme is being replicated with some success by the MFI Bandhan in West Bengal, where Shivia operates.

Even SKS, an Indian MFI best known for its initial public offering in 2010, the first in India, recognises that while microfinance can work for the poor and less poor sections of society, the ultra-poor need much more than finance. They require help in all five types of 'capital' to create stable and sustainable livelihoods for themselves. SKS's NGO, Swayam Krishi Sangam, has worked alongside the ultra-poor in an intensive 18-month programme to increase awareness of government resources, social issues and health care. Upon graduation from the programme, many members may join microfinance organisations or government-sponsored Self-Help Group Bank linkage programmes to sustain their livelihoods and diversify into new opportunities.

'Sustainability' is a desirable goal, but there remains a role for subsidy – or, as it used to be called before the term was discredited, 'charity'. Microfinance institutions should recognise this, and should not be deluded into believing that it is always possible to alleviate poverty and make profits at the same time.

Microfinance from an investor's perspective

Marcus Fedder
International Finance Facility for Immunisation

1. Introduction

Life for investors in microfinance has been difficult recently. Actual defaults are not so much at fault – although those have occurred – but rather the perception that the 'shine has come off the halo'. Stories of Indian microfinance clients committing suicide reached the Western media, and reports of usurious interest rates on microfinance loans in a number of countries alerted investors to the reputational risks associated with this sector. What once seemed an unquestionably positive investment decision has now become more complex. Like certain pension funds, which are themselves under pressure from their constituents, some institutional investors have withdrawn from the sector completely.

The fact that microfinance survived the financial crisis relatively unscathed is most remarkable. There are problems in some countries, mainly due to over-banking, but a complete drying up of funding for microfinance institutions (MFIs) has not taken place. In fact, there is plenty of liquidity in the market to fund microfinance institutions, both debt and equity. CGAP estimated that in 2011 cross-border funders committed at least $25 billion to microfinance or financial services for the poor.[1]

Investors can chose between a relatively secure fixed income or more risky equity-type investments. More passive investors will find a wide range of investment funds – so-called microfinance investment vehicles (MIVs) – that specialise in either loans to MFIs or equity investments. It is now even possible to invest in microfinance funds of funds (eg, Azure Partners) to increase diversity. Apart from a few exceptions, notably Compartamos and Financiera Independencia of Mexico, SKS of India and Equity Bank of Kenya, there are no publicly traded MFIs.

This chapter will look at various aspects from an investor's point of view. It is structured in five sections. The first identifies the gap between demand and supply of financial services and analyses the reasons for it. The second looks at the types of investor and investment that are available. The third compares the experiences of five countries, while the fourth looks at the key factors of a successful MFI and MFI investment, including the issues of majority versus minority stake and exit. The final section turns the focus around to ask what an investor should bring to the table; that is, what added value investors can bring to an MFI.

1 See Estelle Lahaye, Ralitsa Rizvanolli, 'Current Trends in Cross-Border Funding for Microfinance', CGAP Brief, December 4 2012.

Figure 1

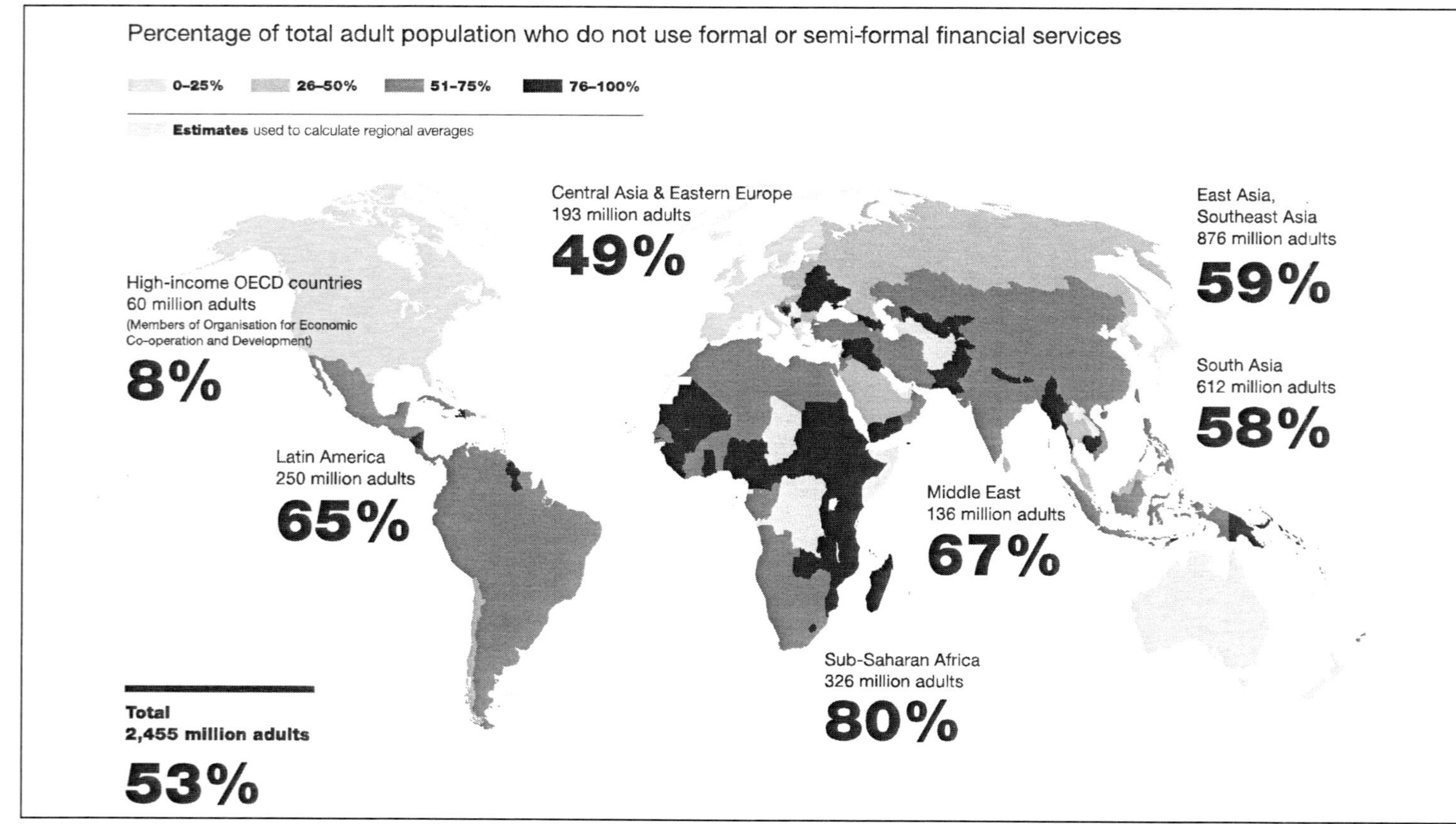
Percentage of total adult population who do not use formal or semi-formal financial services
0–25%
26–50%
51–75%
76–100%
Estimates used to calculate regional averages
Central Asia & Eastern Europe
193 million adults
49%
East Asia,
Southeast Asia
876 million adults
59%
High-income OECD countries
60 million adults
(Members of Organisation for Economic Co-operation and Development)
8%
South Asia
612 million adults
58%
Latin America
250 million adults
65%
Middle East
136 million adults
67%
Sub-Saharan Africa
326 million adults
80%
Total
2,455 million adults
53%

2. The unbanked: a story of a demand and supply gap

According to a study conducted by McKinsey, roughly 2.5 billion people worldwide are unbanked (see the worldmap above).[2] The majority of them live in Africa and Asia. They represent huge remaining opportunities for banking in general and, as most of these unbanked are poor, for microfinance in particular.

Such figures must be compared with microfinance services on the ground in order to show the size of the gap between potential demand and supply. The table below compares the number of unbanked with the number of borrowers and depositors of MFIs reporting to Mixmarket.[3] Today's microfinance industry – despite years of activity – still seems to be a drop in the ocean.

Table 1

	Unbanked	Number of borrowers	Gross loan portfolio	Number of depositors	Deposits
	million	million	billion $	million	billion $
Africa	326	5.8	7.7	18.8	7.4
South Asia	612	6.8	42.1	17.1	1.3
East Asia and Pacific	876	15.5	32.2	14.8	31
Eastern Europe and Central Asia	193	2.5	9.9	2.9	6.8
Latin America and Caribbean	250	18.3	27.9	16.6	18
Middle East and North Africa	136	1.8	1.2	0.03	0.1
Total	**2,393**	**50.7**	**121**	**70.23**	**64**

If only 10% of those without access to banking services became microfinance borrowers, MFIs would have 240 million new loan clients. If each loan is made for an average of $300, then the total volume of such loans would amount to $72 billion. Funding such loans would require $15 billion to $20 billion in equity investments, with the remainder coming in the form of deposits or debt (assuming a leverage of about four to five times equity).

It is clear that such volumes cannot be met by charity and donations alone. This

2 Source: McKinsey research conducted in partnership with the Financial Access Initiative. Financial usage data from Patrick Honohan: "Cross-country variation household access to financial services," *Journal of Banking & Finance*, 2008, Vol 32, No 11. www.mckinsey.com/insights/financial_services/counting_the_worlds_unbanked

3 Numbers reported to Mixmarket as of 2011: www.mixmarket.org.

means that the original concept, promoted by, amongst others, by Muhammad Yunus – that microfinance should not be commercial – is an illusion.

So the question is: why is there such a large gap between demand and supply? It may be because there is not enough capital, or that the risks are too high. Both are valid arguments. But the key obstacle is that there are simply not enough 'investable' MFIs on the ground, particularly in countries in Africa. Again, there are several reasons for this.

First, in many countries the regulatory framework does not allow investors, particularly equity investors, to invest in and build MFIs. This is the case for a number of key countries in Asia, for example. In the Philippines, Indonesia, Vietnam and Sri Lanka foreign (and in some cases also domestic) investors face difficult or even impossible hurdles when trying to invest and build sustainable and competitive institutions. In other countries regulators stipulate high capital requirements for entry that make it uneconomical to operate an MFI. Two laudable exceptions are India and Cambodia, and both countries have an active microfinance sector. Both countries have competent regulatory authorities that understand the value of microfinance and have created frameworks that allow MFIs to be professionally run to the benefit of their clients and allow foreign investors to provide capital.

Second, even in countries where the regulatory frameworks allow MFIs to operate according to commercial criteria and to have foreigners, including MIVs, as institutional investors, other factors can make investments difficult. These include a lack of good governance, the difficulty of employing and retaining professional staff, and poorly defined and executed business strategies. Many MFIs also have founding investors who, even though they themselves have no more to invest in their institutions, are unwilling to open up to new investors. Mission drift and a general loss of control over their company are among their fears. In addition, grant funding from well-meaning donors frequently extends the life of inefficient MFIs, rather than promotes the creation of efficient, client-driven institutions. Such MFIs therefore remain small and inefficient, to the detriment of the poor.

Third, when one looks at portfolios at risk and the profit/loss numbers of certain MFIs, as well as their bad corporate culture, it becomes obvious that commercial investors would only go in if they can see the possibility of effecting a turnaround. For the reasons stated in the previous paragraph, however, this is not often feasible.

3. Types of investor and investment

Many types of investor are involved in microfinance. Private individuals, when they are passive investors, are predominantly invested in debt funds. MFI founders and staff are active investors who often hold direct equity in their institutions. In MFIs that were converted from non-governmental organisations (NGOs) into commercial entities, the NGOs frequently maintain shares in the company. Then there are institutional investors who invest both in MIVs and directly. MIVs are important players. Around a hundred different vehicles invest predominantly by lending to MFIs, although the number of MIVs investing in the equity of MFIs is growing. Last, and probably still the predominant drivers, are governmental and supranational development agencies. These include the International Finance Corporation, the European Investment Bank and regional development banks, as well as CDC, KFW,

FMO, AECID, the Norwegian Microfinance Initiative, Proparco and BIO. These development institutions invest according to commercial principles, looking for MFIs to be profitable, without forcing them to maximise profits. Some lend to MFIs at greatly subsidised interest rates.

3.1 Fixed-income investments

A fixed-income investor has a very wide choice of funds. In turn, these funds have a wide choice of MFIs in which to invest. Most funds are very well diversified, with investments spread over Latin America, Africa, Central and Eastern Europe, and North as well as South Asia. Lending to MFIs is legal in almost all jurisdictions. Where it is not, as it was in India, structures have been created to circumvent the regulatory obstacles. Fixed-income MIVs are the safest investment choice. The flipsides of safety, however, are that financial returns are very low (for example Blue Orchard's flagship fund produced an annual return of just 1.3% over the last three years)[4] and the social element is passive, limited to the fact that the money goes to a cause believed to be worthy of support. Fixed-income lenders have no direct say in the business of an MFI; investors in such funds therefore have no leverage. This is not to say that fixed-income MIVs are not important: most MFIs use leverage (rather than pure equity funding) and MIVs have been one of the key drivers for MFI growth. It is also positive to note that MIVs have changed their product mix. In previous years almost all lending was made in US dollars; now many MIVs offer loans in local currency. This takes the foreign-exchange risk out of the loans and makes MFIs more stable. Unfortunately, so far, there are no 'pure' local currency loan funds, so MIVs have tended to hedge the foreign-exchange risk in the market, adding to loan costs.

3.2 Private equity investments

Equity is key to the health and growth of any MFI. Equity provides money and, with that, responsibility. Unlike lenders, equity investors have a say in the company, and can determine its strategy, mission, product mix, social focus and return targets. Obviously, the larger the stake in the MFI, the better one's views translate into policies and action. Although it is true that only a majority stake will give an investor the final say in a company, smaller shareholders – those holding 10% to 20% – can, via a shareholders agreement and typically board representation, make their views heard and see that the MFI's mission, strategy, return targets or product range are not changed without their specific approval. In practice, this only works if co-investors stick to these agreements and if the country has a legal system that safeguards minority shareholders. If that is not the case – and frequently it is not – minority shareholders are like passengers at the back of the bus: they can enjoy the ride but are unable to drive. Most importantly, they cannot simply get out when they want to.

3.3 Publicly traded MFIs

It is a sign of how under-developed the market still is that there are so few publicly

4 As of March 7 2012: www.blueorchard.com/jahia/webdav/site/blueorchard/shared/Products/DMCF/DMCF%20Presentation/DMCF_general%20presentation_March%202012.pdf

traded MFIs. Few have reached the size or introduced the governance that is required for a listed company. In other markets where MFIs could potentially be listed, such as Cambodia, the stock market either does not exist or is underdeveloped. With the exception of Equity Bank of Kenya, investors who have participated in initial public offerings (IPOs) have had a bumpy ride.[5] SKS has seen a spectacular destruction of its shareholder value.

These figures have to be slightly nuanced. In the case of Compartamos, investors have not had great returns since the IPO. However, those investors who invested $1 million in Compartamos in 2000 would have made $400 million when selling at the time of the IPO in 2007.[6] Such news surely travelled to India.

4. Where to invest

The big problem for equity investors is therefore finding the right institution that is able to employ the capital, and produce a decent return on equity. This search will be determined by the general macro-economic as well as the industry and regulatory environment, and by the particularities of the MFI.

4.1 Country environment

Macro-economic and regulatory environments vary greatly between countries. To illustrate this diversity, we present the example of five countries that provide very different pictures.

(a) India

This used to be the promised land for microfinance: a huge population living in poverty, unbanked. Many MFIs started business there, many with the sole objective of making money. Commercial microfinance started late but soon became a multi-billion dollar business. Nearly 40% of this business was concentrated in the province of Andhra Pradesh. However, the rapid expansion was powered by a production-line type of microfinance, which resulted in frequent multiple lending and the subsequent over-indebtedness of a significant number of borrowers. High interest rates and a lack of transparency in pricing, alongside coercive collection methods, led to defaults and eventually to suicides by borrowers. To stop such practices, and on the basis of the Malegan report, the Indian authorities imposed tight regulation. Lending amounts were limited and, above all, the interest rates MFIs can charge, were capped: for example 24% on individual loans.[7]

At the height of the market – before the Malegan report and the imposition of restrictions – the MFI SKS went public through an IPO. Its share price reached a high of Rs1,400, but is now trading at a price of about Rs140 (see Figure 2).

---

5 Economist Intelligence Unit, Financial Services Briefing and Forecasts, June 21 2012: http://viewswire.eiu.com/index.asp?layout=ib3Article&article_id=269135011&pubtypeid=1132462498&fs=true.

6 Elisabeth Rhyne, *Microfinance for bankers and investors*, McGraw Hill, 2009, p 90.

7 See Malegan report: www.ifmr.co.in/blog/2011/01/19/malegam-committee-report-on-microfinance-released/.

Figure 2

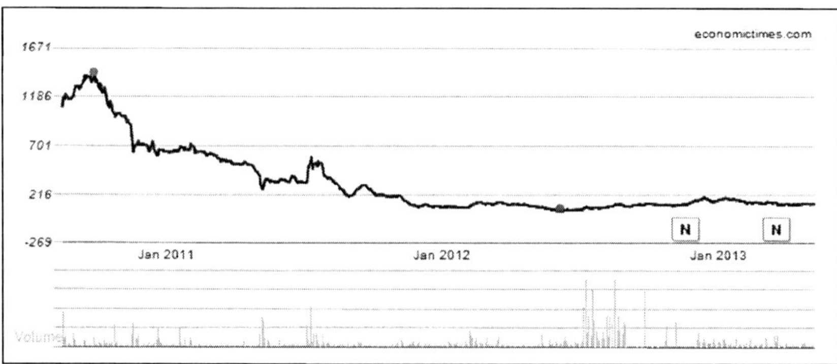

The share price of Rs1,400 depended on unrealistic growth and profit expectations that could only have been realised with dubious lending and operational practices. Today, without the hype and despite tight restrictions, the market in India is functional, meaning that realistic and patient investors can find well-run MFIs in which to invest. The growth of urban microfinance is interesting, and should produce higher returns on equity due to lower operational costs compared to those MFIs operating in the countryside.

Figure 3[8]

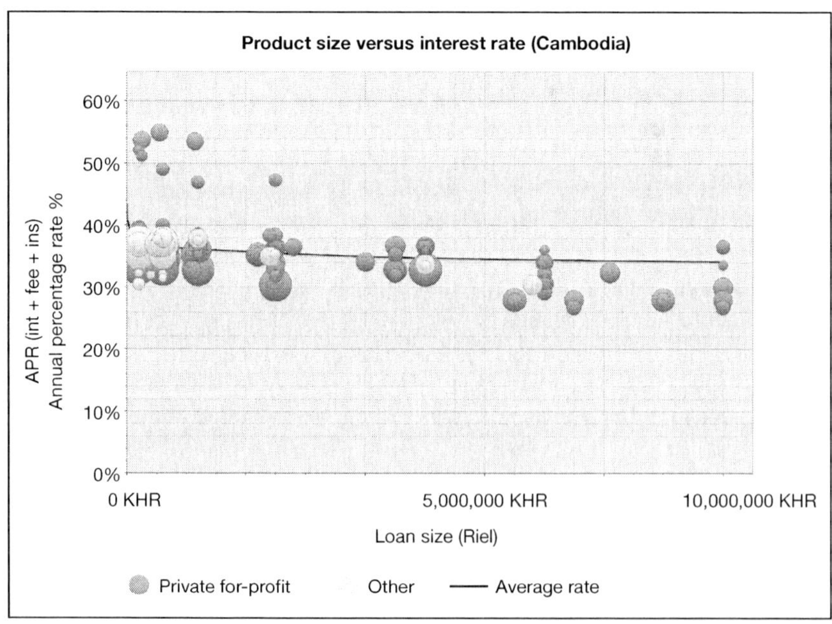

8 See www.mftransparency.org.

(b) ***Cambodia***

Cambodia is another well-developed microfinance market, with a fair number of foreign investors. With 1.4 million microfinance borrowers, $1.6 billion of outstanding loans[9] and a population of 15 million, microfinance has a decent outreach. Cambodia's microfinance is supervised by the highly competent National Bank of Cambodia. The regulator has not imposed caps on interest rates. However, it has helped prevent an Indian-style overheating by introducing a credit agency, which allows MFIs to check whether a new borrower has existing loans from competitors. Interest rates are around 30% to 40% per annum.[10]

Although these rates may at first appear high, they are a result of the high cost of delivering microfinance services in a rural economy where loan officers have to travel long distances by motorbike in order to reach clients. In fact, these rates are relatively low in comparison with interest rates in other countries, and reflect the presence of a competitive market. This requires MFIs to be run efficiently and professionally. As a result, there are a large number of MFIs with distinct profiles in which investors may invest.

(c) ***Philippines***

With more than 3 million borrowers, 4.5 million depositors and $645 million worth of loans outstanding, microfinance in the Philippines is widespread and developed.[11] It is worth noting that the total population is about 92 million, so in relative terms microfinance is in fact still relatively small. The dominant players – that is, those with more than 100,000 clients – are organised as NGOs: Card, ASA, TSPI, KMBI, Life Bank Foundation, TSKI, Pagasa, NWTF or ASKI. Smaller MFIs are incorporated as rural banks and cooperatives. Foreign investor participation in the market is restricted both in terms of the legal entities foreign investors can purchase shares of and in terms of percentage of ownership. As a result, the market is dominated by NGOs. One additional element that makes investing in commercial MFIs less attractive is the fact that commercial MFIs, unlike MFIs run by NGOs, must be regulated by the central bank. This gives them a distinct disadvantage as the regulatory process is slow and bureaucratic. For example, NGO-MFIs can open a new branch without any issues or delays as soon as they have decided to expand into a new geographical area. Commercial MFIs, however, need to apply to the central bank. The approval process generally takes at least six months. Unfortunately, having well-meaning NGOs run microfinance has not led to a competitive environment for interest rates. As MF Transparency's reports show, most lending is done at rates of over 100%; rates of between 200% and 300% are not uncommon.

It should be noted that such usury rates are being charged by benevolent, not-for-profit institutions and not by subsidiaries of hedge funds. Whether such rates are sustainable is another question.

---

9 See www.mixmarket.org; the numbers are slightly distorted as Accleda Bank's loan portfolio accounts for $1.2 billion.

10 See Microfinance Transparency http://data.mftransparency.org/data/countries/kh/.

11 See Mixmarket, 2011 figures.

Figure 4[12]

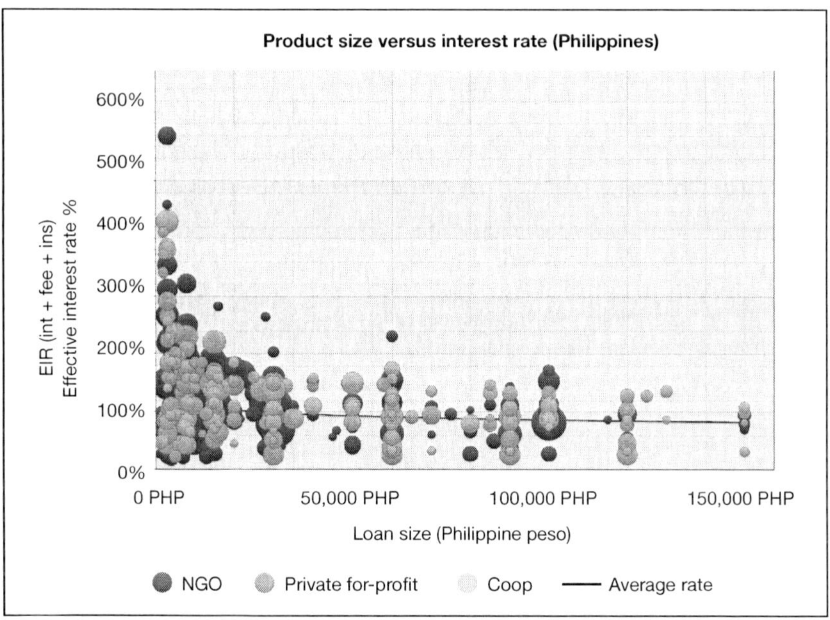

(d) Zambia

Zambia is a contrast with these well-developed Asian markets. With a population of 13 million and an average GDP per capita of about $1,200, the country is poor. Sixty-three percent of the adult population is financially excluded. Interestingly, two-thirds claim they need no bank account.[13] Yet despite – or maybe because of – such attitudes, microfinance has not taken off. There are fewer than 100,000 borrowers, served by a number of tiny institutions. Few institutions are of a size or quality to attract foreign equity investors. The regulatory framework is favourable and the central bank provides appropriate supervision. However, a foreign investor cannot be a majority shareholder, and the percentage a foreigner can hold depends on whether the MFI is deposit taking or not.[14] Low profit margins have been given as a key reason why MFIs have been unable to grow in Zambia, but MF Transparency's data indicates that most MFIs make loans that charge interest rates of between 100% and 300% per annum. Even NGOs with a high social ambition charge 250% interest.

In such a situation, a determined investor is best off starting their own business. However, the question remains whether even interest rates at the lower end of the spectrum, of between 50% and 100%, are sustainable. The challenge for the microfinance industry will be to find businesses to loan to that produce returns greater than 100% (or 250% for that matter). It is not clear that many households

12 www.mixmarket.org.
13 www.mftransparency.org/wp-content/uploads/2012/05/MFT-RPT-108-EN-Country-Survey-Zambia.pdf.
14 25% in case of deposit taking and 50% in case of non-deposit taking.

run businesses that can produce the returns of between 200% and 400% per annum needed to service such microfinance loans and still make a living.

In a recent development, the Bank of Zambia decreed at the beginning of January 2013 that the maximum effective annual lending rate for non-bank financial institutions it designates as microfinance service providers should not exceed 42%. What impact this will have on the development of microfinance in the country remains to be seen. It is obvious, though, that an MFI that requires loans to pay more than 100% interest cannot survive with such capped rates.[15]

Figure 5[16]

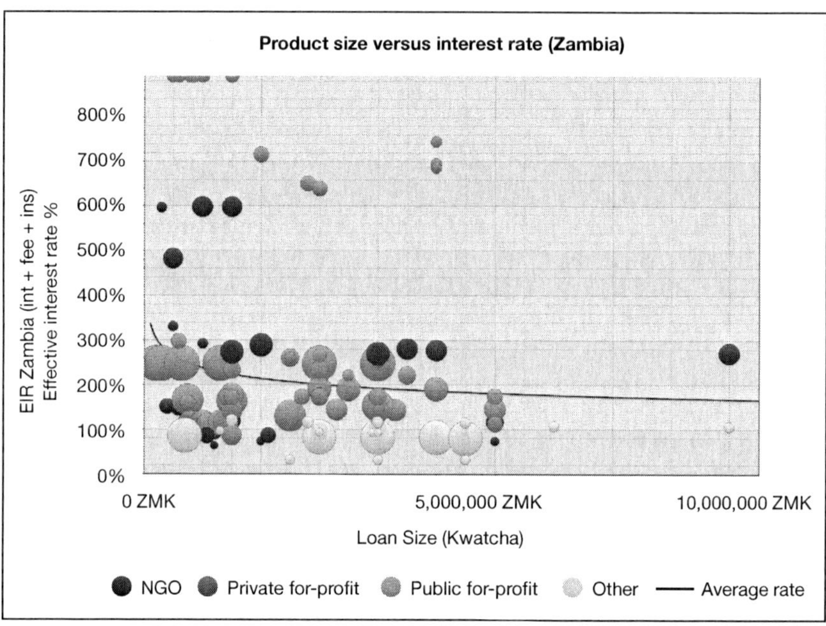

(e) *Kenya*

With a population of about 43 million, Kenya is probably one of Africa's best-developed markets. With 36 MFIs reporting to Mixmarket, many of them organised as investible NBFIs, investors have some choice. The market is well regulated by the central bank but, as in Zambia, there are restrictions for foreign shareholders. Majority shareholdings are not allowed. With $1.7 billion outstanding in loans to 1.1 million clients, the interesting aspect is that the average loan size is relatively high – more than $1,500. The market is dominated by Equity Bank, which has over 630,000 loan customers. Second is the Kenyan Women Finance Trust, with 280,000 clients (both figures as of 2011). It is also interesting that a savings culture has developed, with 6.7 million savers holding deposits worth $2.7 billion. These numbers suggest

15 See www.mixmarket.org.

16 See *Lusaka Times* of January 3 2013.

that the sector could be considered self-funding. Interestingly, as shown in Figure 6, interest rates are at moderate levels. This may be due to the competitive nature of the market.[17] The easiest choice for investors in Kenya is Equity Bank, which is listed and publicly traded.[18] Some other MFIs have been actively seeking private equity funding. One interesting and innovative institution is Musoni.[19] As the only institution that operates on a cashless basis it demonstrates the possibilities provided by mobile banking. Kenya was also the market in which M-PESA pioneered mobile banking. It now has more than 15 million users.

Figure 6[20]

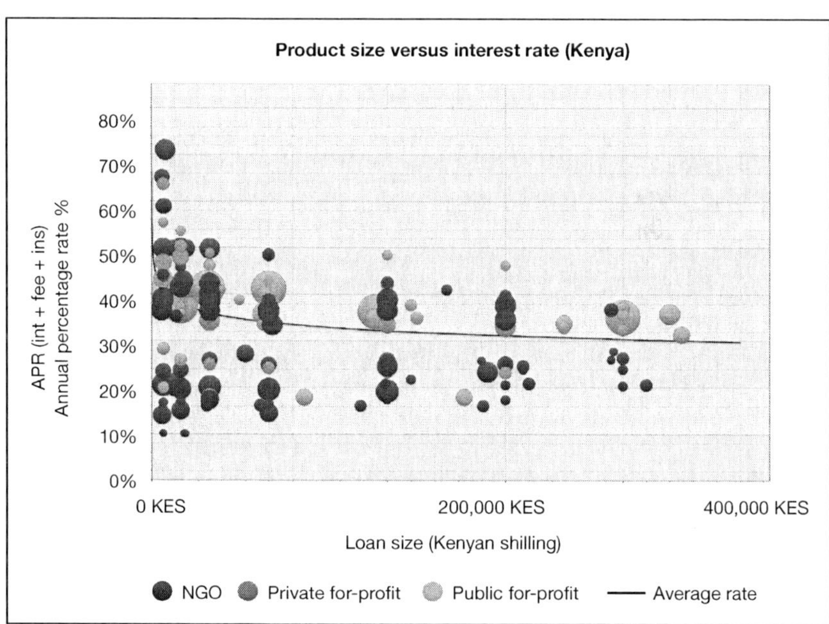

5. Criteria for a successful investment

A range of criteria determine the success of an investment in an MFI. This section will first concentrate on criteria specific to MFIs, then look at the issue of majority vs minority investment as well as exits. Finally it asks what returns an investor can or should expect.

5.1 Criteria for MFI success

Because microfinance is basically a utility business, the key factors determining the return on equity for investors are the growth in the number of customers, the efficiency of the institution, the institution's risk management and the

17 See http://data.mftransparency.org/data/countries/ke/.
18 See www.bloomberg.com/quote/EQBNK:KN.
19 See www.musoni.eu/.
20 See www.mixmarket.org.

diversification of the product range. Also key are the provision of 'microfinance plus' services and social responsibility.

(a) ***Number of customers***

Clearly, the more customers an institution has, the more loans and the higher its profits. Unfortunately, the equation is not quite as simple as this. More customers frequently mean higher acquisition and servicing costs as villages further away from the MFI's branches become targeted. In addition, businesses located away from the commercial centres where MFIs are located are also likely to have lower profit margins. This makes servicing loans more challenging. More customers can also mean that the MFI is moving out of its specific area of expertise, either going more upmarket into SME financing or targeting clients with more difficult credit profiles. SME financing, however, requires loan officers to have a totally different skill-set from 'normal' microfinance, and a number of MFIs have experienced increased loan losses on such new loans. Given that such loans are in most cases much larger, this has had an immediate negative effect on MFIs' profitability.

(b) ***Efficiency of the institution***

A number of factors determine the efficiency of an MFI. One is the type of clients. Rural clients living in villages require loan officers to travel to them in order to make loans, and collect interest and principal. This is costly. MFIs have often tried to improve their efficiency by simply increasing the loan amounts to customers. For the reasons already stated, this is problematic. The cost of funding is another factor. Developing a base of local currency funding from local sources is potentially the most efficient means, but not all markets provide liquidity in the same way as Kenya does. In fact, catering to microfinance clients as depositors entails costs because the amounts saved are mostly relatively small. Furthermore, many MFIs are non-deposit taking, including all non-banking financial companies in India. Automation is another factor. Many MFIs have archaic management information systems that require time-consuming manual intervention. The development of cheap tablets will encourage loan officers eventually to abandon paper and greatly increase efficiency. Mobile money technology – as pioneered by M-PESA – has enabled MFIs to automate the process of money transfers as well as savings. Mobile banking may eventually provide further savings, but so far only Musoni has gone all the way in abandoning cash payments and letting borrowers pay by mobile phone. (Whether the savings of this technology will be outweighed eventually by the fact that customers feel less inclined to repay a loan if the loan officer does not personally come and collect cash still has to be determined.)

(c) ***Risk management***

The importance of independent risk management is not new, and even sophisticated institutions like Lehman Brothers or UBS can fail spectacularly. MFIs have become more sophisticated in analysing and dealing with risks, be they credit, operational or market-related. Although it would be detrimental to eliminate risks altogether, an institution run with a risk-aware culture is well positioned to deal with them. Credit bureaus and specialised FX hedging vehicles like MFX have helped MFIs address the key factors of over-lending as well as foreign exchange risk.

(d) Diversification of the product range

Like any business, diversification in microfinance can increase revenue sources, client loyalty and profit stability. It may also lead to higher returns on equity. Microfinance started off as micro credit. Lending was the name of the game and in most countries is still the most important product. However, both in academia[21] and on the ground, savings are now considered both a useful tool for helping the poor build their livelihoods and an important product for MFIs. Technology can help here too, as savings can be channelled using mobile banking services. Once introduced, these would also allow MFIs to provide money transfer services. Such services would no longer require an MFI branch, but could be handled by local agents, providing local shops and businesses with opportunities to generate extra income while expanding the reach of the MFI. The services provided by this agent of AMK in Cambodia, shown in Figure 7, are self explanatory.[22]

Figure 7

(e) The provision of 'microfinance plus'

Many MFIs pride themselves in providing a number of services to customers, from obligatory education sessions that cover subjects from financial mathematics and

21 See Madeline Hirschland, *Saving Services for the Poor*, Kumarian Press 2005.
22 The local village hairdresser provides these services; many farmers are illiterate.

marketing support to birth control and female empowerment. While all these services may add value (even at a cost of time to the client, who frequently does not have much time to spend on things other than business, field and family), they are a significant cost to the MFI. Someone must cover these costs if grants from donors do not. Unfortunately, in most cases, these costs do not simply constitute a two or three percentage point reduction of the return on equity to investors – which most socially responsible investors would be willing to bear – but a significant increase of the loan margin too. Interest rates of 200% to 400%, as seen in some countries, arise in most cases because the costs of 'microfinance plus' are off-loaded onto borrowers, who have no say in this. It is easy to see that such a practice will be detrimental to an institution's return on equity over the medium and long term. Few sophisticated businesses produce annual returns of 250% – let alone businesses run by the poor in poverty-stricken countries.

(f) ***Social responsibility***

Social responsibility is often seen as detrimental to financial success. This argument was often made in India before the crash. It was clear that if you could roll out one size fits all microfinance across a country, charging an interest rate just marginally below that of the local money lender, then financial success would be guaranteed. The collapse in share price of SKS shows that such a short-term approach does not create long-term shareholder value. For some institutions, like AMK in Cambodia, it has been clear from the start that social responsibility is the basis and guarantee of financially sound microfinance over the long term, and the creation of shareholder value. The following client protection principles, developed by the 'Smart Campaign',[23] have now been generally adopted:

- appropriate product design and delivery;
- prevention of over-indebtedness;
- transparency;
- responsible pricing;
- fair and respectful treatment of clients;
- privacy of client data; and
- mechanisms for complaint resolution.

These principles should be seen only as the basic rules for doing client business and not as the final state of good governance. Sadly, even though these principles are common sense and widely supported, they rely on self-regulation and do not seem to have been fully implemented. Neither are they enforced by the respective regulators; the main driver ensuring compliance is the MFI's investors.

Social performance should not rest with these basic principles but in addition should:

- aim to measure client satisfaction, and use the results to adapt the product base to suit clients' needs better;
- measure changes in the well-being of clients; and
- provide staff with a humane working environment and measure staff satisfaction.

---

23 See www.smartcampaign.org/.

A number of institutions also measure factors related to client outreach in order to be able to evaluate whether they are reaching their target groups.

If properly implemented, these factors will result in a better-run MFI with a better reputation and more loyal clients, and therefore a sustainable and more profitable business and better investment.

5.2 Majority versus minority investment

This question is important to investors and MFIs. For an MFI, having one majority investor would be a positive if there was clear mission alignment and the investor had financial muscle, reasonable expectations and no desire to drive from the back seat. However, having a number of minority investors can make things significantly easier if there is a dominant or founding shareholder who can no longer hold a majority due to capital constraints.

From an investor's perspective, there are advantages and disadvantages to a majority shareholding. The disadvantage is that the majority shareholder is ultimately responsible for the institution. Such responsibility can become costly. On the other hand, a majority shareholder has the power to be more involved in defining the MFI's mission, setting its strategy, business plan and budget, and hiring key personnel. Minority shareholders often have the right to nominate a member of the board, but majority shareholders can be more involved. They can, for instance, be a member of the institution's asset and liability committee, where issues of key importance are discussed and addressed before they become problems. Board members often only see problems when it is too late.

In order to safeguard minority shareholder rights, investors should generally enter into a shareholders' agreement that stipulates that certain key issues require the specific approval of such investors or the consent of at least two-thirds of the issued share capital. Key issues would normally include:

- a change of mission or business strategy;
- the budget;
- disposals of a certain percentage of assets;
- leverage;
- material transactions with related parties;
- dividend payments;
- share buybacks, new share issues and anti-dilution pre-emptive rights; and
- a listing.

It is clear that there are pros and cons to being a minority or a majority investor in an MFI. But it is also clear that a majority investor has the greater opportunity to determine strategy and business. As previously mentioned, the minority shareholder is often just a passenger in a bus, with someone else doing the driving.

5.3 Exits

Any investor will need to ask about potential exits. This is no easier – or more difficult – than for any other emerging market private equity investment. The key exit routes are the following:

- A sale to another specialised microfinance investor. As more and more MIVs include equity in their product range, the number of potential investors grows. In addition, many governmental and supranational development institutions are interested in investing in MFIs directly rather than indirectly through MIVs;
- A sale to a bank expanding into microfinance;
- A merger with another MFI;
- A sale of shares to management and staff;
- A sale of shares to clients; and
- IPO. This route may only be possible for the largest and best-run MFIs that are profitable and have instituted clear best-practice principles of governance – provided, furthermore, that the local stock market and regulatory environment allow for IPOs.

What is important in any sale is the price. Although too low a price obviously reduces the internal rate of return of the investment over the holding period, too high a price can have negative consequences for the MFI: any investor buying shares in an institution at multiples of book value will ensure that the profitability of the institution is maximised so as to receive high dividends and ensure that there is ultimately no capital loss on the investment due to a sale at a lower multiple. A responsible exit is thus as important for the well-being of an MFI, its staff and clients as the responsible running of the institution.

5.4 Returns for investors

The question should perhaps be: what expectations of return should an investor have? Given that it is possible to charge interest rates of 300% and more, very large returns on equity appear feasible. In reality, however, only Compartamos has managed year after year a return on equity of even close to 50%. The bulk of profitable MFIs are in the range of 4% to 18%.[24]

There is also an ethical dimension to consider. Is it correct to make so much money on the backs of the poor? Returns on equity of more than 20% to 25% are generally difficult to achieve. Few hedge funds produce such returns year after year.[25] Deutsche Bank has admitted that it cannot reach its target of 25%, and even Goldman Sachs is only aiming for a return on equity of 20%. On the other hand, efficiently run MFIs that charge loan interest rates of about 35% per annum (in a low interest rate environment) can achieve returns of 15% to 20% if they have a diversified business and can put on a three to four times leverage at decent refinancing rates. The question therefore becomes: is a 15% per annum return on equity enough to attract sufficient investor money to meet the demand?

6. What should an investor bring to the table?

This chapter would not be complete without looking at the key characteristics an

24 Rhyne, Microfinance for Bankers and Investors, *ibid*, p 133.
25 See www.hedgeindex.com/hedgeindex/en/default.aspx?cy=USD.

MFI investor should bring to the table to make the investment mutually successful.

First is financial muscle. Natural disasters or political changes may lead to client defaults and to liquidity crises. In such an event equity investors must be able to step in to prevent default. In addition, most loans today made by MIVs to MFIs contain covenants that give the lender the right to call a loan or even declare it into default on the basis of reasons not directly related to payment default – for example, perceived country credit risk – even if the MFI continues to be solvent. Because MFIs do not usually have large cash cushions, in such a case fresh capital must be provided to prevent the MFI from defaulting, triggering cross defaults and potentially the end of the institution.

The second key element is mission alignment. Different ideas and expectations between investors should be a deal stopper. Under mission alignment come the key questions of expectations of financial returns and social returns.

Third is expertise in financial markets and microfinance. Many MFIs open to new investors as they are upgraded to new legal entities, for example when transforming from an NGO into a non-banking financial company or bank. These institutional transformations generally require a higher level of professionalisation, as complying with regulatory requirements and operating a wider range of products become more complex. In such contexts, MFIs may look for investors with expertise in microfinance, treasury, risk management and general banking who can support the process of building capacity.

7. The future

A lot has been achieved but much remains to be done. It is clear that there is a huge demand–supply gap. Although there are hundreds of MFIs on the ground in developing countries, there is a large unbanked population. Unfortunately, throwing money at the problem is not a solution: money would chase only the few truly investable MFIs, driving up the price. As discussed above, this can be to the detriment of both the institution and its clients.

When analysing the work of MFIs around the world, one can generally see the potential for positive contributions to client livelihoods. In recent years, however, many examples have also shown that these positive effects only happen when MFIs are run professionally, with a high degree of social responsibility and with a mid- to long-term vision.

What are most needed, therefore, are more institutions on the ground in which investors can invest. This requires capital, people, adjusted regulations and patience. It is significantly easier to build a worldwide chain of Starbucks coffee shops than it is to build a worldwide chain of viable and responsible MFIs. Yet this is probably what is needed to give the 2.5 billion unbanked tailor-made loans, savings and other financial products.

Microfinance and capital markets

Juliette Chapelle
Paris Bar School

1. Introduction

One of the biggest challenges to the microfinance sector is to build a strong microfinance market that can alleviate poverty by delivering banking and financial services to the poor, while remaining sustainable for microfinance institutions (MFIs) and financially attractive for investors.

This chapter provides an overview of the role of capital markets in bridging the funding needs of MFIs and the microfinance sector. Capital markets can be broadly subdivided into domestic and international markets. A domestic capital market "operates within the financial system of a single country and is subject to regulation by the national government generally through the central bank or a specialist regulatory agency".[1] International capital markets, however, involve securities issued to and traded by investors in multiple jurisdictions that can be in any major currencies.

The first capital markets transactions relating to microfinance involved bond issues in the international capital markets. For example, in 2004–5, the first collateralised debt obligations based on microfinance risks, BOMS1, issued notes on the international capital market. Although international capital markets transactions have generally been preferred for their access to a broader investor base, more and more transactions are being structured to access investors in domestic capital markets. For example, on November 15 2010 the Promotion for Rural Initiatives and Enterprise, a Tanzanian MFI, issued a local currency bond that traded on the Tanzania Stock Exchange.

There are many advantages to tapping either international or domestic capital markets. Capital markets should provide access to a more diversified source of funding, in a more cost effective way and at better conditions than traditional sources of funding such as commercial loans. Capital markets should also provide a broader range of investors (from business angels to commercially oriented investors), increasing flexibility for the issuer and improving their visibility and information.

2. Debt capital markets transactions in microfinance

A wide range of debt capital markets transactions have been structured in microfinance. These include vanilla bond issues, collateralised debt obligations and securitisations.

1 '*International Capital Markets*', 2nd edn, Self-Study Solutions, p 3.

2.1 Bond issues

(a) *An alternative to commercial loans*

A bond is a debt instrument by which an issuer (the borrower) borrows money from an investor (the lender). The investor will be repaid the principal amount borrowed plus fixed or floating interests over a specified period of time. Bonds are one of the main alternatives to commercial loans.

The microfinance market is predominantly a debt market, with a particular emphasis on loan financing. The MixMarket shows that from 2007 to 2010 debt represented more than one-third of the total funding of MFIs. It increased by $7 billion over the same period.[2] In some regions, especially where deposits are particularly restricted, debt financing is the main way of funding MFIs.

In comparison to commercial loans, bond issues allow MFIs to diversify their funding while accessing funds at lower costs and for a longer term. Most bond issues in microfinance have proved financially attractive while allowing MFIs to access large amounts of capital to develop their activities or improve the conditions for microloans.

In 2005 WWB Cali, an MFI and non-governmental organisation, issued bonds for $52 million. This allowed the organisation to lower its average financing cost by 3.6% and to obtain longer maturity compared to loans. The interest rate charged to micro-borrowers was reduced as a result.[3]

Several such bond issues on the international capital markets have been oversubscribed, demonstrating how well they are perceived by capital market investors. Part of this positive perception is due to the high repayment rate that characterises the microfinance sector.

MFIs that have successfully issued bonds have had a strong financial structure, a well-developed corporate structure and a specific commitment from the board of directors to develop capital market financing.

(b) *The lack of a secondary market*[4]

One of the attractions of investing in bonds rather than commercial loans is their higher transferability. However, the market is still maturing in respect to microfinance. The volume of issues remains quite low, reducing investors' options.

A secondary market in microfinance could be developed in the following ways:

- The implementation of flexible standardisation provided by an international organisation, such as the International Capital Market Association, for both structuring and documentation. This could reduce the costs and risks associated with transactions. Flexible standardisation might direct the use of capital markets in microfinance by providing a transaction outline that deals with the main risks but allows room for negotiation; and
- The creation of specialised platforms to act as intermediaries between the

---

2 R Sapundzhieva, 'Funding Microfinance – a Focus on Debt Financing', *MicroBanking Bulletin*, Nov 2011, available at www.themix.org.

3 'Who Will Buy Our Paper: Microfinance Cracking the Capital Markets?', *ACCION Insight*, April 18 2006.

4 The need to develop secondary markets concerns the whole sector of microfinance.

MFIs and investors. These could be developed by experienced intermediaries in capital markets to strengthen the social and financial performance of microfinance investments. They may also help adapt structures for smaller MFIs.

Box 1: A French initiative: the creation of Microfis[5]

Created in 2010, Microfis is the first French investment provider dedicated to microfinance investment. Its creation meets a demand for socially responsible investment, especially following the global economic crisis. This initiative should help develop the primary and secondary markets in microfinance by enhancing market liquidity and providing financial services such as origination, selection, analysis, monitoring and transformation.

Moreover, Microfis commits to respect:

- the Principles for Responsible Investment established by the Investor Group under the aegis of the United Nations;
- the Consumer Protection Principles established by the CGAP and ACCION INTERNATIONAL; and
- the social performance of MFIs through the implementation of social performance indicators.

The first bonds were issued on the dedicated responsible investment segment of Alternext in May 2011.

2.2 Structured finance

(a) Definition of structured finance

Structured finance is "the creation of complex debt instruments by securitisation or the addition of derivatives to existing instruments. It includes securitisation and collateralised debt obligations as well as other complex structures".[6] Collateralised debt obligations and securitisations in microfinance have been structured since 2005.

A collateralised debt obligation is an asset-backed security based on microfinance receivables (loans, bonds or other debt) that allows those receivables to be packaged in liquid assets that can be sold in different tranches to capital investors. Securitisation is the financial process of transforming homogenous, illiquid financial assets by collecting and repackaging them into marketable securities.[7] This section focuses on securitisation.

One of the main advantages of structured finance is the transformation of illiquid assets into liquid ones. This allows MFIs to access funding at a lower cost and on a longer-term basis compared to other sources. It is also a well-designed tool for managing balance-sheets and risks by transferring the loan pool to a special purpose vehicle (SPV). This transfer allows the MFI to expand its portfolio in terms of

---

5 For more information see www.microfis.com.

6 *Dictionary of Finance and Banking*, 4th edn, Oxford University Press, 2008.

7 S L Schwarcz, *Structured Finance, A Guide To The Principles of Asset Securitisation*, 3rd edn, PLI, 2002 and 2010, §1-1.

geographic target, quality of micro-borrowers and quantity of people served.

The following issues need to be considered.

Chart 1: Securitisation structure

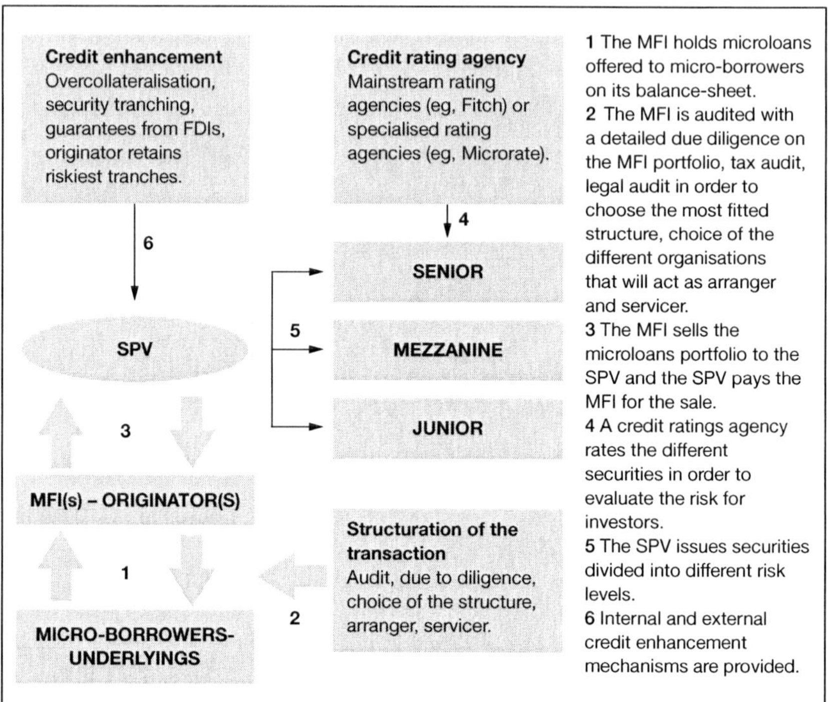

(b) ***Structure of the programme***

There is 'No one size fits all' solution in securitisation. This is particularly true when structuring a microfinance loan securitisation. The programme should be adapted to the features of the underlying microfinance loan portfolio and the legal requirements of the relevant country in which the programme is to be structured. A microfinance loan securitisation typically requires a detailed due diligence to analyse the needs of the MFI and the loan portfolio (eg, default ratio, delinquency ratio, dilution ratio). The due diligence allows the eligibility criteria to be fixed and the different risks and the tools to control them to be assessed. In this way the most appropriate structure (on or offshore securitisation; true sale or synthetic securitisation), and the legal and financial terms (representations and warranties, covenants and guarantees) can be determined.

Under a securitisation programme, an MFI might need to implement new systems or adapt its internal procedures to external standards. The standards of fundamental notions, such as defaulting loans, for example, can differ between the MFI and the capital markets.[8]

(c) *Legal issues*

Securitisation must be legally authorised. The first securitisation based on microfinance receivables, the PCB Bulgaria securitisation in May 2006, was made possible only because the Bulgarian National Bank reviewed its previous restricted regulations.[9] Even if the regulations authorise securitisation, approval can take a long time in developing countries where the national regulatory authorities or supervisors may not be familiar with the process. For example, during the BRAC securitisation, the Bangladesh Bank raised a number of objections and queries, which extended the length of the approval process.[10]

Regulation should allow for the creation of an SPV and the transfer to it of the microloans portfolio by way of true sale. Two risks require specific attention. The first is the impact of the liquidation of the originator on the SPV. Making the securitisation a true sale limits this risk: making transfer of the loan portfolio unconditional prevents the MFI's creditors from claiming the assets against the SPV. The second is the risk of liquidation of the originator when it acts as the servicer. This is also known as commingling risk. Specific mechanisms should be provided to control this risk through, for example, dedicated accounts or a daily cash transfer.

Regulation should be adapted to the specifics of microloans as the foundation of a securitisation transaction. For example, in the aftermath of the banking crisis, the Reserve Bank of India issued guidelines on securitisation for banks and non-banks, including MFIs. These guidelines established a minimum holding period and a minimum portion of loans to be retained prior to securitisation.[11] However, due to the short maturity of microloans and their small number, these guidelines could also prevent the development of securitisation as a means of financing MFIs. Eventually, they were partially revised to suit the particularities of MFIs.[12]

(d) *Rating securities*

The rating process is a fundamental step in structured finance. It helps investors to assess the risks and improves the market quality of the securities issued by the SPV. Fitch, an international rating agency, has identified the difficulty of rating securities that are based on microloans.[13] It has recommended capping the ratings of securitisations transactions to the ratings of the MFI since there is a high dependency between the securitisation structure and the MFI.[14] This is especially true when the MFI acts as a servicer.

Such a cap would restrict the chance of obtaining a higher rating than the

---

8 R. Rahman and S Mohammed, 'BRAC Micro Credit Securitisation Series I: Lessons from the World's First Micro-Credit Backed Security (MCBS)', March 20 2007.

9 S Kyutchukou, 'Securitisation of Bulgarian Bank Assets', Conference SME Asset-Backed Financing Instruments: Opportunities in Europe, Bratislava, May 2008.

10 R Rahman and S Mohammed, 'BRAC Micro Credit Securitisation Series I: Lessons from the World's First Micro-Credit Backed Security (MCBS)', March 20 2007.

11 Securitisation transactions – Draft Guidelines available at www.rbi.org.in.

12 E Macchiavello, 'Securitisation in microfinance and global financial crisis: innovation or Trojan horse?' *Journal of International Banking Law and Regulation*, 2013.

13 FitchRatings, Indian Microfinance Securitisations: Ratings Constrained by Unmitigated Risks, Special report November 16 2010.

14 FitchRatings, Indian Microfinance Securitisations: Ratings Constrained by Unmitigated Risks, Special report November 16 2010.

originator, which is usually one of the key benefits of a securitisation. On the other hand, such a cap takes account of the fact that in microfinance the MFI remains highly involved after the transfer of the loan portfolio. In any case, the ratings can be revised and upgraded according to the robustness of the programme.[15]

(e) *Tranching securities*

Tranching tailors securities to investors' appetite by splitting or directing payments on the bonds among different bond classes. This can be used to create bond classes that appeal to different types of investor and thereby improve the execution of the transaction. The senior tranche is the highest priority debt and the least risky. In case of default, it will be repaid first. The mezzanine tranche is riskier but offers a higher return. The junior or equity tranche is the riskiest.

IFMR Capital usually invests in the junior tranches of transactions. By structuring and arranging these itself[16] it can reassure private investors and enhance the soundness of the structure. Another initiative is the development of specific structures. IFMR Capital has developed multi-originator securitisation, which allows small and medium MFIs to transfer their loan portfolios. The multi-originator model allows a bringing together of competences, a repartition of costs and a reduction of risks that would not be possible with a single-originator securitisation.[17]

Box 2: Is securitisation safe for microfinance?

The US subprime crisis highlighted the negative effects of capital markets. Research into securitisation and microfinance suggests that securitisation is a promising tool for microfinance. However, securitisation and structured finance in general involve large risks that can undermine the microfinance market if regulation is not adapted and strongly supervised. Particular emphasis should be placed on the originate-to-distribute model, the revolving structure and synthetic securitisation in order to avoid risk to the microfinance sector.

3. Equity capital markets transactions

The importance of private equity to the development of sophisticated sources of funding for MFIs is growing. A number of IPOs have highlighted the difficulty of balancing human, social and economic factors when dealing in microfinance.

3.1 Development of private equity

Private equity refers to the activity of investment funds, financial institutions and individual investors that invest equity into MFIs that are operating under a sophisticated corporate structure but which are not publicly listed.

In the area of microfinance, equity financing is less developed than debt financing. It is reported that in 2010 equity represented 18% of the total

15 See, for example, www.ifmr.co.in/blog – ICRA upgraded the ratings on securitisations transactions structured by IFMR.

16 IFMR Capital is a non-banking finance company (NBFC) based in Chennai, see www.ifmr.co.in.

17 V Anand and K Fernandes, 'Multi originator securitisation MOSEC in microfinance", in *The EuroMoney, Securitisation & Structured Finance Handbook*, 2012–13.

composition of microfinance investment vehicles (MIVs).[18] The two largest equity markets in microfinance are India and Peru.[19]

However, if MFIs want to access deeper capital markets as a source of funding and replicate successful debt transactions, then equity financing is vital. This is because:

- equity reinforces the balance sheet of MFIs and provides a strong basis for solvency;
- equity supports debt financing: financial covenants and conditions of loan agreements are based on the solvency of the institution;
- equity helps to increase transparency and information disclosure; and
- equity provides a basis for the development of a consistent strategy through a strong and dedicated shareholding.

Private equity is more demanding and more challenging for both MFIs and investors. For MFIs it is costly and time consuming. Institutions must implement management information systems, accountability standards and higher transparency. For investors it is perceived as more risky, especially in some developing countries, and requires their more active involvement.

MIVs are major actors in developing private equity in microfinance.

Box 3: Diversity of microfinance investment vehicles[20]

MIVs can be classified by:

- Orientation – microfinance development funds (eg, Oikocredit) act as non-profit entities and focus on social returns, quasi-commercial funds (eg, ProFund) seek both financial and social returns and commercial microfinance funds (eg, BlueOrchard) give priority to financial returns; and
- Composition – fixed income funds (eg, Microfinance Growth Fund) specialise in debt instruments, mixed funds (eg, Impulse Microfinance Investment Fund) invest in both debt and equity and equity funds (eg, Goodwell West Africa Microfinance Development Company Ltd) invest more than 65% of their non-cash assets in equity.

The main hurdles to developing equity in microfinance include:

- the lack of historical data and long-term performance data by which to evaluate the MFI;
- the limited number of MFIs that can welcome shareholders; and
- the lack of a secondary market or clear exit opportunities.

However, initiatives have been taken. A number of indexes (eg, WSAS Microfinance Institutions Shareholder Value Indexes) have been developed to evaluate the value of MFIs to investors, and an increasing number of MFIs are

18 Microrate and Luminis, 'The State of Microfinance Investment 2011', MicroRate's 6th Annual Survey and Analysis of MIVs.

19 J P Morgan and CGAP, 'Discovering Limits, Global Microfinance Valuation Survey', 2011.

20 R Dieckmann, 'Microfinance: An emerging investment opportunity', (2007), Deutsche Bank Research; Symbiotics 2011 MIV Survey Report, Market Data & Peer Group Analysis, August 2011.

operating under corporate structures that permit equity investments.

One challenge is retaining dedicated shareholders while attracting external equity funding, but without reducing the control of the MFI. One option is to issue shares without voting rights for investors who are mainly interested in financial returns. Clear exit strategies for investors, especially those without voting rights, should be provided.

Box 4: Why is Peru one of the leading equity markets in microfinance?[21]

The success of the equity market in microfinance in Peru may be mainly explained by:

- the high penetration of microcredit in the population;
- a corporate structure that is favourable to MFIs raising equity;
- the fact that deposits are one of the main sources of funding;
- the importance of local market and local investors; and
- a supportive regulatory framework.

3.2 IPOs in microfinance

The main reason for an MFI to go public is to raise funds to support business expansion by issuing shares listed on stock exchanges. Going public brings many constraints, mainly due to:

- increased pressure from investors to maintain stock price;
- increased pressure from the public regarding important disclosure information;
- loss of strategic independence through a dilution of ownership and a significant number of purely commercially-oriented investors such as hedge funds;
- greater vulnerability to internal and external factors. For example, a dispute between the promoters of SKS and the former CEO led to a drop in its share price;[22] and
- higher volatility and instability as the price of the stock can fluctuate rapidly.

Chart 3 gives details of some microfinance IPOs. Before they went public, the shared characteristics of these MFIs were:[23]

- they were operating under a commercial structure that ensured strong corporate governance and management;
- they had experienced high growth;
- their funding bases were diversified and had a strong level of equity; and
- they were well-known and well-respected in their sector.

---

21 J P Morgan and CGAP, 'Discovering Limits, Global Microfinance Valuation Survey', 2011; Microrate and Luminis, 'The State of Microfinance Investment 2011', MicroRate's 6th Annual Survey and Analysis of MIVs.

22 S Sinha, 'Initial Public Offerings: The field's salvation or downfall?', 2011 Global Microfinance Summit.

23 Information relies on I W Lieberman, A Anderson, Z Grafe, B Campbell and D Kopf, 'Microfinance and Capital Markets: The Initial Listing/Public Offering of Four Leading Institutions', May 2008.

Chart 2: MFIs going public[24]

MFIs	Structure of the MFI	Date of the IPO	Listing
Bank Rakyat Indonesia (BRI)	Full-service commercial bank dedicated to micro, retail and SME loans	October 31 2003	Jakarta Stock Exchange and shares offered under US SEC Rule 144A* to international institutional investors
BRAC Bank	Commercial bank dedicated to SMEs in Bangladesh	December 11 2006	Dhaka and Chittagong Stock Exchanges
Equity Bank	Bank with a focus on small-entrepreneurs	August 7 2006	Kenyan Stock Exchange
Banco Compartmos	Licensed commercial bank with a focus on rural villages and women	April 20 2007	Mexican Stock Exchange and shares offered to international institutional investors under US SEC Rule 144A*
SKS	For-profit non-bank finance company with a focus on low-income households	July 28 2010	Bombay and National Stock Exchange

The macro-economic conditions at the time of each IPO were also favourable.

All five IPOs were financially successful. The Compartamos and the SKS IPOs were oversubscribed. The SKS IPO attracted leading investment groups like JP Morgan and BNP Paribas, and prestigious investors such as Helios subscribed to the Equity Bank IPO.

However, the Banco Compartamos and SKS IPOs highlighted the conflict between financial returns and the social features of microfinance investments, as

24 The table relies on information from I W Lieberman, A Anderson, Z Grafe, B Campbell and D Kopf, 'Microfinance and Capital Markets: The Initial Listing/Public Offering of Four Leading Institutions', May 2008; G Chen, S. Rasmussen, X Reille and D Rozas, 'Indian Microfinance Goes Public: The SKS Initial Public Offering', CGAP Focus Note no 65, 2010, Washington, DC; and the websites of each institution.

well as the potential consequences of 'excessive commercialization'[25] in microfinance.

Both IPOs instituted a crisis of confidence in microfinance. Compartamos had to issue a letter reasserting its commitment to fighting poverty through the delivery of microfinance services.[26] With respect to SKS, the Andra Pradesh government, a region where SKS is particularly involved, began restricting the practice of microfinance. In October 2010 SKS's CEO resigned from his position. The Indian government is currently drafting microfinance regulations that address the possible implementation of an interest rate cap and the restriction of loan collection methods.

Alternatives to an IPO are open to MFIs. One is to offer securities directly to sophisticated investors through a private placement. This should be less costly and more rapid than an IPO, and can be a good way to assess the market before a full public offering.

Box 5: List of first capital markets transactions in microfinance[27]

- 1992: BancoSol is the first NGO to become a commercial bank.
- 1995: ProFund, the first MIV, is created.
- 2003: Bank Rakyat Indonesia is the first bank predominantly dealing in microfinance to be listed on the Nairobi Stock Exchange.
- July 2004: BOMS1, the first collateralised debt obligation based on microfinance risk, is launched.
- April 2006: BOLD1, the first collateralised loans obligation based on microfinance risk, is launched.
- May 2006: ProCredit Bank Bulgaria securitisation, the first securitisation based on microcredit, is structured.
- July 2006: BRAC achieves the first AAA-rated local currency microcredit securitisation.
- April 2007: Compartamos, a Mexican MFI, goes public.

4. The development and enhancement of capital markets transactions

Financing MFIs through capital markets transactions requires the creation, development and/or implementation of a regulatory, supervisory and legal framework in developing countries and a re-assessment of the role of financial development institutions (FDIs).

---

25 Term quoted from C Lützenkirchen and C Weistroffer, 'Microfinance in evolution', Deutsche Bank Research, 2012.

26 C Danel and C Labarthe, 'A letter to our peers', 2008, available on www.compartamos.com.

27 Information relies on multiple sources including B Swanson, 'The Role of International Capital Markets in Microfinance' in S Sundaresan, 'Microfinance Emerging Trends and Challenges', 2008; I Callaghan, H Gonzalez, D Maurice and C Novak, 'Microfinance – on the road to capital markets', *Journal of Applied Corporate Finance*, Vol 19, no 1, Winter 2007; S Stieber, 'Is Securitization Right for Microfinance', Innovations: Technology, Governance, Globalisation Winter/Spring 2007, Vol 2, nos 1–2, 202–213; S. Zaman and S N Kairy, 'Building Domectis Capital Markets: BRAC's AAA Securitisation', *MicroBanking Bulletin*, no 14, Spring 2007, available at www.themix.org; I W Lieberman, A Anderson, Z Grafe, B Campbell and D Kopf, 'Microfinance and Capital Markets: The Initial Listing/Public Offering of Four Leading Institutions', May 2008, and some information available at www.luminismicrofinance.co.

4.1 Developing a strong regulatory and supervisory framework

There are many risks to financing microfinance through the capital markets. These include financial, operational, legal, management and market risks – all of which must be addressed.

The sound development of capital markets transactions in microfinance should mean the implementation of:

- non-prudential regulation to protect micro-borrowers and avoid over-indebtedness;
- prudential regulation to impose solvency requirements on regulated MFIs; and
- supervision to control and assess risks.[28]

Two specific issues should be considered. First, the mechanisms for channeling money into the microfinance sector must allocate sufficient funds. In India the Reserve Bank has issued a regulation, known as Priority Sector Lending, that forces banks to lend money to the microfinance sector.[29] This is problematic because it may lead banks to lend to MFIs that do not need funding while forcing MFIs to lend money to micro-borrowers who cannot repay their loans, therefore creating a vicious circle.[30]

Second, global and regional economic crises have raised concerns about the potential for conflict between the social nature of microfinance and the financial returns of microfinance investment. Calls have been made to develop and implement regulation and oversight that place a premium on the social impact of microfinance investments.[31]

Box 6: Social impact bonds[32]

Social impact bonds (SIBs) are a recent development. The first was arranged in the United Kingdom in September 2010. SIBs allow public entities to finance a social programme with respect to a specific outcome. The public entity raises funds from private investors, and the funds are only delivered in full if the programme achieves its outcome.

SIBs are an opportunity to raise funds in the microfinance sector while creating incentives to achieve financial and social results. They may also provide a new way to channel funds to areas such as in Africa where private sector funding is still developing.

---

28 See for example: 'Microfinance activities and the Core Principles for Effective Banking Supervision' issued by the Basel Committee on August 2010, available at www.bis.org.

29 See, for example, the Master Circular – Lending To Priority Sector dated July 2 2012 and Priority Sector Lending – Targets and Classification as on September 1 2012, available at www.rbi.org.in.

30 Regarding priority sector lending and securitisation see also: B.Swanson, 'Securitization in Microfinance', Microfinance Insights, June 2007.

31 See, for example, X Reille, S Forster and D Rozas, 'Foreign Capital Investment in Microfinance: Reassessing Financial and Social Returns', CGAP Focus Note 71, May 2011, Washington DC; K McKee, E Lahaye and A Koning, 'Responsible Finance: Putting Principles to Work', CGAP Focus Note 73, September 2011, Washington, DC.

32 For more information, see www.gov.uk.

4.2 Enhancing the legal framework

Today, there are an estimated 10,000 MFIs worldwide. At the end of December 2010 2,000 of them reported to MixMarket, serving around 100 million clients,[33] and 3,652 reported to the MicroCredit Summit Campaign and represented more than 205 million clients.[34]

Box 7: Data on the microfinance market

The Microfinance Banana Skins Survey has been conducted since 2008 by the Centre for the Study of Financial Innovation. It aims to evaluate and rank the risks perceived in the worldwide microfinance sector by its major market participants (practitioners, investors, observers and regulators).

MixMarket is a database that provides data and analysis about MFIs, funders, networks and service providers in microfinance. Its aim is to enhance transparency regarding microfinance's main actors.

The MicroCredit Summit Campaign aims to gather microfinance's main actors so as to promote best practices and create an interactive place where experiences, views and opinions can be exchanged.

CGAP is an independent policy and research centre that aims to improve financial access for the world's poor.

MicroRate is the first microfinance rating agency to evaluate the performance and risks of MFIs.

Capital markets impose new burdens, responsibilities and realities on MFIs. Developing a strong legal framework is vital to controlling risks and developing adapted structures in case of problems.

A legal framework should include:[35]

- corporate governance principles that address self-interested transactions, excessive compensation and the protection of shareholders;
- contracts law, property law and administrative law that allow certainty and protect property rights; and
- restructuring and bankruptcy law, including prompt corrective action and emergency lending facilities suitable for MFIs.

Box 8: Liquidation in microfinance: the case of BANEX[36]

BANEX, a Nicaraguan MFI that obtained a banking license in September 2008, was partly financed through international funding via collateralised debt obligations (BOMS1) and collateralised loan obligations (BOLD1 and BOLD2).

---

33 Data available on www.mixmarket.org.

34 J P Maes and L R Reed, 'State of the Microcredit Summit Campaign Report 2012', available on www.microcreditsummit.org/.

35 This list is not exhaustive. For extended law reform studies, see for example: R M Lastra, 'Financial law reform in emerging economies', *Journal of International Banking Law and Regulation*, 2008; J J Norton, 'Financial Sector Law Reform in Emerging Economies', British Institute of International and Comparative Law, 2000.

36 Data collected on the MixMarket and IAMFI and Morgan Stanley, 'Charting the course: Best Practices and Tools for Voluntary Debt Restructuring in Microfinance', 2011.

Although it experienced high growth from 2004 to 2008, BANEX went bankrupt on August 3 2010. In 2009, it started to default due to events both external (global economic crisis) and internal (political instability and concentration of clients).

The BANEX case is a good example of the different trends that lead to crises in microfinance. It highlights the need for not only a smooth channeling of funds but also the development of restructuring and liquidation laws adapted to the microfinance sector. When a restructuring or liquidation is planned the social goals of MFIs should be emphasised, especially during negotiations with creditors.

4.3 The role of FDIs

FDIs are major microfinance funders. A study of the MixMarket shows that in 2010 they injected $28 billion into microfinance – or 19% of the total debt financing.[37]

The interventions of FDIs have been crucial to structuring capital markets transactions in microfinance. However, the growing use in microfinance of capital markets as a source of finance and the involvement of the private sector have raised a number of issues and potential conflicts. An interesting study by MicroRate has questioned the extended role of FDIs in structuring capital markets transactions in microfinance.[38] FDIs do play a fundamental role in connecting capital markets and microfinance, through issuing guarantees or creating innovative structures to reinforce capital markets transactions, such as foreign currency hedging mechanisms[39] and credit bureaus. However, they should avoid entering into conflict with the private sector when financing MFIs.

5. Conclusion

A sophisticated domestic and international microfinance capital market is now emerging, and a significant number of capital markets transactions have been successfully structured. However, there are still hurdles to overcome. The development and implementation of a strong regulatory and supervisory framework that can compromise between social benefits and financial returns would be an important improvement.

---

37 R Sapundzhieva, 'Funding Microfinance – a Focus on Debt Financing', *MicroBanking Bulletin*, November 2011, available at www.themix.org.

38 For a global presentation of FDIs' intervention in microfinance, see J Abrams and D von Stauffenberg, 'Role Reversal – Are Public Development Institutions Crowding Out Private Investment in Microfinance?', MicroRate, 2007; and D von Stauffenberg and D Rozas, 'Role Reversal revisited – Are Public Development Institutions Still Crowding Out Private Investment in Microfinance', Microrate, 2011, available at www.microrate.com.

39 See, for example: D K Dash, 'Capital Markets – Utility for MF', MPRA, 2010; J Abrams and D von Stauffenberg, 'Role Reversal: Are Public Development Institutions Crowding Out Private Investments in Microfinance', Microrate, 2007; D von Stauffenberg and D Rozas, 'Role Reversal Revisited – Are Public Development Institutions Still Crowding Out Private Investments in Microfinance?', Microrate, 2011; and www.mfxsolutions.com.

Governance and the sustainability of microfinance institutions

Melissa Manzo
Allen & Overy LLP

1. Introduction

Governance is relevant to every aspect of the life of a microfinance institution. There are signs that microfinance practitioners are becoming more aware of the importance of good governance in achieving their aims. Yet it continues to be an area to which the industry as a whole could give greater attention.

Why should good governance be high on the list of priorities of microfinance practitioners and stakeholders? Why can it not just be left to the attention of regulators and lawyers? To answer these questions, it is necessary to explore what is meant by the concept of 'governance' and why, in the current climate, issues of governance are becoming increasingly important in the microfinance industry. It is also necessary to examine governance guidelines and specific governance issues in microfinance. This will ultimately show why good governance should be synonymous with the sustainability of microfinance institutions.

2. What is governance?

Numerous definitions of governance exist. One of the most helpful, in the microfinance context, is that offered by Marc Labie and Roy Mersland. Its relevance to the distinctive issues faced by microfinance institutions (MFIs) is that it addresses both the concept of the double bottom line and the need to achieve social as well as financial goals: "corporate governance is a system, or a set of mechanisms, by which an organisation is directed and controlled in order to reach its mission and objectives".[1]

The corporate governance system is made up of several components. These can be categorised into internal controls (such as the board of directors, management, shareholders and employees) and external controls (such as external auditors, market competition, regulators and clients). Although effective governance can only be achieved through interaction between the various internal and external players, the internal controls can be more easily influenced by the microfinance institution itself. The roles of the board of directors and, to a certain extent, shareholders and management, are of particular importance.

More specifically, the functions of governance can be said to be:

---

1 Labie, Marc and Roy Mersland (2011) "Corporate Governance Challenges in Microfinance", *The Handbook of Microfinance*, ed. Beatriz Armendariz and Marc Labie. Singapore: World Scientific Publishing, pp 286 – 287. Every effort has been made to secure the permission of World Scientific Publishing for this citation.

- to uphold the organisation's goals and mission and see that they are implemented;
- to guide the organisation's major strategic decisions;
- to maintain the organisation's health over time and to mitigate risks;
- to ensure accountability throughout the organization; and
- to ensure that the organisation has the necessary human and financial resources to operate effectively.[2]

Most discussions around governance inevitably focus on shareholder-owned MFIs with a corporate existence, rather than ownerless non-governmental organisations (NGOs). Many of the basic principles, however, apply equally to MFIs that are structured as NGOs.

3. The importance of governance

The Microfinance Banana Skins 2012 survey lists corporate governance as its overall number two 'microfinance banana skin', and the number one risk amongst investors, regulators and industry observers. One respondent to the survey offered the following view:

> *the levels of competitiveness, efficiency and scale now required for an MFI to achieve success have increased significantly over five years. The risk is that poor performance in the institutional leadership (executive) has a greater impact on these factors than before.*[3]

Indeed, the last few years have witnessed a dramatic change in the microfinance landscape. A development strategy that was once dominated by NGOs, development finance institutions and aid agencies has been transformed into a multi-million dollar industry. Its stakeholders now come from a large variety of backgrounds. The shift from a donor-led industry to an industry with a significant amount of external investment has raised the standards required of MFIs in relation to governance. The influx of equity investors (for example, through microfinance investment vehicles) has had a particularly notable impact on the industry's governance standards. Whereas donors typically place strict requirements and conditionality on aid/grants prior to making such grants/donations, equity investors tend to insist on constant monitoring of the affairs of their investees through accountable systems of governance. Equity investors will usually demand a more active role than debt investors in the decision-making and monitoring of the microfinance institutions in which they invest.

The number of clients, assets and services offered in today's microfinance industry have increased and the fundraising structures utilised by MFIs have become more complex. The general move towards offering a variety of services to

---

2 Council of Microfinance Equity Funds (2012) *The Practice of Corporate Governance in Microfinance Institutions: Consensus Statement of the Council of Microfinance Equity Funds*, p 4. Available from http://www.cmef.com/document.doc?id=1026.

3 Lascelles, David and Sam Mendelson (2012) *Microfinance Banana Skins 2012: The CSFI Survey of Microfinance Risk*. New York: Center for the Study of Financial Innovation, p 14. Available from http://www.csfi.org/files/Microfinance_Banana_Skins_2012.pdf. The quotation is by Diego Villalobos, analyst at ACCION in the United States.

microfinance clients (such as microinsurance and savings) other than just microcredit has tended to require more rigorous regulation. MFIs' internal governance procedures therefore need to cope with a more sophisticated investor base, a greater volume of clients, more diverse portfolios of products and services, and more interaction with regulatory bodies. Political risk is also a serious challenge in a number of jurisdictions. MFIs are often vulnerable to attack from politicians due to the comparatively high interest rates that they charge to low income populations. Strong boards and effective governance are crucial in such contexts.

The increase in external equity investment in MFIs has undoubtedly raised the overall standard of governance required in the industry. Equity investors usually demand regular reporting, financial monitoring and board representation so as to ensure that MFIs are run in accordance with their investment criteria. In order for such requirements to have a positive effect on governance standards, however, shareholders must actively exercise their rights – particularly in relation to board representation. Equity investors may sit on several boards and may be unable to dedicate the time required to monitor the MFI effectively. Similarly, although they may have insisted on a specified number of board seats, shareholders do not always fully exercise their voting rights as board members to influence decisions. Local board representation, from people with experience of the MFI's local jurisdiction, regulatory requirements and with links to the community, can be helpful to governance. In certain cases, equity investors in microfinance may need to do more to ensure that acceptable governance standards are maintained.

There is an additional ethical reason for the importance of governance within microfinance. Many MFI clients are more vulnerable and MFI governing boards therefore owe them a higher duty of care.[4]

The importance of good governance was highlighted in a 2010 study of Latin American MFIs by Beatriz Marulanda, Lizbeth Fajury, Mariana Paredes and Franz Gomez. The study examined the reasons for MFI failure. ('Failure' here refers to a serious deterioration of the MFIs' capital that jeopardises its solvency and leads to its restructuring, recapitalisation, merger or closure.) One of the study's main conclusions was that governance structure was the main differentiating factor between those MFIs that were able to overcome crises, and those that were not.[5] The suggestion made is that: "The crises are not what cause the failures, but it is the way in which they are faced by the Board, the managers and the staff or a financial entity that explains if an institution overcomes the challenge."[6]

In one of the MFIs studied, its serious crisis was caused by a number of factors:

- none of its founders had a detailed knowledge of the financial sector;
- the institution lost direction when a decision was taken to expand into consumer lending;

---

4 McKee, Katharine (2012) *Voting the Double Bottom Line: Active Governance by Microfinance Equity Investors*. CGAP, p 3. Available from www.cgap.org/sites/default/files/Focus-Note-Voting-the-Double-Bottom-Line-Active-Governance-by-Microfinance-Equity-Investors-May-2012.pdf.

5 Marulanda, Beatriz, Lizbeth Fajury, Mariana Paredes and Franz Gomez (2010) *Taking the Good from the Bad in Microfinance: Lessons Learned from Failed Experiences in Latin America*. Calmeadow, p 47. Available from http://www.calmeadow.com/pdf/failures.pdf.

6 *Ibid.*

- there was a lack of internal controls leading to dishonest practices amongst loan officers and inspectors;
- there were deficiencies in microcredit methodologies; and
- the internal audit department was weak.

When the institution was hit by an economic crisis it found itself in deep difficulties. The local regulator even considered its liquidation. The MFI was ultimately saved by a capital contribution from a financial group (an entity with banking experience) who restructured the institution and refocused it on its microfinance business. Although weak governance was only one of the causes of crisis identified in this case study, it was the intervention and leadership of a new shareholder that eventually saved the institution. It has now overcome this crisis and is aiming to become the best MFI in the country.

The value of good governance in sustaining MFIs during periods of crisis is further highlighted by the case studies in Daniel Rozas' *Weathering the Storm: Hazards, Beacons and Life Rafts*, written for ACCION's Centre for Financial Inclusion.[7] Of the 10 case studies in this paper, the three most successful turnarounds involved particularly strong boards, while major board weaknesses were identified in two of the three MFIs that ultimately failed. Case studies like these reinforce the fact that the key to survival for an MFI in crisis is effective guidance from experienced shareholders and management.[8]

In the context of the recent global financial crisis affecting microfinance, it is even more important for governance systems to be tightened to prevent the large-scale failure of microfinance institutions. Many of the problems faced by microfinance institutions are not of their own making, but strong leadership and adherence to solid governance systems can help prevent similar crises in the future. Guarneri, Moauro and Spaggiari suggest that MFIs have a duty to uphold good governance systems for the sake of the industry in general:

> *The recent crisis in India both shows the extent to which irresponsible practices of some MFIs can damage the overall reputation of the sector and demonstrates that a few specific cases may be generalized by the media and therefore affect the credibility of the entire industry.*[9]

They further observe that a crisis of reputation can have a contagious effect, and translate into a worsening of financial performance, through the degradation of portfolio quality and client drop-out. This crisis also creates the risk of political interference, hindering the sound functioning of the microfinance sector and can ultimately lead to a reduced access to funds.[10]

---

7 Rozas, Daniel (2011) *Weathering the Storm: Hazards, Beacons and Life Rafts. Lessons in Microfinance Crisis Survival from Those Who Have Been There.* Centre for Financial Inclusion at ACCION International. Available from http://centerforfinancialinclusionblog.files.wordpress.com/2011/07/weathering-the-storm_center-for-financial-inclusion_final.pdf.

8 *Ibid*, p 15.

9 Guarneri, Micol, Aldo Moauro and Lucia Spiaggiari (2011) *Motivating your Board of Directors to Actively Promote and Deepen the Social Mission*, p 4. Available from www.globalmicrocreditsummit2011.org/userfiles/file/Workshop%20Papers/M_%20%20Guarneri%20-%20Motivating%20your%20Board%20of%20Directors%20V_3.pdf.

10 *Ibid.*

It is therefore in every MFI's interest to uphold the reputation of the industry as a whole. In today's climate, as a result of the recent crisis in India and beyond, microfinance is no longer the darling of the development industry and microfinance investments are competing with other 'impact investments' for funding and investment. The need for good governance is therefore all the more relevant. Indeed, Marulanda, Fajury, Paredes and Gomez suggest that it is fortunate that those MFI failures experienced to date have not led to more systemic failures in the jurisdictions of such MFIs. This is most likely due to the relatively small size of the MFIs relative to the economies in which they operate.[11]

4. Governance issues in microfinance

What are the specific governance-related issues faced by MFIs? A lot of the literature in this area points to the problems experienced by the industry as a result of the evolution or transformation of MFIs from small, relatively informal organisations to larger, more regulated organisations with a more complex ownership structure. Broadly speaking, many founders of MFIs two decades or more ago came from backgrounds in charity work or international development. They may have had little financial or corporate expertise. The MFIs they founded may have grown and transformed into regulated institutions – something which they may not have anticipated when the organisation was first established. As MFIs evolve, so should their boards and management in order to adapt to the new microfinance landscape and its various challenges. In some cases, however, the problem seems to have been that the original founders sought to maintain control of the MFI and continued to dominate executive decisions, reluctant to relinquish power to the board.

As an institution develops, more formal controls are needed to maintain it. Innovation also becomes key, allowing the institution to keep up with its competitors. When the original founders dominate the institution, too much depends on a few individuals. This imbalance of power means that should those individuals fail – in competence, or in honesty – it can greatly damage the institution. More generally, there are limits to what can be expected of any individual in managing a complex organisation in which formal systems and controls have not been established. There is the danger that ethical standards may suffer, leading to conflicts of interest and nepotism. Some individuals may be motivated by personal goals – the quest for personal recognition, for example – and prevent the institution from operating in a transparent manner. Disturbingly, Marulanda and colleagues cite examples of fraud occurring at the management level. They observe that this was allowed to occur because of an absence of checks and balances implemented through a sound governance system:

> *The multiple cases of fraud and deviation from best governance practices occurred without any suggestion by the Boards that they knew this was occurring at the time. In particular, we found that in many cases the internal auditor or tax supervisor did not report directly to the Board but to the CEO, thus making it easier to manipulate the information.*[12]

---

11 Marulanda *et al* (2010), p 23.
12 Marulanda *et al* (2010), p 49.

In certain cases, the issue is 'board capture'. That is, when the CEO or management have a disproportionate influence on the decisions of the board of directors, who act without question on the instructions of the CEO/management. Indeed, the Council of Microfinance Equity Funds (CMEF) consensus statement addresses this issue: "Maintaining the delicate equilibrium between management versus board capture is at the heart of good governance".[13]

Another recurring governance-related issue in microfinance is the need for the interests between the various stakeholders of the MFI to be aligned. As external investment in microfinance has increased, so has the expectation of a financial return on microfinance investments. It can be difficult to balance the expectations of investors of an acceptable financial return on their investment with the MFI's stated social mission. On the other hand, a disproportionate focus on the social mission, without paying enough attention to ensuring that financial targets are achieved, can lead to the failure of an MFI.

5. Governance codes and guidelines

Although the range of institutions that offer microfinance services makes it difficult to design a one-size-fits-all solution for governance, a small number of governance codes have been developed specifically for microfinance institutions. These are generally inspired by governance codes written for mainstream financial institutions, adapted to highlight certain areas of focus for MFIs, such as the importance of upholding the social mission of the MFI and the management of conflicts of interest. These governance codes offer a useful starting point for MFIs that want to develop governance procedures and good practice.

Board composition and selection is naturally a focus of the various existing governance codes, with an emphasis on the independence of the board from the management and administration of the MFI. Although far from the only microfinance-specific governance code in existence, the CMEF guidelines are designed specifically for MFIs and examine the unique challenges they face. Their focus is on the internal governance controls applicable to an MFI, with a particular emphasis on the role of the board of directors. It offers advice on board composition and guidelines on board and committee meetings. It also outlines key board responsibilities and decisions. The CMEF guidelines were first published in 2005, and were updated in 2012 to reflect the need for greater attention to risk/crisis management and the fulfilment of social missions.

The CMEF guidelines highlight the key role of the board of directors in, among other things, upholding the MFI's social mission, developing strategy, overseeing management (including executive compensation) and, interestingly, representing the MFI to the community and public and ensuring that the MFI fulfils its responsibilities to the community as a whole. The guidelines also state that it is the board's responsibility to ensure that the organisation changes to meet emerging conditions, and to assume management responsibilities, temporarily, if necessary in times of crisis. It suggests that any conflict between financial and social goals can be

13 Council of Microfinance Equity Funds (2012), p 12.

avoided by ensuring that a commitment to the latter is a requirement for board membership, and by putting in place a system to monitor the achievement of social targets and goals. Suggestions are also given for those MFIs in transition from small operations to larger, more sophisticated institutions, with a focus on management succession planning. This is particularly important for emerging MFIs. They provide guidance on structuring an effective board, and advice on responsible exits. Ideally these are to be covered in the shareholders' agreement, so as to ensure that the mission of the MFI is consistently followed despite changes in ownership.

6. Sustainability and social performance

What is the link between good governance and financial sustainability in microfinance? This chapter has illustrated how good corporate governance is crucial for the long-term survival of an MFI, and for the reputation and sustainability of the microfinance industry in general. In terms of financial sustainability, a strong and independent board, supported by experienced shareholders, can help steer a microfinance institution through a crisis. A well-governed MFI should be able to balance the different interests of its stakeholders. In this way it can achieve good levels of growth and efficiency, control default levels, and maintain its social mission. The increasingly widespread adherence to industry-wide client protection principles (such as the SMART campaign) and a growing demand from investors for social reporting and social ratings will help achieve this balance. Governance is therefore essential to the longevity of an individual MFI and to the microfinance industry as a whole in a competitive climate with other forms of impact investment for funding. As a long-standing form of impact investment, microfinance institutions can also lead the way in showing other organisations with social missions how to shape their governance systems.

My thanks to Danielle Donza and Mary Chaffin at ACCION International for sharing their experience and providing their guidance on this topic.

Microfinance regulation: government intervention versus self-regulation

Hajar Barbach
Emma Matebalavu
Clifford Chance LLP

1. Introduction

The regulation of microfinance has become an increasingly topical concern in the wake of the global financial crisis and specific microfinance crises in a number of countries. Global financial standard-setting bodies – including the Basel Committee on Banking Supervision, the Financial Action Task Force and the International Association of Insurance Supervisors – have all issued guidance on the regulation and supervision of the microfinance industry in recognition of the fact that the unique nature of microfinance as an instrument for poverty alleviation and financial inclusion requires special regulatory consideration.

The regulation of microfinance is particularly challenging and arguably more complex to articulate and implement than mainstream finance. As with other forms of financial regulation, the primary concern for regulators is to ensure the stability of the financial system and to protect depositors without imposing undue compliance burdens or stifling lending. The added complexity in microfinance, however, is the delicate balancing act between giving the industry enough flexibility to innovate and grow, while maintaining rules and restrictions to protect low-income and often vulnerable microfinance clients.

Regulation and supervision both entail significant costs, and too much regulation may overburden microfinance institutions (MFIs) with compliance costs and limit their outreach. For this reason it is sometimes argued that the regulation and supervision of microfinance should be left to the industry. Self-regulation would allow a realistic, feasible and cost-efficient regulation of microfinance. Regulators themselves may favour self-regulation as a way of managing their supervisory resources, especially in cases where they feel that they do not have sufficient resources even to supervise adequately the mainstream banks. However, government intervention in the field of microfinance is important in a number of areas, especially in the context of issuing and implementing prudential rules to protect the savings of microfinance depositors.

This chapter analyses the balance between self-regulation and government intervention. It looks at practical examples and attempts at self-regulation, and the ways in which government intervention translates itself in the field of regulation and supervision of microfinance. While this chapter recognises that there is no such thing as an 'off the peg' global recipe for microfinance regulation and supervision, it attempts to draw lessons from examples of regulatory policies as implemented in a few emerging economies.

2. Is self-regulation appropriate for microfinance?

Governments may not consider it politically feasible to leave unregulated an industry that provides finance to low-income and poor citizens. However, those in favour of self-regulation tend to point out that governments have a natural tendency to over-regulate, which can result in unnecessary restraints on innovation. Interest rates caps are often used as an example of a restraint on the development of microfinance. In Tunisia, for example, a 5% cap on interest rates has limited the scope and outreach of the microfinance industry. Advocates of self-regulation point out that most of the growth of microfinance over the last 30 years has taken place in the absence of specific financial policies. They note that in Latin America, a pioneer region for microfinance, pushing for a legal framework in the 1970s and 1980s would have considerably limited the development of microfinance. In Bolivia, which along with other Latin American countries has been a leader in building a legal framework for microfinance, most of the growth in microfinance came before the introduction of regulation.[1]

Governments may also be tempted by their political agendas to subsidise or otherwise champion certain MFIs, which may distort competition between microfinance providers and discourage new MFIs from entering the microfinance market. The range of microfinance services offered in Vietnam, for example, is limited, as the state-owned banks that dominate the sector focus on providing microloans which are heavily subsidised by the government. This results in a monopoly of very few microfinance actors, at the cost of broadening the microfinance industry beyond just microloans to include other products such as savings.[2] Some experts therefore argue that it is better for governments to exercise 'benign neglect', or 'regulation by winking', thereby removing microfinance from the political radar.[3]

However, government intervention in microfinance has not always led to over-regulation, restraint of innovation or distortion of competition. In the Philippines, for example, in the early 1990s the government took a pro-microfinance stance. The industry was given enough flexibility to develop, and the government intervened only when required to create an enabling regulatory environment. A national strategy for microfinance was formally adopted in 1996. Among its key features was an exemption from rules on interest rates. The government also removed itself from direct involvement in providing microfinance and eliminating subsidy-based microfinance programmes. Legal structures were developed that recognised MFIs' need for suitable legal vehicles in order to operate. The variety of legal structures available meant that strong microfinance non-governmental organisations (NGOs) were able to convert to other more formal structures, without necessarily having to

---

1 Imboden, K and Barry, N "Policies, Regulations and Systems that Promote Sustainable Financial Services for the Poor and Poorest" (2002).

2 The Economist Intelligence Unit "Global Microscope of the Microfinance Business Environment 2011" (2011).

3 Peck Christen, R and Rosenberg, R "The Rush to Regulate: Legal Frameworks for Microfinance" (1999).

become fully fledged commercial banks and incurring the corresponding costs of compliance, reporting and taxation. The microfinance sector still enjoys the legacy from this pro-microfinance stance adopted by government, and the Philippines were recently described as having had "a strong enabling environment for microfinance for more than a decade."[4] In several other countries, including Ghana, Uganda, Zambia, Bolivia or Peru, governments have adopted measures to create microfinance-friendly legal structures that have enabled regulated MFIs to mobilise equity, savings and borrowings.[5] With respect to the available legal structures, clearly MFIs would not be able to operate properly without government intervention, since these structures can be implemented only by way of formal legislation. The lack of appropriate legal structures has been identified as an obstacle to the development of microfinance in certain countries, such as Egypt, where the only available entities to provide microfinance services are either NGOs or fully regulated banks.[6]

Creating a clear legal and regulatory framework that balances the objectives of improving access to finance with the soundness of the financial system at large is an important factor in the stability and attractiveness of the microfinance industry of a particular country. This is especially true given the increasing involvement of commercial actors and international development financial institutions in the financing of MFIs.

Government intervention in financial regulation at large may also be necessary to correct market imperfections. This became particularly apparent in the context of microfinance following the crises of 2008 and 2009 in various countries (including India, Morocco and Bosnia and Herzegovina), which saw indebtedness rise to unsustainable levels amongst microfinance borrowers. Although, as discussed later in this chapter, these crises also revealed the relevance of self-regulation efforts, most governments in the affected countries responded by reinforcing the regulatory framework and strengthening consumer protection, with measures including requiring MFIs to exchange credit information about borrowers to prevent multiple lending and over-indebtedness, and banning abusive collection practices and unfair and high-pressure selling practices.

3. Prudential and non-prudential regulation

As in mainstream finance, the distinction between prudential and non-prudential regulation in microfinance is key. Many of the regulatory concerns relevant to other financial institutions also apply to microfinance. It is therefore instructive to consider the types of regulation which apply generally to financial institutions, and more particularly those institutions which deal with individuals.

---

4 The Economist Intelligence Unit "Global Microscope of the Microfinance Business Environment 2011" (2011).

5 In Bolivia, for example, private financial funds were created, which are formal financial institutions licensed to engage in a wide range of lending and some saving activities. They are an intermediary legal form between an NGO and a fully licensed bank. Their minimum capital requirements are lower than those for commercial banks, and they are not allowed to provide certain services that banks provide (eg, underwriting, asset management) (Malamut, G "Microfinance in Brazil, Bolivia and Bangladesh" (2005)).

6 USAid and CGAP "The Legal and Regulatory Environment for Microfinance in Egypt – diagnostic study with focus on NGO-MFI transformation issues" (2009).

Prudential regulation seeks to protect the soundness, financial health and stability of the financial system. It ensures that financial institutions behave without taking excessive risks that could affect their performance and endanger the safety of small deposits. Prudential regulation includes rules on reporting, as well as capital adequacy and liquidity requirements. In the case of prudential regulation, the regulator vouches for the soundness of the licensed financial institutions. This 'guarantee' implies that the licensed institution complies with the prudential norms, and in turn that the supervisor dedicates resources to ensure adequate supervision and, if necessary, enforcement. As a result, compliance with prudential rules is costly for both the supervised institution and the supervisor.

The cost of prudential regulation is clearly justified when the stability of the financial system or the safety of depositors is at risk. One of the key objectives of prudential regulation is to ensure that deposits are protected, and in the vast majority of jurisdictions it applies only to institutions (including MFIs) which take savings from the public. Because credit-only MFIs (that is, MFIs that only lend) do not take deposits, in most countries they are not prudentially regulated. However, these MFIs are often subject to non-prudential regimes intended to protect consumers from mis-selling, coercive lending practices and other abusive practices. Such regulation seeks to promote good behaviour in the financial system, and includes rules on consumer protection, information disclosure, fair business practices, prevention of fraud and financial crimes and the implementation of credit bureaux. Non-prudential rules allow credit-only MFIs to evolve sustainably within a structure of regulatory requirements and guidelines, while protecting the interests of vulnerable customers.

4. Can prudential regulatory norms be subject to self-regulation?

Prudential regulation requires government intervention in order to provide a consistent framework. Capital adequacy, liquidity ratios and other prudential rules are almost universally established by either primary legislation adopted by governments, or in some cases by secondary legislation adopted by government regulatory authorities. Due to the systemic importance of prudential norms, it is difficult to argue that prudential norm-making should be left to industry bodies without any government intervention.

However, a distinction needs to be drawn between making prudential rules on the one hand, and enforcing and monitoring them on the other. While government intervention is largely accepted in respect of the former, banking supervisors may not view the supervision of deposit-taking MFIs as the best allocation of their resources and may consider that the monitoring and enforcement can be carried out by the industry.[7]

Some countries have tried self-regulation as an alternative way of prudentially regulating deposit-taking MFIs, especially in cases where the regulator was already over-stretched by regulating and enforcing prudential norms for the traditional banking system. This was the case, for example, in the Dominican Republic and

7 CGAP "A Guide to Regulation and Supervision of Microfinance – Consensus Guidelines" (2011).

Guatemala, where strong MFIs created federations whose missions included monitoring and enforcing prudential rules.[8]

However, as noted by the World Bank's Consultative Group to Assist the Poorest (CGAP), prudential self-regulation has been tried several times, especially in developing countries, and has not yet been effective in protecting the soundness of the regulated entities.[9] One central issue (examined in more detailed later in this chapter) is the inherent conflict of interest due to the supervisor being controlled by the supervised entities. Other issues include enforcement – that is, the fact that the supervisor is likely to prove powerless when a supervised entity does not comply with the rules. This is especially likely in the case of large federations whose board members also run large MFIs.

5. Prudential regulation for all deposit-taking MFIs including small entities?

Small deposit-taking MFIs pose a practical problem for regulators. Some regulators might be inclined to take the view that all deposits, no matter how small and no matter how poor the depositor, should be protected and therefore prudentially regulated. From this perspective, entities which cannot comply with prudential rules are not deemed safe enough to take deposits, and therefore should not exist (at least not as deposit takers). However, the argument that all deposit-taking institutions, regardless of their size, should be effectively supervised becomes more difficult in the case of member-based deposit-taking MFIs that are so small, and so geographically remote, that it might not be cost-effective for the regulator to supervise them[10] effectively.

While in theory the principle that any institution that cannot be prudentially regulated should not exist might seem reasonable, it does not take into account the realities of the market which microfinance providers try to serve. As demonstrated in countless studies, poor people can and do save.[11] Where formal deposit accounts are not available, they use savings instruments such as putting cash under the mattress, joining informal rotating savings, or placing money with neighbours or relatives. These vehicles are often expensive. In most cases they are also riskier than opening a formal account with a small unsupervised intermediary. Eliminating the small local deposit-taking MFI may therefore increase the risks faced by poor savers by forcing them back into informal savings systems.

Under this perspective, a self-regulation system for small deposit-taking member-based intermediaries might be better than no regulation at all. This ensures that these small entities have a set of rules to follow designed by industry players, even though they are not formally licensed by the regulator. In Ghana, for example, the Ghana Cooperative Susu Collectors Association is an umbrella organisation for Susu collectors (ie, individuals who collect small savings from customers) which seeks to encourage and mobilise savings and improve public confidence in the Susu system

8 Peck Christen, R and Rosenberg, R "Regulating Microfinance – The Options" (2000).
9 CGAP "A Guide to Regulation and Supervision of Microfinance – Consensus Guidelines" (2011).
10 CGAP "A Guide to Regulation and Supervision of Microfinance – Consensus Guidelines" (2011).
11 See http://econ.worldbank.org/.

by imposing a number of barriers to entry to the association. This cooperative effectively regulates the operations of Susu collectors.[12] The lack of prudential licensing might seem detrimental to the depositors at first, but it may in fact be better not to create an expectation in depositors that the government is effectively overseeing and guaranteeing their deposits.

Thus, although the case for government intervention in the case of prudential regulation is compelling, it might not be so obvious in the case of small deposit-taking MFIs which do not necessarily pose a systemic risk on the financial system, and for which forced closure might be more detrimental to the consumers which the microfinance industry tries to serve. This shows that the issue of government intervention or self-regulation in microfinance is not all black and white, and needs to be carefully considered in light of the variety of actors active in microfinance.

6. Self-regulation and financial cooperatives

Financial cooperatives are particularly pertinent to an analysis of government intervention versus self-regulation of the microfinance industry. Financial cooperatives are entities which are owned and run by the borrowers and depositors. In many countries they are the main providers of financial services to the poor, and they may sometimes, together with other forms of microfinance providers, hold deposits that exceed in number those held by banks.[13] In developed countries, financial cooperatives that lend to and take deposits from their members tend to be prudentially regulated, regardless of their size, with prudential norms adapted to the nature, size and impact of the relevant financial cooperative.[14] In most developing countries, however, federations of financial cooperatives[15] are more likely to be self-regulating and self-supervising.

As financial cooperatives use members' deposits to fund their lending activities, it can be argued that they do not need to be prudentially regulated because they are not endangering the public's deposits. However, as noted by CGAP, when membership is open to anyone living in a particular geographic area there is not much difference between the public and members of the cooperative (anyone can make a deposit simply by paying the membership fee and joining the cooperative). The Basel Report on microfinance notes that even though cooperative members have the power to elect the management, the cooperative structure implies an inherent conflict of interest because the "owners are also borrowers and depositors". This can lead to "poor credit underwriting and management, inappropriate loans to related parties, and fraud". In practice, members might not take the time, or have the expertise, to oversee the actions of the board effectively. As such, members of a

---

12 See www.accion.org/Page.aspx?pid=1470.

13 The Basel Report "Microfinance Activities and the Core Principles for Effective Banking Supervision" (2010) cites the example of Nicaragua where the microfinance sector serves around 53% of all borrowers in the financial system. Looking at loans specifically, the Basel Report further notes that sometimes the number of loans from non-regulated banks may surpass those granted by conventional banks. The Basel Report cites the example of Bangladesh, where recent figures show microcredit providers hold nearly 7 million outstanding loans, compared to around 4.5 million in regulated banks.

14 Basel Report "Microfinance Activities and the Core Principles for Effective Banking Supervision" (2010).

15 Gallardo, J. "A Framework for Regulating Microfinance Institutions: The Experience of Ghana and the Philippines" (2001).

financial cooperative might not be more able to oversee the governance of the board than depositors of a conventional bank (except perhaps in the case of very small financial cooperatives). Thus, the fact that financial cooperatives are run and operated only by their members does not necessarily mean that they should not be prudentially regulated and that they can be left to be self-regulation.

7. Non-prudential regulation

Non-prudential regulation is about ensuring the good behaviour of the financial system. It is often referred to as 'conduct of business' regulation. It does not require the government to intervene to ensure the stability of the financial system or protect small depositors. As such, it is often described as a type of regulation that can largely be self-executed.[16] Credit-only MFIs are generally subject only to non-prudential regulation, as it would be too burdensome and unsustainable for entities which do not take deposits from the public to comply with prudential rules.

Several non-prudential regulatory issues are relevant to microfinance. These include permission to lend, consumer protection, credit information services, prevention of fraud and financial crimes, and setting up interest rate policies.

The recent crises of over-indebtedness in the microfinance industry, and the reported cases of unethical lending practices have highlighted two non-prudential regulatory issues that are especially relevant to microfinance:

- protecting borrowers against abusive lending and collection practices; and
- protecting both borrowers and MFIs against multiple lending by promoting credit information services and general transparency about the cost of loans.

Self-regulation, particularly when it is implemented by large microfinance associations or networks, can contribute significantly to the promotion of effective client protection practices and the building of expected behaviour in the local microfinance market. As highlighted in the SEEP Network study,[17] although regulators have a role in pointing out unacceptable practices and setting out the rules, industry players have a greater impact on determining the best way to implement those rules, and on translating general concepts around unethical lending into specific rules regarding training and internal controls.[18]

Efforts at self-regulation often materialise in large microfinance associations producing codes of conduct, or codes of ethics. In Mexico, for example, the largest microfinance association (ProDesarollo) helped to build a standard of MFI behaviour by adopting a code of ethics with different levels of certification according to the standards of client protection and transparency committed to by each MFI.

The examples of self-regulation in India, Mexico, Pakistan, Ghana and other countries have shown the potential benefits of self-regulation. These include a more cost-effective management of a larger number of MFIs than is possible under more general and inflexible global standards, and a feasible alternative to official

16 CGAP "A Guide to Regulation and Supervision of Microfinance – Consensus Guidelines" (2011).

17 SEEP Network "Codes of Conduct and the Role of Microfinance Associations in Client Protection" (2012).

18 As above.

supervision in environments where the government's supervisory capacity may be limited. Efforts at self-regulation, especially when they are carried out by a network covering the majority of MFIs, can help individual MFIs strengthen their reputation and inject credibility into the national microfinance industry. The Ghana Microfinance Institutions Network, for example, was created out of a research programme sponsored by the World Bank that was designed to strengthen MFIs. It now represents the majority of institutions in Ghana that provide microfinance services, and has established a number of policies to, among other things, educate MFIs on best practices and enhance integration between the formal and informal sector.

8. Self-regulation in the aftermath of the microfinance crises

The crises in the microfinance industries of countries including India, Pakistan, Morocco, Nicaragua and Bosnia and Herzegovina have arguably highlighted the relevance of self-regulation efforts through microfinance networks. In each of these countries, the crises occurred after a period of intense growth in the microfinance sector. An examination of the causes of these crises has shown some fundamental weaknesses within the microfinance industry of each of these countries.[19] These include:

- multiple borrowing with little or no control over the borrower's credit profile;
- overstretched MFI internal systems and controls due to rapid growth; and
- weakening of MFI lending discipline.

As pointed out by the SEEP Network study, each of these vulnerabilities can be addressed through the type of self-regulation that is often contained in a code of conduct.

The Indian Microfinance Institutions Network (MFIN) has shown the role that self-regulation can play in building (or restoring, as the case may be) the reputation of the microfinance industry. The MFIN was created in 2009 by a group of MFIs which saw the need for an industry body which could show their commitment to good practices, at a time when the Indian sector was expanding rapidly with many MFIs growing at over 100% per year. The rapid and intense growth of the Indian microfinance industry had several unintended negative consequences, culminating in a crisis that gained international attention in late 2010, and which causes included, among others, severe competition between MFIs and a geographic concentration of client loans, multiple lending with clients unable to repay multiple loans, and coercive collection practices with allegations of abusive practices. The lack of effective credit information sharing became apparent in the aftermath of the crisis. In seeking to address this issue, the MFIN now requires its members to join a credit bureau, and to submit action plans to the association to ensure the sharing of credit information.

When Pakistan's local microfinance industry experienced a crisis of its own, the

19 SEEP Network "Codes of Conduct and the Role of Microfinance Associations in Client Protection" (2012).

Pakistan Microfinance Network (PMN) also undertook considerable self-regulation efforts to improve the health of the sector. By 2008 increased competition between MFIs resulted in high levels of parallel borrowings by clients, which was increasingly tolerated by the MFIs themselves. The PMN launched a pilot credit bureau in 2010, and MFIs are now required to report to this credit bureau as a condition of their membership to the network. The PMN also developed an innovative way to monitor bad practices in the market by putting in place a 'staff bureau'. This is based on the same idea as a credit bureau, but tracks past and current employees of PMN members who have committed fraud at work to warn other MFIs against hiring them.

9. The limits of self-regulation

Notwithstanding its flexibility, pragmatism and cost-effectiveness, there are very clear limits to self-regulation. Most prominently, these include challenges relating to monitoring, enforcement and conflicts of interest. The absence of enforcement powers may leave MFIs with few incentives to comply with codes of conduct. This could in turn lead to a significant number of institutions falling outside the orbit of the voluntary associations and continuing to use price obfuscation and other unethical practices that tarnish the reputation of the industry as a whole. It can also be difficult for associations to achieve consensus amongst their members on standards for codes of conduct.[20] Even where consensus is achieved, the associations may not cover the majority of MFIs in the market. The ProDesarollo network in Mexico, for example, covers around 85 financial institutions, which includes many leading MFIs, but does not cover hundreds of other MFIs and consumer credit institutions in the Mexican microfinance market.[21]

Along with the issue of monitoring MFIs' behaviour and adherence to codes of conduct, conflict of interest is an inherent issue when those who are responsible for promoting, overseeing and enforcing a code are also running the institutions that must be bound by it. A 'supervisory' entity put in place by the members being supervised may not command credibility, and may be tempted to promote rules more convenient to larger MFIs that are more strongly represented in the federation.

Even in the area of pricing transparency, disclosure and consumer protection,

---

20 In Bolivia, for example, the largest microfinance network in the country (ASOFIN) has yet to issue a clear consumer protection policy (www.centerforfinancialinclusion.org/publications-a-resources/client-protection-library/99-summary-of-client-protection-in-bolivia).

21 SEEP Network "Codes of Conduct and the Role of Microfinance Associations in Client Protection" (2012).

22 The 'flat rate' method refers to a method of calculating the interest rate on a loan where interest is charged on the full original loan amount throughout the loan term, rather than on the money that is actually on the borrower's balance at any one time. On the contrary, using the 'declining balance' method, the interest rate calculation is based on the outstanding loan balance. As the borrower repays instalments, the remaining loan balance declines over time, so although the interest rate remains the same, it represents a smaller amount of money because the balance is less than the original amount. Therefore, the interest payments under the flat rate method tend to be significantly higher than under the declining rate method. Interestingly, the flat rate calculation is widely used in microfinance, but it is much less used in countries which operate under legislation that promotes the use of the declining balance method (eg, Latin American countries). For example in Colombia only about 3% of MFIs use the flat rate method, whereas the percentage is as high as 81% in Kenya (MFTransparency, www.mftransparency.org/wp-content/uploads/2012/05/MFT-BRF-205-EN-Flat-versus-Declining-Balance-Interest-Rates-What-is-the-Difference-2011-09.pdf).

regulatory rules can achieve wider market coverage than most association-driven efforts. In 2001, for example, the National Bank of Cambodia prohibited the use of flat interest rate calculations.[22] Analysis by MFTransparency[23] has shown that this measure helped to increase pricing transparency and diminish borrowing costs across the entire microfinance sector, something which is not always feasible for even the most powerful national MFI association.[24] Since non-prudential rules such as transparency and disclosure of the cost of loans are relatively rules-based, some experts have argued that where clear guidance can be established for all institutions, such rules lend themselves well to a legal and regulatory approach to developing market standards that can be applied broadly and enforced effectively.[25]

10. The importance of the market context

The success of self-regulation will largely depend on the local context, in particular the balance between political stability, resources of the financial regulator and level of influence and market share coverage of microfinance associations. In politically volatile markets, mature microfinance associations can have a very significant impact in promoting the credibility and contributing to the health of the local microfinance industry.

The existence of a clear client protection legal framework (or lack thereof) also greatly determines whether self-regulation is necessary. In Bosnia and Herzegovina, for example, there are no specific laws for consumer protection in financial services. The country's primary network (AMFI), which covers 98% of MFI clients in Bosnia, has adopted a code of business ethics that includes provisions on transparency of pricing and conditions and resolution of consumer complaints.[26] Haiti offers another example, where the absence of legislative or regulatory leadership has led MFIs themselves to promote and implement standards that protect client interests.[27]

11. Partnership between public and private bodies

There are several examples of effective partnerships between private microfinance actors and governments in the areas of consumer protection, transparency and other non-prudential issues, especially in countries with more mature microfinance industries.

Financial literacy and consumer protection are two areas that offer opportunities for public and private bodies to partner and develop joint initiatives. The consultation of private bodies allows for flexibility and realistic attention to the actual issues that need to be addressed, while the intervention of a regulator may allow initiatives to achieve a national scale in their outreach. In Peru, one of the few countries where the regulator is committed to financial education programmes, the central bank, in consultation and coordination with industry players, has devised a

---

23 See www.mftransparency.org/resources/cambodian-law-calculation-interest-rate-microfinance-loans/
24 Mazer, R "Can Self-Regulation work to protect Clients?" (2012).
25 As above.
26 See www.accion.org/Page.aspx?pid=1417.
27 See www.centerforfinancialinclusion.org/publications-a-resources/client-protection-library/104 summary-of-client-protection-in-haiti.

wide range of financial education campaigns (including broad advertising campaigns informing the general population of the benefits and risks of financial products).[28]

Self-regulation efforts through codes of conduct are useful in the area of over-indebtedness because they allow the sector itself to define the boundaries around reckless and responsible lending. Microfinance associations can identify issues and establish industry standards, but regulators can champion transparency on costs of loans and lending practices, encourage the use of credit bureaus and supervise and enforce guidelines.

Approaching non-prudential regulation as a partnership between governments and private actors permits another view of regulation beyond the binary distinction of self-regulation or government intervention. A 'delegated supervision' model can be envisaged, for example, whereby the regulator maintains legal responsibility for the supervised institutions, but delegates site visits and general monitoring to a third party. Peru offers an example, where the financial regulator has delegated day-to-day supervision to a federation of savings and loan institutions.[29] Despite delegating supervision, the Peruvian financial regulator retains control over the independence and quality of the federation's supervisory work, and performs an annual on-site supervision visit of each supervised institution.

In establishing self-regulatory norms, some microfinance federations recognise that they cannot replace the prudential regulation and supervision of a government regulator, and view their self-regulation efforts as a complement rather than a replacement. In India, for example, regulatory licensing by the Reserve Bank of India (RBI) is a pre-requisite for membership in the MFIN. Membership does not replace compliance with government regulation, but it means that the MFIN's members are already compliant with the prudential rules of the RBI, and have in addition chosen to become members of the MFIN as a sign of their commitment to good practice in the areas of client protection, sharing of client information and prevention of over-indebtedness.[30]

12. The importance of proportionality in the context of microfinance regulation

Flexibility is key to the growth of microfinance. This has been explicitly recognised by international financial sector standard-setting bodies, including the Basel Committee on Banking Supervision, the Financial Action Task Force and the International Association of Insurance Supervisors. All have endorsed the principle of proportionality – that is, the balance of risks and benefits against the costs of regulation and supervision.

The Basel Report on microfinance recommends that non-banks that mobilise deposits from the public should be subject to prudential regulation and supervision, but such regulation and supervision should be proportionate to the type and size of their transactions. The report distinguishes between the following sets of core principles:

28 CGAP and World Bank "The State of Financial Inclusion through the Crisis" (2010).
29 Peck Christen, R and Rosenberg, R "The Rush to Regulate: Legal Frameworks for Microfinance" (1999).
30 SEEP Network "Codes of Conduct and the Role of Microfinance Associations in Client Protection" (2012).

- those that should apply equally to banks and other deposit-taking institutions in microfinance regardless of the nature of microfinance activities and the size of MFIs (including principles relating to independence, transparency and cooperation, or major acquisitions); and
- those that require a tailored approach to ensure proportional regulation and supervision (including principles relating to permissible activities, licensing criteria or capital adequacy).

The report further emphasises that compliance with prudential rules and other requirements can be costly for both supervised institutions and supervisors in comparison to the risks posed. It recommends that regulators focus their attention on the prevention of systemic risks so as to allow the microfinance industry enough flexibility to innovate and grow.[31]

In the debate between self-regulation versus government intervention, the principle of proportionality requires regulators to realise the feasibility of regulating and supervising a microfinance industry that is comprised of many small, unconventional financial institutions. Rather than leaving the industry to be regulated by industry players, or imposing heavy government regulation, some regulators have embraced a 'tiered' approach, proportionate to the type, complexity and size of each MFI's transactions. This adaptation to regulatory norms means that in some instances, the regulator might employ a light-touch, leaving more scope for industry players to establish self-regulated industry norms.

Flexibility can be achieved by creating a special regulatory framework tailored to the characteristics and risk profile of MFIs. This approach is known as the 'special window' for microfinance and allows MFIs to be inserted into the regulatory structure according to the range of financial services they provide. Peru provides an example of this approach, where the regulatory regime depends on the range of financial services MFIs provide. Other countries which use a tiered financial and regulatory structure include Bolivia, Ghana, Uganda, Zambia and the Philippines. Although there are considerable variations between these systems, one common denominator is the adaptation of banking laws and regulation to microfinance. Prudential requirements such as minimum capitalisation are significantly lower for MFIs than those for conventional commercial banks. The countries with 'special windows' for microfinance have also adopted microfinance-friendly legal structures to allow MFIs to graduate from NGOs and semi-formal MFIs into legitimate institutions under a clear regulatory framework with greater access to funding from commercial markets.[32] In Zambia, for example, MFIs that are not yet safe for deposits from the general public can be granted a 'halfway banking licence', which sets out which transactions (and of what size) the MFI can and cannot do according to the risk profile of the institution.

Interestingly, the Basel Report is cautious in its praise of tiered structures within a special window: "tiered frameworks have had mixed results, since in some

31 The Basel Report "Microfinance Activities and the Core Principles for Effective Banking Supervision" (2010).

32 Gallardo, J "A Framework for Regulating Microfinance Institutions: The Experience of Ghana and the Philippines" (2001).

countries there are... too few qualifying entities to justify the resources expended to licence and oversee them".[33] From this perspective, the constraint appears to be a shortage of licensable MFIs, rather than the absence of a regulatory regime specific to microfinance. This may in turn add support to arguments for self-regulation, to let the industry develop and allow new players to enter a market free from government intervention. However, in the long run, MFIs need to evolve within a stable and clear regulatory framework that is adapted to their activities (and clients). This is even more true for deposit-taking MFIs.

13. New regulatory challenges: mobile banking

Mobile banking has emerged in recent years as an innovative and powerful way to implement financial inclusion and reach remote rural areas where the poorest are often located.

However, regulators face the challenge of defining a regulatory regime for mobile network operators and telecommunication companies which were not previously subject to financial regulation and supervision.

Given their limited activities and the small funds involved, non-bank e-money issuers do not necessarily present a systemic risk. Most countries in which they operate have so far taken a minimal approach to their regulation and supervision.[34] This is consistent with the principle of proportionality, where the regulator recognises that burdensome regulation and supervision may restrain the industry and disincentivise new market entrants.

Does this mean that mobile banking should be free from government intervention and regulated solely by market actors? The CGAP Microfinance Consensus Guidelines point out that "in many countries, industry innovation has been ahead of policy makers... and in some countries, branchless banking has thrived because of the absence of regulation". However, if the mobile banking industry is to grow, adequate, but proportionate, regulation and supervision will be key to its safety and credibility.

Non-bank e-money issuers face two risks in particular:

- significant or total loss of customer funds due to decapitalisation or failure of the issuer; and
- loss of liquidity due to the unavailability of customer funds.

Customer protection and transparency measures are also particularly important as mobile banking presents clear risks of fraud. In this context, the creation by the government of an enabling regulatory environment can help the wide-scale use of mobile banking in the financial inclusion agenda, as opposed to limited and *ad hoc* initiatives. In Mexico, for example, recent regulations on branchless banking have created a framework for the industry to develop a variety of branchless banking services.[35] Equally, in Pakistan, new regulations allow telecommunication companies

---

33 The Basel Report "Microfinance Activities and the Core Principles for Effective Banking Supervision" (2010).

34 CGAP Brief "Supervising Nonbank E-Money Issuers) (2012).

35 Faz, X and Breloff, P "Mexico: Promising Moves Towards New Banking Models" (2011).

to take ownership in banks and observers have noted that the market has since developed in several directions, with some banks leading their own branchless microfinance services, and some telecommunication companies acquiring microfinance licences.[36]

14. Conclusion

Self-regulation can be important to the development of the microfinance industry and standard-setting, especially in countries where governments do not have the resources or political appetite to devise a regulatory framework for microfinance. However, as argued in this chapter, except in limited circumstances, self-regulation is not appropriate to designing and enforcing prudential laws, which are too important to the stability of the financial system and to the protection of small deposits.

In the long run, the microfinance industry cannot grow, innovate and reach its full potential unless it benefits from a clear regulatory environment that balances the needs of advancing financial inclusion and the social goals of microfinance with the stability of the financial system. The need for a clear regulatory framework does not make self-regulation irrelevant, or redundant. Rather, the most effective regulation of microfinance seems to be one which recognises that regulation and supervision imply significant costs (including non-financial costs such as restraint of innovation) and creates a realistic and proportionate regulatory framework, which may involve removing government intervention in areas where the industry needs to self-regulate, but also implements clear and consistent rules, especially in those areas that require prudential attention.

---

36 Rotman, S "Variations on a Theme: Business Models in Branchless Banking" (2012).

Microfinance and the empowerment of women

Tara S Nair
Gujarat Institute of Development Research, Ahmedabad, Gujarat

1. Introduction

The idea of empowerment gained currency among women's movements during the 1980s, drawing upon the ideas of liberation theology and the renewed interest in Gramsci's concepts of cultural hegemony and the subalterns. Its origins, however, can be traced back much further to the 16th-century European Reformation. It evolved through many social justice movements through the subsequent years and across continents before it acquired political vigour in the 1960s and 1970s, the decades when liberation theology held sway as the revolutionary religious movement that upheld the hopes and the ambitions of the poor.[1]

Empowerment emerged as a dominant theme in the discourse on women, gender and development during the 1990s thanks mainly to the efforts of women's movements around the world and the active involvement of non-government organisations and people's movements. Special mention must be made of the International Conference on Population and Development held in Cairo in 1994. Here was articulated in concrete terms the significance of women's empowerment as a development goal worth pursuing for its intrinsic worth.

> *The empowerment and autonomy of women and the improvement of their political, social, economic and health status is a highly important end in itself... The power relations that impede women's attainment of healthy and fulfilling lives operate at many levels of society, from the most personal to the highly public. Achieving change requires policy and programme actions that will improve women's access to secure livelihoods and economic resources, alleviate their extreme responsibilities with regard to housework, remove legal impediments to their participation in public life, and raise social awareness through effective programmes of education and mass communication. In addition, improving the status of women also enhances their decision-making capacity at all levels in all spheres of life.*[2]

Subsequently, the Human Development Report 1995 focused on the theme of gender and human development. It made the revolutionary statement that human development "if not engendered, is endangered".[3] "Women must be regarded as

1 Batliwala, Srilatha (2007) "Taking Power out of Empowerment: An Experiential Account", *Development in Practice*, Vol 17, No 4/5, pp 557–565. This article is based on an unpublished work by John Gaventa that describes the evolution of the concept of empowerment.

2 United Nations (1994) "Report of the International Conference on Population and Development (Cairo, 5-13 September 1994)", United Nations Population Information Network (POPIN), p 25. Available at www.un.org/popin/icpd/conference/offeng/poa.html (accessed February 28 2013).

agents and beneficiaries of change", it went on to state. "Investing in women's capabilities and empowering them to exercise their choices is not only valuable in itself but is also the surest way to contribute to economic growth and overall development".[4] The report introduced two measures for capturing gender disparities – the gender-related development index (GDI) and the gender empowerment measure (GEM). While the GDI is a modification of the Human Development Index that takes account of the inequality between women and men as well as the average achievement of all people taken together, the GEM focuses on variables that reflect women's participation in political decision making, their access to professional opportunities and their earning power.[5] Thus, the GDI concerns the development of capabilities and the GEM concerns their use in accessing economic, political and professional opportunities.[6]

The first Microcredit Summit, held in early 1997 in Washington, DC, adopted "reaching and empowering women" as one of its core themes. The special focus of microfinance on women was justified on the following bases:

- women are better credit risks than men;
- women-run businesses are more likely to benefit families directly; and
- economic returns help women improve their status not only within their families, but also within their communities and nations.

Studies of the association of microcredit with poverty and women's status and empowerment had already begun to appear in the mid-1990s. This was thanks to the convergence in interests of feminist scholars who were grappling with the challenges of developing the concept and measurement of empowerment, and microfinance researchers who wanted to explore how credit and saving services served women's interests. Microcredit is a market-led approach to development, and these enquiries contributed to the wider discussion on the relationship between the spread of pro-market economic ideology and women's participation in markets, in terms of both productive and reproductive activities. Feminist scholarship around development planning received a further boost thanks to a general rise in interest in understanding of the dynamics of 'women and finance'.

Before reviewing some of the important observations about the relationship between microfinance and empowerment, it is appropriate to discuss the concept of empowerment in some detail.

2. Empowerment: the conceptual boundaries

The term 'empowerment' encapsulates the process of redistribution of power in favour of previously powerless individuals and social groups so that they can start to exercise greater control over their lives.[7] The gendered meaning of empowerment is

---

3 United Nations Development Programme (1995) *Human Development Report 1995*. New York/Oxford: Oxford University Press.

4 *Ibid*, p 2.

5 *Ibid*.

6 It must be noted that promoting gender equality and women's empowerment is among the eight Millennium Development Goals (MDG) adopted by the United Nations in 2000.

therefore "the transformation of the relations of power between men and women, within and across social categories".[8] This process is critical to the development of a gender-equal society in which rights, obligations and opportunities are enjoyed equally by men and women. According to Batliwala the process of empowerment rearranges social power in three ways:

> *by challenging the ideologies that justify social inequality (such as gender or caste), by changing prevailing patterns of access to and control over economic, natural, and intellectual resources, and by transforming the institutions and structures that reinforce and sustain existing power structures (such as the family, state, market, education, and media).*[9]

In other words, power needs to be understood in two ways. First, as control over physical, financial, human and intellectual resources or extrinsic control. Second, as control over ideology – that is, values, beliefs and attitudes, or intrinsic control.[10] Gaining control over one's physical and material resources and expanding one's self-consciousness are closely connected. Neither improving access to material resources without helping women to be or to express themselves, or changing awareness and building confidence without removing barriers to resources, can sustain empowerment.[11] In both of these situations others would gradually take control away from women's hands.

Kabeer explores the concept of empowerment through three closely related dimensions: agency, resources and achievements. "Agency represents the processes by which choices are made and put into effect... Resources are the medium through which agency is exercised; and achievements refer to the outcomes of agency".[12] Kabeer's scheme highlights that in understanding empowerment it is not enough to identify whether individuals make choices. More critical is the concept of agency: how individuals see themselves or their self worth, and the terms on which resources are made available to individuals.

3. Evidence from research

Several studies published between 1996 and 2005 sought to scrutinise the potential of microcredit initiatives to empower women. They helped highlight those aspects of microfinance that were most important to transforming the lives of poor women. According to Doward, Kidd, Morrison and Poulton,[13] these included:

- the provision of small, short-term loans;
- compulsory and regular savings and repayments;

---

7 Sen, Gita (1997) "Empowerment as an Approach to Poverty", Working Paper Series No 97.07. Bangalore: Indian Institute of Management; Sen, Gita and Srilatha Batliwala (2000) "Empowering Women for Reproductive Rights", *Women's Empowerment and Demographic Processes: Moving beyond Cairo*, ed. Harriet B. Presser and Gita Sen. Oxford: Oxford University Press.

8 Batliwala (2007).

9 *Ibid*, p 560.

10 Sen (1997).

11 *Ibid*; Sen and Batliwala (2000), p 18.

12 Kabeer (2005a), p 14.

13 Doward, Andrew, Jonathan Kydd, Jamie Morrison and Colin Poulton (2005), "Institutions, Markets and Economic Co-ordination: Linking Development Theory and Praxis", *Development and Change*, Vol. 36, No 1, pp 1–25.

- the gradual building up of individual and group funds to act as loan collateral and to meet emergencies;
- preference for production loans;
- group lending to reduce transaction costs for the microfinance institution and to encourage peer pressure;
- graduated access to increasing loan sizes;
- effective management information systems; and
- socially and geographically accessible loan officers with clear incentives and delegated authority.

Some researchers[14] saw that the inflexibility of loan purpose and insistence of small loan size created bottlenecks for those women who possess entrepreneurial skills but lack the necessary capital. Although the indicators chosen and methodologies adopted varied between studies, they raised critical questions about the role and limits of microfinance in affecting not only the historically gendered distribution of formal financial resources, but also the structures of subordination of women in general. Field studies carried out in Asia, Africa and Latin America examined critically the rationale for targeting microcredit exclusively at women, suggested frameworks to operationalise and measure 'empowerment' and analysed the impact of microcredit on the economic functioning and social wellbeing of households as well as the personal endowments of women.[15]

Most of the earliest studies examined the relationship between women's participation in credit programmes and their empowerment in the context of rural Bangladesh, in particular the Grameen and BRAC interventions.[16] One group of studies showed these programmes to be effective in empowering women. They showed that the programmes increased women's contribution to household consumption, expenditure, hours devoted to production and the value of their

---

14 For example, see Joekes, Susan (1999) "Diminished Returns: Increasing Women's Access to Capital Resources", *Harvard International Review*, Fall, pp 54–58.

15 See: Goetz, Anne Marie and Sen Gupta, R (1994) "Who Takes the Credit? Gender, Power and Control over Loan Use in Rural Credit Programmes in Bangladesh", *World Development*, Vol 24, No 1, pp 45–63; Hashemi, Syed M, Sidney Ruth Schuler and Ann P Riley (1996) "Rural Credit Programs and Women's Empowerment in Bangladesh", *World Development*, Vol 24, No 4, pp 635–653; Hunt, Juliet and Nalini Kasynathan (2001) "Pathways to Empowerment? Reflections on Microfinance and Transformation in Gender Relations in South Asia", *Gender and Development*, Vol 9, No 1, pp 42–52; Kabeer, N (2001) "Conflicts over Credit: Reevaluating the Empowerment Potential of Loans to Women in Rural Bangladesh", *World Development*, Vol 29, No 1, pp 63–84; Kabeer, N. (2005a) "Gender Equality and Women's Empowerment: A Critical Analysis of the Third Millennium Development Goal", *Gender and Development*, Vol 13, No 1, pp 13–24; Kabeer, N (2005b) "Is Microfinance a 'Magic Bullet' for Women's Empowerment? Analysis of Findings from South Asia", *Economic and Political Weekly*, Vol 40, Nos. 44/45, pp 4709–4718; Kabeer, Naila and Helzi Noponen (2005) "Social and economic impacts of PRADAN's Self Help Group Microfinance and Livelihoods Promotion Program: Analysis from Jharkhand, India", Working Paper No 11, Improving the Impact of Microfinance on Poverty: Action Research Programme. Brighton: Institute of Development Studies; Mayoux, Linda (1998) "Women's Empowerment and Micro-Finance Programmes: Strategies for Increasing Impact", *Development in Practice*, Vol 8, No 2, pp 235-241; Mayoux, Linda (2003) *Sustainable Learning for Women's Empowerment: Ways forward in Microfinance*. New Delhi: Samskriti; Pitt, Mark M and Shahidur R Khandker (1998) "The Impact of Group-based Credit Programs on Poor Households in Bangladesh: Does the Gender of Participants Matter?", *Journal of Political Economy*, Vol 106, No 5, pp 958–996; and Aminur Rahman (1999) *Women and Microcredit in Rural Bangladesh: Anthropological Study of the Grameen Bank Lending*. Colorado: Westview Press.

16 Goetz and Sen Gupta (1996); Hashemi, Schuler and Riley (1996); Pitt and Khandker (1998); Rahman (1999).

assets. Pitt and Khandker[17] observed that borrowing by women in Bangladesh increased household consumption significantly more than borrowing by men. Their estimates showed that every loan of 100 taka given to women increased spending on household consumption by 18 takas; for men spending increased by only 11 takas. Pitt and Khandker reiterated the positive empowerment effects of microfinance in Bangladesh in a later paper:

> *Credit programs lead to women taking a greater role in household decision making, having greater access to financial and economic resources, having greater social networks, having greater bargaining power vis-à-vis their husbands, and having greater freedom of mobility. They also tend to increase spousal communication in general about family planning and parenting concerns.*[18]

According to Joekes[19] microfinance has generally led to positive outcomes for women. These include increasing their purchasing power, enhancing their non-land asset holding and enabling them to support their own expenditure priorities. In many contexts, women's supply of labour power has also increased marginally. Kabeer makes a persuasive case in favour of microcredit, arguing that lending to women is more efficient and has greater gender-transformatory potential than lending to men. This is because "the entire family is much more likely to benefit economically and women are much more likely to benefit personally and socially".[20] The rationale for such lending need not always be empowerment per se; any intervention that can help reallocate resources in favour of women constitutes a more sustainable route to empowerment.

In another study set in Bangladesh, Goetz and Sen Gupta[21] found that most female borrowers of microcredit exercised little or no managerial control over their loans. This was especially true of those who were married. The women were either unaware of the purpose for which the loans were actually used or had no labour involvement in the activities that the loan was meant to support.

Rahman observed that Bank's methods also contribute considerably to the disempowerment of poor women. Because the model's financial sustainability rests on high levels of loan disbursement and a high rate of recovery, bank workers and borrowing peers put excessive pressure on their female clients. This leads to conflicts between men and women within households and an escalation in domestic violence. In the absence of other options, women enter loan-recycling processes to maintain their regular repayment schedules. This intensifies their debt liability and further increases household tensions and frustrations. Rahman noted the double bind in which poor women find themselves: "In the household they [women] are powerless in relation to their husbands and in the loan centres they are powerless before influential members and bank workers who are mostly men."[22]

More detailed evidence of female empowerment resulting from participation in microfinance has come from India. This can be attributed to the wide variety in

17 Pitt and Khandker (1998).
18 *Ibid*, p 817.
19 Joekes (1999).
20 Kabeer (2001), p 83
21 Goetz and Sen Gupta (1996).
22 Rahman (1999), p 75.

legal/organisational forms of microfinance activity and the considerable diversity in social-cultural forces that influence women's participation in economic activities across the country. Moreover, the use of credit and savings as a strategy to mobilise, organise and empower women took shape in India much earlier, around the mid-1970s. Organisations like the Self Employed Women's Association, Women's Working Forum and Annapurna Parivar have worked since then to mobilise women around issues that impede their economic participation, and make them aware of the significance of saving. The self-help group-bank linkage programme launched in the early 1990s by the National Bank for Agriculture and Rural Development helped galvanise the efforts of many non-governmental organisations, including PRADAN and MYRADA, to dovetail microcredit and thrift approaches with larger programmes of local economic regeneration.

Some studies that have examined these initiatives have found that women with a longer engagement with microfinance organisations gradually come to play a greater role in household decision-making.[23] Kabeer and Naponen found in the case of PRADAN in Jharkhand that those women who were members of self-help groups and also participated in the income generation activities promoted by the organisation "had higher levels of participation in public life and greater likelihood of sole decision making role in the household".[24]

Several studies into the working of microfinance and the self-help group model in India have reported positive effects on the protection of the basic livelihood of poor households. Among the positive economic outcomes mapped at the household level are increased savings, asset holding, the adoption of better production techniques, livelihood diversification and reductions in both poverty and dependence on informal credit agents. However, there is as yet no conclusive evidence that these household gains are shared equally between men and women. In terms of non-material gains, studies indicate that women's participation in microfinance has given them opportunities to engage with public institutions until now inaccessible, such as banks and public offices, in states like Andhra Pradesh, Kerala and Tamil Nadu.

Evidence from India also suggests that organisational philosophies affect the practice and outcomes of microfinance. Chari-Wagh made a comparative study of two organisations, one an NGO with an instrumentalist view of microfinance and the other an organisation driven by feminist political ideals.[25] She argues that the latter has substantial transformatory potential while the former is more transactional in its orientation. Similarly, Kalpana's study of self-help groups in Tamil Nadu contends that self-help promotional organisations that are ideologically founded in women's movements tend to engage with women seeking microfinance with a perspective that extends well beyond assessing the their financial viability.[26] Based on a detailed review of findings from a set of microfinance institutions in India, Kabeer

---

23 Kabeer and Naponen (2005).

24 Kabeer and Naponen (2005), p 32

25 Chari-Wagh (2012) "The Transformational Potential of Microfinance: Two Case Studies", unpublished draft.

26 K Kalpana (2012), "SHG Intermediation and Women's Agency: A View from Tamil Nadu", unpublished draft.

argues that organisations that approach microfinance from the perspective of poverty lending are more likely to improve empowerment than those that follow a minimalist financial system approach and provide solutions that are 'market like'.[27]

Mayoux[28] emphasises the importance of the approach towards performance outcomes that microfinance institutions adopt. She distinguishes between 'empowering' and 'instrumentalist' approaches. Many microfinance organisations target women because they are more docile and are willing to commit more resources in terms of time and energy to reduce programme costs. In other words, such organisations perceive women as relatively cost-efficient, convenient and risk-free instruments for reaching out to households and men. Organisations that follow the empowering approach, on the other hand, target women with the goal of bringing about fundamental changes in gender relations. This requires, among other things, a radical reordering of social and developmental priorities – the attitudes and behaviour of men, the structure and organisation of microfinance institutions and a realignment of the development priorities of donor agencies.

The question of whether microfinance actually empowers women hinges on the delicate relationship between the power to access resources and the power to be oneself. According to Sen[29] one danger of microcredit is that although it focuses on providing access to resources, assets and services, it fails to create spaces in which women can build their self-esteem and self-confidence. Microfinance clients are committed in a rather passive manner despite the use of terms like 'participation' and 'ownership'.

Summarising the experiences of microfinance initiatives in India, Mayoux[30] explains why microfinance does not contribute directly to the development of critical self-consciousness. Women access loans but do not use them. Even when they do, they tend to choose activities that are considered feminine and that yield low incomes, over which they have limited control. Moreover, as male indifference to the changes brought about by the increasing participation of women continues, and the gender division of labour and resources persists, women's workload may increase alongside a rise in domestic disharmony and violence against women. Thus it is not enough to have only a progressive vision regarding empowering women.

Studies of microfinance institutions, like those by Ackerly and Mayoux,[31] have brought forth another set of factors that would make microfinance markets work better for those with few assets. They argue that access to credit must be combined with other services, such as voluntary savings, non-productive loans, insurance, business development services and welfare related services. Many studies have emphasised the advantage that integrated packages have over minimalist credit in making visible changes to clients' lives. Similarly, greater social and financial intermediation has been found to be more empowering than direct banker-client models of delivery.[32]

---

27 Kabeer (2005b).
28 Mayoux (2003).
29 Sen (1997).
30 Mayoux (2003).
31 Ackerly (1995); Mayoux (1998)
32 Holvoet, Nathalie (2005) "The Impact of Microfinance on Decision-Making Agency: Evidence from South India", *Development and Change*, Vol 26, No 1, pp 75–102.

4. Conclusion

There is enough evidence to suggest that access to microfinance can and does make an important contribution to the economic productivity and social wellbeing of poor women and their households. The evidence so far does not suggest that financial markets can adequately address the structural aspects of intra-household relations. It is now acknowledged that easing women's access to credit alone does not translate unproblematically into their control over its use. In other words, access to microfinance for women does not automatically translate into empowerment – any more than do education, political quotas, access to waged work or any of the other interventions that feature in the literature on women's empowerment. There are "no magic bullets, no panaceas, no blueprints, no readymade formulas which bring about the radical structural transformation that the empowerment of the poor, and of poor women, implies".[33]

The social and cultural norms that affect the integration and exclusion of women, the gendered division of labour and the gendered distribution of roles, resources and responsibilities all remain untouched by policies and initiatives that focus mechanistically on increasing women's participation in financial markets. Some have pointed out that improvements to women's productivity in home-based economic activities facilitated through credit may subvert the strategic developmental goal of redistributing power and resources between men and women. Researchers and practitioners are therefore reluctant to place exclusive emphasis on such improvements as a benefit of credit.

As poverty, particularly as experienced by women, has increasingly come to be understood as a multidimensional phenomenon, faith in microfinance as a panacea for the social and economic subordination of women has been greatly moderated. The importance of organisational understanding and philosophy with respect to the links between women, poverty, finance and empowerment is now more greatly appreciated. So too are the processes followed to get women to participate in microfinance activities and organisational strategies needed to mediate the provision of financial services to produce empowering outcomes.

As explained at the start of this chapter, true empowerment means meeting both the practical and strategic gender interests of women. Fulfilling strategic gender interests requires fundamental changes to patriarchal power structures and gendered social relations, and the norms and practices that reinforce them. Such restructuring is only possible over an extended period of time. For this reason, it is important that analyses of empowerment take account of the more modest and incremental improvements in the circumstances that financial access can bring about to improve women's agency to negotiate the practical needs of everyday survival. The opportunity to save in small amounts in self help groups provides poor women in India with some degree of freedom in household decision making. Such small changes can create pathways to empowerment by transforming gender ideologies and building women's confidence to take greater control over their life choices. Efforts are however needed to build on and document evidences of the changes –

33 Kabeer (2005b).

both marginal and substantial – that are valued by women who are part of the microcredit movement.

Microfinance investment vehicles and social performance

Jean-Marie De Corte
Marc Labie
Ludovic Urgeghe
University of Mons, Warocqué School of Business and Economics
Jean-Claude Vansnick
Value Focused Consulting SPRL

1. Introduction

Microfinance investment vehicles (MIVs) have developed tremendously over the last 10 years. This trend has translated into the establishment of more funds (there are now more than 100) and a greater diversity of structures. There are also many more assets under management: $8 billion in 2011 compared to $1 billion in 2004.[1] MIVs are now perceived as key players in microfinance. As well as loans they also – but to a lesser extent – provide equity and guarantee funds.

Although the development of MIVs has been impressive, it has raised questions for the future. Notable among these is the relevance of this means of financing for microfinance institutions (MFIs). Indeed, as already observed in many different countries, MFIs tend in the long run to favour local funding over the use of MIVs, either through the establishment of their own savings products or by contracting local debt from the traditional banking sector.[2] This leaves the question of which MFIs should be targeted for MIV funding.

In theory, there are two basic answers to this question. The first is those MFIs that operate in an environment where local debt from regular commercial banks may not be available. The second is those MFIs that come from what are often called 'second and third tiers' – that is, MFIs that have not yet reached a level of development that allows them to connect directly through the banking and financial markets. Unfortunately, the ability of MIVs to focus on those segments has so far proved limited. In the current market too many funds are going after the same MFIs. This results in a crowding-out effect, where the supply of funds is too great for the amount of demand. The market is thus experiencing bottlenecks and questions are being asked about how future developments should take place.

Different evolutions are possible. A first and logical one would be to assist a

1 Reille X, S Forster and D.Rosas (2011) "Foreign Capital Investment in Microfinance: Reassessing Financial and Social Returns", *CGAP Focus Note*, No. 71. Washington, DC: CGAP.

2 Portocarrero Maisch, F, A Tarazona Soria and GD Westley (2006) "How should microfinance institutions best fund themselves?", *Inter-American Development Bank, Sustainable Development Department, Best Practices Series*. Washington, DC: Inter-American Development Bank.

major consolidation trend among funds so as to match better the number of funded organisations and the number of funding operators. However, the funding operators do not appear to be willing to consider this option.

Another possibility is a more mature segmentation of the market, with different MIVs specialising in niches in order to prevent themselves from all chasing the same MFIs. Some MIVs have already taken steps in this direction; however, the number of niches so far appears quite limited.

In fact, considering the present state of microfinance, the available strategic options involve either a better focus on rural development or a deeper social commitment. This last option in particular has been a subject of study. The reason for this is simple. At first, any investment in microfinance was considered socially responsible, microfinance itself being perceived as social.[3] However, as time has passed, increasing concern has been expressed about the heterogeneity of the industry. Socially responsible investors – who represent a major stake of the funders of MIVs – have become more interested in confirming that their investments in MIVs have indeed resulted in financing for socially oriented MFIs. The search for good procedures by which to assess the social performance of MFIs has therefore become an increasingly high priority when reviewing the strategies and policies of MIVs.

In parallel to these developments, many tools have been created with which to assess MFIs' social performance. While these initiatives have taken the microfinance sector a long way in defining the multiple dimensions that compose social performance, they are still insufficient for making investment decisions. These methods are not tailored to the investors' specific values, and they suffer greatly from technical issues related to performance measurement.

It is in this context that this chapter suggests a new way for MIVs to review the social performance of MFIs, and presents a first application of this new method based on the MACBETH (Measuring Attractiveness by a Categorical Based Evaluation Technique) approach.[4] This is a decision-supporting method that is already widely used in public and private sector investments and whose application to microfinance could deeply improve the way double (or even triple) bottom-line objectives are aggregated.

There are five sections to the chapter.

In the first, we review the development of MIVs and highlight the major trends that characterise them. We explain why the 'double bottom-line' debate that has been so strong for MFIs is now being passed to the MIV industry, with the result that more attention is being given to how MIVs ensure that their investments are 'socially responsible'.

In the second section, we present various methodologies that have so far been used to assess the level of social performance in microfinance. We then try to identify

---

3 Urgeghe, L (2010) "*Les véhicules d'investissement en microfinance et le défi de la performance sociale*", *Mondes en Développement*, Vol. 38, No. 4, pp 69–82; Mersland, R and L Urgeghe (forthcoming) "International Debt Financing and Performance of Microfinance Institutions", *Strategic Change: Briefings in Entrepreneurial Finance*.

4 Bana e Costa, C A, J M De Corte and J C Vansnick (2005) "On the Mathematical Foundations of MACBETH", *Multiple Criteria Decision Analysis: State of the Art Surveys*, ed Figueira José, Salvatore Greco and Matthias Ehrgott. New York: Springer, 409-442.

the strengths and limits of these approaches, emphasising the mathematical limits of most of the techniques that are used to aggregate social data.

The third section introduces an alternative approach that may allow MIVs correctly to express their social values in a set of criteria, and aggregate the information they collect on financial and social performance in a mathematically relevant way. It is based on the MACBETH approach.

The fourth section then presents a first empirical case of the MACBETH procedure being used in microfinance. This case has been developed in partnership with a major microfinance funds manager and has been designed for debt investments, the most frequent case in the MIV industry. This section presents not only the results of this application but also some consideration of the advantages and limits of such a procedure for MIVs.

The fifth section concludes the study and establishes an agenda for further research.

2. The development of MIVs: financial development and double bottom-line goals

Having been created with the aim of connecting MFIs to capital markets, MIVs have had a relatively short history. Yet they have experienced many developments over the last 10 years. The first established funds mainly worked with equity investment, and sought to show that it was possible to invest in microfinance. The story of PROFUND is illustrative of these origins. PROFUND was created in the early 1990s by a set of leading players in the microfinance industry for the purpose of investing in Latin American MFIs and establishing the fact that 'investing in microfinance' was a real possibility. The fund was soon followed by other, slightly different initiatives. The following pattern is typical. One or a few known player(s) in the United States or Europe establish a fund with the technical collaboration of some major actors of the finance and banking industry, usually involved in such deals as part of their own social responsibility involvements. The fund receives starting capital either from donors (often already involved in microfinance projects) or from the partner bank itself. The fund is capitalised over time through calls for investments, most of which come from the socially responsible investment community. The funds are then provided to MFIs, most often for the short or medium term. Finally a new type of socially responsible investor is established in Europe and/or the United States and a new source of funding for MFIs in developing countries.

The growth of such funds over the last 10 years has been impressive in terms of both number of MIVs and assets under management. Today, more than 100 MIVs finance MFIs around the world, mainly through debt and to a lesser extent equity investment. A study by MicroRate found that in 2010, 82% of these investments were made through loans and 18% through equity.[5] For some, these funds play a crucial role in the growth of MFIs as they are the only ones capable of coping with the future potential growth of MFIs.[6]

---

5 MicroRate (2011) *State of Microfinance Investment 2011 – Microrate's 6th Annual Survey and Analysis of MIVs*. Available from www.MicroRate.com.

There are many sources for these funds. In 2010, the mix was as follows: 42% institutional investors, 34% individuals, 21% DFIs and 3% others.[7] As already mentioned, growth has been impressive. Between 2004 and 2011, the total assets under management multiplied eight-fold, to a total of $8 billion.[8]

Over time the types of MIVs have also evolved, and there is now greater heterogeneity in the commercial strategies and instruments used. Indeed, the first study on MIVs identified three types of investment fund – development funds, semi-commercial funds and commercial funds – distinguished mainly by differences in expected returns for the investors. In this classification, development funds invest through subsidised instruments (return expectations limited to inflation rate) while commercial funds aim at fully sustainable MFIs that provide competitive financial returns.[9] As the MIV industry grew, the Consultative Group to Assist the Poor (CGAP), an initiative of the World Bank) actualised this typology.[10] This classification, which is still in use, comprises six categories. These are no longer based on investment returns, but on the types of financial instrument used (fixed-income or equity investments) and on the complexity of their structures and legal forms (mutual funds, holdings, collaterised debt obligations and so on). The six types of MIVs are as follows:

- registered fixed-income mutual funds;
- commercial fixed-income investment funds;
- structured finance vehicles;
- blended value fixed-income and equity funds;
- holding companies of microfinance banks; and
- private equity funds.[11]

While the Goodman framework[12] paved the way for a clear segmentation of funds based on expectations of return, the current typology makes it harder for investors (and industry observers) to distinguish 'social' from 'commercial' MIVs.

Finally, the MIV market is highly concentrated. The total assets under management of the 10 largest players amount to 58% of the total. Geographically speaking, 73% of MIV investments are made in Eastern Europe, Central Asia and Latin America.[13]

---

6 Daley-Harris, S (2009) State of the Microcredit Summit Campaign Report 2009, the Microcredit Summit Campaign, Washington DC, United States; Swanson, B (2008) "The role of international capital markets in microfinance", Chapter 2 in Sundaresan, S, (2008) *Microfinance: Emerging Trends and Challenges*, Edward Elgar, Cheltenham, UK, Northhampton, United States, 129 pages.

7 MicroRate (2011).

8 Reille, Forster and Rosas (2011).

9 Goodman, P (2003) *International Investment Funds: Mobilizing Investors towards Microfinance*, Luxumbourg: ADA.

10 Reille, X, Forster, S (2008) "Foreign Capital Investment in Microfinance: Balancing Social and Financial Returns", Focus Note 44. Washington DC: CGAP.

11 *Ibid.*

12 See Goodman (2003).

13 MicroRate (2011). Based on total assets under management in December 2009, the five largest MIVs were: European Fund for Southeast Europe (€836 million), Oikocredit (€770 million), Dexia Microcredit Fund ($541.7 million), ResponsAbility Global Microfinance Fund ($489.4 million), and SNS Institutional Microfinance Fund I ($261.2 million); CGAP CGAP (2010b) *Challenging Times: Do MIVs Need a New Investment Strategy?*. Available from http://cgap.org.

Of course, if the development of MIV industry has been impressive, the challenges it faces are also of some importance. Three major challenges are:

- mismatches between supply and demand;
- product development; and
- social and financial return expectations.

First, mismatch issues. MIV managers usually want to put prime, or 'first-tier', MFIs in their portfolio. These institutions offer excellent track records, and because they appear to be of a lesser risk their profile is easy to market. The problem is that these 'top of the class' institutions are usually not those that most need MIV funds. Indeed, when a MFI is a market leader, has been operating for some time and is perceived as relatively 'low risk', it usually has access to other (cheaper) sources of funding either through the local banking sector or through direct issuing of bonds or certificates on the financial markets. For top-tier MFIs, it seems that maintaining a contact with MIVs is more a way to diversify their sources of funds ('keeping a window opened in case extra funding would become urgently necessary') than it is a vital source of funding itself. This is the origin of the first mismatch, since MIVs tend to focus not on those MFIs that most need them. Focusing on 'tomorrow's stars' (fast-growing but sound second and third-tier MFIs) would probably be more appropriate, although it is harder to do, as identifying tomorrow's stars is more difficult than spotting those of today.

A further mismatch between supply and demand occurs at the institutional level. There are presently just over 100 MIVs, but the number of MFIs providing the type of profile for which MIVs are looking is several hundred. No exact figure is available, but as an approximation one study shows that for 2009 the top seven MIVs were financing 574 MFIs, of which 85.35% came from tier one.[14] A more recent study conducted by the ratings agency MicroRate and the Microfinance Information Exchange (the MIX) platform[15] showed that in 2010, 90.04% of total MIV funds was allocated to 200 MFIs. Compared to the more than 2,000 MFIs reported by the Mix Market (www.mixmarket.org) this indicates that demand is limited, while supply is diverse. One might ask if this should not lead to some consolidation between MIVs; even more so when it seems that some funds are very small in comparison to all the costs normally associated with their activity. Such a trend has not yet begun, however.

Another way to consider mismatch is to compare supply and demand in terms of products. Indeed, MIVs have so far focused on senior debt and, to a lesser extent, equity investment. For debt, MIVs are usually created in hard currencies (even though local currency funding initiatives have been developed over the last few years), for the short or medium term (generally one to three years). The demand is different, however: MFIs usually prefer longer-term loans without having to take a

14 Wiesner, S and D Quien (2010) "Can 'Bad' Microfinance Practices Be the Consequence of Too Much Funding Chasing Too Few Microfinance Institutions?", *ADA Discussion Paper No. 2, Appui au Développement Autonome*. Available from www.lamicrofinance.lu. Wiesner and Quien consider tier 1 as MFIs with total assets of more than $30 million, tier 2 as MFIs with total assets of between $30 million and $10 million, and tier 3 as MFIs with total assets of less than $10 million USD.

15 Viada, L A and S Gaul (2011) "The Tipping Point: over-indebtedness and investment in microfinance", *The Microbanking Bulletin*, Microfinance Information Exchange, MicroRate.

foreign exchange risk. Besides, in the context of interest rate decreases, the interest charged by MIVs is sometimes perceived as too high.[16]

Last but not least is the focus on the double bottom line. The expected returns for MIVs are also linked to social performance. For MIVs that focus on debt, the issue is reasonably simple. Assurances are needed that MIVs do in fact finance MFIs that are themselves considered 'socially responsible'. Because microfinance has often been considered 'social *per se*', there has so far been little pressure to justify it. However, there is good ground to believe that this may soon change. MIVs should be prepared to prove that MFI investments are socially responsible because they offer a good financial/social mix.

The question may become even more urgent for those MIVs that focus on equity. These are developing rapidly and use a variety of philosophies. Some consider themselves as patient capital, acting as true partners and with a double bottom-line approach. Others seem more interested in the ability of microfinance to generate profits within a fast-growing industry, and consider it an investment more like risk capital. In such cases, the chances of mission drift may increase and some MFIs may even begin to focus primarily on creating value for their shareholders, forgetting the improvement of services to clients and the original goal of providing efficient financial services at the lowest possible cost. This has happened frequently in mainstream finance.

In summary, given the mismatch and the heterogeneity of the industry, those MIVs that want to prove that they are socially responsible investors should ensure that their policies and procedures clearly reflect their commitment to social returns.

The next section builds on the debate about measuring social returns by MIVs, and discusses the main flaws of the currently used methods.

3. Assessing social performance: a challenge for MIVs

The origin of socially responsible investment lies in the concept of corporate social responsibility (CSR). Indeed, Penalva defines 'socially responsible investment' as the "financial translation of corporate social responsibility".[17] The idea behind CSR is that firms, beyond their economic objectives, also have ethical obligations and must respond adequately to pressures from society.[18] At first, CSR was limited to corporate philanthropy.[19] The concept then evolved into the idea that true social responsibility involves not only giving away money to charities, but also investing in projects that yield social and economic benefits.[20]

The double bottom-line mission of MIVs lies at the core of corporate social

---

16 Labie, M, Urgeghe, L (2011) "*Investissements socialement responsables et microfinance*", *Management et Avenir*, 46, 280-297.

17 Penalva E (2009, p41), "*Un exemple emblématique de la RSE : l'investissement socialement responsable et son mythe progressiste*", in Boidin B, Postel N, Rousseau S (2009), "*La responsabilité sociale des entreprises – Une perspective institutionnaliste*", Presses Universitaires du Septentrion, France, 199 pp 41-67.

18 Sethi, SP (1975) "Dimensions of corporate social performance: An analytical framework" *California Management Review*, Vol 17, No 3, pp 58–64; Carroll, A B (1979) "A three-dimensional conceptual model of corporate performance", *Academy of Management Review*, Vol. 4, No 4, pp 497–505.

19 Cochran, P. L. (2007) "The Evolution of Corporate Social Responsibility", *Business Horizons*, No 50, 449–454.

20 Porter, M E and M R Kramer (2002) "The competitive advantage of corporate philanthropy", *Harvard Business Review*, Vol 80, No 12, 56–68.

responsibility. It reinforces the need for them to justify their position as socially responsible investors. Schepers and Sethi[21] even argue that socially responsible investment fund managers have a double mission: screening the investments that best fit the values of the investors they represent, and influencing corporate behaviour through the application of CSR practices.

In comparison with socially responsible investment practices, MIVs have to choose between two approaches for the screening of their investments: the negative one or the positive one.[22] In the negative approach, exclusion criteria are applied. Those investments that do not match the criteria are considered 'bad' and are excluded from the investment horizon, while the others go through a classical financial analysis. Typical negative criteria in socially responsible investments screen tobacco, gambling or weapons companies out of the investment possibilities. In the positive approach, investments are selected because they meet higher performance levels on the desired criteria. This approach requires an ability to measure performance on the selected screening criteria (eg, social or environmental performance), and to compare potential investments to benchmarks.

So far it seems that most commercial investment strategies in microfinance have followed the negative screening approach. The first concern was to exclude anything that is not microfinance, and then to consider any remaining investment as potentially valid without considering its social impact any further.[23] This is no longer enough. More and more, the public is asking for greater justification and more frequent reporting.[24] The positive approach is increasingly expected from MIVs. In order to do meet this demand, they must be able to measure the social returns of their investments.

Two categories of tool are usually discussed. First are social performance indicators based on quantitative and standardised measures, such as percentage of women clients or average loan size of the investee MFIs. These indicators, although easy and inexpensive to obtain, are biased for two principal reasons: they do not consider the social and cultural context and, more importantly, the concept of 'average' can be strongly criticised from a qualitative point of view. These indicators are therefore weak for making international comparisons between potential investments.[25] Second are social performance tools that match the 'new vision' of social performance. These are defined as:

- effectively translating an institution's social mission into practice in line with accepted social values such as serving larger numbers of poor and excluded people;

---

21 Schepers, D H and S P Sethi (2003), "Do Socially Responsible Funds Actually Deliver What They Promise? Bridging the Gap Between the Promise and Performance of Socially Responsible Funds", *Business and Society Review*, Vol 108, No 1, pp 11–32.

22 O'Rourke (2003) "The message and methods of ethical investment", *Journal of Cleaner Production*, No 11, 683-693. Renneboog L, Ter Horst J, Zhang C (2008) "Socially Responsible Investments: Institutional aspects, performance and investment behavior", *Journal of Banking and Finance*, No 32, 1723-1742.

23 Mersland, R, Urgeghe, L (2013) International Debt Financing and Performance of Microfinance Institutions, Strategic Change: Briefings in Entrepreneurial Finance, No 22, 17-29.

24 CGAP (2010a) *Microfinance Investment Vehicles Disclosure Guidelines – Consensus Guidelines 2010*. Available from http://cgap.org.

25 Urgeghe (2010).

- improving the quality and appropriateness of financial services;
- creating benefits for clients; and
- improving the social responsibility of an MFI.[26]

The new vision combines qualitative and contextual approaches. Social audits, social ratings and social performance management are the current tools used by microfinance practitioners. These relatively new approaches better embrace the nature of social performance, but they suffer from biases originating from the aggregation of the many dimensions of social performance.[27] Other tools have been designed to assess social performance at the level of the MIV, such as the Social Audit tool for MIVs from CERISE[28] and M-CRIL's first initiative for an MIV rating.[29]

Such initiatives aim to assess the social responsibility of MIVs, a whole new field that will not be discussed in this chapter. We will focus on the tools used by MIVs to reach their dual objective of financial and social returns.

More specifically, we discuss the difficulties in measuring and aggregating multiple criteria in social performance assessments. The assessment of MFIs' social performance contributes to the wider technical debate on how to aggregate the performance of different properties that are all measured in a different manner. Whatever the property concerned, however, the key issue is always the same: in order to measure something, you need to have a unit of measurement. So far, such a unit does not exist for social performance in microfinance.

An example is the social performance tool that we believe that is most likely to be used by MIVs to select and monitor their investments. This is the Social Performance Indicators (SPI) tool developed by CERISE.[30] The SPI is designed to help microfinance institutions evaluate their intentions, systems and actions, and so determine whether they have the capacity to meet their social objectives. The tool is based on a questionnaire divided across four dimensions:

- targeting and outreach, which defines the specific mission of the MFI and the corresponding target population;
- products and services, which assesses the fit between the MFI's products and services and the needs of its clients;
- benefits to clients, which examines the empowerment of clients; and
- social responsibility, which evaluates the degree of responsibility of the MFI towards its staff, its clients, the community and the environment.[31]

---

26 See www.sptf.info.

27 Van den Bossche, F, N Rogge, K Devooght and T Van Puyenbroeck (2010) "Robust Corporate Social Responsibility Investment Screening", *Ecological Economics*, No 69, pp 1159–1169; Chatterji, A K and M W Toffel (2010) "How firms respond to being rated", *Strategic Management Journal*, No 31, pp 917–945.

28 Lapenu, C (2008) *"Performances sociales en microfinance: perspectives et enjeux pour les investisseurs"*, *European Dialogue*, No 1 European Microfinance Platform, 121 pages.

29 Sinha, F and S Sinha (2010) "Rating of Microfinance Investment Vehicles: a pilot initiative by M-CRIL", *European Dialogue*, No 3, pp. 27–41.

30 CERISE *(Comité d'Echanges de Réflexion et d'Information sur les Systèmes d'Epargne-crédit)* is a knowledge exchange network for microfinance practitioners. See www.cerise-microfinance.org.

31 CERISE (2008) *Operational Guide to the SPI Questionnaire Version 3.0*. Available from http://cerise-microfinance.org.

Each dimension is composed of three sub-dimensions containing the criteria on which the MFI is assessed. There are 71 criteria in total.

The SPI has been elaborated over the years in collaboration with MFIs and other microfinance actors, and benefits from great legitimacy within the sector. It is currently integrated into the Mix Market[32] in the form of Social Performance Standards, which are publicly available in a database of 415 MFIs evaluated between 2008 and 2009.

Although it is widely recognised, however, we believe that the way SPI assesses social performance is more a way to define a social MFI, determined by respect for the 71 rules, than a true instrument of measurement.

Let us take two examples of such rules to illustrate our point.

Example 1 (related to savings products):
2.6 Does the MFI propose voluntary saving products. directly or in partnership with other institutions, or actively promote savings?
☐ 0 = No voluntary savings products (or voluntary saving concems either less than 5% of clients or less than 5% of the volume of the loan portfolio).
☐ 1 = Voluntary savings services are provided by the MFI, or through an operational partnership with another fmancial institution. Or, the MFI provides information or training session to promote saving (in conjunction with savings institutions).

Source: CERISE (2008), p 41

This rule stipulates that to qualify as social, "Voluntary savings services are provided by the MFI, or through an operational partnership with another financial institution. Or, the MFI provides information or training sessions to promote savings (in conjunction with savings institutions)". Note that the rule also considers that there are no voluntary savings products if they involve less than 5% of the MFI's clients or less than 5% of the loan portfolio.

Example 2 (related to the prioritisation of where the MFI is to work):
1.1 Does the MFI select operating areas based on criteria of poverty/exclusion?
☐ 0 = Not a criteria.
☐ 1 = One of the criteria but not the most important one.
☐ 2 = One of the most important criteria, reflected in the strategic planning of the MFI.

Source: CERISE (2008), p 17

This rule stipulates that in order to be social, the MFI must select operating areas based on poverty or exclusion as one of its most important criteria, and this should

32 The Mix (Microfinance Information Exchange) is an online platform for information exchange on the microfinance sector at a global scale (www.themix.org).

be reflected in the strategic planning.

If all 71 rules are satisfied, the MFI receives 100 points. This means that it can be considered to be "100% social". In other cases, SPI calculates a "percentage of social orientation" of the MFI by giving:

- 1% of satisfaction for each Boolean rule respected (a rule is Boolean when the choice is dual, between respected (+1%) or not (+0%), as in Example 1); or
- 2% when it relates to rules where non-satisfaction can be split into "partial non-satisfaction" (+1%) and "total non-satisfaction" (+0%) (as in Example 2, where 2% is the maximum, 1% is attributed for "a selection criteria but the most important one" and 0% is given for "not a selection criteria").

The scores are then presented graphically as a spider's web, which is often regarded as easy to visualise.

This kind of aggregation is not rigorously valid for screening investments by socially responsible investors who want their choices to clearly reflect their social values. We see two major problems: an inappropriate weighting system, and the lack of a unit of measure.

Regarding the weighting system, let us return to the examples. In Example 2, fulfilling the rule provides twice the satisfaction (+ 2%) than fulfilling the rule in Example 1 (+ 1%). Does that mean that having selection criteria based on poverty or exclusion (Example 2) is twice as important as proposing voluntary savings products (Example 1)? Unless this difference of satisfaction is clearly stated and justified by the decision maker, the numbers make little sense. In other words, adding the numbers (0, 1 or 2) for each of the 71 rules to arrive at a total out of 100 raises questions about the sense of the numbers. More weight is implicitly given to some criteria due to the introduction of intermediary levels of performance (such as in Example 2). We argue that in line with the missions of socially responsible investment[33] this weighting system must be decided by investors according to their values.

The SPI does not provide a measurement as such, which is fundamental for any mathematical treatment. The method is rather like comparing apples with oranges. In Examples 1 and 2, for example, we are adding one number that measures the range of products to another number that measures whether the MFI applies poverty criteria to select where it is going to work. What is the real meaning of adding these two values?

A property can only be measured on a scale of 0 to 100 if it is clearly specified in what case a '0' will be given and in what case it will be '100'. To aggregate various performance levels across various characteristics – such as the social aspects of microfinance – we need a reference scale that is common to all characteristics. In the next section, we introduce the decision-supporting tool MACBETH (Measuring Attractiveness by a Categorical Based Evaluation TecHnique). This was developed to measure the 'attractiveness' of alternative courses of action, but it also has the

33 Renneboog *et al.* (2008); Schepers and Sethi (2003).

34 Bana e Costa, C A, J M De Corte and J C Vansnick (2011) "MACBETH (Measuring attractiveness by a Categorical Based Evaluation Technique", *Encyclopaedia of Operations Research and Management Science*. New York: Wiley.

potential to measure rigorously any well-defined characteristics.[34] We believe that this approach can complement existing social performance initiatives in microfinance such as SPI. Indeed, SPI has contributed much to the identification and definition of the multiple dimensions of social performance. We believe, however, that it is better suited as an internal rating system for the MFI itself than an international assessment tool for investment screening. As will be presented in the next section, MACBETH also resolves the methodological issues related to the measurement of a characteristic and, most importantly, its meaning for the decision maker. Issues related to the aggregation of several dimensions and sub-dimensions are also addressed in a mathematically relevant way.

4. A complementary approach: MACBETH

MACBETH was inspired by multiattribute value theory,[35] and was developed with two objectives in mind:

- from the social point of view, to facilitate the process of multicriteria assessments by minimising the risk of the assessment procedure being impeded by conflicting interests between decision makers; and
- from the technical point of view, to ensure the consistency of decisions' outputs with the decision makers' system of values, on behalf of which the assessment is made.

The method consists of a set of procedures which aim to help decision makers through each stage of a multi-criteria assessment process.

The first step consists of making explicit all those aspects that assessors wish to take into consideration, and constructing from these a set of criteria. A criterion is a focus point for the assessors (either a single aspect or a combination of aspects) that can be used as a basis for making a judgment. This means that those involved in the assessment are able to specify for each criterion a number of levels of performance that can be reached, and can rank these performances by decreasing attractiveness.

In the MACBETH approach, assessors are invited to 'operationalise' each criterion by specifying at least two levels of performance. The first is what they would consider 'good to reach' ('good level'); the second is the level below which they would not like to go ('neutral level'). This identification needs to be precise enough for everyone to have the same understanding of what the two levels are. These two benchmarks not only give meaning to the criterion, but also allow for the definition of a 'unit of measurement'.

The procedure is similar to that implemented by Celsius in the 18th century for measuring heat. Celsius took the boiling and melting points of water as benchmarks, and from there defined the 'Celsius degree' as a hundredth of the difference of heat between these two references. Two comments should be made here. First, even though people usually speak of measuring heat, the Celsius degree is really a unit measuring the variation in heat, and not the heat itself. Second, the temperature of

35 Belton, V amd T J Stewart (2002) "*Multiple Criteria Decision Analysis. An Integrated Approach*". Norwell, MA: Kluwer Academic Publishers.

an object (expressed in degrees Celsius) is defined as the difference of heat between this object and the melting point of ice.

Figure 1

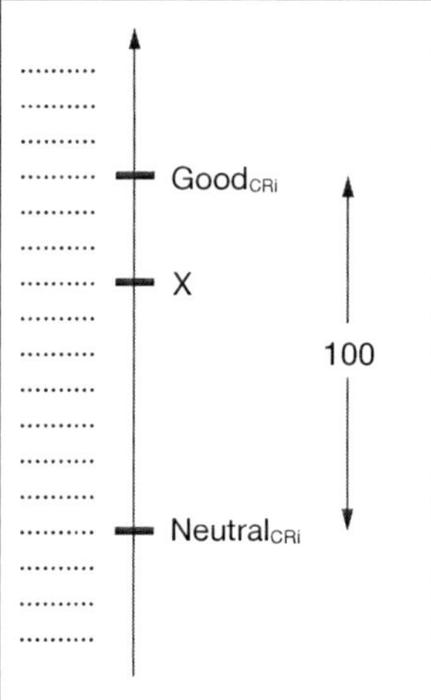

In measuring the attractiveness of an element X on a criterion CRi we can, for example, define:

- the unit of measurement of the difference of attractiveness on CRi (notation: pt_{CRi}) as a hundredth of the difference of attractiveness between $Good_{CRi}$ and $Neutral_{CRi}$; and
- the attractiveness of an element as the measure of the attractiveness difference between this element and $Neutral_{CRi}$.

To identify the attractiveness of X, we only need to know the position of this element respective to the levels $Good_{CRi}$ and $Neutral_{CRi}$: in Figure 1, $Att_{CRi}(X) = 70\ pt_{CRi}$. This definition immediately implies that: $Att_{CRi}(Good_{CRi}) = 100\ pt_{CRi}$ and $Att_{CRi}(Neutral_{CRi}) = 0\ pt_{CRi}$.

The attractiveness of an element can also be negative (if the performance of CRi does not reach $Neutral_{CRi}$) or higher than 100 pt_{CRi} (if the performance of CRi is better than $Good_{CRi}$).

When various elements must be assessed simultaneously on a criterion CRi, MACBETH can help by asking for qualitative opinions on the differences of attractiveness between these elements (as well as $Good_{CRi}$ and $Neutral_{CRi}$). At the same time, it will test the consistency of all the judgements already expressed.

In order to make these opinions easier to express, six categories of difference of attractiveness are introduced:

- very weak;
- weak;
- moderate;
- strong;
- very strong; and
- extreme.

It is this specific procedure that gives its name to the methodology.[36]

Once the attractiveness of an element X [notation: $Att_{CRi}(X)$], has been identified for each criterion CRi, MACBETH uses a weighted average to aggregate this local information and obtain the overall attractiveness of X [notation: AttG(X)].

For the three criteria CR1, CR2 and CR3, the model takes the following presentation: $AttG(X) = p_1.\ Att_{CR1}(X) + p2.\ Att_{CR2}(X) + p_3.\ Att_{CR3}(X)$.

In this formula, p_1, p_2 and p_3 are technical parameters whose function is to convert

36 Bana e Costa, C A, J M De Corte and J C Vansnick (2003) "MACBETH", *Working Paper LSEOR 03-56*, London School of Economics. Available from www.m-macbeth.com.

the various units of measure pt_{CRi} in a single unit of measure (of the difference of global attractiveness). Were this not the case, we would not be able to add those three local attractivenesses, as they are expressed in different units (apples and oranges again!). In contrast to what many people believe, those parameters that are part of a weighted sum do not characterise the relative importance of these criteria. As one famous American consultant has put it, this is "the most common critical mistake in decision making".[37]

We can use different methods to set the value of each technical parameter, pi. One of these (used in MACBETH) consists in asking the assessors to determine the overall attractiveness of some simple hypothetical elements, with each defined by its performance on each criterion.

In the case of N criteria, these hypothetical elements are N+1; they are written as [Neutral] and [CRi], i being able to take the values 1, 2, ..., N. [Neutral] is a hypothetical element whose performance on each criteria CRi is NeutralCRi. Whatever the value of i ∈ {1,2, ..., N}, [CRi] is an hypothetical element whose performance on CRi is GoodCRi and whose performance on any other criterion CRk is NeutralCRk. For the three criteria, the hypothetical actions are therefore

- [CR1] ≡ ($Good_{CRi}$, $Neutral_{CR2}$, $Neutral_{CR3}$)
- [CR2] ≡ ($Neutral_{CRi}$, $Good_{CR2}$, $Neutral_{CR3}$)
- [CR3] ≡ ($Neutral_{CRi}$, $Neutral_{CR2}$, $Good_{CR3}$)
- [Neutral] ≡ ($Neutral_{CRi}$, $Neutral_{CR2}$, $Neutral_{CR3}$)

Since two hypothetical elements may only differ on a maximum of two criteria, it is easy for assessors to compare them in pairs, to rank them by decreasing attractiveness and to give qualitative opinions on the differences in overall attractiveness that they perceive between these elements. The MACBETH procedure then allows them to place the hypothetical elements on an axis, with the relative distances between these elements indicating the relative differences in attractiveness perceived by the assessors. To match the aggregation model perfectly to the assessors' perception (in particular on the respective roles they intend to give to each criteria at the time of the assessment), the relative values of parameters pi (i ∈ {1,..., N}) must be proportionate to the relative distances between [CRi] and [Neutral] (i ∈ {1,..., N}).

Figure 2 (on the next page) illustrates, for the case of 3 criteria, the process of determining the values for parameters p1, p2 and p3.

Using MACBETH has been made easier thanks to purpose-built software (see http://m-macbeth.com). This software allows some sensibility and robustness checks to be made, and can present most results in easily understandable graphics. It has been widely used in many decision processes to date, notably in the field of public investments. It has also been used twice in finance.[38] The following section attempts to show how it can also help MIVs grasp the double bottom line of microfinance.

37 Keeney, R L (1996) *Value-focused thinking: a path to creative decisionmaking*. Cambridge, MA: Harvard University Press, p 147.

38 Bana e Costa, C A, J C Lourenço and J O Soares (2002), "Qualitative modelling of credit scoring: a case study in banking", *European Research Studies Journal*, Vol 5, No 1, pp 37–51; Bana e Costa, C A, J C Lourenço and J O Soares (2007) "An interval weighting assignment model for credit analysis", *Journal of Financial Decision Making*, Vol 3, No 2, pp 1–9.

Figure 2

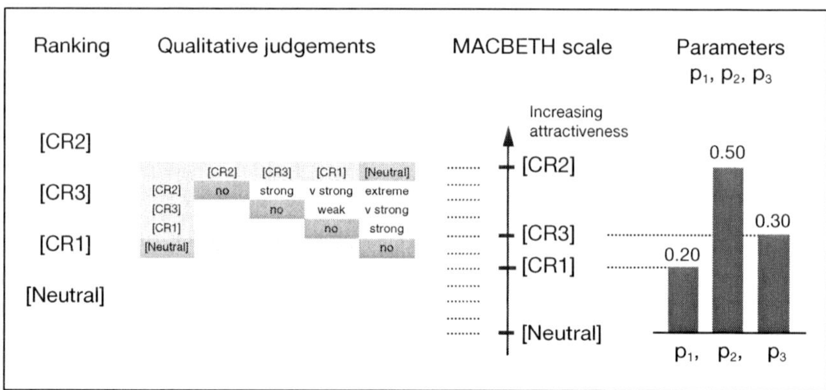

5. First lessons from a practical application

Here we present a first empirical case of the MACBETH procedure being used in microfinance. It has been developed in partnership with a major microfinance funds manager and has been designed for debt investments, the most frequent case in the MIV industry.

5.1 Context of the case study

For reasons of confidentiality our partner MIV will remain anonymous. Like many others, this MIV has a mission statement declaring the objective of double bottom-line returns for its investors, and has the clear intent to translate this mission into practice when it comes to selecting investment projects.

To date, the investment decision-making process at the MIV has taken place as follows. The first screening of MFIs is undertaken by a team of investment officers. Having made selections according to the MIV's eligibility criteria, the team proceeds to a 'pre-due diligence' analysis. Two distinct in-house tools are used: a financial risk tool and a social performance assessment tool, initially inspired by the CERISE SPI (in common with many MIVs).

These tools are used to assess each pre-selected MFI, and each receives two separate scores: one financial and one social. Each tool is composed of several dimensions, which are in turn composed of several sub-dimensions. Each sub-dimension contains the decision criteria on which investment officers make their assessment. Figure 3 gives an idea of the existing social performance tool used. Taking into account all the criteria that have to be assessed for both financial and social assessments (73 criteria for financial performance and 43 for social performance), a total of 116 assessments are needed for each potential investment. The performance on each criterion is then aggregated at each level using a weighted sum to provide the final score. The weights used in the aggregation formula are set by the MIV team itself and reflect its strategic priorities regarding investment policy. The final scores are percentages, often ranging between 60% and 80%. Investment officers then suggest the files to the investment committee, which makes the final decision.

Figure 3: The social performance tool

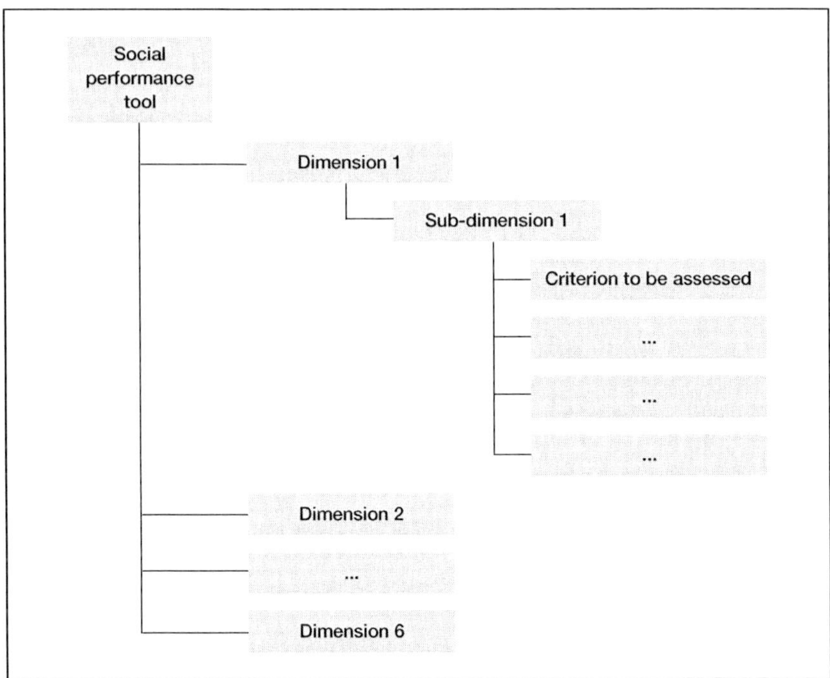

In our first meeting, the MIV's investment team said that the investment committee had often made complaint about their 'apparent subjectivity' regarding the scores provided. Indeed, the committee found it difficult to understand that a 70% score provided by one investment officer did not mean the same (in terms of the financial and social characteristics of the underlying MFI) as a 70% score provided by another officer. The investment team explained that because the final score aggregates many different dimensions, different MFIs can happen to reach the same score. As Figure 4 on the next page shows, both MFI A and MFI B have an average score of 25, but their performance on each of the four dimensions is very different.

In addition, the committee wanted to understand why the scores so often sat between 60% and 80%, and was worried about that assessments might be biased in some way by the 'assessment style' of each investment officer. The team therefore needed to be able to present a detailed profile of each MFI to the committee to help it better understand the origin of the scores. It was also in need of a way to prove the consistency of its assessments with respect to the double bottom line.

Figure 4: Different profiles leading to the same scores

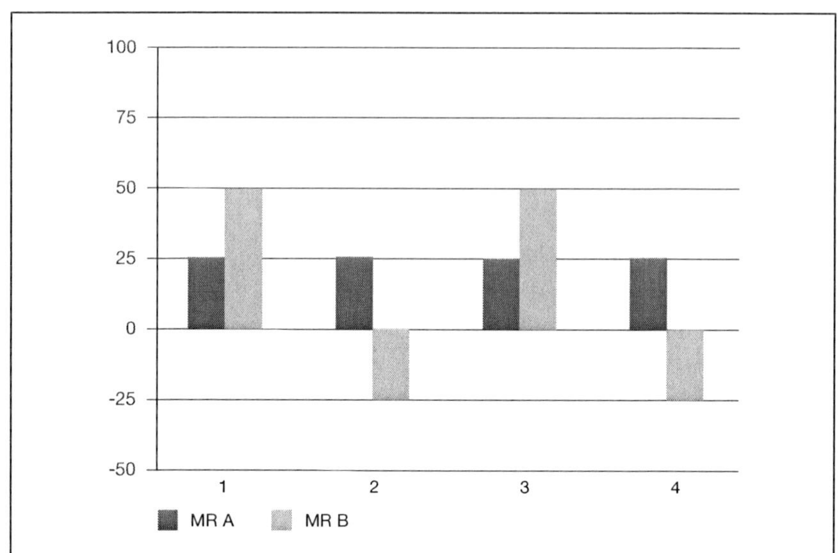

5.2 Applying the MACBETH methodology

This case study was carried out in four phases, corresponding to the different steps of the MACBETH procedure.

(a) Step 1

The first phase consisted of discussion and analysis of internal documents to understand the decision-makers' system of values and the decision-making process of the organisation.

(b) Step 2

The second phase consisted of extensive discussions with the investment team. These took several full working days. The objective was to review all the existing decision criteria one by one and to make them operational for the MACBETH procedure. The investment team had to agree on two performance levels (neutral and good) for each of the 116 criteria that made up their performance assessment tools. The MIV already had a functioning tool, and had set a range of possible values for each criterion and their corresponding score (see the example of the OSS below). Following the MACBETH process, each criterion was given a new performance scale simplified to two levels, neutral and good. The difference of attractiveness will be used as a unit of measurement for comparing one MFI with another. The MACBETH approach permits as many intermediary performance levels as the decision makers wish, but it is important to understand that the numerical treatment is based on the difference of attractiveness between the good and neutral levels and, most importantly, that these two levels correspond to the values of the investment team.

Figure 5 shows the initial criterion regarding operational self-sustainability (OSS).

Figure 5: Initial criterion for operational self-sustainability

Is the OSS:	5	$x > 130\%$
	4	$120\% \geq x \geq 130\%$
	3	$110\% \geq x > 120\%$
	2	$100\% \geq x > 110\%$
	1	$90\% \geq x > 100\%$
	0	$x < 90\%$

The column in grey shows the score scale used by the MIV for this criterion. The score obtained by the MFI is determined by one of six performance levels and is then averaged against the score on all the other criteria. The new criterion for OSS is shown in Figure 6.

Figure 6: New criterion for operational self-sustainability

OSS		
Reference levels		Attractiveness
Good	115 %	100
Neutral	100 %	0

During the procedure, the team discussed and agreed on acceptable (neutral) and desirable (good) levels of performance. Note that the attractiveness of these levels are 0 and 100, respectively. As the only thing that matters in the MACBETH approach is the difference of attractiveness between neutral and good and the positioning of options regarding these levels, the numbers 0 and 100 are not important as such. Good references are levels of performance that decision makers 'feel' the difference between a good one and a 'just acceptable' (neutral) one. For instance, we initially suggested 60 (as a 'satisfactory grade' at university) and 90 (for 'the highest honors'), but the investment team decided to adopt 0 and 100 as a norm as it was easier for them to visualise. These two reference numbers only have to make sense to the decision makers.

In our example of the OSS, the neutral level is situated at 100% and the good level is at 115%. This indicates that an MFI with a performance higher than 115% provides little additional satisfaction to the assessors. In the former criterion, a 115%

performance level was situated at the middle of the scale and the satisfaction was allowed to improve by almost twice as much (5 points for the highest level compared to 3 points for the '110% ≥ x > 120%' level).

As shown in Figure 7, the scale has been adjusted in the new definition of the OSS criterion to fit the actual preferences of the decision makers. While satisfaction increases significantly between 100% and 115% (the passage from neutral to good), the additional satisfaction provided by an OSS beyond 115% gradually decreases. For an OSS beyond 140% the attractiveness even declines to reflect the preferences of the MIV: an MFI with an OSS higher than 140% will be penalised in the final score, which may eventually lead to its rejection. The value of the MACBETH approach at this stage is that it can take into consideration the fact that the satisfaction of decision makers regarding performance is in most cases non linear. The new criterion therefore reflects more accurately the assessors' system of values.

In the same figure, we also show the MACBETH scale for the social performance criterion 'client desertion rate'. On this scale, the MIV team expressed their values through the fact that their satisfaction increases as client dropout reduces, but below 20% the satisfaction increases less and less, and below 5% it stops increasing altogether.

Figure 7: Fitting the performance levels to the decision makers' satisfaction

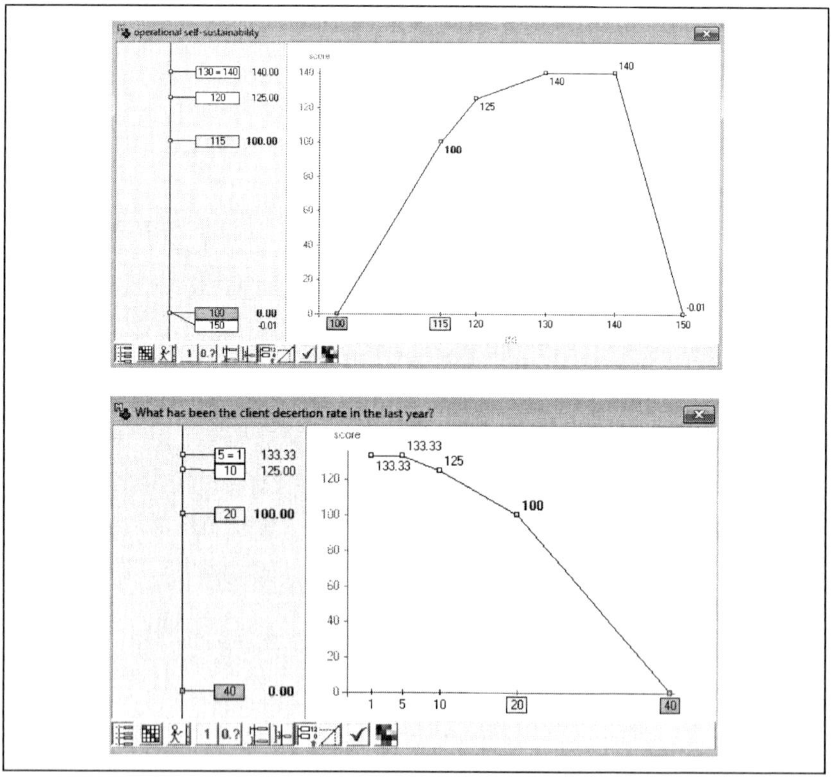

These in-depth discussions helped the team clarify how it defined many of its criteria. They also helped it to agree on many issues that, for some team members, had never been discussed before, such as the minimum acceptable age of MFIs, the requirements in terms of regulation and the importance of training.

The team also decided to change some criteria after realising that they were not operational in terms of available information or simply because the meaning of the criteria needed to be clarified. For example, the team realised that they were not able to measure objectively the two governance criteria "Does the MFI have reputable shareholders with experience in microfinance/banking and financial backbone?" and "Quality and support from shareholders and promoters". These they decided to replace a single new criterion, "Percentage of equity in hands of professional shareholders", which can be measured more accurately.

The former criteria regarding the quality of support and the experience of shareholders are given in Figure 8, and the new MACBETH criterion in Figure 9.

Figure 8: Initial criteria for quality of support and experience of shareholders

Does the MFI have reputable shareholders with experience in microfinance/ banking and financial backbone?	5	Yes
	2.5	Partly
	0	No

Quality and support from shareholders and promoters: Does the MFI receive significant financial, strategic and/or technical support from its shareholders and/or promoters?	5	Yes
	2.5	Partly
	0	No

Figure 9: New criteria for quality of support and experience of shareholders

Percentage of equity in hands of professional shareholders		
Reference levels		Attractiveness
Good	More than 50%	100
	Between 25% and 50%	
Neutral	Between 5% and 25%	0
	Below 5%	

With this new criterion, the team expressed its preferences in terms of acceptable and desirable levels of professional shareholding in an MFI's equity. This criterion is qualitative, and therefore cannot be illustrated on a curvilinear graph. Instead it is illustrated using a 'thermometer' graph on which the relative distances between the qualitative performance levels represent the differences of attractiveness of these levels compared to the neutral level. Figure 10 shows two criteria: equity (financial side) and training (social side). Decision makers are now able to see the distances between the different levels on the scale, and can therefore adjust them according to what they feel best matches their expectations.

Figure 10: Relative distances between performance levels

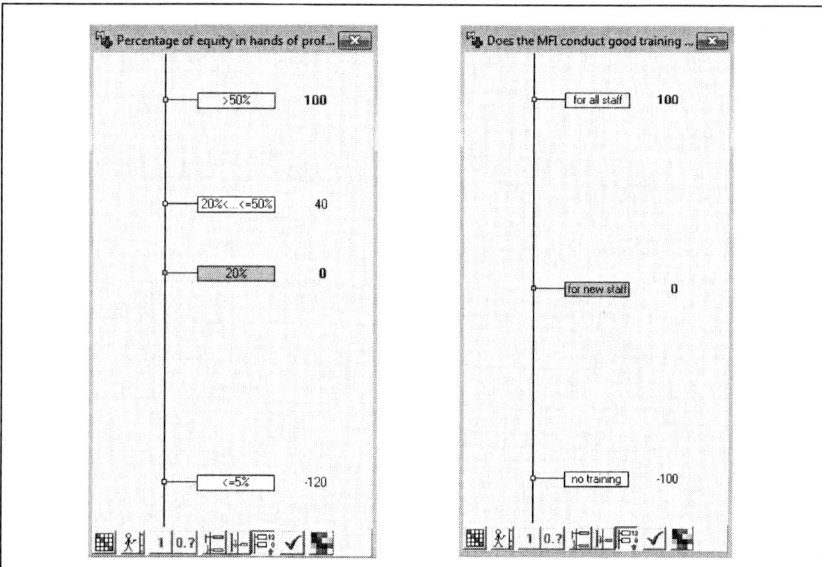

This second phase also allowed the team to consider dropping or merging some criteria. We were struck by the very large number of criteria that the team had to assess for each potential investment file. As suggested in Figure 3, there are many different levels and any weighting allocated to one of the 116 criteria at the end of the tree will be extremely low, making its relative importance difficult to grasp.

With this in mind, we tried to understand at what level of the tree decisions were actually taken by investment officers for each dimension and sub-dimension. When it was thought to be relevant, we encouraged them to assess the performance of the MFI at a higher level of abstraction, for example directly at the level of the sub-dimension instead of at the level of each small criterion. The team was able to do this for some cases, such as the assessment of the country risk: for this only one indicator is now used, which summarises the information previously contained in five indicators.

(c) ***Step 3***

In the third phase, the 'weights' of the criteria were determined. This was done by adjusting an additive aggregation model to the decision makers' system of values, based on a comparison of some hypothetical options. We brought the team together to discuss the weightings between each category of criteria, asking them for their preferences among a number of fictitious MFIs, each one being 'good' at a certain dimension and 'neutral' at all the others.

This allowed the team to discuss and agree on its preferences for each dimension of their assessment tool. For their social performance assessments, for instance, they agreed that they preferred MFIs to be 'good' at the sub-dimension 'Outreach and access' and 'neutral' on all other criteria, rather than 'good' at 'Human resources' and 'neutral' on all other criteria. Likewise, the sub-dimension 'Quality of customer services' was ranked higher than 'Social mission and vision'. By stating preferences between the different dimensions and sub-dimensions, the team was able to express a system of values. From these qualitative judgments, the MACBETH procedure then derived the weighting of each criterion.

Perceptions and opinions regarding how criteria should be assessed change from person to person. During the course of the present research, some people from the investment team left the company and some newcomers had arrived. It was difficult to arrive at a 'generally agreed' opinion on preferences because the new team members didn't always agree with the former team on criteria that had already discussed. This highlights the difficulty of structuring a decision-making methodology that will be followed by everyone within an organisation. It encourages the implementation of methodologies such as MACBETH, which place the organisation's system of values at the core of its decision making and makes them transparent to everyone.

(d) ***Step 4***

The last phase consists in assessing real investment cases using the 'new' weightings established by the MACBETH procedure. The objective here is to use the new investment approach to re-assess past investment files, and find out whether the decisions made would have been different. Would the investment have been rejected instead of accepted or, even if accepted, would its score have been lower or higher? For this empirical test, we obtained 45 investment files from 2008 to 2010 and all the information necessary to assess the financial and social performance on each criterion using the MACBETH methodology. All 45 MFIs were selected and financed by the MIV.

Figure 11 shows the financial scores obtained by the MFIs using the previous assessment tool, and the scores for the same MFIs obtained using the MACBETH approach. The graph presents MFIs sorted from the best financial score (MFI 1, score 80) to the worst (MFI 45, score 53).

Figure 11: Financial scores: MIV in-house tool versus MACBETH

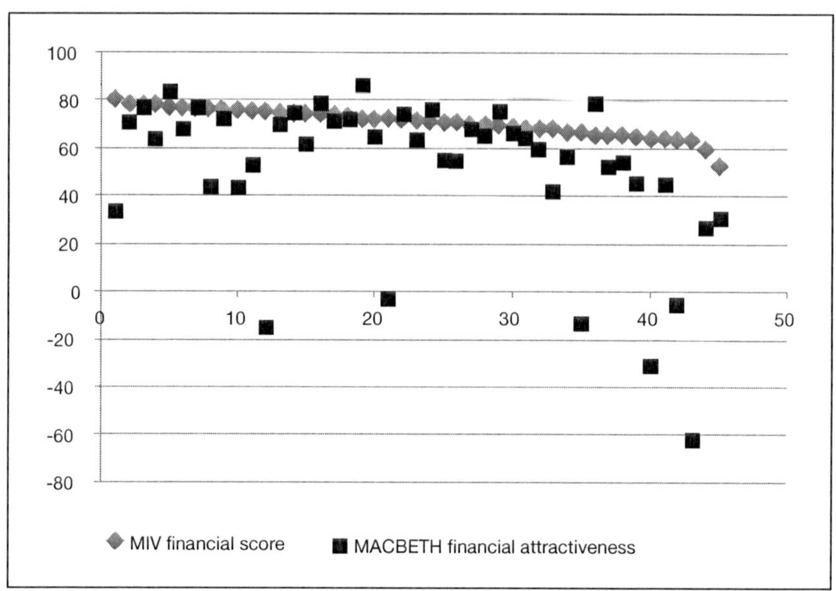

Figure 12 shows the social scores of the MFIs, presented in the same order (from MFI 1 to MFI 45), obtained using the previous tool and the MACBETH approach.

Figure 12: Financial and social attractiveness with MACBETH

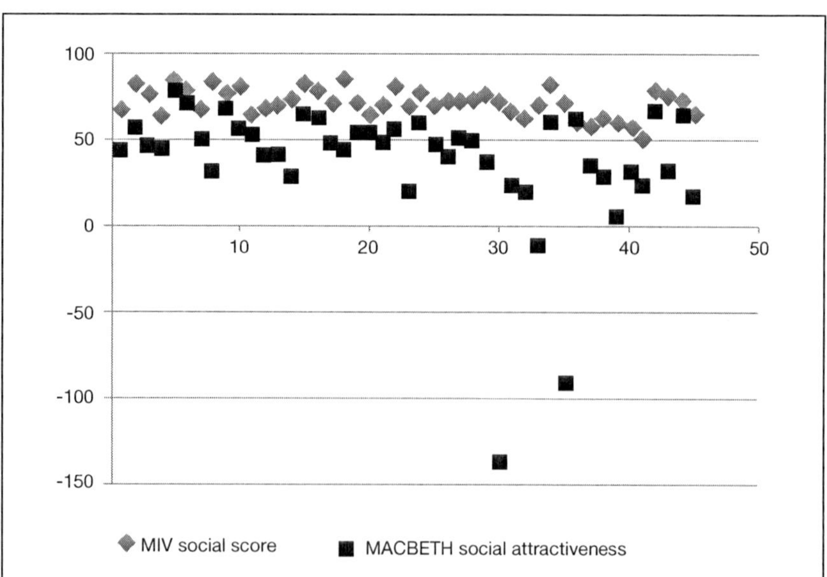

The first observation is that the MACBETH approach creates a greater dispersion in both financial and social scores than the previous tools. The ranking of MFIs has also completely changed (see the Appendix for rankings before and after MACBETH). This outcome was expected, since the overall decision making system is now more 'sensitive' to the MIV values, which have been coded into every performance criterion. Indeed, by using the new weighting system to express the MIV's values and by adjusting the non-linear satisfaction of the MIV, potential investments are more penalised when they do not meet expectations, and more rewarded when they do.

Second, we can see clearly that for both assessments, nine MFIs are now ranked below the neutral level of performance (0 on the graph). These nine MFIs do not reach the MIV's minimal expectations in terms of financial or social performance. Note that only one MFI (MFI 35) is below neutral on both financial and social performance. Figure 13 combines the MACBETH financial and social attractiveness of all 45 MFIs on the same graph.

Figure 13: Financial and social scores with the MACBETH approach

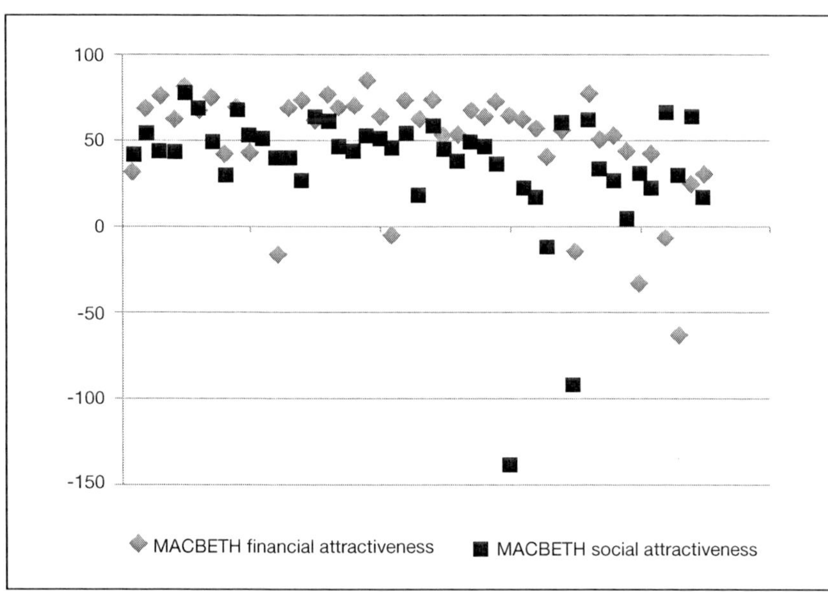

From this information, the investment committee can immediately spot those options that do not meet their minimal expectations for an investment. The MACBETH software also allows the profile of each MFI to be displayed, showing in detail the performance on each criterion.

As an illustration, here is a part of the financial profile of one MFI.

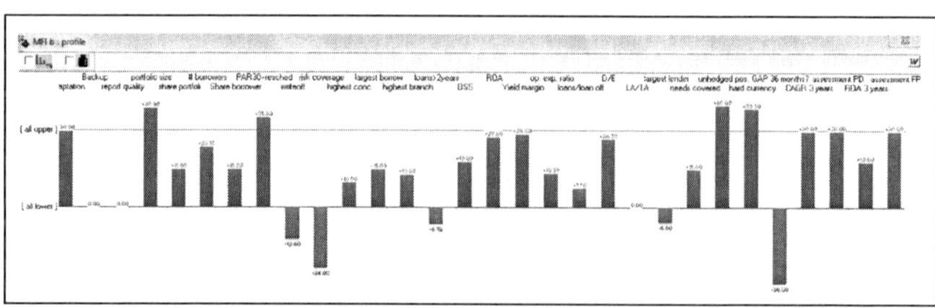

With profiles like these, investment officers can show the investment committee why an MFI has obtained a certain score, and in which areas it is strong or weak.

5.3 Lessons learnt from the application of MACBETH

The MACBETH approach has provided solutions to the two problems stated by the investment team at the beginning of the process. First, it addressed the apparent subjectivity of their assessments. Indeed, the method provides assurance that how performance is measured is consistent with what the whole team has agreed for each decision criterion. More importantly, the satisfaction provided by a certain level of performance has become more objective because it is now clearly reflected in the neutral and good reference levels, and in the adjusted curve (if the criterion is quantitative) or the relative distances between the performance levels (if the criterion is qualitative). In other words, the organisation's values regarding desired performance are embedded in the tool, and the decisions that will be made using it will reflect these values. Second, the investment committee can now understand the meaning of the scores provided thanks to their understanding of the neutral and good performance levels. The investment team can now justify exactly what a 70% score represents, and what are the strengths and weaknesses of a given MFI.

The approach has also given the investment team a clearer view of their daily decisions. They have been obliged to think deeply about the meaning of each decision criterion in their assessment tool. In doing so, they have realised that some were not easy to use or lacked consensus on how they should be evaluated on the field, or that some of them were useless because they were not able to express a 'neutral' or 'good' level of performance for them.

Most importantly, the MACBETH approach creates sense and meaning. The investment team can now clearly define what are neutral or good levels of performance for every criterion of their decision-making tool.

The values of an organisation as stated in its mission are difficult to incorporate into everyone's behaviour and decision making. Indeed, we often observed strong differences of opinion between team members with regard to acceptable levels of performance on certain criteria. This exercise has therefore benefited the team, who are now able to spot where the strongest divergences are and so fix them.

6. Conclusion

As MIVs face several bottlenecks regarding their future role in the microfinance industry, this chapter suggests a new way of reviewing their commitment to double bottom line returns.

MIVs face a difficult task when it comes to measuring and aggregating data on the financial and social performance of MFIs. They are often criticised for a lack of transparency in their methods. The existing social performance assessment tools have been beneficial to the microfinance industry, but unfortunately suffer from mathematical flaws that undermine their usefulness for investors, who need robust methods.

The present research, in partnership with a major microfinance fund manager, has implemented the MACBETH approach for the first time in helping choose debt investments in microfinance. Beginning from lengthy discussions with decision makers, it can be seen that the MACBETH approach allows the double bottom line mission of an MIV to be translated into operational decision criteria. These can then be weighted through an innovative and rigorous methodology based on qualitative judgments.

This methodology creates a meaningful unit for measuring performance on any criterion, financial or social: the difference of attractiveness between two reference levels, the acceptable (neutral) and the desirable (good). Indeed, to assess an option, decision makers must first define lower and upper levels of performance; the MACBETH approach provides exactly this, just by asking for qualitative judgments. Moreover, by being able to calibrate accurately the satisfaction provided by a given performance on any criterion, the assessment of potential investments precisely reflects the values and expectations of the decision makers.

The MACBETH approach also requires the whole decision-making team to agree on two major questions for each criterion: "How do we measure it?" and "What performance do we want?" Every decision taken will therefore reflect the organisation's objectives and values. As a consequence, MIVs will be able to show transparently that their investments match the interests of their investors. Our belief is that a combination of MACBETH with existing tools such as the SPI, which have made large advances in defining social performance, can create the transparency that MIVs need to assure the whole sector that their commitment to double bottom line returns is real. Moreover, there are different types of MIVs with varying degrees of profit motivation. The MACBETH approach would allow greater transparency regarding this diversity, simply by adjusting its performance scales to the different profit expectations.

There are some limitations to the approach. First, it allows only one system of values at a time to calibrate and weight the decision criteria. A fund manager in charge of several funds with different objectives, for example, will have to use a different MACBETH application for each fund. Second, this first application was tested for debt investments only. Equity investments follow a different logic. For these, more attention is given to the development prospects of the MFI rather than its current performance (financial or social). The MACBETH tool would need to be adapted to take this difference into account.

Finally, assuming the availability of data, future research can compare the subsequent performance of investments that have been screened using the MACBETH approach with those screened using classical techniques.

7. Appendix

Financial and social performance rankings before and after MACBETH are shown on the next page.

The authors are very grateful to their anonymous MIV partner. Without the time and effort put into this project by the investment team, this study would not have been possible. By participating in this innovative and challenging project, our MIV partner has demonstrated its strong social values and its willingness to build on new knowledge to further develop its own decision-making tools.

Financial performance				Social performance			
MFI	Financial score (before)	MACBETH financial attractiveness	Ranking (MACBETH)	MFI	Social score (before)	MACBETH social attractiveness	Ranking (MACBETH)
MFI 1	80	33	37th	MFI 1	85.4	78.96	1st
MFI 2	79	70.89	14th	MFI 2	84.9	45.07	25th
MFI 3	79	77	5th	MFI 3	84.2	31.33	33rd
MFI 4	79	64	21st	MFI 4	83.1	56.26	11st
MFI 5	77	84	2nd	MFI 5	83.0	64.73	6th
MFI 6	77	44	35th	MFI 6	83.0	61.74	9th
MFI 7	77	67	17th	MFI 7	81.3	55.67	12th
MFI 8	77	77	6th	MFI 8	80.8	55.19	13th
MFI 9	76	44	34th	MFI 9	79.0	67.67	4th
MFI 10	76	72	11th	MFI 10	78.8	70.9	2nd
MFI 11	76	52.65	30th	MFI 11	78.6	62.71	8th
MFI 12	75	75	9th	MFI 12	77.6	60.27	10th
MFI 13	75	71	15th	MFI 13	77.5	68.48	3rd
MFI 14	75	-16	43rd	MFI 14	76.0	45.65	23d
MFI 15	74	72	12th	MFI 15	76.0	31	34th
MFI 16	74	61	24th	MFI 16	75.7	37.48	30th
MFI 17	74	78	4th	MFI 17	74.3	28.52	35th
MFI 18	74	71.06	13th	MFI 18	73.9	65.62	5th
MFI 19	73	86	1st	MFI 19	73.3	48.42	19th
MFI 20	73	-3	40th	MFI 20	73.0	39.5	29th
MFI 21	73	65	20th	MFI 21	72.0	50.0	18th
MFI 22	72	74	10th	MFI 22	72.0	-137.8	45th
MFI 23	72	63	23rd	MFI 23	71.1	54.8	14th
MFI 24	71	76	7th	MFI 24	71.0	48.0	21st
MFI 25	71	55	27th	MFI 25	71.0	-91.0	44th
MFI 26	71	54.43	28th	MFI 26	70.5	-11.3	43d
MFI 27	70	65	19th	MFI 27	70.3	48.1	20th
MFI 28	70	67	16th	MFI 28	70.0	40.8	28th
MFI 29	69	75	8th	MFI 29	69.9	46.12	22nd
MFI 30	69	66	18th	MFI 30	69.8	18.67	40th
MFI 31	68	42	36th	MFI 31	69.4	41.08	27th
MFI 32	68	63.84	22nd	MFI 32	68.0	51.30	17th
MFI 33	68	59.33	25th	MFI 33	67.6	43.40	26th
MFI 34	67	56.24	26th	MFI 34	65.7	23.90	37th
MFI 35	67	-13.63	42nd	MFI 35	65.0	18.11	41st
MFI 36	66	54	29th	MFI 36	64.8	52.85	16th
MFI 37	66	78.56	3rd	MFI 37	64.4	53.82	15th
MFI 38	66	52	31st	MFI 38	64.0	45.6	24th
MFI 39	65	46	32nd	MFI 39	63.0	18.96	39th
MFI 40	64	-32	44th	MFI 40	62.0	28.52	36th
MFI 41	64	45	33rd	MFI 41	60.0	5.55	42nd
MFI 42	63	-6	41st	MFI 42	58.2	62.88	7th
MFI 43	63	-63	45th	MFI 43	58.0	31.48	32nd
MFI 44	60	27	39th	MFI 44	57.9	34.39	31st
MFI 45	53	31	38th	MFI 45	51.6	23.52	38th

The strength of weak ties in microfinance

Cornell Jackson
Kings College London
Ana Marr
University of Greenwich

1. Introduction

Microfinance, typically provided through credit, has the goal of reducing poverty in a financially sustainable way. Many of the early pioneers of modern microfinance thought they had an effective way to deliver poverty reduction. For example, Rupert Scofield, the CEO of FINCA, an international microfinance network, has described the excitement of seeing the dramatic positive impact of loans on reducing the poverty levels of the entrepreneurial poor.[1]

Over time, however, microfinance has proved to have only a limited ability to reduce poverty significantly. Scofield himself observes that the entrepreneurial skills of the additional microfinance clients diminished, as did the impact of microcredit on poverty. Studies like his help explain why the impact of microcredit on poverty is currently under question. They appear to validate Bateman's argument[2] that the microfinance pioneers have fallen victim to the fallacy of composition; that is, the assumption that if microcredit works for the most entrepreneurial of the poor, it will also work for most of the poor. Also seemingly validated is Banerjee and Duflo's argument[3] that microfinance practitioners are guilty of promising too much.

Traditionally, microfinance has focused on financial mediation. Much of the research on poverty alleviation, however, indicates that it is not just a lack of access to finance that causes poverty. Poverty has multiple causes, a number of which are social in nature. In order to achieve greater poverty reduction microfinance needs to add social intermediation to its toolset.

The convention in microfinance is to provide working capital loans to clients to help them start, maintain or grow their businesses. However, in order to succeed these businesses need more than financial access. The success of these businesses is very important to microfinance institutions because, among other things, the greater the success, the higher the repayment rates on the loans by clients.

---

1 Scofield, Rupert (2012) Remarks made at the FINCA UK Breakfast Symposium – "Social Entrepreneurship: A Solution to Poverty Alleviation?" Held in London, UK on March 21 2012.

2 Bateman, Milford (2010) *Why Doesn't Microfinance Work: The Destructive Rise of Local Neoliberalism.* London: Zed Books.

3 Banerjee, Abhijit V. and Esther Duflo (2011) *Poor Economics: A Radical Rethinking of the Way to Fight Global Poverty.* New York: Public Affairs.

2. Low-entry-barrier and low-growth businesses

Most microenterprises are not very successful, however. Banerjee and Duflo[4] identify two main reasons for this. First, the businesses typically run by the poor are tiny. Second, these businesses make very little money. These businesses tend to have a high failure rate.

Bhagavatula and Elfring[5] show that this is because of a tendency among the poor to start low-entry-barrier businesses that are vulnerable to competition. It is therefore not surprising that microfinance clients are not able to achieve much poverty reduction through such businesses. Banerjee and Duflo, and Bhagavatula and Elfring agree that one of the main problems for microfinance clients is that they tend to start businesses that suffer from low growth, limiting the impact of financial intermediation.

As well as starting businesses that have low barriers to entry and are low in growth, the poor tend to open businesses that are the same as each other. Spears[6] attributes this tendency to "present bias". This is a tendency to focus on a business that will produce money in the present, rather than wait for a more valuable business that will produce more money in the future. However, Spears found an exception to this tendency. Microfinance clients who were literate, who treated their water before drinking it, who reported wanting to cut any category of spending – or who reported wanting to cut spending on intoxicants – were more likely to have an uncommon, rather than a common, business. These markers also indicate a significant commitment to the business.

Banerjee and Duflo argue that the real problem is that growing a business is too difficult for most poor people. They cannot borrow enough to grow the business to a reasonable size, and unless the business is extremely profitable it takes too long to save that amount. This can lead to a lack of commitment to and a lack of enthusiasm for the business. This is exacerbated by a tendency to run multiple businesses as a way to mitigate risk. Such individuals are unable to commit enough to one business to specialise and become good in one area. In addition, the structure of the typical microcredit product discourages the taking of large risks. Loan repayments usually have to start soon after the loan is given, meaning that the client needs a business that generates cash right away. This leads to Spears's present bias tendency.

Bhagavatula and Elfring argue that the only advantage a poor microentrepreneur can acquire in a low-entry-barrier environment are the social and business networks they nurture.

3. The importance of social networks

Social networks are defined and measured as connections among people, organisations, political entities (states and nations) and/or other units. These relationships can be studied using the theory and techniques of social network

---

4 *Ibid.*

5 Bhagavatula, Suresh and Tom Elfring (2010) "The Structure of Content in Multiplex Ties: Exploring the Advantages for Entrepreneurs in Rural India". Found on the Indian Institute for Management Bangalore Website at www.iimb.ernet.in/research/working-papers/structure-content-multiplex-ties-exploring-advantages-entrepreneurs-rural-india.

6 Spears, Dean (2009) "Dosas by the Dozen: Theory and Evidence of Present Bias in Microentrepreneurs", Institute for Financial Management and Research Centre for Microfinance Working Paper Series No 27.

analysis.[7] Christakis and Fowler[8] claim that the science of social networks provides a distinct way of seeing the world because it concerns individuals and groups, and how the former become the latter.

Social network analysts view society through a structural lens that says that the structure of society and the relationships within it are as important as the attributes of individuals in explaining what happens in society. Valente quotes Borgatti, Mehra, Brass and Labianca: "One of the most potent ideas in the social sciences is the notion that individuals are embedded in thick webs of social relations and interactions."[9]

What makes the structural view so important? What makes the relationships that form social networks so important? According to Valente, relationships matter because they influence a person's behaviour above and beyond the influence of his or her attributes. A person's attributes influence who they know and who they spend time with: their social network.

Social networks are important because human beings are ultra-social animals.[10] Christakis and Fowler[11] add that human beings don't just live in groups, they live in networks. Geoffrey Cohen, quoted in Syed[12] concurs: "The need to belong, to associate, is among the most important human motives. We are almost certainly hardwired with a fundamental motivation to maintain these associations."

Social networks are relevant to microfinance clients because their microenterprises need the latest information on markets, finance, customers, suppliers and the competition – information that often comes from a social network.

So, how do the dynamics of the network affect the poor? Price was the first to apply the process of cumulative advantage or preferential attachment to networks.[13] Preferential attachment, he argued, explains why the millionaire earns income more quickly than the beggar. This is now known as the rich get richer effect, and it produces what is known as a scale-free network. A scale-free network is one whose degree distribution follows a power law; that is, the number of nodes having a certain number of connections is found to vary as a power of the number of connections. Put more simply, they are networks in which a few nodes possess an overwhelming number of network connections. Barabási has argued that scale- free networks occur because people want to connect to networks at their most central locations.[14] This results in a strengthening of those locations' central positions.

In such a situation the rich maintain their position at the centre of the most important networks while the poor find themselves on the periphery. Christakis and Fowler argue that this social network dynamic reinforces two different kinds of

7 Valente, Thomas W (2010) *Social Networks and Health: Models, Methods and Applications*. Oxford: Oxford University Press.

8 Christakis, Nicholas and James Fowler (2010) *Connected: The Amazing Power of Social Networks and How They Shape our Lives*. London: Harper Press.

9 Borgatti, S P and A Mehra, D J Brass and G Labianca (2009) "Network Analysis in the Social Sciences", *Science*, Vol 323, pp 892–895, cited in Valente (2010).

10 Haidt, Jonathan (2006) *The Happiness Hypothesis: Finding Modern Truth in Ancient Wisdom*. New York: Basic Books.

11 Christakis and Fowler (2010).

12 Syed, Matthew (2010) *Bounce: The Myth of Talent and the Power of Practice*. London: Fourth Estate.

13 Price, Derek de Solla (1976) "A General Theory of Bibliometric and Other Cumulative Advantage Processes", *Journal of the American Society for Information Science*, Vol 27, No 5–6, pp 292–306.

14 Barabási, A -L (2003) *Linked: The New Science of Networks*. Cambridge, MA: Perseus.

inequality.[15] The first is situational inequality, meaning the socioeconomic inequality between individuals. The second is positional inequality, meaning an inequality in terms of individuals' network position. Christakis and Fowler further argue that the rich get richer dynamic means that the positive feedback loop between social connections and success concentrates even more power and wealth in the hands of those who already have it.

For Christakis and Fowler, the ability of network inequality to create and reinforce inequality of opportunity comes from the tendency of people with many connections to be connected to other people with many connections. The reverse is also true: those who are poorly connected usually have friends and family who are themselves disconnected from the larger network. This feature distinguishes social networks from neural, metabolic, mechanical and other non-human networks. Christakis and Fowler argue that in order to reduce poverty, the personal connections of the poor must be addressed. Poverty reduction measures should focus not only on monetary transfers or even technical training, but on helping the poor form new relationships with other members of society. When the poor on the periphery of the network are reconnected, the whole fabric of society benefits, not just those disadvantaged individuals at its fringe.

While there has been growing recognition of the role social intermediation plays beyond preparation for financial intermediation, there has been little recognition in the literature of the role of networks in social intermediation and helping microfinance institutions (MFIs) connect their microentrepreneur clients to the larger network. In order to determine how network theory contributes to an understanding of how microfinance can benefit clients who own their own businesses, we will now focus on the contribution of network theorists such as Granovetter and Burt, and how their concepts of weak ties, brokerage and closure help to answer to this question.

Granovetter's main contribution to social network theory has been his description of the role of weak ties. In a seminal paper[16] he identified the strength that weak ties can have in a network. Before Granovetter, in Wirth,[17] for example, weak ties were seen as a source of alienation. Gravonetter, however, saw their key strength as transmission routes, or bridging ties, for non-redundant or new information. Weak ties that are bridges – connections that carry information – actually strengthen a network. When he revisited his theory in 1983, Granovetter pointed to research by Coser[18] that suggests that because bridging weak ties link different groups, they are far more likely than other weak ties to connect individuals who are significantly different from one another.

For his 1973 paper Granovetter conducted a thought experiment to demonstrate why strong ties do not serve as transmission routes for non-redundant information.

15 Christakis and Fowler (2010).

16 Granovetter, Mark S (1973) "The Strength of Weak Ties", *American Journal of Sociology*, Vol 78, No 6, pp 1360–1380.

17 Wirth, Louis (1938) "Urbanism as a Way of Life", *American Journal of Sociology*, Vol 44, No 1, pp 1–24.

18 Coser, Rose (1975) "The Complexity of Roles as Seedbed of Individual Autonomy", *The Idea of Social Structure: Essays in Honor of Robert Merton*, ed L Coser. New York: Harcourt Brace Jovanovich.

Let us take a trio of people called A, B and C. If A has strong ties to both B and C, then it is very likely that B and C will also have a strong tie between them. This is because the stronger the tie between A and B or A and C, the more similar A and B or A and C will be. This logic leads to B and C being similar and therefore having a strong tie between them too. Granovetter says that this is confirmed by Heider's thesis of cognitive balance,[19] in which non-similarity among people with strong ties introduces stress into the relationships. This is also shown by the transitivity of interpersonal choices, where if P chooses O and O chooses X, then P chooses X. This occurrence is most likely where the ties between P and O and between O and X are strong. The more similar people are, the more likely it is that these people will have the same or redundant information. Therefore, except in unlikely conditions, strong ties do not act as bridges. It is for this reason, Granovetter says, that the removal of an average weak tie will do more damage to transmission probabilities than the removal of an average strong tie.

Granovetter found empirical evidence for the strength of weak ties from a random sample of technical, professional and managerial job changers who found employment through contacts. By using the number of times the job seeker had seen the contact recently as a measure of the strength of the tie, Granovetter found that most of the job seekers found work through their weak ties. The reason for this is that those to whom we are weakly tied – acquaintances, rather than close friends, for example – are more likely to move in circles different from our own. They will therefore have access to information different from that which we normally receive.

In his later paper,[20] Granovetter points to research by others that shows that poor people tend to rely more on strong ties. Ericksen and Yancey, for example, found that less well-educated respondents were those most likely to use strong ties for jobs.[21] In a separate study conducted in Philadelphia, they found that the "structure of modern society is such that some people typically find it advantageous to maintain strong networks and we have shown that these people are more likely to be young, less well educated, and black".[22] Two ethnographic studies demonstrate the same point: Stack studied a black, urban American, Midwestern ghetto; Lomnitz a shantytown on the fringes of Mexico City.[23] Both found that the poor relied on networks of strong ties that focused on reciprocal relationships.

Granovetter concludes that this pervasive use of strong ties by the poor and insecure is a response to economic pressures.[24] They believe themselves to be without alternatives, and the adaptive nature of these reciprocity networks is the main theme of the analysts. Granovetter also suggests that the heavy concentration of social energy in strong ties fragments poor communities into encapsulated networks that

---

19 Heider, F (1958) *The Psychology of Interpersonal Relations*. New York: Wiley.

20 Granovetter, Mark (1983) "The Strength of Weak Ties: A Network Theory Revisited" *Sociological Theory*, Vol 1, pp 201–233.

21 Ericksen, E and V Yancey (1980) "Class, Sector and Income Determination", unpublished manuscript, Temple University.

22 Ericksen, E and V Yancey (1977) "The Locus of Strong Ties", unpublished manuscript, Department of Sociology, Temple University, p 23.

23 Stack, Carol (1974) *All Our Kin*. New York: Harper & Row; Lomnitz, Larissa (1977) *Networks and Marginality*. New York: Academic Press.

24 Granovetter (1983).

are poorly connected to one another. Individuals encapsulated in this way may then lose some of the outreach advantages associated with weak ties. This may be another reason why poverty is self-perpetuating.

Network structure can also affect the creation of social capital. Burt observes that two network structures have been proposed as creators of social capital.[25] Under the closure argument, social capital is created by a network of strongly interconnected elements. Under the structural hole argument, social capital is created by a network in which people can broker connections between otherwise disconnected segments. Structural holes are holes or gaps in the social network, and social capital comes from bridging these structural holes with weak bridging ties like those described by Granovetter. Burt draws from a comprehensive review made elsewhere[26] to support two points: that there is replicated empirical evidence on the social capital of structural holes; and that the contradiction between network closure and the structural holes network can be resolved in a more general network model of social capital. Brokerage across structural holes is what adds value, but closure can be critical to realising the value buried in bridging structural holes. Burt also argues that network closure creates advantage by lowering the risk of cooperation. It also facilitates sanctions that make it more likely for people in the network to trust one another. Brokerage across structural holes creates advantage by increasing the value of cooperation.

Microfinance clients in groups are therefore probably generating social capital simply through their frequent meetings and lending. However, does the social structure around them impede or help the creation of social capital and accessing opportunities? Many microfinance clients live in hierarchical cultures. Theory seems to suggest that getting information from vertical links in the network is difficult. Does this mean that clients who need to bridge the structural holes around themselves using vertical ties because they live in a hierarchical society face a near impossible task? Is this especially so if few or no solidarity networks already exist in their area? These are key questions – particularly so if social capital is essential for microentrepreneurial success, as Gomez and Santor suggest.[27]

In summary, microfinance clients need to add weak bridging ties to their social networks to help them access the latest business information, strengthen their social networks and gain competitive advantage in businesses with low barriers to entry.

This leads us to two questions, which will be addressed in the remainder of this chapter:

- How does a MFI help its clients bridge structural holes?
- How can a MFI socially intermediate to help clients establish weak bridging ties?

---

25 Burt, Ronald S (2000b) "The Network Structure of Social Capital", *Research in Organisational Behaviour*, ed Robert I Sutton and Barry M Staw, pp 345–423. Greenwich, CT: JAI Press.

26 Burt, Ronald S (2000a) "Structural Holes versus Network Closure as Social Capital", Chapter 2 of *Social Capital: Theory and Research*, ed Nan Lin, Karen S Cook and Ronald S Burt New York: Aldine de Gruyter.

27 Gomez, Rafael and Eric Santor (2001) "Membership has its Privileges: The effect of social capital and neighbourhood characteristics on the earnings of microfinance borrowings", *Canadian Journal of Economics*, Vol 34, No 4, pp 943–966.

4. Visualisations

Before going any further, however, it should be noted that one of the key advantages of social network analysis is the ability to visualise the network using software. Features that are not readily apparent from the numbers can become very apparent in a visualisation. The popular SNA software package UCINET[28] was used to map and analyse the networks of the sari sellers. Its companion software component NetDraw[29] was used to visualise the networks.

On a field trip to India during research to answer the above questions,[30] each respondent was asked to identify which members of the self-help group did the most work. In looking at the visualisations below, it is important to note that direction is important. In this case, the base of the arrow is at the respondent and the arrowhead points to the people the respondent thinks are important. The more arrowheads a person has, the more important the person is within the self-help group.

Figure 1 is the visualisation of the answers for the male self-help group, and Figure 2 is that for one of the female self-help groups.

Figure 1: Male self-help group: who does the most work?

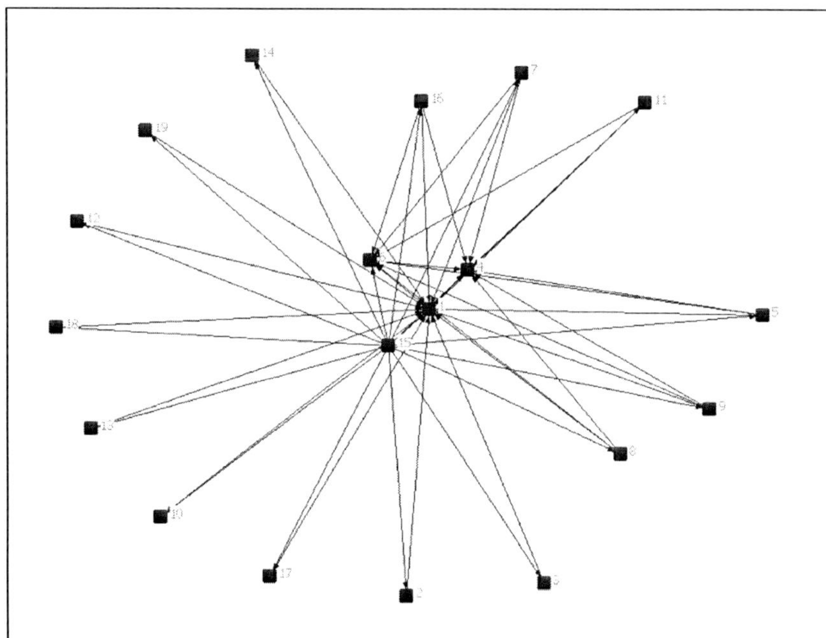

28 Borgatti, S P and M G Everett and L C Freeman (2002) *UCINET for Windows: Software for Social Network Analysis*. Harvard, MA: Analytic Technologies.

29 Borgatti, S P (2002) Netdraw Network Visualization Harvard, MA: Analytic Technologies.

30 See: Jackson, Cornell (2012) "The Strength of Weak Ties in Microfinance", doctoral dissertation, London: University of Greenwich.

Figure 2: Female self-help group: who does the most work?

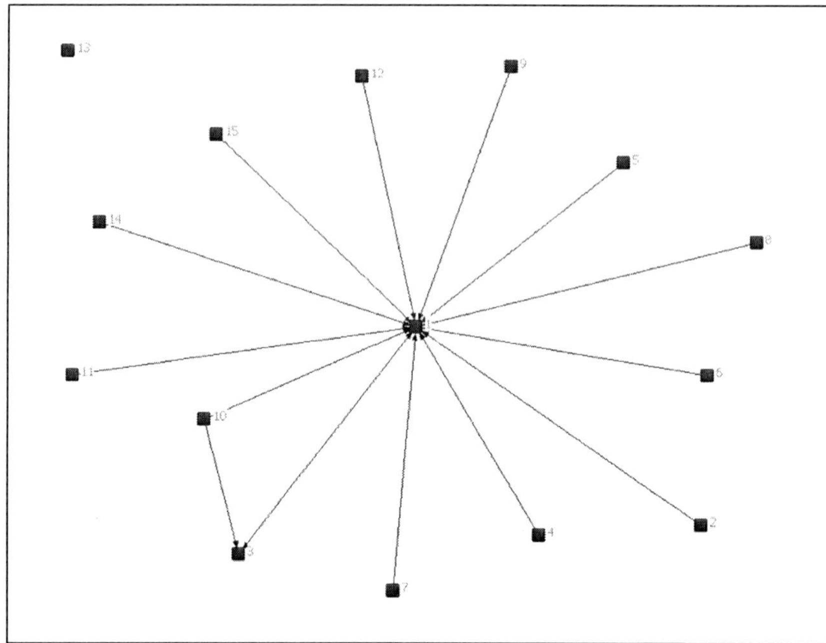

In Figure 1, most of the arrows point to the animator (self-help group leader) and the two representatives (deputy self-help group leaders). In Figure 2, almost all of the arrows point to the animator. In one sense, it is not surprising that the leaders have the most arrows pointing to them. However, another interpretation is to say that if anything happened to the leader of the male self-help group, there are two ready replacements. The female group, on the other hand, would be in considerable difficulty if its leader disappeared. These two figures show the power of visualisation in social network analysis.

5. Sari seller example

The Bullock Cart Workers Development Association (BWDA) based in Villupuram, Tamil Nadu in India agreed in 2009 to participate in the research project. BFL, the associated MFI, has more than 400,000 clients, more than 200,000 of whom have loans out at any one time. More than 21,000 self-help groups are associated with BWDA. The purpose of identifying which businesses were started and the number of them was to identify those businesses where the strength of weak ties could be used to improve a significant number of BWDA's clients.

Saris selling exhibited potentially interesting value chains and networks. Furthermore, not much research has been done on the sari industry in India. One sari seller confirmed that sari selling is a low-entry-barrier business by complaining that her sales remained flat because three new sari sellers were now operating on her street.

Because of the portability of saris, sari sellers can develop rich and interesting networks that would be able to test the theoretical framework. For these reasons, the decision was made to focus the research on sari sellers who were clients of BWDA. BWDA was asked to identify all self-help group members who sold saris in the Cuddalore and Villupuram Districts in the state of Tamil Nadu and the Union Territory of Pondicherry. There were a total of 111 sari sellers in the research population.

Sari sellers were asked about their network connections for information on the market, finance, customers and suppliers. However, respondents often could not remember all of the relevant connections when asked. In order to get a more complete network picture other methods were used. One such method was the reverse small world method.[31] In this technique, respondents were asked to name people who can carry information to persons outside their network. Although this method was conceived as a way of identifying the scale and nature of a respondent's global network of the respondent, Freeman and Thompson have made it clear that it only captures part of the global network.[32]

To measure the poverty level of each sari seller, the decision was made to use the Progress out of Poverty Index (PPI), an instrument created by the Grameen Foundation.[33] Using data from the national household surveys of India, PPI provides a scorecard of 10 simple criteria that estimates the likelihood of a household in India having an expenditure below a given poverty line.

When a sari seller identified an organisation as a link on the second field trip, she was asked to name a person in that organisation with whom she usually worked. If she was unable to name an individual, the link was dropped. This left the individuals identified during the second research field trip and individuals from organisations identified during the third research field trip. Using the technique created by Kahn and Antonucci[34] and also used by Hogan, Carrasco and Wellman,[35] respondents were asked to place these individuals to whom they were linked on a target diagram. How close they were to them was indicated by the distance they were placed from the central circle, representing the sari seller herself. The respondents were then asked to connect those people who know each other by drawing a line between them. The target diagrams were generously provided by Dr Paola Tubaro of the University of Greenwich; an example is shown in Figure 3. This diagram was typical of the networks of the sari sellers. These were small and focused on their strong ties. If they

31 Killworth, Peter D and H Russell Bernard (1978) "The Reversal Small World Experiment" *Social Networks*, Vol 1, No 2, pp 159–192; Bernard, H. Russell and Eugene C. Johnsen, Peter D. Killworth, Christopher McCarthy, Gene A. Shelley and Scott Robinson (1990) "Comparing Four Different Methods For Measuring Personal Social Networks", *Social Networks*, Vol 12, No 3, pp 179–215.

32 Freeman, L. C. and C. Thompson (1989) "Estimating Acquaintanceship Volume", Chapter 8 of *The Small World*, ed Manfred Kochen. Norwood, New Jersey: Ablex Publishing.

33 Schreiner, Mark (2008) "Progress out of Poverty Index: A Simple Poverty Scorecard for India". Found on the Progress Out of Poverty Website at: http://progressoutofpoverty.org/system/files/PPI_Design_Documentation_for_India_1.pdf.

34 Kahn, R L and T C Antonucci (1980) "Convoys over the life course: Attachment roles and support", *Life Span Development and Behaviour*, ed P B Baltes and O G Brim, Vol 3, pp 253–286. San Diego: Academic Press.

35 Hogan, Bernie and Juan Antonio Carrasco and Barry Wellman (2007) "Visualising Personal Networks: Working with Participant-Aided Sociograms", *Field Methods*, Vol 19, No 2, pp 116–144.

have weak ties, these tended to be individuals of the kind identified on this diagam (relatives and officials). However, the position of the bank official in this particular network indicates that a weak tie can become a strong tie. The local government minister was added as a result of the reverse small world method. When asked why he was placed so far away, the seller's reply was that in the latest elections he had been voted out of office.

Figure 3: Example of sari seller target diagram

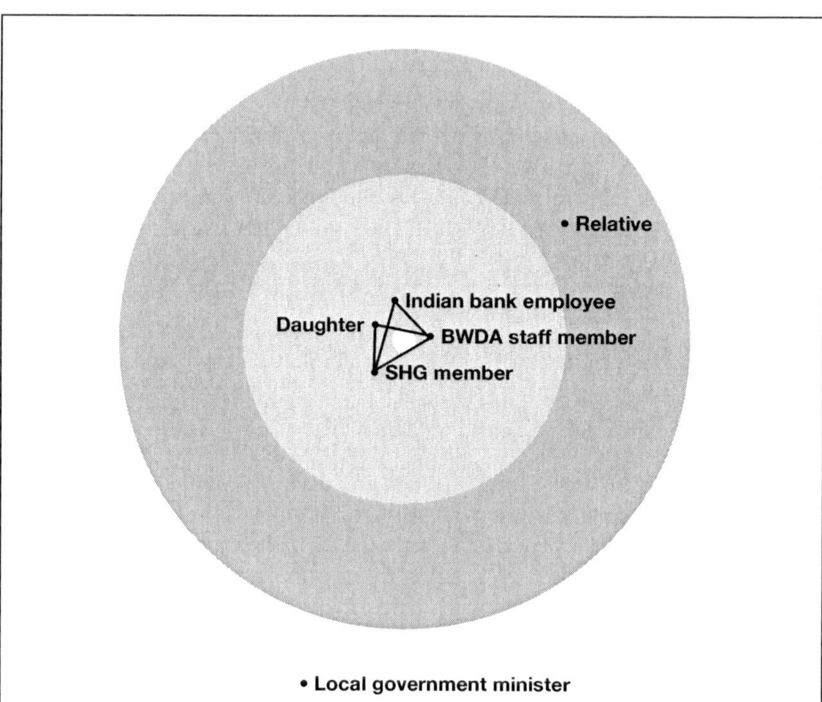

An intervention was made to see if weak bridging ties among the sari sellers could be established, and whether the the sari sellers saw an improvement in their business as a result. All the sari seller clients of BWDA in the Cuddalore and Villipuram Districts in Tamil Nadu and the Union Territory of Pondicherry were asked if they were willing to share information and/or skills with other BWDA sari sellers. They were allowed to put constraints on who they were willing to share information with. For example, they may not have wanted to share with nearby sari sellers who may have been seen as competitors. However, they may have been more willing to share with those further away.

A list of those sari sellers willing to share information was assembled, along with their contact details. This list was given to sari sellers in the Villipuram District only. Sari sellers in the other districts effectively served as a control group. Because what was being offered were information and skills, the contacts should have formed weak bridging ties. It was also assumed that the typical social hierarchy issues would not come up because of the castes to which the sari sellers belonged. Of the 111 sari sellers, only two were Brahmin. The overwhelming majority of the sari sellers came from the backward castes. After the intervention the sellers' social networks were remapped to see if there had been any changes to the PPI score and to see if the sari sales for Diwali in 2011 were higher, lower or the same as the sari sales for Diwali 2010.

6. Sari seller findings

A key finding is that the sari sellers relied mostly on strong ties. Granovetter showed how the poor often rely on strong ties.[36] Burt predicts that individuals who depend on mostly strong ties will be surrounded by structural holes.[37] This will tend to lead to exploitation as the poor have few ties and options available to them. This research has found what appears to be a number of structural holes within the sari sellers' network.

When the networks of the sari sellers are combined with their BWDA contacts, the resulting network is fragmented and contains a number of structural holes. There are no ties between branches of BWDA in the network except through the BWDA head office. In this way, the full network resembles a command and control structure in which the different silos join only at the top. There are almost no ties between sari sellers of different branches. The establishment of weak ties between sellers should be able to bridge the structural holes and help stabilise the network.

The intervention was timed to take advantage of the Diwali sales. Diwali, the Hindu festival of lights, is one of the biggest sari-selling seasons in Tamil Nadu. (The other is Pongal, the Tamil harvest festival, usually held in the middle of January.) The hope was that this festive season would encourage sellers to contact other sari sellers to establish weak bridging ties to get information and so increase their sales.

The proxy for the improvement in the sari selling business was a year-on-year improvement of the number of saris sold for Diwali. Of the 30 sari sellers, only three saw an increase, and all three were in the treatment group. An increase in the number of customers was the explanation for all three of them. Only two sari sellers saw a year-on-year decrease in Diwali sales. One sari seller said that this was because the designs of the saris her supplier sells is unpopular. She said that she did not know another supplier who sold more popular designs. This situation cries out for a weak bridging tie to allow the seller to access the necessary information on suppliers.

However, one sari seller from Villapuram and an incident that took place while interviewing members of the control group in Pondicherry provide indications that the theory of the strength of weak ties holds for microfinance clients who have low-growth, low-entry-barrier businesses.

The incident in Pondicherry occurred during the course of interviewing 15 sari sellers at the BWDA branch office there. One seller asked the translator why BWDA was not buying saris in bulk for all of the sari sellers, so obtaining a big discount

36 Granovetter (1983).
37 Burt.

which would increase the profit margins for all sellers. The translator stopped the interview and told everyone the question that had been asked. The translator, who was very familiar with the research, said that BWDA was working on this suggestion but that it would take some time. He asked in the meantime whether anyone in the room knew of anyone living in Surat, Gujarat. Surat is now the centre of sari production in India. It is over 1,500 kilometres away from Pondicherry on the west coast of India. One sari seller raised her hand to say that her son lived there. The translator then told everyone to give this woman their mobile telephone numbers so that she could coordinate a bulk order of saris that her son could purchase. The effect on the room was electric. It was obvious that no one had thought of this before. The sari sellers, being less powerful, were depending on the more powerful BWDA to solve this problem for them. They had never thought of organising a solution themselves. They were so excited about organising a bulk purchase among themselves that the translator had to ask them to be quiet so that he could continue to conduct the interviews.

In this case, the translator provided the mechanism to create weak bridging ties among the sari sellers that brought them new, non-redundant information. This included identifying a seller with a link to Surat and finding ways to combine their efforts to buy saris in bulk and increase their profit margins. With a large enough increase in margins, the sari sellers would start to see a real reduction in poverty. One can imagine what could happen if this scenario had been repeated with other BWDA sari seller clients. This case shows why microfinance theory needs to take into account social networks and the strength of weak ties in microfinance.

For the sari seller from Villupuram, the increase in Diwali sales can be tied to the addition of weak bridging ties to her social network. Both her PPI score and her Diwali sales were up. When asked why her 2011 Diwali sales had increased, she said that she had added a new friend to her social network who had introduced her to a lot of new customers. It was these new customers that led to a large increase in sales. This new friend started as a weak tie, but is now a strong one. The introduction to new customers is probably what strengthened the tie between the two. One can imagine the benefits of other BWDA sari seller clients having weak bridging ties that could introduce them to new customers. Once again, this case shows how concepts of social networks and the strength of weak ties can increase the potential of microfinance.

7. Strengthening microfinance clients' networks

So, how does a MFI help its clients bridge structural holes and socially intermediate to help them establish weak bridging ties? This research identifies five ways this may be done:

- Assistance swaps – those with the information or skills needed for sari selling can offer these to other sari sellers who need them. Because this would entail passing information between people who may not know each well, the link has the potential to become a weak bridging tie.
- Acting as a broker – the MFI is to act as a broker between its clients and the mainstream markets. In this case, BWDA can act as a broker between the sari

sellers and the sari industry and negotiate large discounts on bulk orders of saris for all of its sari sellers. However, it is important that someone with industry experience is negotiating on behalf of the MFI so that neither the MFI nor its clients suffer from the vagaries of the industry.

- Sector-based networks – the MFI is to build a sector-based network. There brings two benefits to the clients. First, clients can build weak bridging ties among other clients in the same sector. Second, these clients can obtain closure (Burt, 2005) by learning from other clients in the network.
- Mentoring – the MFI is to provide mentors from the industry to their clients most likely from people retired from the industry. Again, the client gets closure from being trained by the mentor. The client can also gain from the status of the mentor, allowing them to establish weak bridging ties based on the mentor's recommendation.
- Increased security – the MFI can help its clients establish weak bridging ties by making them feel more more secure. Granovetter (1983) said that the main reason that the poor relied on strong ties was insecurity. Therefore, the more secure a MFI can make its clients feel, the more they will feel free to explore establishing weak bridging ties for their businesses.

8. Summary

The key problem for microfinance is that it has not achieved the degree of poverty reduction envisioned by its founders. One key reason for this is the low-growth, low-barrier-to-entry businesses often started by microfinance clients. Microfinance theorists have previously focused on financial intermediation. Using Granovetter's thought on social networks, however, the present chapter reveals the necessity of emphasising the social intermediation aspect of microfinance. In this context, social intermediation adds weak bridging ties to the social networks of microfinance clients. These in turn lead to improvements in their businesses and the reduction of poverty.

Our research has identified five ways in which MFIs could accomplish this goal. The main implication is that if placing an emphasis on social intermediation works for sari sellers, it will work for other low-growth, low entry-barrier microenterprises. By using the strength of weak ties, microfinance can achieve its goal of helping reduce poverty among its clients.

The authors are grateful to the Leverhulme Trust for its financial support (Research Grant Ref F/00 345/D) to the project Optimising the Dual Goals of Microfinance.

Microfinance and the impact of mobile banking

Cameron Goldie-Scot
Musoni BV

1. Introduction

Much has been written about the success of Safaricom's mobile money transfer (MMT) service M-PESA and the different ways it has transformed the lives of ordinary Kenyans. The simple act of being able to send money from one person to another, over a mobile phone and as easily as sending a text message, has not only revolutionised the payments environment in Kenya, but has also led to the creation of many new businesses that take advantage of the new technology. These include microfinance institutions.

From improving back office efficiency and reducing costs, to penetrating rural areas and improving the client experience, the advantages of linking mobile money to microfinance are clear. Nevertheless, many microfinance institutions have been slow to adopt mobile banking technology, and very few have been able to take full advantage of its potential. In this chapter, I hope to explain the fantastic opportunity that linking microfinance and mobile money provides to improving both the quality and availability of financial services delivered to the poor, informal sector. I will cover the benefits for a microfinance institution (MFI) of partnering with MMT services, as well as the challenges faced when doing so. In particular, I will draw upon my experiences with Musoni, the world's first MFI to be completely mobile, carrying out 100% of its loan repayments and disbursements through mobile money.

2. Problems with traditional microfinance

Access to financial services plays a key role in alleviating poverty and improving lives. It enables individuals to stabilise their sources of income, to build up assets, to plan for the future and to manage emergencies such as a fire, a death in the family or an unplanned hospital bill. It provides a safe place to save money, and makes people feel more empowered and secure. And yet there are still one billion people without access to financial services. In sub-Saharan Africa alone this equates to more than 75% of the population, or roughly 500 million people. There are many reasons for financial exclusion, but one of the main ones is the limited availability of financial services. Most of the unbanked live in remote rural areas with no access to bank branches or ATMs. Setting up branches in remote locations can be prohibitively expensive for traditional financial institutions, and as a result most sub-Saharan Africans have to travel long distances to reach their nearest bank.

While microfinance institutions play a key role in expanding financial inclusion, all too often they are expensive, inefficient and bureaucratic. This can mean poor products and services for clients, who are left servicing loans that are expensive and confusing. Most microfinance branches also tend to be concentrated in urban and peri-urban areas. Few (albeit with some notable exceptions) have really been able to penetrate rural communities meaningfully. Microfinance institutions also tend to compete for the same clients as traditional banks, leaving large numbers of the population without access to formal financial services.

At the same time, however, mobile phones have penetrated the continent over the last decade. By the end of 2012, a massive 73% of African owned a mobile phone. Many of the one billion people who do not have a bank account do have a mobile phone.

Mobile money transfer services have rapidly taken off alongside this growth in mobile phone penetration.

3. Success of MMT services

To date, over 18 million Kenyans use M-PESA on a daily basis. There have been similar successes in other countries. Vodacom Tanzania recently announced that the number of people using its MMT service had risen to 4.4 million and that more than $22 million was transferred between people each day. Similar successes can also be seen in Uganda (where MTN has approximately 3 million MMT customers) and indeed all across sub-Saharan Africa. A recent study by the Gates Foundation, the World Bank and Gallup discovered that in 15 African countries, at least 10% of people had used mobile money in the previous 12 months. The implications of this for financial inclusion are huge. Unlike traditional banking infrastructure (bank branches and ATMs), the extensive network coverage, huge agent networks and rapid increase in mobile phone penetration means that MMT services are able to leapfrog the traditional barriers of distance and poor infrastructure to bring financial services directly to those living in the most remote locations, or at least those locations not served by traditional financial institutions. In Kenya, for example, there are over 40,000 M-PESA agents (used to cash-in and cash-out from the platform) compared to approximately 1,163 bank branches and 2,205 ATM machines.

4. Microfinance and mobile banking

In spite of the potential that mobile banking brings to the financial sector, many microfinance institutions have been slow to adopt MMT services. It is therefore ironic that M-PESA began life in 2005 as a project funded by the UK Department for International Development specifically targeting the microfinance community, and funded with the aim of providing affordable financial services to those at the bottom of the pyramid. However, as Claire Penicaud of the Mobile Money for the Unbanked programme at the GSM Association has argued, this is not surprising: "typical mobile money services have not been designed with the vision of serving MFIs, but rather individuals, and using mobile money to supplement their operations presents a number of challenges for MFIs". In addition, microfinance institutions are generally cautious. This is a good thing when dealing with credit, but less so when dealing with new working methods. Change can be slow, and moving away from cash requires a huge leap of faith for many MFIs. In spite of these obstacles, the

Department for International Development's original idea remains valid, and the benefits that mobile money can bring to MFIs are very real.

5. Benefits of mobile money

Apart from a pilot between Faulu and Safaricom, the first MFI to allow its clients to repay their loans using M-PESA was SMEP, based in Nairobi. During this trial, many of the benefits of linking mobile banking to microfinance began to make themselves clear. On September 10 2008, instead of carrying cash to his weekly meeting, Mohammad Githio Yunus, a SMEP client (who coincidentally shares a name with the father of modern microfinance), used his mobile phone to repay his microfinance loan. What had previously been a manual, time-consuming and occasionally risky cash process became safer, faster and more efficient.

In traditional microfinance, loans are disbursed to individuals who co-guarantee each other within a group structure. To repay a loan installment, each member of the group carries their weekly profits through the streets or on local public transport until they reach the place where their group is meeting. Carrying bundles of cash around the low-income areas of Kenya is inherently risky, and it is not unknown for clients to be robbed on their way to the group meeting, or indeed for entire groups to be robbed while at the meeting itself. Each individual's repayment is collected, counted and confirmed at the meeting. As a result, meetings frequently last upwards of an hour, and occasionally even longer. Once this laborious process has been completed, one of the leaders of the group will normally take the entire group's bundle of notes down to the bank before queuing – again for up to an hour – and finally depositing the group's money and collecting a deposit receipt. For those micro-entrepreneurs who are servicing loans, the whole process is a waste of precious time.

In contrast, by using M-PESA, SMEP clients were able to load their money onto their phones at nearby M-PESA agents, and with the click of a button, send their weekly repayment directly into their SMEP account. This allowed them to spend more time running and growing their businesses. Feedback from clients was extremely positive. Nelly Barati, the owner of a small tailoring business, commented "Before, weekly meetings took two hours, now they only take 30 minutes", before adding, "With M-PESA lots of time is saved." Elizabeth Nyambura, who ran a phone accessories shop, agreed, but believed that the ease and flexibility of M-PESA were its most important benefits. "As soon as I make my money, then I put it on my phone and send it to SMEP: it is very safe and secure."

Despite such positive responses, early attempts to integrate mobile banking and microfinance also encountered some challenges. During the Faulu/Safaricom pilot, it was noticed that Faulu's back office system could not handle electronic payments or record keeping. As a result, every transaction had to be manually logged before being entered into the computer. Similar problems occurred at SMEP, where the integration between M-PESA and their system still involved many manual processes and was prone to errors. Because mobile money transactions still needed to be physically entered into the system, the back office efficiency gains the MFIs hoped to realise failed to materialise. Additionally, handling mobile money payments alongside cash repayments caused confusion both for wealth creation officers, who struggled to keep track of who had repaid and who had not (with some clients saying that they had paid on M-PESA when in fact they had not), and clients, for whom the technology was still new. As some clients still repaid cash at group meetings, the reductions in group meeting time were also limited. Management also feared that removing the cash repayments from group meetings would reduce the incentive to turn up to the group meeting at all, and therefore affect the quality of the portfolio.

All the same, these early pilot programmes demonstrated the potential of introducing innovative new technologies to the microfinance industry. I was part of the team that decided to set up a new greenfield MFI that would be completely cash-free. From day one it would use mobile money for all loan repayments and disbursements, as well as the depositing and withdrawal of savings. In September 2009, after almost a year of preparations, Musoni BV was founded. By May 2010, Musoni Kenya had disbursed its first loan and at the end of 2012 it had established five branches and successfully disbursed over 25,000 loans (roughly $8.5 million) entirely through MMT services.

Musoni's decision to use MMT services for all transactions meant that it was able to realise immediately many of the benefits that had been seen in the earlier pilots. Because it did not have to worry about handling cash alongside mobile payments, it was also able to avoid many of the problems that these projects had encountered. Musoni clients are still required to meet regularly with their Wealth Creation Officers, either on a weekly basis, or fortnightly/monthly for more experienced clients. This ensures that the close relationship between the client and the officer is maintained, which in turn is important to ensure repayments continue to be made and the portfolio remains healthy. However, by completely cutting out the act of handling cash from the group meetings, and instead requiring clients to repay their loans in advance of the group meeting using M-PESA, the amount of time spent in each meeting is greatly reduced. This allows wealth creation officers to focus their efforts where they are needed most – working with difficult clients and attracting new clients, rather than wasting time counting cash.

By completely removing cash from all operations, the company also benefits from the reduced potential for fraud. One of the most common acts of fraud in microfinance institutions involves deals struck between the loan officer and the client, a common example being the loan officer keeping part of the client's repayment for himself in exchange for approving the loan. When all repayments are handled electronically over a mobile payments channel, clients are able to repay straight into the system of the MFI itself, bypassing the loan officer and leaving a clear electronic trail for auditors or members of management to follow.

Making clients repay with mobile money significantly reduces the number of manual errors. In a traditional microfinance institution, all loan repayments are physically entered into the banking system by tellers, located either at the branch or in Head Office. Each day the tellers receive a pile of repayment slips indicating the details of every individual client and the amount they have repaid. One by one, each repayment is entered. Occasionally mistakes are made. When you are entering your one hundredth repayment of the day, it is easy to add on an extra zero by mistake, allocate the money to the wrong client's account, or even forget to complete the process itself. These errors not only result in incorrect information being presented to staff and clients, but also make reconciling mobile money accounts with the banking system extremely difficult. At Musoni, each day around 1,000 M-PESA repayments are automatically processed in a single batch. The system is able to recognise the client making the repayment through their phone number, and automatically allocates the repayment to the correct account. In this way, Musoni, and any other MFI using MMT for repayments, is able to immediately reduce the number of manual errors made each day, improve the ease of reconciling accounts, and of course avoid hiring large numbers of data entry clerks.

Automatic processing of mobile repayments improves the reliability of the data available to wealth creation officers and members of management. Officers are able to check each morning which clients have repaid and which have not, while members of management can monitor staff performance on a real-time basis. In comparison to traditional microfinance, where it can take days for all repayments to be manually processed, with loan officers never aware of their key performance indicators, making reliable information available throughout the institution in real time makes it much easier for the core microfinance operations to function smoothly.

The ability to repay on a mobile phone also increases the flexibility of repaying for clients. Rather than tying repayments specifically to a group meeting at which cash is handed over, clients can use mobile money to repay from anywhere in the country, at any time of day or night. Elizabeth Nangila, one of Musoni's early clients, described this benefit at one of Musoni's promotional filming sessions: "You can pay anywhere, even if you are in the vehicle you can pay, at night you can pay. Even if you are in the bathroom and you feel like you have money, you can ask for your phone and pay."

You can not only repay your loan from anywhere, but also receive it wherever you are. Because Musoni can disburse loans straight to the client's mobile phone, there is no need to meet physically to hand over a cheque or cash. This means that clients can receive their funds on the same day as they apply for a loan. Comparing this with more traditional options, where they cannot receive their loan until at least their next group meeting, clients regard this as a key benefit of linking microfinance with mobile banking. Collins Karanja, who runs a stall selling bananas and sweet potatoes, argues that "the greatest advantage of Musoni is that their loans are processed fast. If you apply today, by tomorrow you receive the money."

Eliminating the need to handle and store cash significantly reduces the costs of setting up new branches. This is another potential way in which the success of MMT services can help expand financial services into rural areas. MFIs that use mobile money no longer require strong rooms or safe deposit boxes. They do not need to employ professional couriers to transport their cash to the nearest bank, and of course do not need to recruit tellers or build banking halls as no transactions actually take place at a branch level. Instead, branches effectively become marketing outlets, acting as a brick and mortar presence in local communities, and serving as a base from which field staff can operate. This should make it much cheaper to expand into areas that are hard to reach, both opening up more business for the MFI and increasing its social impact.

Perhaps most importantly from a social impact perspective, however, the back office efficiency gains that Musoni has been able to realise have enabled it to charge clients lower interest rates than those charged by other microfinance institutions. Compared to an average annual flat interest rate of approximately 25% in the Kenyan market, Musoni charges an average of 21% and is looking to reduce these rates further once it reaches profitability.

6. Challenges

Why then have MFIs been so slow to adopt mobile money? The benefits seem overwhelming: less time spent in group meetings, lower costs, reduced risk, improved efficiency, a better client experience and cheaper rural expansion.

One of the main challenges, especially for early adopters and smaller MFIs, whose IT systems are or were not built to handle mobile payments, is the difficulty of efficiently processing large numbers of mobile payments. Even today, many of the MFIs in Kenya who enable their clients to repay using M-PESA still require a team of data entry clerks to record each mobile payment manually and then enter the same details again into their IT system. Without more intelligent integration between the two platforms, many of the gains in reducing fraud and manual errors will not materialise. Even when the MFI is able to process incoming repayments efficiently, a number of complicating factors still need to be considered. Most mobile money services have multiple transaction states, for example 'authorised', 'cancelled', 'completed' or 'expired'. On some occasions, a repayment will be made by a client and be given the status 'authorised', but may change in status to 'cancelled' a few days later. An MFI needs to decide at what point these transactions should be allocated to a client's account, and at what point has the client actually repaid. This requires additional business rules to be built into the system. MFIs also need to find ways to automatically handle transaction reversals, account transfers and many of the other different transaction types that can occur on the MMT platforms in order to get the maximum benefits out of partnering with MMT services. Fortunately there are now a number of companies, such as Kopo Kopo or Software Group, operating in Kenya that are able to help MFIs link to mobile payment platforms. Indeed, Musoni BV now also licenses its IT system to other MFIs.

Microfinance clients also make mistakes. Many are not technically literate, and they can often struggle to use technology with which they are not familiar. When making a repayment, most MFIs using mobile money tend to require clients to enter a unique identifier so that the institution knows which account to allocate the funds to. These unique identifiers can be complex, often involving more than 11 characters in a combination of numbers and letters. It is easy for a client to enter a single digit incorrectly, and for the incoming repayment to then either be allocated to the wrong client's account, or to be unable to allocate it at all. At Musoni, rather than have clients enter a unique identifier, clients instead enter 'LR' for loan repayment. The system then recognises the client using the mobile phone number from which the payment has been received. Even with this simple approach, some clients still make errors, and additional intelligence has had to be added to the system to ensure that a client entering '...—L.r.r' still has their payment allocated correctly. In spite of this, Musoni still is unable to allocate about 10 repayments each day. In these instances it is necessary to call the phone number from which the payment originated to determine where to allocate the funds.

These technical challenges can be overcome. There is no reason why many more microfinance institutions should not begin to partner with mobile banking channels. Across East Africa, and indeed the rest of the continent, MMT services are becoming increasingly commonplace. As clients become more familiar with the services in their day-to-day lives, it becomes easier for MFIs to persuade them to use their phones to carry out financial transactions. In Kenya now, most microfinance institutions have partnered with M-PESA and have embraced mobile microfinance to varying degrees. As one Kenyan practitioner recently put it, if you are not offering mobile money services in your MFI, then you have a problem. All the same, there is still a long way to go, and there is a big difference between enabling existing clients to transact using their mobile phone, and actively using mobile money to extend financial inclusion and reach previously unserved areas.

In Africa, the impact of mobile money on microfinance has so far been limited largely to Kenya. There is great potential for the lessons learnt over the last few years to be applied to the rest of the continent. As mobile money technology continues to develop, and as agent networks continue to expand, microfinance institutions can use MMT services to reduce their costs, grow their client base and improve the quality of the client experience. At Musoni, we are seeking to expand the number of products we offer through mobile telephones. We have also recently started using tablet devices to enable wealth creation officers to carry out their work without needing to come back to their branches every day. The aim is to continue penetrating rural areas, and to use technology to do so.

MFIs in India in the aftermath of the crisis

Sanjay Sinha
M-CRIL

---

1. The new Microfinance Act

Micro-credit Ratings International Limited's (M-CRIL) integrated financial and social review of Indian microfinance in 2012 analyses the performance of Indian microfinance institutions (MFIs) in the new regulatory environment that emerged from the crisis that began in October 2010.

The review concludes that while MFIs continue to be a significant component of the financial system and their contribution to financial inclusion continues to rival, if no longer exceed, that of the rural banking system, their efficacy has been undermined by the crisis and its aftermath. The government has now proposed a new Microfinance Act, which would:

- bring the sector under the jurisdiction of the Central Bank;
- enable MFIs to offer at least limited deposit services to low-income families (recognising their need for savings facilities); and
- protect MFIs from the whims of local government by clarifying that microfinance is governed by national laws and is therefore not a state-level concern.

In so doing it would remove the perception of political risk that has made commercial banks hesitate in lending on funds to MFIs. The bill contains all the legislation and regulation necessary to safeguard and stabilise the provision of microfinance services in India.

2. The microfinance crisis

With the phenomenal growth of microfinance in India in recent years (see Figure 1) – 62% per annum in terms of numbers of unique clients and 88% per annum in terms of portfolio over the five-year period 2005-2010, and around 32 million borrower accounts as of October 2010 – India had the largest MFI sector in the world. This high growth rate was fuelled by commercial bank funding, which gravitated towards for-profit institutional structures. This led to an India-wide trend towards the transformation of MFIs into for-profit non-bank finance companies (NBFCs) so that over 73% – 41 of the 56 MFIs in this year's M-CRIL analysis – now consist of such institutions. Both the transformed and new, start-up MFIs were able to grow rapidly through a combination of easy access to funding and by using the proven methodology of a mono-product offering rolled out over large numbers of branches in diverse locations using standard processes. This often took place in an environment of restricted staff-client interaction.

Figure 1: CRILEX, M-CRIL's growth index, March 2003

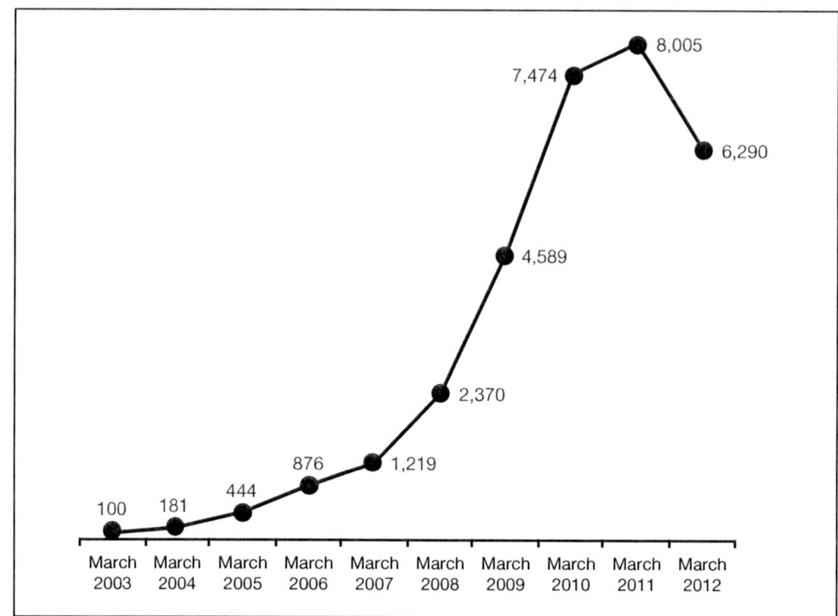

The current crisis is partly the result of the over-simplification of the MFI-client relationship. While large numbers of low-income families were reached, the fleeting nature of the instant relationship between MFI and borrower resulted in a lack of commitment on both sides, which led to substantial multiple lending. This prompted concern in the wider community about the rights of clients who had been oversold microcredit. Some clients became over-indebted as a result of the free access to debt and the media attention generated by the phenomenal success of the initial public offering (IPO) of SKS Microfinance (at the time, the largest microfinance non-banking financial company (NBFC) in India) only led to further discussion about the status of microfinance clients. Microfinance was blamed not only for this but also for reports of suicides in rural Andhra Pradesh (AP) – something that regrettably happens every year for a variety of reasons. Given the populist nature of state-level governance in India, conditions were ripe for intervention and the AP Microfinance Ordinance of October 14 2010 was the result.

This effectively banned the offering of financial services by MFIs in AP, halting the growth in Indian microfinance. The drying up of commercial bank funding to MFIs all over the country in response to the crisis has caused the sector to fall by nearly one-third from its peak in October 2010; the CRILEX, M-CRIL's index of microfinance growth (Figure 1) shrank from 9,000 at the end of September 2010 to an estimated 6,300 just 18 months later.

3. Still a significant part of the financial system

The number of effective client accounts served as of the end of March 2011 was nearly 35% lower than in the previous year. This is on account of the write-off (or dormancy) of a large number of client accounts in AP and also due to the reduction of funding for MFIs elsewhere as the AP government's action raised the commercial banks' perception of risk in lending to MFIs.

Figure 2: MFI credit accounts compared with other banks less than Rs25,000 (million accounts)

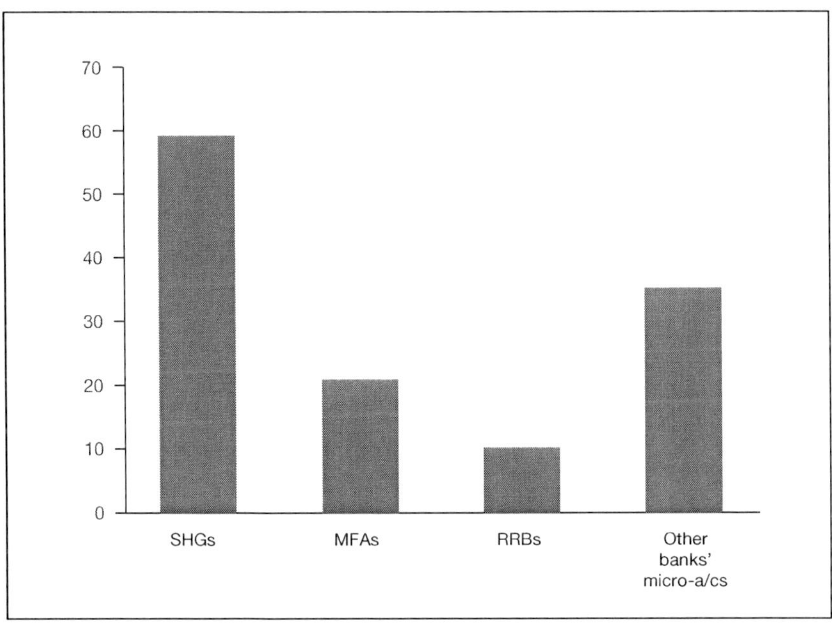

Even with only 21 million borrower accounts by the end of March 2012, the microfinance sector more than matches other significant parts of the Indian financial system in terms of the number of citizens affected. This is still more than twice the number of micro-credit accounts (ie, less than Rs25,000 or $500) serviced by the regional rural banks (as shown in Figure 2). In spite of the loss of all MFI operations in AP, MFI borrower accounts are still more than 60% of the total number of micro-accounts with commercial banks. If allowed to be seen as part of the mainstream financial system, the microfinance sector would have over 30% of the total number of formal micro-credit accounts; due to the recent decline of MFIs this proportion has fallen from around 45% in March 2011. Including self-help groups (SHGs), the total of micro-credit accounts in India held in the formal and semi-formal financial system is around 126 million.

4. MFIs and outreach

The intended income profile of MFI clients targeted by MFI managements is presented in Figure 3. After many years of debate on the feasibility of reducing poverty through microfinance, significant numbers of MFIs have realised the need to focus on low-income clients – whose incomes may or may not be below national or international poverty lines but who are, nevertheless, excluded financially. However, despite this, relatively few institutions systematically target poverty and M-CRIL's client analysis – based on social rating data – shows that a significant number of MFI client profiles are now close to matching the national poverty profile but are rarely able to reach beyond to the poorest families.

Figure 3: Stated client focus of reporting MFIs

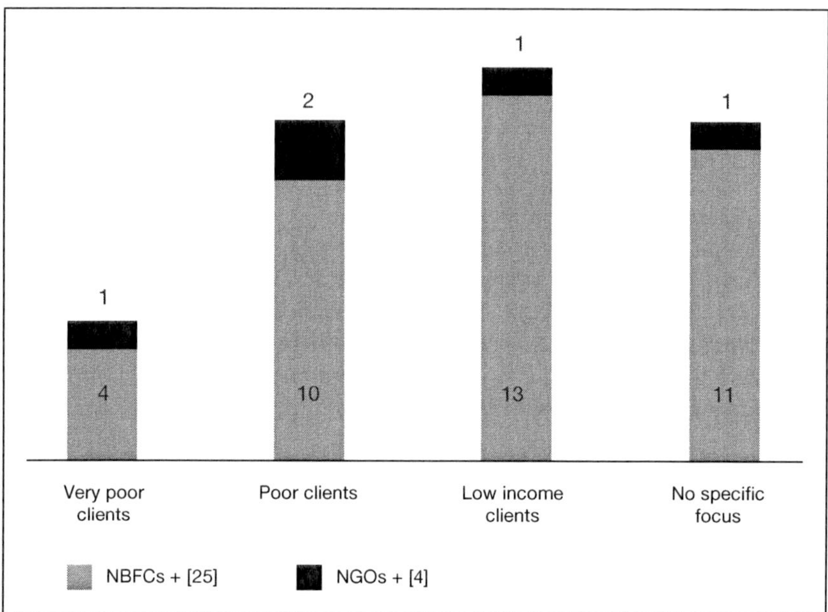

5. Reasons behind the crisis

The disruption caused by the AP law is substantial. The apparent reasons for this intervention were allegations of:

- excessive lending by MFIs in the state of AP leading to over-indebtedness, which caused distress to low-income microfinance borrowers; and
- coercive behaviour by MFI staff in collecting from these over-indebted borrowers.

Whether there was excessive lending in AP (and in other states) and who was responsible for it has been analysed in this year's M-CRIL Microfinance Review. The state-wide picture is disquieting. While the number of MFI loans in AP was just over 80% of the number of eligible financially excluded families in late 2010, SHG loans were actually 250% of that. More importantly, to the extent that microfinance loans were not evenly distributed this means that there were a significant number of financially excluded families in AP that had as many as five or six loans at any one time, a number of these being SHG loans. This raises the question of whether it was government-promoted SHG lending rather than MFI lending that was responsible for multiple lending in AP. The analysis reveals that even if the debt were distributed equally among all eligible families there would just be a balance of indebtedness in AP (in 2010-11) – assuming that 40% is the maximum reasonable debt servicing capacity at the income levels of typical financially excluded families. It is apparent that not only is debt distributed unequally but also, at lower assumed levels of debt servicing capacity, there is a significant degree of over-indebtedness.

6. The principle of responsibility

Since the crisis, new concern for responsible microfinance is reflected in the codes of conduct developed by MFIN and Sa-Dhan, and internationally in the client-protection principles developed through the Smart Campaign. M-CRIL had already included evaluation of responsibility to clients as part of its social rating. Starting this year M-CRIL, along with other specialist rating agencies, has launched the Microfinance Institutional Rating (MIR), an enhanced service that incorporates client protection, indebtedness and mission orientation as an integral part of output. Issues covered include integrity, transparency, governance, competition, client protection, appropriate staff behaviour and resolution of complaints. Most leading MFIs are taking action to improve performance in all these areas.

7. Falling cost efficiency

Figure 4: Cost per borrower (Rs)

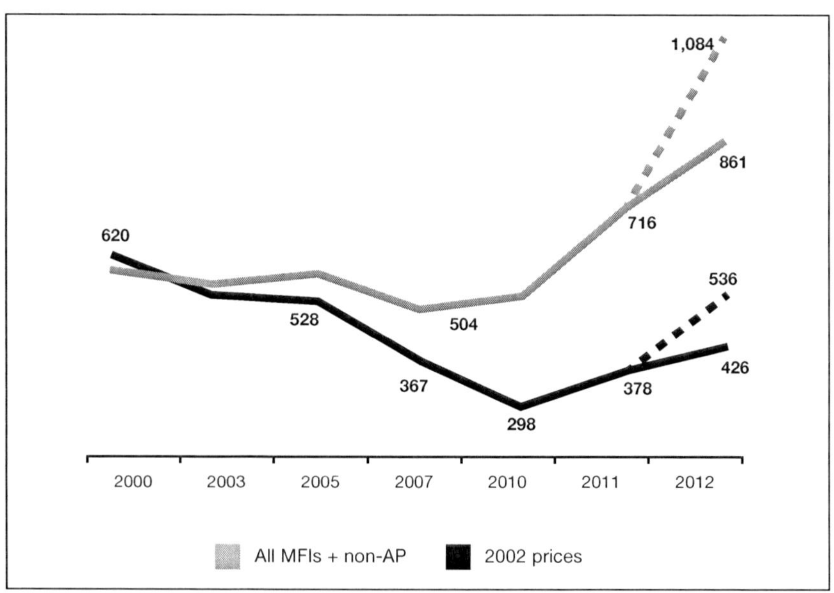

The cost incurred by Indian MFIs in servicing loan accounts is low compared to the global benchmark of $85 on the MIX. Even when compared to other Asian MFIs, the cost per borrower (Rs1,084 or $21) amounts to just 34% of the East Asian median of

$61 and is also substantially lower than the median for low-end MFIs internationally ($64). However, since the crisis, the cost per borrower for Indian MFIs has risen substantially. Even for non-AP MFIs, the Rs861 average cost per borrower for the delivery of micro-loans in India has increased by 60% over the past two years (Figure 4). This is attributable to the high "growth at all costs" pursued by MFIs in the first half of 2010 as the larger ones chased the chimera of an IPO, while the latter half of the year as well as 2011-12 was spent fire fighting, trying to persuade borrowers in AP to repay and those elsewhere to maintain their payments.

The weighted average operating expense ratio (OER) has also risen for Indian MFIs but is still significantly lower than those set out in the 2007 analysis by M-CRIL. The weighted average is now around 12% for both AP and non-AP MFIs but the typical non-AP MFI – as measured by the simple average across MFIs – had an OER of 17.3%, up from 15.6% last year.

8. Reversing the widening trend in the yield-OER margin

Figure 5: Trend in portfolio yield and OER

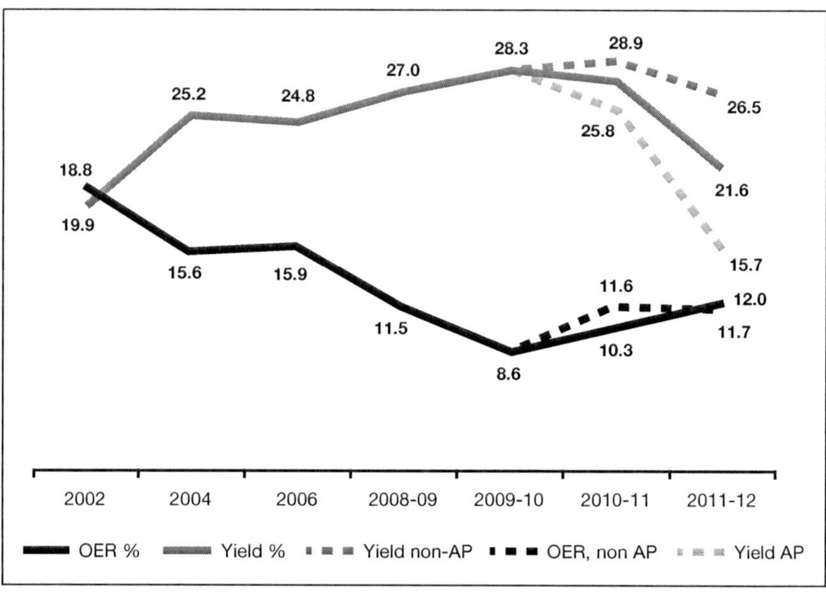

The weighted average yield of 26.5% for non-AP MFIs (compared to 28.3% last year) has declined further in response to the controversy about interest rates in the lead up to and immediately following the AP ordinance. Figure 5 shows the trend in portfolio yield and OER of Indian MFIs over the past 10 years. The portfolio yield increased significantly in recent years, largely because of changes in fees charged and sometimes on account of a change in the loan term when, say, a reduction in the term from 50 weeks to 45 weeks can have a significant impact on the yield, even though the change appears to be small. With this fall, the average yield earned by MFIs in India continues to be lower than the global median of 28%. On account of the interest and margin caps for microfinance NBFCs, the squeeze on margins is likely to continue during the current financial year (2012-13).

9. Portfolios outside AP

Figure 6: Long-term trend in the quality of portfolio

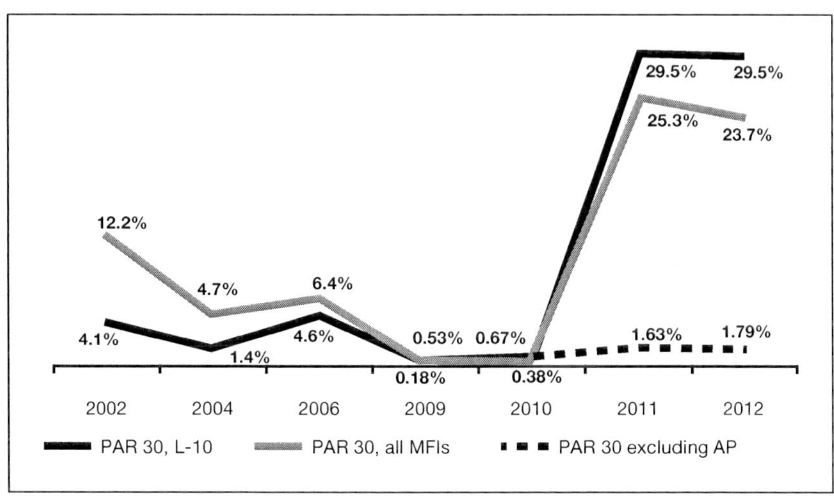

The unspoken message of the AP state law to clients was that MFIs would not be allowed to operate and, therefore, there was no need to repay MFI loans. Analysis indicates that as a group MFIs in India now have among the worst portfolio quality ratios in the world. The sample average of par 30 at 23.7% for the end of March 2012 (after significant write-offs) is in sharp contrast to the reported portfolio quality ratio of 0.67% for the end of March 2010. Given the reality of the AP situation, this presents a bleaker picture than is justified. Figure 6 shows that the aggregated par value for the portfolio of non-AP MFIs is just 1.79% compared to the 90-day par of 6.1% for loans from banks to SHGs in India.

Exceptional circumstances aside, the client retention rate is generally accepted as being a key indicator of client satisfaction. While the available data does not provide for a strong correlation between retention rate and portfolio quality, it does indicate a significant positive relationship. In particular, it suggests that as client satisfaction increases portfolio quality improves – as shown in the M-CRIL Review. However, overall, the 64% average client retention rate for Indian MFIs is quite low.

The aggregate write-off ratio of 34% for AP MFIs in 2011-12 is as expected and it is now clear that the eventual write-off resulting from the crisis will be far higher. Despite the Reserve Bank of India (RBI) initiating debt restructuring, a haircut for both the MFIs caught in the crisis and for their lenders is inevitable. It is only the closeness of the cut (ie, the proportion of investment lost) that remains to be determined. M-CRIL estimates that, in addition to the Rs42,700 million ($821 million) already written off, another Rs42,000 million ($808 million) of bad debt remains and will need to be written off in subsequent years – a total loss of Rs84,700 million ($1.63 billion). This is nearly 40% of the March 2011 portfolio of Indian MFIs.

10. The price of relying on commercial banks for funds

The distribution of sources for microfinance funds, presented in Figure 7, shows that the share of debt in MFI finances is still high. However, the current level of debt, amounting to Rs155,000 million ($3 billion) or 67.5% of total MFI funds represents a reduction from the highest level of around 80%, which was reached in 2008. Also it includes the Rs42,000 million ($808 million) of portfolios financed by bank funds yet to be written off in AP. The effect of an immediate write-off would be for bank funding of microfinance to fall below 60%.

Even so, the extent to which commercial debt continues to dominate the financing of Indian microfinance is apparent. Indeed, the domination of commercial bank funds is underplayed in this analysis since it excludes off-balance sheet financing via portfolio sales and securitisations of portfolios undertaken by some of the leading MFIs with the commercial banks. A separate compilation of the portfolio managed by MFIs for others – securitised portfolios that are not on MFI balance sheets – shows that the amount added some 7.6% to the total portfolio managed by MFIs.

Figure 7: Sources of funds for microfinance operations

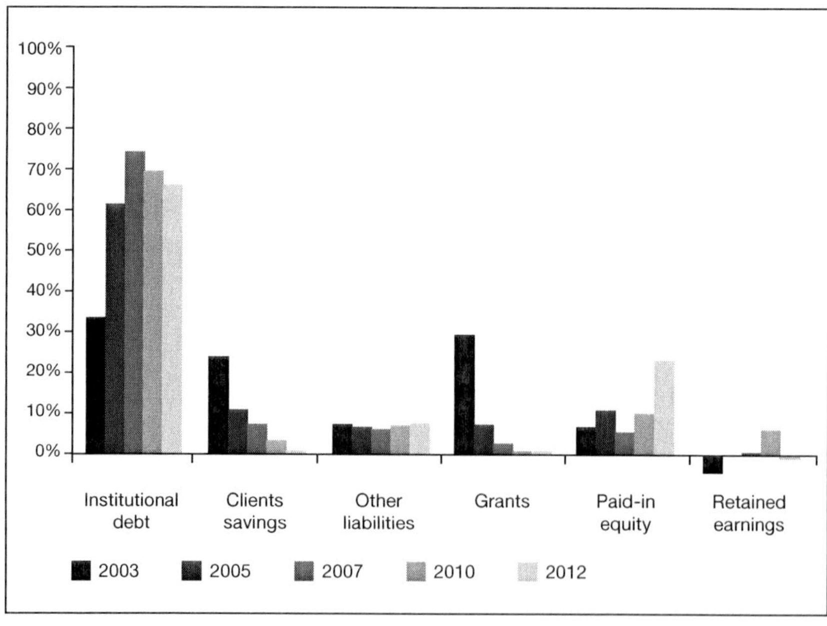

By the end of financial year 2011-12 the net worth of Indian MFIs amounted to 22.9% of total funds but its composition changed dramatically. Equity now amounts to over 23% of total funds, while the recent crisis mean that a positive 6.6% of funds as retained earnings in March 2010 has turned negative. This is likely to fall further as the full effect of the AP portfolio collapse becomes apparent through more write-offs during 2012-13.

11. Funds being squeezed by cash constraints

Figure 8: Use of funds by Indian MFIs, 2012

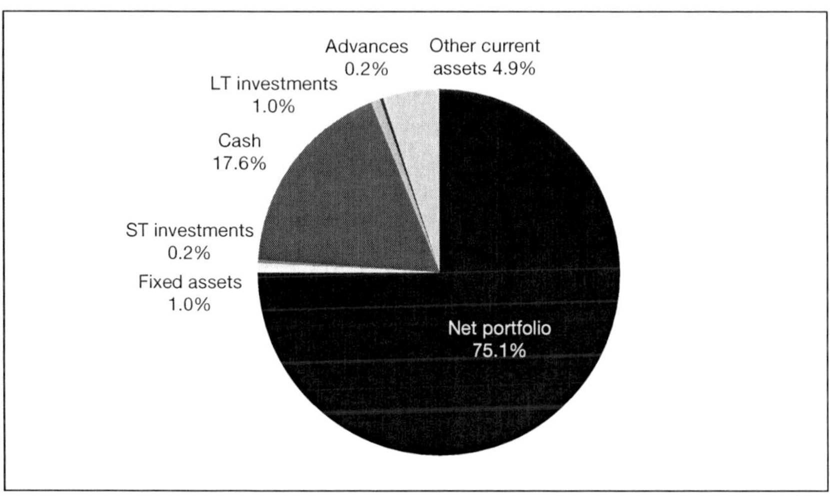

The allocation of funds by Indian MFIs has conformed fairly well to international best-practice norms in recent years. However, the exceptional circumstances of the 18 months leading up to March 2012 resulted in exceptional measures. Of the total resources of Rs224,710 million ($4.4 billion) deployed in microfinance by sample MFIs, just over 75% was in loans to clients as of the end of March 2012 (Figure 8). Two years ago this was 69%, which was below the portfolio allocation level of the MIX international median of 76.8%, largely because of the practice of making substantial disbursements of loans to MFIs in the last week of March, the end of the financial year.

As discussed earlier, the effect of the AP crisis soon spread far beyond the state. This was not due to contagion but rather the drying up of bank funds to MFIs. Thus, the banks' perception of political risk in the AP Ordinance resulted in the whole sector reducing its loan approvals for MFIs during 2011-12, while privately owned banks withdrew almost completely. This had an impact on MFIs all over the country and is the primary reason for the nearly 35% decline in net portfolio of the leading MFIs during the year. Since there is a limit to the equity that can be raised and it takes longer to mobilise, while deposits are not allowed by the regulator, MFIs were forced to shrink their portfolios. It is remarkable that this shrinkage did not cause contagion – where clients (outside AP) refuse to repay loans, assuming that they are unlikely to receive fresh ones. The fact that non-AP MFIs were able to manage this situation is to their credit.

12. A win for prudential management

In order to ensure prudential management, banks in India are expected by the RBI to maintain capital adequacy ratios (CAR – ie, net worth as a proportion of risk weighted assets) of 9% and NBFCs of 15%. While equity was a constraint in the early years of Indian microfinance, this has eased considerably in recent years. Although investors became very cautious after October 2010, the weighted average CAR for Indian MFIs was over 28% by March 2012 – well ahead of the banking sector. However, it is the decline in portfolio over the following 18 months that was largely responsible for this increase from the 18% average MFI CAR of March 2010.

While securitisation may offer a short-term solution to the capital problem, it cannot resolve the issue in the long term. For commercial banks, it provides the benefit of inclusion in the priority sector lending requirement (though that is now being re-assessed by the RBI in the context of the crisis). A surfeit of lending funds leads MFIs to:

- induct clients without due care and relationship building;
- lend beyond their clients' capabilities and means; and
- resort to coercive practices when the clients expressed their inability to pay.

The emergence of client protection issues and the related political risk in AP and Karnataka (and, by extension, elsewhere in India) can largely be attributed to this. In this context, the reduction in the proportion of the managed portfolio from 53% of the owned portfolio in 2005 to 7.6% is now a welcome development. However, it is worth remembering that until March 2010 the absolute amounts of managed portfolio had increased to such an extent that the proportions become meaningless from the perspective of an over-heated economic sector. In the authors' opinion, securitisation dilutes the prudential effect of the CAR requirement and should be carefully monitored by regulators.

13. Falling returns due to write-offs and squeezed margins

The financial viability of microfinance institutions in India, apparent in the early 2000s, was under threat in 2007. While this situation was dramatically reversed in 2009-10 – with average returns on assets of Indian MFIs rising to nearly 7% (Figure 9 below) – the current crisis has caused another reversal. This is apparent in considering the returns that MFIs earn net of all costs – operating and financial – and has been caused by the substantial write-offs necessitated by the collapse of microfinance in AP. The high efficiency (low OER) of Indian MFIs played a key role in their profitability, as did the significantly increased portfolio yield since 2007 (as seen in Figure 5 above). However, substantial current write-offs (included partly in operating expenses and partly in loan-loss provisioning) have increased the total expense ratio significantly. As discussed earlier, the crisis has not only halted microfinance in AP, it has also caused a sudden attack of prudence in commercial bank lending to MFIs (at the same time as a hardening in inflationary conditions in the country) resulting in an increase in lending rates and causing a significant increase in the financial expense ratio of MFIs. Unsurprisingly the average return on assets for Indian MFIs in 2011-12 resulted in a large loss (7.4%) of assets. However,

MFIs not directly affected by the crisis (non-AP) still earned a good 3.9% average return on assets in the year under review.

14. The long-term implications of the crisis

Figure 9: Trends in returns on assets (%)

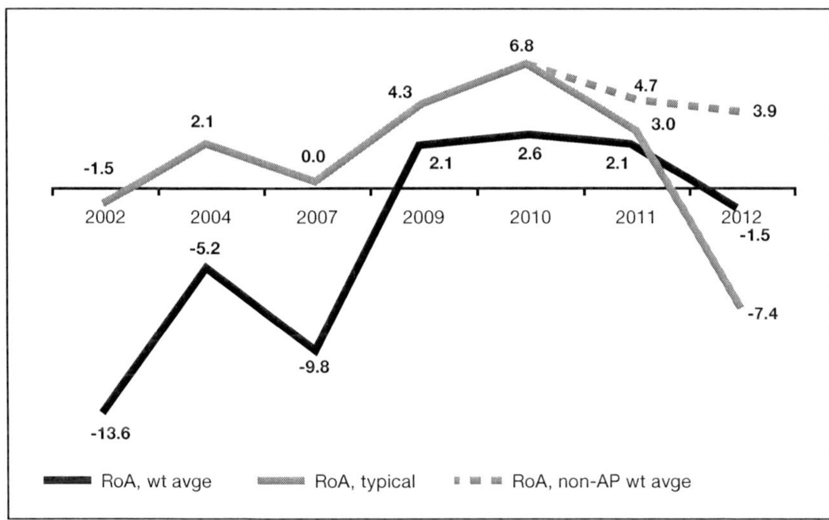

Given the actions of the AP government and the collapse of portfolios in the state as a result, it is quite likely that the write-off and provisioning expenses of MFIs with operations in AP will increase even further. At the same time, as indicated above, M-CRIL expects another decline in portfolio yield on account of the limits set by the RBI on the margins of microfinance NBFCs.

The implications of the drastic intervention of the AP government and slow progress towards resolving the crisis for the long-term future of financial inclusion are still difficult to predict. It has already resulted in a substantial decline in capital – both debt and equity – available for microfinance and has reversed the financial inclusion effect of MFI operations. Whether MFIs can continue to contribute to the financial inclusion process in India now depends on the passage of the Microfinance Bill by the Indian Parliament – a process that is currently moving extremely slowly. In the meantime, most low-income families in AP have been thrown back into the not-so-benevolent arms of moneylenders. As this discussion has shown, many low-income families elsewhere have also suffered collateral damage as the drying up of on-lending funds from commercial banks has caused a reduction in MFI operations throughout the country. It is apparent that the economic future of low-income families has not received adequate attention from policy makers and needs to be brought immediately to the forefront of financial policy making so that the poor can receive practical support for their lives and livelihoods.

The future of microfinance

Ian Callaghan
Shorebank International

1. Microfinance is not new

It is easy to be gloomy about the future of microfinance. One moment it is the miracle machine that will consign global poverty to the museum, lauded by everyone from presidents to venture capitalists to popstars; the next it is characterised as a catastrophic failure, with no development value and plagued by greed, aggressive lending practices and even physical violence.

In the sorry tale of the scores of suicides among poor rural borrowers in Andhra Pradesh, the resulting near-catastrophic shutdown of large sections of the microfinance industry in India, leading to decimation of the fortunes of its most garlanded microfinance institution SKS, and in the fortunes of the person often feted as the pioneer of microfinance, Mohammed Yunus, finally driven out of the Grameen Bank which he created and with which he won the Nobel Peace Prize in 2006, we seem to see an entire cycle for microfinance from invention to scale to boom to bust played out in little more than a few decades.

Like many, I came into microfinance in the mid-2000s – specifically in the UN-proclaimed 'Year of Microfinance' in 2005. I was instrumental in getting my then employers Morgan Stanley to see the industry as one in which it could be a commercial participant. For too long I took it for granted that the business model had somehow arisen fully formed, like some Venus Anadyomene of development finance, in the 1970s or 80s. Although there were different claims as to where and by whom this spectacular birthing had been brought about, it was easy at that time to accept a narrative for microfinance in which it emerged from its non-governmental organisation origins and established a sustainable model during the 1990s, then grew in the 2000s and beyond into scalable, commercial and even highly profitable sector of the global financial industry.

It was tempting to interpret the series of crises that struck microfinance operators between 2008 and 2010 (in Andhra Pradesh and elsewhere in India, as well as in Nicaragua, Pakistan, Nigeria and Bosnia-Herzogovina) in the context of this narrative and within the context of the hype and over-confidence that precipitated the crash of 2007. That is, to read these events as part of a classical cycle of inevitable progress from hubris to nemesis.

Although some fragments of the past emerged as I became more deeply engaged – I found out, for example, that what eventually became the Bank of America had its origins as a micro-lender after the San Francisco earthquake of 1906 – it was not until the publication in 2011 of David Roodman's *Due Diligence: An Impertinent Enquiry into*

Microfinance[1] that I realised that my view of the business was almost entirely separate from the reality. Far from having been invented a few decades ago, microfinance in fact had a deep-rooted pre-history. Indeed, Roodman unearths an archaeology for microfinance that extends at least to the days of ancient Athens and Rome. From these times he then traces a richly varied tradition that extends through the middle ages and encompasses initiatives ranging from the *monti de pieta* (a kind of church-organised pawnshop) in 15th-century Italy, to the activities of trade guilds throughout medieval Europe. He identifies the efforts of the satirist Dean Jonathan Swift in the 1720s to lend to the famine-struck poor of Ireland using the "social collateral" of mutual guarantees. He notes the gradual institutionalisation of financial services for the poor in Britain during the Industrial Revolution, right through to the establishment of building societies, cooperatives and credit unions in Europe and the United States in the 19th and 20th centuries. Although the book does not cover them, similar developments could doubtless be traced in the rest of the world.

Since any useful discussion of a future needs to be informed by a past, and since one of the problems that has beset judgements on the uses and abuses of microfinance has been what turns out to have been a deracinated view of its present, understanding the pre-history of modern microfinance is critical.

2. What is the essential value of microfinance?

Viewed against this backdrop, it is evident that the present difficulties of microfinance are more like molehills than mountains. For many, indeed, the disappearance of hyperbole from the discourse on microfinance is welcome. So too, probably, is the retreat of the 'summer soldiers' among what had become an army of investors,[2] leaving a more battle-hardened (if battle-weary) cadre to continue the campaign.

A campaign for what, though? Again, Roodman captures what I think is becoming the mainstream view of microfinance among its committed investor base. (A base in which I include, by the way, philanthropic and donor investors as well as commercial investors.) "Poor people," Roodman says,[3] "need financial services even more than rich people do. For people navigating an unpredictable and unforgiving terrain of poverty, any additional room for maneuver, any additional control, can be invaluable ... Overall, history suggests that the real strength of microfinance ... is in bringing formal financial services to millions of people in minimally subsidised, business like ways".

When it is set against ambitions to end poverty itself, a mission to widen financial inclusion may seem humdrum or even inadequate. Yet it is that very financial inclusion that over time creates economic opportunity. Moreover, this economic opportunity beyond the narrow lens of micro-credit and micro-entrepreneurship.

---

1 Centre for Global Development.

2 Scores of specialist microfinance investment funds were established between 2005 and 2007 alone. Many more were either fundraising or in preparation to fundraise when the crash occurred.

3 *Due Diligence*, pp 34 and 39.

The following are some of the ways to widen such inclusion and increase the empowerment of the poor:

- Products that provide savings and insurance (these are almost always the top two in surveys of the actual wants as opposed to the perceived needs of the poor);
- Delivery channels that reduce transaction costs, both directly in terms of cash and indirectly through more time-efficient access – that is, through requiring the poor to spend less of their time (often their only asset) actually using the service;
- Improved financial literacy and consumer protection; and
- 'Soft' empowerments such as the dignity of being a valued customer.

Through this kaleidoscope of inclusion, it can be seen that the developing modern microfinance industry is beginning to address the needs of the poor. The complexity of these needs, as well as the ingenuity with which the poor already address them through informal mechanisms, has been expertly and vividly captured in studies such as The Poor and Their Money[4] and Portfolios of the Poor.[5]

Since coming across these works, it has become my habit to use one of the case studies presented in Portfolios of the Poor to 'personalise' my own thinking on how we approach the formalisation of financial inclusion.

The case study is that of Hamid and Khadeja. Hamid and Khadeja live in a slum in Dhaka, Bangladesh, with their young son. Their home consists of cement block walls and a tin roof. They share bathroom and kitchen facilities with eight other families. Hamid is a reserve motorised rickshaw driver; Khadeja supplements his unpredictable income with earnings as a seamstress. On average the couple earns $70 per month,

Financial assets	**Financial liabilities**
Microfinance savings	Microfinance loan
Savings with a moneyguard	Private interest-free loan
'Mattress' savings	Wage advance
Life insurance	Savings held for others
Remittances to family	Shopkeeper credit
Loans out to others	Rent arrears
Cash in hand	

4 Stuart Rutherford, 2009.
5 Daryl Collins and others, 2009.

20% of which is spent on rent and much of the rest on food. The family of three survives on an average (and uncertainly timed) sum of $0.78 per person per day.

Yet as we can see from the listing of their financial assets and liabilities on the previous page, Hamid and Kadeja are extremely active managers of what little wealth they possess.

On the assets side – what they own – they use or have created seven different savings and insurance products. Of these, only two – the microfinance savings and the life insurance – are formal products. The other five are informal arrangements of one kind or another, mainly made with friends, family and co-workers.

On the liabilities side – what they owe to other people – they have found six different ways to finance temporary shortfalls in their income, which as we have seen is highly unpredictable. All of these except the microfinance loan are informal.

3. Future pathways for microfinance

From the point of view of formalisation, then, what strands can we identify, and what themes might we develop from these, as pointers to a future for microfinance?

I would pick the following four themes. Since the scope of this chapter also covers other 'base of pyramid' (BOP) products and services,[6] I will discuss at least some of them with respect to these other sectors as well:

- the increasing involvement of strategic commercial actors;
- the continued evolution of financial products beyond micro-credit;
- innovations in the way that such services are delivered, improving both their benefits and their value to poor consumers; and
- necessary developments in the financing of commercial enterprises in the BOP arena.

Most of the observations below arise from my own daily engagement as an adviser in this sector, involved in mobilising of capital for microfinance and, increasingly, other BOP products and services, as well as with corporate finance activity such as acquisitions and disposals of stakes.

3.1 Increasing involvement of strategic commercial actors

Our first theme is the appearance of what are termed 'strategic' investors. These are investors with the depth, breadth and weight of financial resources, management experience, operational capability and sector contacts to single-handedly take an entire institution to a new level of scale, efficiency and sustainability. In the microfinance arena, such investors are usually commercial banks or other large financial institutions. Typically they will replace either a founding investor group, or, more usually, a group of perhaps up to six or seven financial investors (that is, investors without an operational or management dimension to their engagement). There are a number of reasons why this is happening in the microfinance sector.

The first is simply the passage of time. With the significant growth of the industry since the 1990s, a meaningful number of microfinance institutions have

---

6 Affordable housing, health, education, water and sanitation, domestic energy etc.

now reached a level of maturity that makes them ready for investment by a strategic partner. Indeed, these institutions, having outgrown the competencies of their founder or purely financial investors, actively require such strategic investment in order to progress.

At the same time, many of the specialist microfinance investment vehicles formed in the early to mid-2000s were structured as closed-ended vehicles – that is, funds with a limited investment period and lifespan. In many cases, the investment periods of these funds have now ended or are nearing their end, and managers are seeking alternative investment options. In other cases, where funds have longer life cycles, their mission governance may require them to recycle their capital from maturing institutions to earlier-stage entities or even start-ups.

The second reason for the entry of strategic investors reflects both a success and a partial failure on the part of microfinance institutions. When strategic partners come to assess microfinance institutions as potential investees, they see on the one hand a viable business model in microfinance, but on the other the fact that microfinance institutions have not fully dealt with their targets for scalability, sustainability and portfolio performance. This is of course precisely the scenario that offers a strategic investor the opportunity to create real added value, not only by adding its financial resources but also through the injection of its core commercial skillsets and, in some cases, more disciplined and decisive cultures.

At the same time, strategic investors also appear to be seeing such value maximised not through takeovers or mergers, but rather via corporate arrangements. These draw on their own strengths as commercial financial institutions – regulatory familiarity, internal auditing, management information systems, core banking systems, operations, capital raising, etc – while at the same time allowing the microfinance institutions to do what they do best, such as creating and managing client relationships and designing innovative products. Typically, therefore, the entry of strategic investors is preserving separate brands for the microfinance operations.

One significant commercial dimension for strategic investors may be the opportunity to link 'alternative' delivery channels developed by banks (eg mobile and internet platforms) with the mass outreach potential of microfinance institutions. Combinations like this can provide commercial banks with the large client numbers that such platforms need to be financially viabile, while at the same time offering the microfinance partner the chance to reduce transaction costs and improve access to financial services for its clients.

If the Pralahad thesis[7] – that microfinance is merely one (and the first) of a range of 'mainstream' products and services that can be re-engineered to be affordable by the poor – is to be believed, then we would expect other sectors to follow where microfinance leads. It is therefore not surprising that beyond microfinance we can also see strategic interest from large, established commercial enterprises and brands in the development of partnerships in sectors such as housing, clean water, healthcare and nutrition, food products and domestic energy.

7 In works such as *The Fortune at the Bottom of the Pyramid*, 2004.

In part this trend is related to the emergence of an identifiable low-income sector in many developing countries. The existence of such an identifiable sector (the bottom end of emerging middle classes in such places) is very different, in terms of its accessibility to large players, from a non-homogeneous mass of 'the poor'. Nevertheless, such players lack confidence in their ability to tap such new markets. Their interest is therefore in forming connections with those who have, or are developing, the re-engineered business models that will successfully address BOP markets.

SBI is presently working on projects as diverse as dairy, energy, health insurance, clean water and even the creation of employment opportunities among people with autism spectrum disorders. Large corporations are playing a variety of roles in these projects. These may involve their financial resources, as investors or co-investors; their operational capabilities, especially their distribution chains; or their management capabilities and industry contacts.

In some cases, the partner may be one of the foundations established by many large corporations to implement their CSR agendas. These often provide 'smart subsidy' grants that can be critical to building capacity and testing business models. Corporate foundations sometimes complement commercially delivered services with programmatic support for education and similar campaigns surrounding the product or service that especially need funding. For example, the PepsiCo Foundation supports, through the Safe Water Network, the village-level clean water facilities being built in Africa by Waterhealth International. Among other things, it funds education programmes regarding the safe storage and usage of clean water in homes. These programmes doubtless significantly increase the health benefits of the commercially provided services.

I regard this as a major trend. It means that all market participants should reassess their definition of what constitutes an 'investor'. That word may no longer relate only to providers of cash but equally to contributors of any combination of brand, talent, culture, market access and operational support.

3.2 Continued evolution of financial products beyond micro-credit

The importance of such products has been clear to me ever since I was involved, as an investment manager, in financing the first specialist microinsurance fund, Leapfrog Investments. While working on the Leapfrog project, I saw in survey after survey that microfinance clients ranked savings and insurance products ahead (often well ahead) of micro-credit as a desired financial product. The lives of poor people such as Hamid and Khadeja in the case study above illustrate the need for ways to smooth their income receipts. Indeed, for many borrowers one suspects that micro-loans – rather than being taken principally for enterprise reasons – are really a kind of savings product in reverse. In their balance sheet we also one formal insurance product (life insurance) that is likely to have been bundled with the micro-loan. This means there is there more to protect the lender than the borrower. Nevertheless, we can probably be sure that if other insurance products, especially health insurance, were available at affordable prices, these clients would use them.

Many of the general trends that we identified above are also evident in this dynamic of product development. Strategic investors are starting to appear. A number of insurance companies and reinsurers are investors in the LeapFrog fund, for example. In the arena of savings we see the substantial presence of the Bill and Melinda Gates Foundation, a powerful signal to similar market participants of the importance of making focused and – even more importantly – long-term commitments at a sectoral level.

As well as new products that are directly aimed at low-income consumers, there is encouraging evidence of new sector-level infrastructure developments that indirectly benefit these consumers too. These include credit bureaus – which have contributed to the stable growth of the Peruvian market – and platforms and methodologies for consumer protection. These include, for example, the SMART campaign, which in 2011 had signed up some 600 microfinance institutions to endorse and practise six principles of responsible lending.

It is even more encouraging to see that such initiatives appear to be the result of the microfinance landscape being more expertly mapped and divided up between partners with different strategic interests and skillsets.[8] These developments in sector infrastructure are often instigated by foundations and similar players. Previously they may have supported the microfinance institutions themselves, but these are now better served by a different set of more financially oriented investors. Added to these highly desirable infrastructure developments are, of course, a plethora of 'impact' measurement initiatives, the value of many of which remains to be proven.

3.3 Innovations in service delivery

Despite their very late appearance on the scene, telecommunications services have already outstripped banking services in most of the developing world. This is a startling fact. Over half the world's population lacks reliable banking services, yet more than 5 billion people have cell phones. Due to this bizarre dynamic, using mobile technology to transfer small amounts of money may be the best way to bridge the gap between the haves and the have-nots. But 'mobile money' gives the have-nots far more than access to microfinance. It reduces their daily costs and gives them a channel through which holistic, customer-focused benefits may be delivered.

Mobile banking has already met with real-world success. Following the lead of pioneering innovators such as GCash, SMART, M-PESA, WIZZIT and others, more than a hundred mobile and branchless platforms are being developed and introduced to dozens of developing countries. Many of the players are social investors who are focused on BOP financial inclusion; others are more aggressively commercial. Between them, and despite the many practical difficulties of implementation, we can safely say that mobile banking is here to stay.[9]

One reason that mobile banking and payment systems have led to better

8 It is worth saying that microfinance has been singularly well-served by its think tanks, principally CGAP, which have been responsible not just for excellent research but also for a number of intelligently targeted funding interventions that have enabled market participants to identify trends, focus their own initiatives and avoid at least some of the pitfalls inevitably present in any largely unmapped territory.

9 Readers with a particular interest in this topic can find more on the SBI blog/website at http://bankingbeyondbranches.com/.

customer solutions is that, generally speaking, situations cannot be improved unless they can be measured first. Data collection systems are required to gain critical information about those whose needs are being served. Such systems can be embedded in cellular technology (through targeted surveys via SMS messages, etc). For instance, the start-up Grameen Foundation makes a data collection mobile app used by loan officers in rural areas to aggregate household data. This provides a richer understanding of the poor's financial behaviour and requirements and ensures that microfinance service providers are delivering products based on their customers' underlying demands and requirements.

Mobile money also significantly decreases the customer's transaction costs, which in emerging economies are often prohibitive. Of course costs are reduced directly in terms of lower cost of transport, lower ATM fees and other cash savings for the consumer. But the indirect cost reductions might be even more significant. There are vast increases in savings and security – cash stuffed under the mattress is more likely to get stolen than cash digitised in a mobile phone. Mobile banking can be used to improve governance, track funds, transfer cash, and make welfare and salary payments (which prevents scammers from siphoning off funds). All of these lead to enhanced savings. The security benefits to people in the developing world, and particularly to women, are tremendous. Apart from not having to bear the risks that come with carrying cash on her person, a woman with a mobile phone is ensured of being able to access her accounts and deposits, repay loans directly, receive salaries and so on. None of these should be taken for granted in parts of the developing world.

Another benefit of mobile money is that other solutions can be bundled onto it. Mobile technology spurs the invention of new products and services that can be delivered on the same platform. Since the incremental costs of adding services to mobile banking are negligible, many derivative benefits are accruing and fuelling the inclusive finance revolution. For instance, the Kenya Women's Finance Trust, which controls 70% of the microfinance market in Kenya, has a child and maternal health platform. The trust sends its female customers health and service updates through mobile phones, giving women benefits from the technology beyond banking. The insurance provider MicroEnsure protects the poor from the daily risks they face by giving them a free month of life insurance, reinstated every month, as long as they use $3 worth of airtime on their mobile phones. (MicroEnsure's Africa client base is currently 2.5 million; they have seven mobile insurance products and are profitable.) Customers are deriving entirely parallel benefits through using their mobile phones.

The above trends are sure to continue and expand. Lowering transaction costs in the microfinance sector (alongside reducing telecom unit costs and increasing capacity) will ensure that the space becomes increasingly competitive. This, in turn, will drive transaction costs and barriers to entry down still further, and the cycle will continue. Many new entrants will not be social impact players, but rather 'single-bottom-line' participants, such as Visa, which recently acquired the mobile banking platform Fundamo. This may make customers more vulnerable in some ways. On the other hand, the enhanced competition and ensuing commodification of financial services will increase choice and make them more empowered.

Certain subtle risks and rewards are difficult to foresee: a disruptive product may be potentially socially dislocating, or socially cohering. For instance, mobile phones in Africa are playing a big role in love and courtship – is this good or bad? The long-term implications of the financial inclusion revolution are unknown to us. But one thing is certain – (micro) financial investment is not enough to satisfy the needs of the poor. Many types of investment, both soft and hard, must be bundled together to make solutions in the developing world sustainable. An alternative delivery channel such as mobile technology (due to its ubiquity and scalability) allows a wide array of holistic, cost-effective, customer-centric solutions to be delivered through it. On balance, this must be a good thing.

3.4 Financing commercial enterprises that provide BOP products and services

In this final section, I will focus on one market failure (of many that could be advanced) and one suggested 'big picture' change that I believe is necessary for this market to succeed in the future.[10]

The market failure in question is the almost total absence of finance for recently formed businesses to fund the proof-of-concept stage of their lifecycles; that is, the stage between initial start-up (financed by friends and family) and the ability to generate sustained revenue. In many markets, next-stage financiers are queuing up to fund the handful of opportunities they might see emerge from this stage each year. There is a real role for public and not-for-profit actors to nurture enterprises to readiness for market capital. Addressing this need successfully would greatly increase the flow of quality deals downstream, where there is substantially more funding available.

That said, it is important that the type of financing that small and growing enterprises receive is appropriate to their circumstances and needs. All too often it is not. At present, almost all the financing offered to such businesses is based on a very US/European model of venture capital and private equity. Time frames that are very short, relatively speaking, and financial return expectations (despite the providers asserting double- or even triple-bottom-line objectives) are often far higher than BOP businesses could ever realistically hope to achieve. The terms on which such financing is based can therefore profoundly distort the underlying business model. Often they will lead an enterprise to develop far more quickly than is realisable given the practical and market challenges it is likely to face. These are, of course, much more extensive and, in the case of corruption and suchlike issues, far more insidious than in developed markets. Worse still, enterprises may even be led to chase unachievable financial returns, changing the fundamental value proposition to the customer and thus the economic viability and long-term social impact of the company itself. Less fundamental but nevertheless challenging issues posed by such forms of financing include the valuation of early stage business and the arrangement of what can be highly complex exits for early stage investors. Both can consume a lot of management energy and time that could be better spent on growing the business.

---

10 For a study on this issue see the Monitor Group's report, published in association with the Acumen Fund, "From Blueprint to Scale", 2012.

Financing BOP businesses therefore requires a form of capital that is:

- patient (ie, operating over a seven to 10 year span, or even longer);
- which seeks reasonable financial returns (probably in large single figures);
- which offers continued interest for the founders and key staff (by not being diluting);
- which does not require valuation; and
- whose exit is in-built.

One form of such capital is subordinated debt. This may have an equity-like feature such as a 'kicker' (additional return) if the business is especially successful and can offer such an additional return without distorting its models or consumer objectives. Such capital is already being offered by innovative funds such as Den Sociale Kapitalfond of Denmark.[11]

My prediction for the next decade is that this form of capital will slowly become a substantial – and highly liberating – source of capital for those seeking to provide goods and services to the poor around the globe. Such a development would perhaps finally make it possible for such communities to be served by sustainable businesses that provide affordable and well-designed products of mass appeal and therefore great impact.

The author would like to thank Jan Piercy, Jesse Fripp, Shamik Desai and other colleagues at Shorebank International for their input and comments on this chapter.

11 This has been extensively written about by John Kohler and colleagues at the Centre for Science, Technology and Society of Santa Clara University in the United States.

Microfinance 3.0

Phyllis SantaMaria
Microfinance without Borders

1. Introduction

Modern microfinance is entering a truly exciting era, for all of us. On an individual level, more of the world's professionals are connecting directly with the world's poorest communities, not to just raise or donate funds, but to contribute their time, talents and technical skills interactively at the grass roots of the developing world. People living on different continents, from opposite ends of the financial spectrum, are learning together as they collaborate on enterprise projects, co-create financial products and platforms, connect to build essential infrastructure, and share and develop skills.

Perhaps even more significantly, the world's poor now have a chance to move from being passive, dependent recipients of credit from microfinance institutions (MFIs), donors and investors (which I here call 'Microfinance 1.0'), to becoming voluntary savers through a savings model in contrast with a credit model ('Microfinance 2.0'), and ultimately becoming entrepreneurs who use mobile platforms for finance and business management to connect and achieve sustainability (the more developed 'Microfinance 3.0'). As they move through these phases and gain access to vital financial infrastructure, the poor are creating assets, taking owningership of the means of production and distribution, increasing their skills, and moving towards financial sustainability for their families and communities.

This new era of innovation and transparency is driven by new technologies, a global will to learn from the past, and a large growth in the desire of professionals the world over to play a direct and practical role in sustainable international development. More than any before it, the era of Microfinance 3.0 is creating opportunities to fill infrastructure gaps in health and livelihood protection through microinsurance and provide access to regional and global markets through payment systems.

Modern microfinance was created 300 years ago by teachers, local government officials and clergy (including the satirist and writer Jonathan Swift) in the British Isles and Germany in response to the plight of the poor as those countries modernised. Much later, in the 1970s and 80s, professionals from Bangladesh, India, Latin America and Africa, such as former Shell executive Fazle Hasan Abed and economics professor Mohammed Yunus, developed a business-like microfinance model that initially used small amounts of subsidy. This model has grown in scale and now reaches almost 200 million people who live on between $2 and $4 a day.

The involvement of microfinance, whether 300 or 30 years ago, or as part of 'Microfinance 3.0', can transfer knowledge and create opportunities for sustainable solutions by providing access to financial and information gateways.

This chapter provides examples of how professionals from financial services, information technology and healthcare are becoming involved. Will you be inspired to take action as a modern Swift, creating a lending platform for poor tradesmen as he did in Dublin in 1720? Or will you be like Abed, who returned home to Bangladesh in response to its crisis? Or will you create a partnership to develop a micro-health insurance programme?

Microfinance 3.0 is our era. Whether we are rich or poor we all have the potential to connect and build together as never before. My own journey with microenterprise began when I worked from 1965 to 1967 as a US Peace Corps Volunteer with Mayan women weavers in San Juan Comalapa in Guatemala. We invented micro handwoven purses – 'monederos'. I have since seen these around the world, a reminder of their role in the long-term economic and social empowerment of Mayan women. Over the decades, monedero weaving grew into small businesses, symbols of sustainable enterprise rather than charity.

Today in Comalapa historical murals adorn the entrance walls, painted by the community at the end of 30 years of civil war, so that children and their parents could remember and learn from the past. The project to paint this mural was the creation of Maria Soledad Icù Peren, a second generation member of our weaving club, who became an anthropologist before unfortunately passing away at the age of only 35.

As a professional capable of making a difference, how will you co-create with the poor and other professionals like Maria?

2. Microfinance 1.0: professionals responding to crises with microcredit

Bangladesh was the birthplace of 20th-century microcredit, where it was developed as an answer to the war, famine and floods that gripped this new nation in the 1970s. The 'Bangladesh Big Three' MFIs – Grameen, BRAC and ASA – each developed their own distinctive model. They attracted support from international donors and funders who were impressed by the business-like ways that these pioneers recycled loans to poor people.

Mohammed Yunus, a US-educated economics professor, started Grameen in the 1970s, using trial and error to develop the 'solidarity group lending' model of lending that ensured high repayment rates. Grameen Bank, founded in 1983, now has 8.4 million female and 315,000 male members as of April 2013.

Abed started BRAC as a form of disaster relief, and eventually brought microcredit into its education, health and grassroots development programmes. Today BRAC is the world's largest development organisation in terms of the scale and diversity of its interventions. Together with BRAC Bank, which services small and medium-sized enterprises, it employs over 100,000 staff and reaches 100 million people.

Shafiqual Haque Choudhury, a non-governmental organisation (NGO) professional, built on Grameen's model to found ASA, now one of the leanest microcredit organisations in the world. By 2007 ASA ranked highest in the Forbes 50 list of MFIs for efficiency and profitability.

As the microfinance movement grew in Bangladesh, other professionals in India, Indonesia and Latin America created cost-effective ways to reach an untapped market of poor people, mainly women.

Ela Bhatt, a professional woman in Gujarat, India, developed SEWA Bank in 1974 for self-employed women in trade cooperatives. She saw early on that financial services were central to the economic emancipation of women. Today, SEWA Bank holds 26,000 loan accounts and 348,000 savings accounts.

From the early 1970s Indonesian microfinance developed an individual loans and savings model in which loan officers would go directly to their customers to collect savings and loan payments. Bank Rakyat Indonesia (BRI) was started by professionals as a small microfinance bank, and today services 4.5 million loan accounts and 21 million savings accounts. This is about as many small accounts as in all of Bangladeshi microfinance, and makes BRI the second largest bank in Indonesia by assets.

Acción first started microlending in Brazil in 1973, led by the American Joseph Blatchford. Today it has helped build 62 MFIs in 31 countries, and has an active loan portfolio of $4.6 billion.[1]

FINCA's village banking model – another form of microcredit – was started in 1984 by the former US Peace Corps Volunteers John Hatch and Rupert Schofield in response to the Bolivian drought and economic crisis. Today it has 21 host country affiliates; along with Acción and Grameen it is considered one of the most influential MFIs in the world.[2]

As part of this history of microfinance in the 1970s and 80s, let us look at the characteristics and limitations of Microfinance 1.0:

- Consumers, mainly women, were organised into groups to make the task of training, distributing loans and collecting payments easier for MFIs.
- Potential borrowers, organised in groups to guarantee each others' loans, made compulsory savings until they reached a suitable percentage of the loan they wanted to receive.
- Borrowers started with small loans, gradually increasing in size, as they repaid each loan on a regular (usually weekly) basis. This enforced discipline generally worked until microfinance penetration in urban areas increased sufficiently to enable borrowers to take credit from several MFIs, thereby increasing the risks for lenders and borrowers.
- Little thoughtful product development took place, and MFIs instead created what they believed customers wanted.
- A full range of products was not offered, with the exception of BRI in Indonesia, which offered voluntary savings and credit on an individual basis, enforcing a discipline of using local savings for loans rather than going to investors outside Indonesia.

---

1 See www.citigroup.com/citi/press/2011/111024b.htm.
2 See http://en.wikipedia.org/wiki/FINCA_International.

Figure 1 illustrates the roles of consumers and MFIs in Microfinance 1.0 with consumers as the recipients of credit and MFIs 'pushing' credit to consumers. This form of microfinance, still used throughout the world, was the foundation for further developments, as we will see in Microfinance 2.0 and 3.0.

Figure 1

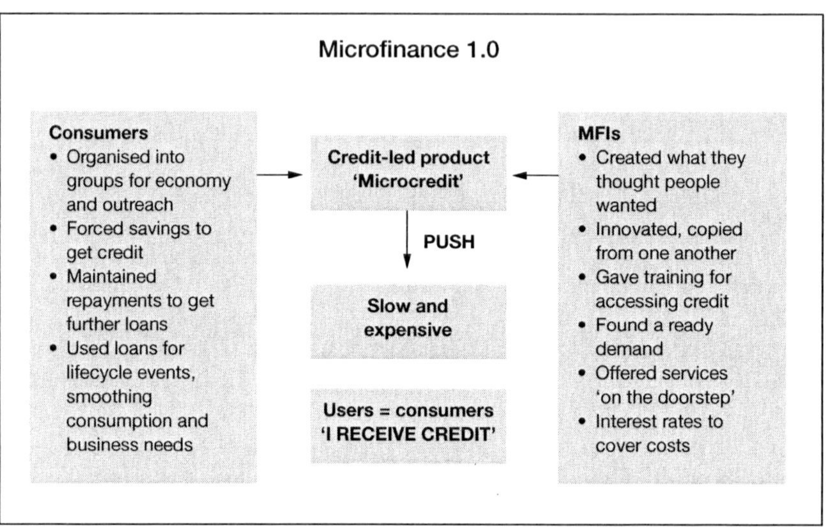

2.1 Getting involved in Microfinance 1.0

Despite its limitations and overuse in some areas, the effectiveness of Microfinance 1.0 in recycling loan money makes it still the most common form of microcredit in use today. The best models reduce interest rates through greater efficiencies and by measuring social impact; the worst maintain high interest rates with little social concern. Here I outline some case studies, based on real examples, of how volunteers, donors or investors can get involved in Microfinance 1.0, and help through targeted investment or by improving performance.

(a) Lending platforms

Chris, who lives in a village in Wales, has some funds that she would like to invest, but she cannot afford to give them away completely. For this reason she would like to invest in a microfinance borrower who is running a microenterprise. She would also like to be connected in some way with helping women in villages abroad get ahead. Chris is using a lending platform, lendwithcare.org, to invest in a chosen entrepreneur. This will help her recover her investment or recycle it. Other lending platforms include Oikocredit, Kiva, Deki, MyC4, Opportunity International and Kubaru. Some of these have opportunities to volunteer with their partner MFIs.

(b) Developing microfinance skills alongside your career

Professionals in finance, law, health and other sectors who want to make a difference can find ways to develop their skills in microfinance without giving up their day job. For example, John, a risk management specialist in a European bank, adds unpaid leave days onto his bank assignments in West Africa to perform due diligence work with local MFIs. He also heads the Special Interest Group for Microfinance and Social Impact Investment at his bank in the United Kingdom and keeps up to date with developments through the UK Microfinance Club.

Others professionals take on short-term assignments for MFIs in the United Kingdom with their partners in Africa or Asia. They may include specialists in financial regulation who advise on government regulation issues, teachers who help develop enterprise training for microfinance clients or filmmakers who create documentaries.

(c) ***Developing microfinance projects***

Professionals with financial, marketing, consulting or international development experience have invested in or donated to major microfinance projects. These may already exist, such as Opportunity International, or they may have been created specially, such as the Microloan Foundation, which was started by a group of UK volunteers and today operates in Malawi and Zambia on an operationally sustainable basis.

Figure 2

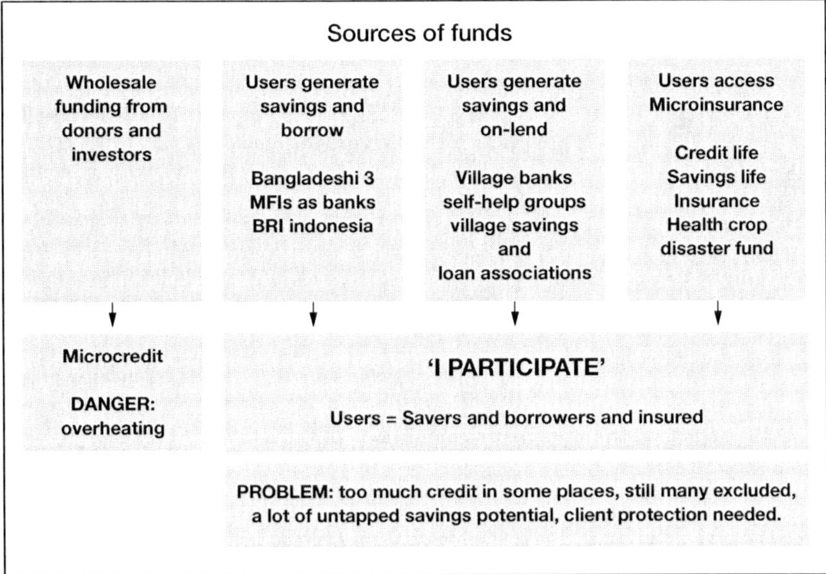

3. Microfinance 2.0

The era of Microfinance 2.0 saw the development of voluntary savings and insurance products. These evolved in places like Bangladesh in response to the needs of poor customers for a safe, long-term place for their savings, as well as safeguards against shocks and emergencies such as illness, death, livelihood losses and natural disasters.

Figure 2 on the previous page summarises developments in Microfinance 2.0. It begins on the left with classic microcredit, often on the Grameen model of group lending. The increased flow of money from outside investors and donors increased the risk of overheating in urban areas flooded with microcredit competitors.

Voluntary savings and borrowing appear as we move to the right. Reforms made by the Bangladeshi Big Three in the 1990s allowed for voluntary savings, flexibility in loan products and the shedding of 'solidarity group lending', but the retention of regular meetings. As an example of the major shift that Microfinance 2.0 represented, Grameen, a legal bank able to mobilise savings for lending, reported in 2005 that it had taken 26 years to reach 2.5 million members, but just 31 months to reach 5 million once a range of savings and loan products had been introduced. As of April 2013 96% of Grameen's 8.4 million members are women.[3]

MFIs in Latin America and elsewhere became banks, enabling them to take voluntary savings and offer a wider range of credit products.

BRI in Indonesia has long had a model of individual microbanking in which borrowers had to be savers as well have individual accounts. In fact, BRI has nine times as many savers as borrowers. ProCredit has disbursed individual savings and lending to poor people internationally, although it does not lend to the poorest.

Moving further to the right in Figure 2, we see user-generated savings and on-lending in village banks beginning in Latin America and spreading worldwide through FINCA and others. Some of these village banks have graduated to regulated banks.

About 60 million women in India are members of self-help groups, and together they comprise the largest number of microfinance users worldwide today.[4] Women are organised into such groups by NGOs, who then create a group account for them with a bank. Once the members of a group have saved a certain amount, they can borrow four times their savings from the bank.

Members of village savings and loan associations (VSLAs) save and then lend from these savings to members and non-members. CARE and PLAN, large NGOs, are now working with Barclays Bank to spread such associations to slums and remote areas in Africa and Asia with links to group accounts at Barclays. The model was developed by CARE International in Niger in 1991 and has spread to at least 61 countries in Africa, Asia and Latin America. There are more than 6 million active participants worldwide.[5]

The furthest arrow on the right is microinsurance. Its most common form is 'credit life': microcredit lenders offer a simple policy to cover the cost of the loan in case the borrower dies. This generates funds for the MFI with relatively little risk.

Other forms of microinsurance include savings life (endowment), health, crop,

---

3 Grameen Bank monthly reports for January 2003, www.grameen-info.org/index.php?option=com_content&task=view&id=159&Itemid=422; August 2005, www.grameen-info.org/index.php?option=com_content&task=view&id=93&Itemid=422; and April 2013, www.grameen-info.org/index.php?option=com_content&task=view&id=453&Itemid=422.

4 'Microfinance in evolution: an industry between crisis and advancement', Deutsche Bank Research, 13 September 2012. http://tinyurl.com/MF-stats-DB

5 http://vsla.net/

disaster and funeral insurance. These entail higher risks than credit life insurance and need special design and collaboration with a range of partners. These will be discussed further in the section on Microfinance 3.0.

The big change between Microfinance 1.0 and Microfinance 2.0 is the wider range of products available, notably savings, and the development of microinsurance and mobile payment systems. Simplified models of Microfinances 1.0, 2.0 and 3.0 exist side-by-side, depending on the region or level of maturity of the market.

Microfinance 2.0 in Figure 3 illustrates the growing demands from consumers for a variety of loan products and savings in parallel with their increased use of mobile phones. We will see in Microfinance 3.0 how microfinance starts taking advantage of the increased use of mobile phones by consumers. For example, in Kenya the demand for more financial products and use of mobile phones fuse in a mobile phone payment system known as MPESA. At the same time as consumer demand has increased, investors and donors are developing new platforms for peer-to-peer lending, and are investing in, client protection, investor standards and better regulation.

Figure 3

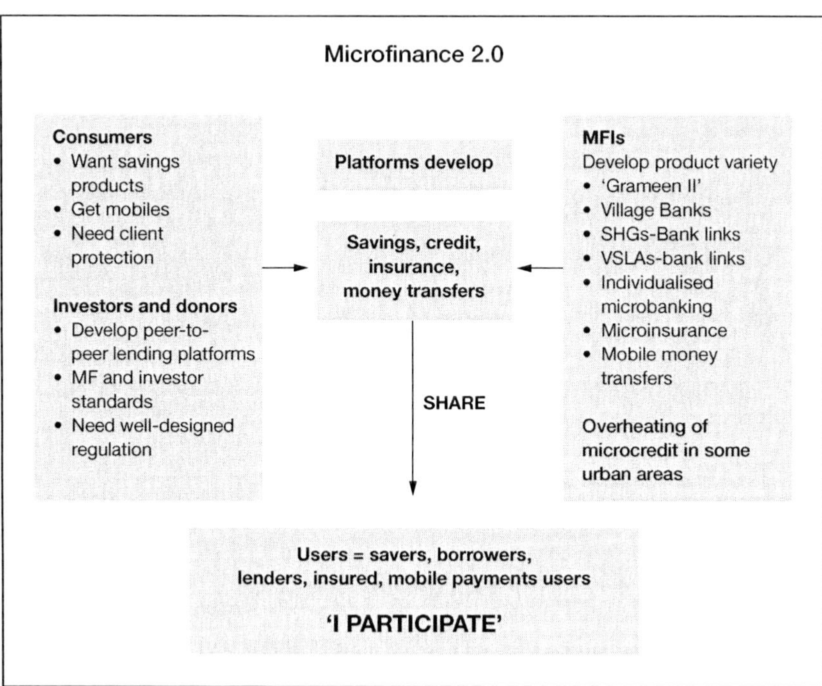

Looking at the MFIs, we see the larger MFIs developing a variety of products, including voluntary savings and microinsurance, in response to consumer demand. At the same time, self-help groups in India and VSLAs are developing a cost-effective way for microfinance services, including savings, without the need for banking licences. Microinsurance and mobile money transfers are starting to progress, although these services are not widespread. Microfinance 2.0, in summary, involves greater participation by consumers, investors' and donors' growing awareness of the need for consumer protection and regulation, and response by MFIs to develop more products. There is still the overall danger of overheating by microcredit, as more MFIs operate competitively in urban areas

3.1 Getting involved in Microfinance 2.0

(a) Start-up microsavings in Ghana

When he arrived in the United Kingdom from Ghana in the early 1990s, Thomas Donkor was shocked by a TV programme about street children in his home town of Kumasi. He vowed to do something for them. The school he set up is now in its eighth year, and he also established a traditional 'susu' savings-led microfinance programme. Unfortunately, the microfinance operation had to be closed down in 2009 due to an embezzlement, and Donkor repaid the clients from his own funds. Then in 2010 former clients asked him to restart the susu as it fulfilled their demand for doorstep savings. He has since done this, and with help from consultants with whom he took a microfinance course in London he is restructuring. "It's challenging to manage from the UK", he says. "We're hampered in our growth, but both the school and susu are operationally sustainably. Both provide needed services."

(b) Social impact measurement at a small MFI in India

Nora, a full-time credit manager with a UK bank, eventually wants to return to her home country in the Middle East to begin offering microfinance. After completing a microfinance course in the United Kingdom and two fieldwork assignments in Kenya, helping to develop an enterprise course for microfinance borrowers in the slums of Nairobi, she designed a social impact study for a small MFI in India that greatly improved their client tracking. Now that she knows the range of challenges that credit- and savings-led microfinance organisations face she is able to develop a career in the microfinance sector.

4. Microfinance 3.0

Landing in Dhaka, Bangladesh, in February 2013, I was greeted by 'BRAC Bank' signs, and 'Grameen' popping up as my mobile provider. I jostled for my luggage with Bangladeshi migrant workers returning from Dubai, remembering how poor families send a member to work in the city or another country and their need for reliable payment systems. As we all checked our mobiles, I imagined a future Microfinance 3.0 of mainstream information and financial services – the 'bank in everyone's pocket'.

The areas developing as Microfinance 3.0 include mobile money, platforms for e-commerce and open payment systems, microinsurance, lending platforms, and microfranchises. Figure 4 illustrates how platforms are developing, with investment from donors and investors shifting from wholesale lending for Microfinance 1.0 credit, to support for Microfinance 2.0 savings systems such as village savings and loan associations, and on to Microfinance 3.0's needs for infrastructure.

On the right are a variety of products, ranging from user-generated savings as in village banks and savings and loan associations, to mobile-based services, microinsurance and eBay-type business services. On the left are the infrastructure platforms. These range from mobile services to microfinance and industry standards. This evolution depends on the collaboration of many partners, each focusing on what they do best. It also requires co-creation with users, illustrated by village savings and loan associations or with merchants using integrated payment systems, as outlined below.

Figure 4

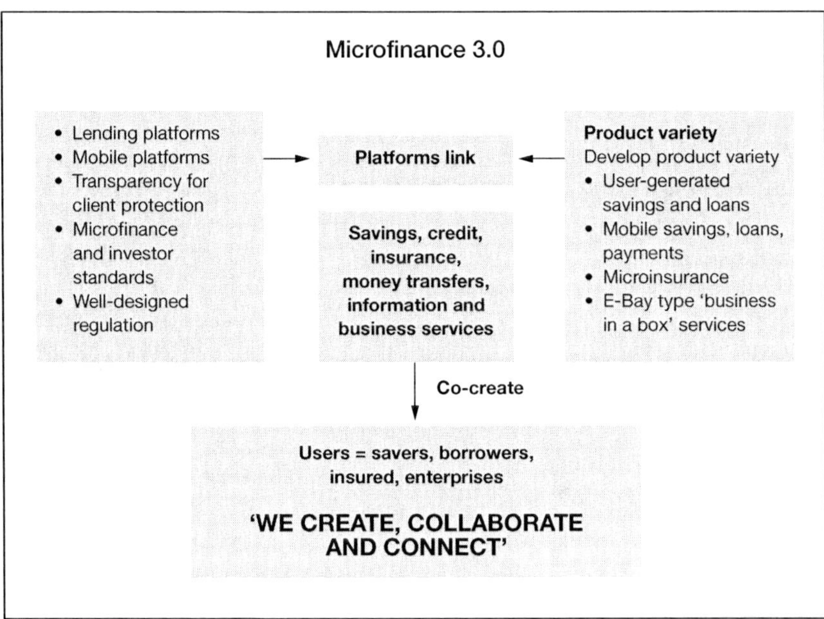

4.1 Mobile money for branchless banking

Bank customers in developed markets are used to using ATMs, debit or credit card payments and online banking. However, this is not the case for the up to 80% to 90% of unbanked citizens in the world's developing countries. Yet there is hope for banking services with mobiles. This revolution is already happening in Kenya and is spreading fast around the world. There are already 160 deployments in mobile money worldwide, and another 110 are planned in the next two years.[6]

Most Kenyans lack bank accounts, yet 75% of the unbanked have M-PESA accounts, using Safaricom mobile services to make money transfers or store savings. As of April 2012, Kenya has over 15 million M-PESA users, and the system is now operational in Uganda and Tanzania.[7] This revolution has taken place thanks to

6 See http://microfinancewithoutborders.com/mobile-money-in-the-ebrd-region-conference-overview/.
7 'Time to Cash Out?' Kara Platoni, *Stanford Magazine*, Sept–Oct 2012, http://tinyurl.com/time-to-cash-out.

collaboration between mobile phone providers, technology experts, banks and MFIs, regulators, and donors such as the UK's Department of International Development, which has invested £1 million in infrastructure.

Under M-PESA, an M-PESA account holder in Nairobi deposits money with a Safaricom mobile kiosk operator, and the operator then notifies the recipient via SMS message that they can collect the funds from any agent. The method is a simple, safe and time-saving way to save money, handle loans or transfer money.

M-PESA has joined with Equity Bank, Kenya's largest MFI, to produce M-KESHO. This allows qualified account holders to save and get loans from any Safaricom mobile phone agent, found in small shops throughout Kenya.[8]

Musoni, a Kenyan MFI with 10,000 customers that has made more than $6.3million in loans since its launch in May 2010, has moved to a completely electronic transfer system. This provides traceability of funds, security and greater efficiency. Better still, loan officers armed with tablets and wireless connectivity can assess the business prospects of future borrowers, store interview data immediately, refer to borrowers' payment history and send text messages. This allows them to cultivate relationships with a larger number of customers. Musoni will soon license its technology to other MFIs, which will help to bring down the cost of credit.[9]

BASIX microfinance in India is developing branchless banking, using voice recognition in mobiles[10] for savings accounts so that savers can deposit as little as $10 at a shop and get an immediate receipt. Using a network of corner shops, BASIX will have at least one branch per square kilometre throughout India.

4.2 Platforms for e-commerce and open payment systems

Consumers in developed markets take online shopping using PayPal for granted. Not so in Africa. Intra-African trade accounts for just 2% of Africa's GDP, and there is a desperate need for online payment solutions. FloCash has been founded by Sirak Mussie, a telecoms and payment systems professional of Ethiopian origin based in the United Kingdom. An online payment solution founded in the UK in 2010, FloCash answers the need for an African PayPal. It currently has more than 5 million customers in ten African countries,[11] and partners with banks, mobile network operators and credit card providers to create a seamless payment system.

FloCash originated from Sirak's ambition 'to link up businesses and consumers in a seamless and convenient way though the converging mobile and payment technologies.'[12] The company is working with partners to develop 'business in a box' solutions for African merchants to trade online – a prime example of Microfinance 3.0. Users can co-create businesses, connect through payment systems and collaborate to access international markets. In another example of involvement, professionals in banking, marketing, payment systems and capacity building are working together to develop FloCash's platform for training merchants.

---

8 See www.cgap.org/photos-videos/m-pesa-mobile-money-0.
9 See www.economist.com/blogs/schumpeter/2013/02/microfinance.
10 See www.cgap.org/photos-videos/sub-k-seeking-next-breakthrough.
11 See www.humanipo.com/news/124/FloCash-Africas-Answer-to-Paypal, February 23 2012.
12 See www.adventurenetwork.org/en/emprendedor-en-africa-iii-flocash/.

4.3 Microinsurance

The 'sleeping giant' of microfinance, microinsurance, is ready to grow through streamlining processes, innovation and collaboration. MFIs have long used 'credit life' policies to cover the cost of borrowers' loans in case of death. This is relatively easy to develop, and borrowers pay a 1% premium on their loan. This is a good source of extra revenue for MFIs and is virtually risk-free as the insurance is valid only while the borrower has a loan.

The 2.6 billion low income people worldwide make up an insurance market that is worth an estimated $40 billion.[13] New insurance products include health, index-based weather (drought or excessive rainfall), loss of assets and education. This area is ripe for development – even large MFIs such as the Bangladesh Big Three are only now beginning to offer microinsurance products.

(a) *Getting involved in microinsurance*

The following are some examples of partnerships between banking, healthcare, insurance and capacity building professional that provide microinsurance programmes for health and agriculture.

A banker used a career gap between jobs to find partners from the pharmaceutical sector, individuals in the local community who were involved with Microfinance without Borders enterprise training, and local healthcare professionals to develop a sustainable clinic in Kibera, Nairobi, Africa's largest slum. The project is working with a microinsurance expert to gather data for a micro-health insurance product that it will develop with an insurance company that serves the Kenyan market. The banker, now in a full-time job in London, supervises operations in Nairobi over the Internet, and has developed security systems including fingerprint recognition to guard against fraud, both by clinic attendees and staff.

A UK general practitioner with extensive public health experience and a long-term association with an Indian ashram is developing the ashram's primary health care facilities and a micro-health insurance programme for its 80,000 microfinance members. The microinsurance expert who is consulting on the Kenyan project is also advising this one.

Insurance professionals at Green Delta in Bangladesh are working with a team to pilot a micro-health insurance project designed to provide a cushion against risk factors and minimise household healthcare costs, which could wipe out a family's income without insurance. Many organisations with health schemes for the poor offer discounted health services, but not insurance services.[14]

Mobile and microinsurance products are developing through partnerships between telecom companies, microinsurance expert MicroEnsure and the insurer. Index based insurance for farmers in Kenya[15] uses weather stations to collect rainfall data and pays premiums via mobile phone when crops are damaged by drought or excessive rainfall.

---

13 Swiss Re, 2010 in 'The 2012 Research Conference on Microinsurance', http://tinyurl.com/SwissRe-microinsurance.

14 See www.socialenterprisebuzz.com/2012/04/09/microinsurance-pilot-for-health-in-bangladesh/.

15 See http://tinyurl.com/Kenya-index-insurance.

Life insurance via mobiles is being piloted in Ghana,[16] where lessons are being learnt about the need to 'sell at scale and educate well' to maximise the opportunity for mobile insurance.

Microinsurance's challenges are many in getting low-margin, high-volume products to the low-income market, especially a lack of trust in the insurance sector, and mobile-delivered solutions are gaining a foothold. Resources for getting involved can be found at the Microinsurance Innovation Facility.[17] This is one of the most exciting developments of Microfinance 3.0 – protecting low-income families with against risk and helping them stay over the poverty line once they have risen above it.

4.4 Microfinance lending platforms

Lending platforms make it possible for individuals to lend to MFIs and receive reports that are typical for the borrowers who receive the loans. Known as peer-to-peer or peer-to-institution lending, the oldest of these is Oikocredit.[18] Others include KIVA,[19] Lend with CARE[20] and Deki.[21]

These platforms work through MFIs, which administer the loan and eventually pay it back. There are several advantages to using a lending platform rather than going directly to an MFI:

- The lending platform's vetting process and expertise with exchange rate risks reduces overall risk
- MFIs receive technical assistance both for improving their financial and social impact performance and for communicating stories of the entrepreneurs who receive loans
- The lending platforms conduct fundraising for grants, corporate sponsors and foundations to cover the costs of their operations.

(a) Getting involved with lending platforms

Professionals can get involved by investing or donating to a lending platform or an MFI umbrella organisation in the United Kingdom. Examples of these include the MicroLoan Foundation, Five Talents Opportunity International, or UK subsidiaries of Grameen, BRAC and FINCA UK. The CARE-PLAN-Barclay's 'Banking on Change' project will extend village savings and loan associations with savings-led services to half a million people in 11 countries over three years.

4.5 Micro-franchises

BRAC, one of the Bangladesh Big Three, invented micro-franchising as a way to revolutionise, among other sectors, healthcare, livestock and poultry rearing. It developed a system for training micro-entrepreneurs in basic skills, enabling them to

---

16 See http://tinyurl.com/Ghana-life-insurance-mobile.
17 See www.ilo.org/public/english/employment/mifacility/.
18 See www.oikocredit.org/.
19 See www.kiva.org/.
20 See www.lendwithcare.org.
21 See www.deki.org.uk/.

sell services such as poultry vaccinations, financed through microfinance. BRAC has extended its micro-franchising system to other countries in which it operates, such as Haiti.

Other organisations, such as Living Goods in Uganda, are partnering with BRAC to develop BRAC-type micro-franchising for health and energy entrepreneurs.[22]

(a) *Professional involvement in linking franchises with microfinance*

By June 2013, Brian Shaad, a UK-US social entrepreneur, and his business partner Nikhil Jaisinghani had installed low-cost solar-powered microgrids in over 300 northern India villages to provide clean light and phone charging. Their partnerships with local NGOs and a grant from USAID[23] made this infrastructure change possible, resulting in clean lighting and savings on unhealthy kerosene. These rural villagers on less than $0.40 per day use microfinance-type groups to collect payments and have a surplus from their government subsidy for kerosene, enabling them to lend small sums to others without access to solar microgrids. This franchise system illustrates how an infrastructure change enables growth, along with lifestyle improvements and microfinance-type innovation.

(b) *Payment systems and solar by professionals in Ethiopia*

German organisation Stiftung Solarenergie has developed a revolving fund as a sustainable financing model for solar lights for rural Ethiopians. It has added an intelligent change controller in the installed solar system to ensure punctual repayments for the system.[24] This integrated system of microfinance and solar energy with in-built controls illustrates how Microfinance 3.0 can provide platforms for new enterprises, benefiting and involving people directly at the bottom of the pyramid. Investment is aimed at infrastructure development and not at subsidising credit, the original Microfinance 1.0 model. Poor people need a range of financial services, especially savings as illustrated by the solar-microfinance models, where they are no longer dependent on kerosene and can thus make savings on a daily basis.

5. Conclusion

Our journey from Microfinance 1.0 to 3.0 is illustrated in Figure 5. We started with microfinance innovation in the 1970s, predominately in Bangladesh in response to crisis, with microcredit. This 'pushed' credit to consumers, eventually developing the group lending model, with women proved to be more reliable and consistent customers than men. By the 1990s, consumers were demanding voluntary savings and Microfinance 2.0 responded as some MFIs became banks. Experimentation with microinsurance and village savings and loans associations showed how new savings models could develop. By 2007 MPESA, the Kenyan mobile phone payment system, illustrated the potential of linking technology with microfinance. Today, Microfinance 3.0 is developing, as pan-African payment platforms such as FloCash

---

22 See http://livinggoods.org/what-we-do/micro-franchise-business-model/

23 See www2.technologyreview.com/article/427670/solar-microgrids/

24 See www.solar-energyfoundation.org/Microcredit,605.html?syndicat=d7f7add1939ecc8fa3ac9813a8806793

couple with 'business in a box' platforms to open the way for development for micro, small and medium-sized enterprises. Microfinance 1.0 at the level of microloans to market stall traders will not in itself bring massive economic development. Mobilising savings and disciplined use of finances in Microfinance 2.0, in response to users' demands, is making the next step forward. Microfinance 3.0, linking mobile phone, credit cards and banks with franchising systems and platforms will open new markets.

Figure 5

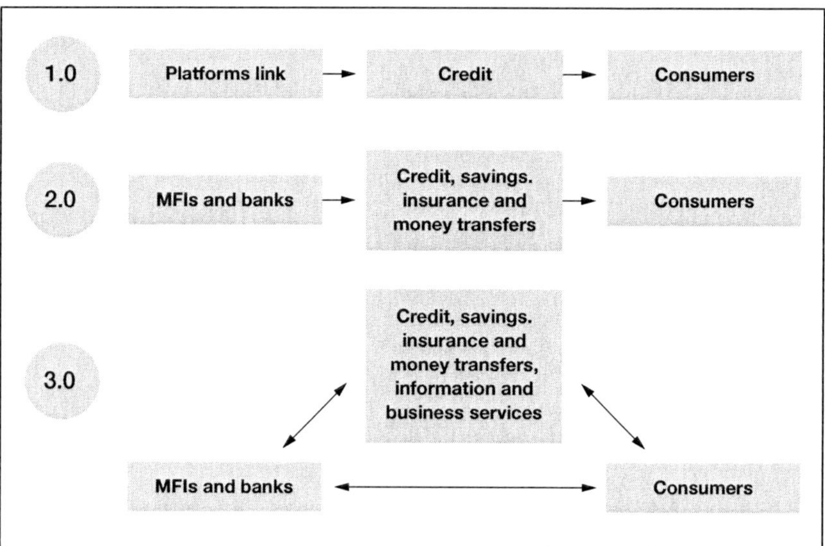

People at the bottom of the pyramid have lacked access to financial services, crippling their ability to plan and to recover from shocks – whether lifecycle events, health or disasters. They are demanding services, including connectivity, to expand their microenterprises and safeguard against shocks as their governments cannot provide the needed health, education or social security infrastructure. Microfinance 3.0 needs skilled professionals around the world to expand the range of socially conscious financial services available to the working poor, thereby enabling us all to co-create, collaborate and connect.

Appendix of resources for involvement in microfinance

Research

The best online source is the Consultative Group to Assist the Poor (CGAP),[25] the independent policy and research centre dedicated to advancing financial access for the world's poor. Its MIX Market lists financial reporting data from major MFIs. As an example, one financial lawyer has used CGAP's MIX Market for advanced research about the securitisation of a large MFI by a microfinance fund.

It is also possible to interview people involved in microfinance and attend the networking events suggested below.

Special interest groups

These range from advocacy groups to microfinance and social impact investment groups that can be joined on LinkedIn.

- Advocacy: RESULTS[26] campaigns on microfinance and is part of the Microcredit Summit.[27]
- Clubs and events: the UK Microfinance Club, the All Party Parliamentary Group for Microfinance and WAM (Women Advocating Microfinance) host events in London. Large law firms have special interest groups for microfinance and social impact investment, as do universities.

Funding

Oikocredit, Lend with Care, KIVA and Deki all have investment platforms. It is possible to get involved in fundraising for specific projects for microfinance umbrella organisations such as Five Talents, Opportunity International and the MicroLoan Foundation.

Microfinance learning programmes, coaching, mentoring and consultancy

- The Rural Finance Learning Centre[28] is a free, comprehensive learning resource that includes excellent online microfinance lessons, reference materials, videos and a list of training opportunities.
- The UK MF Club[29] website also lists courses in the United Kingdom.

Volunteering

Research your local resources for MFIs that may welcome volunteers, especially for funding and specialist skills.

Pro bono work

Advocates for International Development (A4ID), the special interest groups of legal firms and Bankers without Borders all offer pro bono opportunities for lawyers and bankers.

---

25 See www.cgap.org.
26 See http://results.org.uk/.
27 See www.microcreditsummit.org/state_of_the_campaign_report/.
28 See www.ruralfinance.org/training/.
29 See www.mfclubuk.org/.

Diaspora

London has diaspora groups from all continents working to create sustainable projects that can benefit groups 'back home'. These include Donkor's Life Link 'susu' for Ghana, and Mussie's FloCash for all of Africa.

Hands on experience: short- to long-term

Fieldwork may be undertaken in your own country or abroad. A general principle is to prepare yourself in advance with financial and social impact measurement tools so that you can ask better questions while in the field. Some avenues to investigate include:

- universities,[30] which offer fieldwork or competitions for funding to do projects through their undergraduate societies;
- Vodafone's 'World of Difference' Scheme; a graduate of MFIA and LSE graduate is currently working with a UK MFI on social impact measurement under this scheme;
- Grameen training programmes linked to fieldwork;[31]
- Bankers without Borders, part of Grameen Foundation that offers virtual projects and engagements in developing countries;
- long-term health and microinsurance projects created by MWB graduates who are developing projects in Kenya and India, being mentored by an expert in microinsurance; and
- Volunteering to develop project proposals and participate with microfinance organisations.

30 See http://oxfordmicrofinance.org/get-involved/oxford-students/; www.cusu.cam.ac.uk/societies/directory/beyondprofit/; http://groupspaces.com/lsemicrofinancesoc/.

31 See http://tinyurl.com/Grameen-training.

About the authors

Mosleh Uddin Ahmed
Chief executive officer, Microinsurance Research Centre
mosleh.ahmed@btinternet.com

Mosleh Uddin Ahmed is a microinsurance specialist. He qualified as a chartered accountant in 1970. He is founder and chief executive officer of the Microinsurance Research Centre based in the United Kingdom, with a presence in Bangladesh, India, Kenya, Nigeria and Sri Lanka. He is also a director of Microfinance without Borders.

Mr Ahmed has more than 20 years' international experience in microinsurance, having acted as an independent consultant for the Asian Development Bank, the German Agency for International Cooperation, the International Finance Cooperation, the International Labour Organisation, the World Bank and the United Nations Development Programme in development projects in Armenia, Bangladesh, Brazil, Croatia, Georgia, India, Indonesia, Kazakhstan, Kenya, Mongolia, Moldova, Nepal, Nigeria, Pakistan, Sri Lanka, Tajikistan and Uganda.

Mr Ahmed has co-authored a book entitled *Protecting the Poor – a Microinsurance Compendium*. He is a member of the UK All Party Parliamentary Group on Microfinance, the Microinsurance Network and the UK Microfinance Club.

Hajar Barbach
Associate, Clifford Chance LLP
hajar.barbach@cliffordchance.com

Hajar Barbach is a lawyer in the banking department of Clifford Chance in London, specialising in development finance and emerging markets financing. She also runs the microfinance group at Clifford Chance and has advised on a number of microfinance transactions, acting for a wide range of participants, including international commercial banks, global development institutions, microfinance organisations and governments.

Ms Barbach holds an undergraduate degree in international relations and history from the London School of Economics and master's degrees in law and economics from *Sciences Po* Paris and international business law from *Université Paris I Panthéon-Sorbonne*. She speaks fluent French, English and Arabic and is proficient in Spanish. Ms Barbach is a visiting lecturer on microfinance at the Centre for Commercial Law Studies at Queen Mary, University of London and sits on the steering committee of the UK chapter of Women Advancing Microfinance.

Ranajoy Basu
Senior associate, Reed Smith LLP
rbasu@reedsmith.com

Ranajoy Basu is a senior structured finance and capital markets lawyer who also spearheads Reed Smith's global social impact finance group, which provides legal advice on structuring innovative social impact finance solutions and microfinance projects. He has worked with microfinance institutions in Asia, Africa and South America, and regularly advises arrangers, charitable institutions, funds and investors on innovative social impact finance projects, including social impact bonds, funds, renewable energy and emerging market transactions relating to social impact finance. He regularly speaks at events and writes on microfinance and impact investment.

Mr Basu studied law at Calcutta University in India and has an LLM in banking and finance law from King's College London.

Ian Callaghan
Head of capital advisory services, Shorebank International, [London]
icallaghan@sbksbi.com

Ian Callaghan is head of the capital advisory services practice at Shorebank International and brings more than 20 years' expertise as a business owner, consultant and banker to the areas of small and medium-sized enterprise finance, microfinance and finance for other 'base of pyramid' products and services.

Between 2005 and 2008 Mr Callaghan led investment bank Morgan Stanley's efforts in the field of microfinance, latterly as head of its microfinance institutions group. During this period he arranged some $250 million in loans for some 35 microfinance institutions in 20 countries, including the two largest transactions ever completed in the sector.

During 2008 and 2009 Mr Callaghan was senior director of investments at the Omidyar Network. He began his banking career with the financing of the Eurotunnel Channel Tunnel – then the largest privately funded infrastructure project in the world.

Juliette Chapelle
Trainee lawyer, Paris Bar School
julchapelle@gmail.com

Juliette Chapelle is studying law at the Paris Bar School and will qualify at the end of 2013. She has a particular interest in development law, as well as social and solidarity-based economy.

Ms Chapelle is also undertaking an internship at an international law firm specialising in business law. She was previously an intern at a French corporate and investment bank. She holds two master's degrees – one in business law from the University of Paris I *Panthéon-Sorbonne* and one in private international law and international trade from the University of Paris II *Panthéon-Assas* (both *cum laude*) – and an LLM in banking and finance law from Queen Mary University of London (distinction). During her LLM, Ms Chapelle wrote her thesis on securitisation in microfinance.

Jean-Marie De Corte
Lecturer, Warocqué School of Business and Economics, University of Mons
Jean-Marie.DECORTE@umons.ac.be

Jean-Marie De Corte is a lecturer in mathematics at the Warocqué School of Business and Economics, University of Mons, Belgium. He holds a PhD in mathematics and specialises in multi-criteria decision-making support. He is a co-author of the Measuring Attractiveness by a Categorical Based Evaluation Technique (MACBETH) multi-criteria decision analysis approach. Dr De Corte created and coded the M-MACBETH software based on the MACBETH approach. The continual improvement of this software allows public and private entities to apply the MACBETH approach. In addition, numerous scientific papers have been published based on its practical applications.

Olly Donnelly
Chief executive, Shivia
olly@shivia.com

Olly Donnelly is chief executive and founder of Shivia, a UK charity with operations in India and Nepal. She previously worked at Accenture Strategy in London and the World Bank in Washington DC.

Ms Donnelly has worked on issues related to microfinance, HIV/AIDS, women, education and caste, and with disadvantaged children. She is involved with several charities, including Familia, a foster home in West Bengal, India, and is a trustee of UK charity Multi-Agency International Training and Support. She previously sat on the Leonard Cheshire international committee and the Moonpig Foundation board of trustees. Ms Donnelly is the UK ambassador for BASE, a leading non-governmental organisation in western Nepal. Ms Donnelly holds a first-class honours degree in geography and achieved a distinction in her master's degree, both from Oxford University. She sits on the alumni committees of her former college, St Edmund Hall, and school, St Mary's Ascot.

Marcus Fedder
Director, International Finance Facility for Immunisation
marcus.fedder@gmail.com

Marcus Fedder is a former banker with more than 20 years' experience. He is a director of the International Finance Facility for Immunisation and previously co-founded Agora Microfinance Partners in 2009. Until recently he was also a board member of Angkor Mikroheranhvatho Kampuchea, a major Cambodian microfinance institution, and of Jaghdan Finance, a Mumbai-based MFI.

Dr Fedder previously held senior positions at several financial institutions: Toronto Dominion Bank – vice chair of TD Securities, responsible for all businesses in Europe and Asia-Pacific; European Bank for Reconstruction and Development – treasurer, responsible for investment of the bank's liquid assets, bank funding, asset and liability management and client advisory; World Bank – advised governments and central banks on debt management and asset and liability management; Canadian Imperial Bank of Commerce – executive director, responsible for derivatives in London; and Deutsche Bank – worked in capital markets.

Dr Fedder holds a PhD in politics from the *Freie Universitaet* Berlin and postgraduate degrees in international relations from Cambridge University and the London School of Economics.

Cameron Goldie-Scot
Chief operating officer, Musoni BV
cameron.goldiescot@gmail.com

Cameron Goldie-Scot is co-founder and chief operating officer of Musoni BV. In 2009 Musoni BV established the first completely cashless microfinance institution in the world, using mobile payments for all transactions. Since then, Musoni has disbursed more than 35,000 loans totalling in excess of $10 million to Kenyan micro entrepreneurs entirely through their mobile phones. Mr Goldie-Scot is responsible for the development and licensing of Musoni's technology platform to MFIs around the world.
Previously, Mr Goldie-Scot worked as an independent consultant for Triple Jump Advisory Services. From July 2008 he was responsible for facilitating the introduction of mobile payment services to microfinance clients in Kenya and Tanzania. These were the first successful partnerships of their kind and have survived to this day. During this period, when he was based permanently in East Africa, Mr Goldie-Scot gained first-hand experience of the challenges faced when implementing mobile banking services, as well as the key factors necessary for success.

Atif Hanif
Partner, Allen & Overy
atif.hanif@allenovery.com

Atif Hanif is a partner in the banking department of Allen & Overy's London office and is head of the firm's European Islamic finance practice. He advises on a wide range of banking, finance and debt capital markets transactions. He has extensive experience of acting for financiers, borrowers, issuers and project sponsors.

Mr Hanif is recognised as a leading Islamic finance specialist by the *International Financial Law Review* (2010), *Islamic Finance News* (2012), *Legal 500* (2012) and *Chambers UK* (2012).

Malcolm Harper
Chairman, M-CRIL; Emeritus professor, Cranfield University
malcolm.harper@btinternet.com

Malcolm Harper was educated at Oxford, Harvard and Nairobi universities. He initially worked in marketing in the United Kingdom and subsequently taught at the University of Nairobi and was professor of enterprise development at Cranfield School of Management (UK). Since 1995 he has worked independently – mainly in India. He has published extensively on enterprise development, microfinance and livelihoods and child protection issues.

Mr Harper was formerly chairman of Basix Finance in India for 10 years and is currently chairman of Micro-Credit Ratings International Ltd, an international microfinance and social rating company.

He is chair, trustee and board member of a number of institutions in the United Kingdom, the Netherlands and India, and has worked on poverty issues in Bangladesh, Pakistan, Africa, Latin America, the Caribbean, the Middle East, Southeast Asia, China and the United Kingdom.

Cornell Jackson
Research associate, Kings College London
cornell.jackson@kcl.ac.uk

Cornell Jackson is a research associate in social network analysis for historical data at Kings College, London. He holds degrees in computer science and engineering from the University of Pennsylvania and has an MBA from the *Ecole Nationale des Ponts et Chausées*, France.

Dr Jackson was awarded a PhD in microfinance and social network analysis from the University of Greenwich in 2012. His research focused on measuring the social networks of microfinance clients in India, which had microenterprises selling saris, and how such networks can be improved in order to increase business and reduce poverty. The research showed that such methods can improve other low-growth, low-entry-barrier businesses established by microfinance clients. It was funded by a three-year grant from the Leverhulme Trust.

Dr Jackson has 25 years' experience in information technology, including nine years' experience as a project manager in an international IT consultancy.

Marc Labie
Associate professor, Warocqué School of Business and Economics, University of Mons
marc.labie@umons.ac.be

Marc Labie is an associate professor at the Warocqué School of Business and Economics, University of Mons, Belgium, where he teaches organisation studies and management. He is also a visiting professor at the Solvay Brussels School of Economics and Management. He previously lectured in various other universities, including the *Université de Liège* and Harvard University (Financial Institutions for Private Enterprise Development Executive Programme at the Kennedy School of Government). He is co-founder and co-director of the Centre for European Research in Microfinance based in Mons and

Brussels. Dr Labie has worked in Benin, Bolivia, Burkina Faso, Colombia, the Democratic Republic of Congo, Indonesia, Kenya, Madagascar, Mexico, Morocco, and Peru. He has co-authored numerous articles on microfinance, mostly focused on corporate governance issues. In 2011 he co-edited *The Handbook of Microfinance*, published by World Scientific Publishing.

Melissa Manzo
Senior associate, Allen & Overy LLP
melissa.manzo@allenovery.com

Melissa Manzo is a senior associate at international law firm Allen & Overy LLP, specialising in debt finance and restructuring. She co-founded the firm's microfinance and social investment group and has acted on a variety of microfinance-related transactions.

Ms Manzo is a trustee of UK registered charity Bidna Capoeira, an organisation that uses the afro-Brazilian martial art/dance of capoeira to enhance the lives of children in conflict situations around the world.

Ms Manzo studied at Oxford University and BPP Law School, London.

Ana Marr
Associate professor in international development economics, University of Greenwich
a.marr@gre.ac.uk

Ana Marr is a principal economist specialising in microfinance, development economics, enterprise promotion and social research. She holds a master's degree from the London School of Economics and a doctorate degree from the School of Oriental and African Studies, University of London. Dr Marr has more than 15 years' experience of working in developing countries, including long and short-term assignments in Asia, Africa and Latin America.

She is director of the International Microfinance Research Group at the University of Greenwich, which has most recently been running a large research project in India, Peru and Tanzania supported by the Leverhulme Trust. She also lectures on microfinance on various master's programmes and supervises a number of PhD students.

Dr Marr has published extensively on the subject of microfinance, covering issues related to social performance, poverty reduction and social network analysis.

Emma Matebalavu
Partner, Clifford Chance LLP
emma.matebalavu@cliffordchance.com

Emma Matebalavu is a partner at Clifford Chance, London specialising in real estate finance and all types of structured debt. Ms Matebalavu is a co-sponsor of the Clifford Chance microfinance group and a trustee of Grameen Foundation Scotland.

Sam Mendelson
Financial inclusion and microfinance consultant
sam@arcfinance.org

Sam Mendelson is the current UK Department for International Development/Citi development fellow and co-author since 2009 of *Microfinance Banana Skins* – the gold-standard survey of industry risk. He is co-founder and director of Social Performance Advisory and leads monitoring and evaluation at Arc Finance – an energy microfinance NGO with sector-support projects in Africa, Asia and the Americas. He previously ran the research programme at the Centre for the Study of Financial Innovation.

Mr Mendelson writes regularly for *Financial World*, *Africa Investor*, *Prospect* and other publications on development, financial inclusion, technology and geopolitical issues. In 2011 he was nominated for a Foreign Press Association Feature of the Year award for his Prospect piece on Qatar.

Mr Mendelson has undergraduate degrees in psychology and law from the University of Western Australia and an LLM in public international law from University College London.

Tara S Nair

Associate professor, Gujarat Institute of Development Research
tara01@gmail.com

Tara Nair is associate professor at the Gujarat Institute of Development Research, Ahmedabad, India. She holds MPhil and PhD degrees in economics from the Jawaharlal Nehru University, New Delhi. Her research interests and publications span areas such as micro and rural microfinance, financial inclusion, microenterprise development, gender and entrepreneurship and political economy of media. She has been part of large-scale field studies on the impact of microfinance in India, Myanmar and Bangladesh.

Pete Power

Former chief executive officer, Angkor Mikroheranhvatho Kampuchea Co, Ltd
pete.power@amkcambodia.com

Pete Power is the outgoing chief executive officer of Angkor Mikroheranhvatho Kampuchea Co, Ltd (AMK). With more than 300,000 clients, AMK provides microfinance services to approximately 10% of households in Cambodia. Between 2010 and 2012 Mr Power led AMK's 1,200 staff through a strategic transition, transforming the company from a rural credit organisation into a provider of a broad range of microfinance services, including savings, credit, money transfer, mobile banking and various other innovations.

Mr Power holds degrees in international relations and European integration, as well as an MBA. He has significant international experience, having worked and lived in Ireland, China, Vietnam, Cambodia and the United States. He has also completed short-term assignments in approximately 15 other countries, primarily in the developing world.

Edana Richardson

Trainee solicitor, Allen & Overy
edana.richardson@allenovery.com

Edana Richardson received her PhD from Trinity College Dublin in 2012 for her thesis entitled "The Integration of Islamic Finance into the Irish Legal System: Current Issues and Future Challenges". She is a scholar of Trinity College Dublin and her doctoral research was funded by a humanities and social sciences postgraduate scholarship which she received from the Irish Research Council. In 2011 she taught Islamic finance as part of an LLM course on Islamic law at Trinity College Dublin. Dr Richardson currently works as a trainee solicitor in Allen & Overy's London office.

Phyllis SantaMaria

Founder-director, Microfinance without Borders
phyllis@microfinancewithoutborders.com

Phyllis SantaMaria founded London-based social enterprise Microfinance without Borders to deliver quality education, mentoring and partnership programmes for microfinance, including microinsurance.

Dr SantaMaria holds a BA in history (Wellesley College, United States), an MA in linguistics and a PhD in education (both Exeter University, United Kingdom). She has specialised in microfinance capacity building since 2000, based on her experience in international development in Latin America, Africa and Asia, her education and training in the United Kingdom, Germany and Kenya and her involvement with professional interactive multimedia at the BBC and for various corporate and EU projects.

She has led microfinance and microinsurance projects in East and West Africa, India, Nepal and China, and was the UK coordinator for the UN International Year of Microcredit 2005. Dr SantaMaria has participated in award-winning teams for interactive multimedia titles for the BBC's ground-breaking Domesday Project and the EU Lingua Project.

Sanjay Sinha
Managing director, M-CRIL
sanjaysinha@m-cril.com

Sanjay Sinha is managing director of Micro-Credit Ratings International Limited (M-CRIL) – a company that undertakes financial and social ratings of microfinance institutions and provides research and other services designed to promote the flow of investment in microfinance and microinsurance. Mr Sinha has more than 30 years' economic and development research experience and has worked in more than two dozen countries. In addition to microfinance, he specialises in the analysis of value chains relevant to the livelihoods of poor people and microenterprise promotion. He was involved with M-CRIL's launch of a pioneering programme to assess the performance of private schools aimed at low-income students in developing countries.

In 1983 Mr Sinha co-founded Economic Development Associates Rural Systems, a premier development consulting company in Asia. Between 2006 and 2008 he was a member of the UN advisory group on inclusive financial sectors. He has an MPhil in economics from Oxford University.

Ludovic Urgeghe
Researcher, Centre for European Research in Microfinance
ludovic.urgeghe@umons.ac.be

Ludovic Urgeghe PhD is a permanent researcher at the Centre for European Research in Microfinance. In addition, he is a PhD student at the Warocqué School of Business and Economics, University of Mons, Belgium, where he is also a teaching assistant in management. His PhD research focuses on microfinance commercialisation and aims to explore the role of socially responsible investors in the microfinance sector.

Jean-Claude Vansnick
Consultant, Value Focused Consulting SPRL
vfconsulting@voo.be

Jean-Claude Vansnick is a consultant at Value Focused Consulting SPRL. He was previously professor of quantitative methods at the Warocqué School of Business and Economics, University of Mons, Belgium, with a main interest in multi-criteria decision analysis. Dr Vansnick received his doctor of science degree in mathematics from the *Université Libre de Bruxelles* in 1973. He has widely published in the area of decision making and his paper "Strength of Preference: Theoretical and Practical Aspects" was selected as Belgium's national contribution for the 10th triennal conference of the Internal Federation of Operational Research Societies. Dr Vansnick is a member of several research groups on multi-criteria analysis and has been a visiting professor at several international summer schools on multi-criteria decision-making support. He is a co-author of the Measuring Attractiveness by a Categorical Based Evaluation Technique approach and has extensive experience in applying this in real decision contexts.

Index

[all references are to page number]